Greater Than Equal

Greater Than Equal

AFRICAN AMERICAN STRUGGLES

FOR SCHOOLS AND CITIZENSHIP IN

NORTH CAROLINA, 1919–1965

Sarah Caroline Thuesen

The University of North Carolina Press / Chapel Hill

Library of Congress Cataloging-in-Publication Data
Thuesen, Sarah Caroline.
Greater than equal : African American struggles for schools and citizenship
in North Carolina, 1919-1965 / Sarah Caroline Thuesen.
page cm.
Includes bibliographical references and index.
ISBN 978-0-8078-3930-0 (cloth : alk. paper)
1. African Americans—Education—North Carolina—History—
20th century. 2. African Americans—North Carolina—Politics and government—
20th century. 3. Segregation in education—North Carolina—History—20th century.
4. Education—North Carolina—History—20th century. 5. Public schools—
North Carolina—History—20th century. I. Title.
LC2802.N8T58 2013
371.829'960756—dc23 2013004074
17 16 15 14 13   5 4 3 2 1

For my children,
Henry and Ida,
and their generation of
schoolchildren

Contents

Illustrations and Tables

TABLES

Acknowledgments

Throughout the process of writing this book, I have wrestled with the dilemma of knowing that I had more stories to tell than any reasonable editor would permit. Nowhere is that more true than in the acknowledgments. These few paragraphs can only begin to convey my gratitude for the many people who have helped with what has truly been a collaborative effort. This book's merits rest on countless shoulders; its shortcomings rest on mine alone.

Several institutions and organizations provided critical financial assistance. I was especially lucky to have the support of a Spencer Foundation Dissertation Fellowship and a National Academy of Education/Spencer Foundation Postdoctoral Fellowship. In addition to generous stipends, both of these fellowships provided invaluable opportunities to discuss my project with senior and beginning scholars from across the disciplines. Many thanks to James Anderson, Karen Benjamin, Elizabeth Cascio, Michael Clapper, Ruben Flores, Adam Gamoran, Maureen Hallinan, Carl Kaestle, Adam Laats, Dan Lewis, Nancy MacLean, William Reese, Bethany Rogers, Sarah Rose, John Rury, Margaret Beale Spencer, Maris Vinovskis, and Heather Williams for their collegiality and compelling critiques. How fortuitous it was for me that my initial Spencer cohort included Heather Williams and that she subsequently moved to Chapel Hill, where she has inspired me with her work and cheered me with her encouragement.

I was also generously assisted by both a Small and Large Mowry Grant from the University of North Carolina History Department, a Latané Interdisciplinary Summer Research Grant from the UNC Graduate School, an Archie K. Davis Grant from the North Caroliniana Society, an Albert J. Beveridge Grant from the American Historical Association, and summer research grants from UNC's Center for the Study of the American South and the Rockefeller Archive Center in Tarrytown, New York.

My greatest intellectual debts are to my mentors. At the University of North Carolina, my adviser, James Leloudis, gave me the idea for this project and urged me to dig into the papers of North Carolina's Division of Negro Education. I used his scholarship on southern schools as a critical foundation for my work. Even more important, I first became inspired to pursue a career in history during a college seminar with him. For his early and unwavering confidence in me, as well as his careful reading of many drafts and his countless words of encouragement, I owe him a world of thanks. Jacquelyn Hall has mentored hundreds of students at UNC, but she has the remarkable ability to make each one of us feel at the center of her universe. I am so thankful for her thoughtful reflections on my work, her lessons in the value of oral history, and her many gestures of support and friendship. Several other mentors read this book in its formative stages and merit special thanks: Jerma Jackson, for always asking the toughest questions and for sharing her boundless enthusiasm; Walter Jackson, for steering me to new sources with his encyclopedic command of intellectual and southern history; and Kenneth Janken, for challenging me since my undergraduate days to think critically about the southern past from an African American perspective. Donald Mathews offered cheerful guidance as I designed an early research proposal. A memorable seminar with Robert Korstad at Duke University immersed me in intellectual literature about life "behind the veil." For my early training in American history, I am grateful to William Barney, Peter Coclanis, John Kasson, William Leuchtenburg, John Nelson, and Harry Watson.

In this book's early stages, I was quite fortunate to be in writing groups with Melynn Glusman, David Sartorius, Brian Steele, Michele Strong, and David Voelker. I benefited enormously from their friendship and detailed observations. David Sartorius's work on race and loyalty in Cuba was particularly influential in my development of chapter 1. Karin Breuer also served at various moments as a writing companion and has been a consistent source of wit and wisdom.

David Cecelski, William Chafe, and Jerry Gershenhorn graciously gave of their time and read portions of this book. Their collective wisdom on race and education in the South prompted me to ask fresh questions of familiar material. Karl Campbell, Pamela Grundy, Lydia Claire, Malinda Maynor Lowery, and Ken Zogry shared ideas from allied projects. James Anderson, Prudence Cumberbatch, V. P. Franklin, Valinda Littlefield, and Kate Rousmaniere offered helpful comments on related conference papers. Anne Whisnant was my resident expert on all matters of book production and child rearing (and how to combine the two).

Since beginning this project, I have had the pleasure of working at several institutions. At the University of North Carolina, a semester's work with James Leloudis and George Noblit's study of southern school desegregation gave me a foundation for further exploration of the post-*Brown* South. During two years of postdoctoral work with UNC's Southern Oral

History Program at the Center for the Study of the American South, I had the privilege of engaging with a broad network of scholars doing similar work. I learned a great deal during that time from David Cline, Jacquelyn Hall, Beth Millwood, and Joe Mosnier about the art of oral history. Joe also shared his deep knowledge of educational litigation in North Carolina—plus bushels of produce from his garden. I was also lucky to be working at that time with Dwana Waugh and Rachel Martin, two fellow historians of education. I am very grateful to students and colleagues at Wabash College, Warren Wilson College, William Peace University, and Guilford College. Having the opportunity to teach this story's broader context enriched my telling of it in many ways. Philip Otterness at Warren Wilson and Stephen Morillo at Wabash deserve special thanks for years of professional encouragement.

Well before I became a historian of the North Carolina public schools, I attended them as a student. Many teachers from those twelve years stand out in my memory, but at St. Stephens High School in Hickory, B. C. Crawford, Loyd Hoke, and the late Beth Haunton had a particularly direct and important influence on my later work. I hope that in some small way my work is a tribute to them and the vital role that all teachers play in schooling future citizens.

I am extremely indebted to the many librarians, archivists, and other individuals who shepherded me through a maze of sources. Joe Mobley introduced me as a college student to the North Carolina State Archives, where I later spent many hours researching this project. At the State Archives, Debbi Blake, Kim Cumber, and Earl Ijames were especially diligent in locating sources, as was Elizabeth Hayden at the North Carolina State Library. At UNC's North Carolina Collection, Robert Anthony, Alice Cotton, Eileen McGrath, Harry McKown, and Jason Tomberlin have supported me since this project's inception. Andre Vann at North Carolina Central University went above and beyond the call of duty in pointing me to sources and connecting me with his network of veteran educators and NCCU alumni. At the administrative offices of the Hickory City Schools, Mary Duquette and Ann Stalnaker were most welcoming, and Ann generously shared research from her dissertation. Lorraine Nicholson granted me access to the papers of the North Carolina Congress of Colored Parents and Teachers. Marsha Alibrandi and Candy Beal shared materials from their oral history project of Ligon Middle School.

Others who helped locate sources and photographs include Jean Bischoff of the G. R. Little Library, Elizabeth City State University; Diana Carey of the Schlesinger Library at the Radcliffe Institute; Janey Deal of the Patrick Beaver Memorial Library in Hickory; Michael Evans of the Wake County Public Schools; Stephen Fletcher of the North Carolina Collection Photographic Archives; Andrea Jackson of the Woodruff Library, Atlanta University Center; Linda Richardson of the Durham Public Library; Tommy Richey of the Raleigh City Museum; Mildred Roxborough of the NAACP; Arlene Royer of the National Archives at Atlanta; Traci Thompson of the Braswell Memorial Library in Rocky Mount; and Helen Wykle of the Ramsey Library, UNC-Asheville. I also am thankful for able assistance from the staffs of the Manuscript Division of the Library of Congress; UNC's Southern Historical Collection; the Rockefeller Archives in Tarrytown, New York; and the Special Collections of Perkins Library, Duke University.

Some of my most important lessons in history came not in classrooms or libraries but in the homes of people I interviewed. I also made essential use of interviews conducted by others, most of which are housed at the Southern Oral History Program Collection at UNC. All interviews are listed in the bibliography, but a few extra words of thanks are in order. The first person I interviewed for this project was Ruth Lawrence Woodson. I am sure that my questions at that stage betrayed my relative inexperience, but she graciously answered each one and inspired me to dig deeper into the history of North Carolina's Division of Negro Education. Also in Raleigh but quite a few years later, Joseph Holt Jr. similarly inspired me, put me in touch with others to interview, and generously shared a wealth of clippings and documents from his personal files. In Hickory, Catherine Tucker invited me for lunch at her home, where she introduced me to other Ridgeview School alumni, all of whom taught me that I had still had a lot to learn about my hometown's history. In Lumberton, Alice Briley and Elizabeth Kemp invited me to attend a reunion of Redstone/Thompson alumni, where I also had the good fortune of meeting Lillian McQueen. I could not have told the story I tell in chapter 5 without their help.

I was so pleased as a historian of North Carolina to have the privilege of working with the University of North Carolina Press, an institution whose own rich history has intersected with my research on more than one occasion. My editor, Chuck Grench, along with Paula Wald and Sara Cohen, promptly and patiently answered many questions and in all respects made this a better book. Ellen Goldlust's expert copyediting improved this book in both style and substance. My thanks to Mary Caviness for proofreading the page proofs and to Kay Banning for preparing the index. I am also most grateful to the press for enlisting Adam Fairclough and Vanessa Siddle Walker as readers. I have long admired their influential histories of

African American education and hope that I have done justice to their insightful suggestions.

My historical curiosity about education no doubt has much to do with being the child of educators. My parents, Mary Wise Thuesen and Theodore Johannes Thuesen, read a draft of this manuscript when they should have been enjoying their retirement, and they have always taken great interest in my interests at every stage of my life. They, of course, were my first teachers and will always be my most important. Peter Thuesen, my brother and fellow scholar of the American past, is already a far more prolific author than I will ever be, and how fortunate for me that this is so. I have shamelessly exploited his expertise on many occasions. He, too, read parts of this manuscript and provided much-needed humor along the way. Also cheering me at every step were members of my extended family, including Sarah Benbow, Mills Bridges, Paula Clarke, Steve Clarke, Sheila Kerrigan, Jane Kenyon, and the late Heidi Salgo.

In writing a book that at its core is about children, I would be especially remiss if I did not give prominent acknowledgment to several first-rate child care providers. While I was writing, Corrie Finger, Leslie Fox, Tulani Hauger-Kome, Janis Leona, and my sister-in-law, Patricia Mickelberry, had the harder—and more important—task. They gave my children the thoughtful attention and me the peace of mind that made this book's final stages possible.

My husband, Scott Clarke, also provided countless hours of child care while I labored on this book, but that was only one of his many contributions. I met him just as this project was beginning, and even though we inhabit very different professional worlds, he has always been my most enthusiastic fan. I will never be able to thank him enough for his love and support. The births of our children, Henry Thuesen Clarke and Ida Caroline Clarke, slowed down the birth of this book in many ways, but in many more ways they have brought me immeasurable joy and deepened my sense of investment in the future of public schooling. It is to them and their generation of schoolchildren that I dedicate this book.

Greater Than Equal

Map of North Carolina

And the children of the white race and the children of the
colored race shall be taught in separate public schools; but there shall be
no discrimination made in favor of, or to the prejudice of, either race.
—Amendment to Article IX of the
North Carolina State Constitution, added in 1875

[The Negro's] educational development may be temporarily retarded by
unconstitutional and unchristian legislation, but his citizenship is a fixture.
—*The Progressive Educator*, the organ of the North Carolina
Teachers Association, 1888

The new choice, it seems, is between separate but equal [schools]
and separate but unequal.
—Journalist James Traub, on the occasion of
Brown v. Board of Education's fortieth anniversary, 1994

Introduction

Like many children of the post-1960s South, I was first struck as a student
of history by the profound difference that one generation can make. My
mother began public school in South Carolina in 1943, at the height of
racial segregation. When she began her senior year of high school in North
Carolina in 1954, the Supreme Court had just ruled "separate but equal"
schooling unconstitutional, yet another two decades would pass before
the region's schools desegregated on a meaningful level. By contrast, I
began my public school career in North Carolina as levels of school integration were approaching their historic peak. In 1980, the year I completed
the first grade, North Carolina could boast of having the most integrated
schools in the South and some of the most integrated schools in the nation. Yet not quite two decades later, another sea change was emerging. As
journalist James Traub concluded in 1994, "The new choice, it seems, is between separate but equal [schools] and separate but unequal." Two years
later, *Time* magazine headlined a cover story, "Back to Segregation." By
the end of the decade, Charlotte, North Carolina, was taking center stage
in this national debate over the future of school integration. When a 1999
court decision allowed that district to suspend busing plans designed to
achieve racial balance, the local schools quickly resegregated.[1] By *Brown*'s
fiftieth anniversary in 2004, similar trends could be found across the nation, and countless observers tempered their tributes to the ruling's architects with data indicating America's rapid retreat from its goals.

Having once viewed my generation as the first (of presumably many) to attend integrated schools, I began to wonder if we were instead an aberrant blip on the radar of educational history. Indeed, now it seems quite likely that my children, born in 2009 and 2011, will attend a public school system that is legally bound to provide all students with "equal opportunity" but not necessarily the experience of classroom diversity.[2] To be sure, school resegregation has unfolded alongside competing evidence of a more racially inclusive society, including the historic election of the nation's first African American president and, by a number of measures, the "softening" of white racial attitudes. My children will without question grow up in a nation where race plays a very different role than it did during their grandmother's—or even their mother's—childhood. Yet recent litigation surrounding the schools is raising anew once settled questions: Can racially separate schools ever be truly equal? How can equality be measured? Can "separate but equal" schools prepare children for full citizenship? Or, as a forum in a local newspaper asked, "Is Diversity Worth the Effort?"[3]

Some of the most important answers to those questions derive not from the present but from the past. At a time when policymakers across the country seem to be rehabilitating the notion of separate but equal, I have looked closely at the men and women who understood firsthand both the possibilities and the profound limits of school equalization as a strategy for securing first-class citizenship. In focusing this study on the last decades of segregated schooling in the South, I have explored how black North Carolinians pressed for equalization at the level of curricula, higher education, teacher salaries, and school facilities; how white officials coopted the strategy as a means of forestalling integration; and, finally, how black activism for equalization evolved into a fight for something greater than equal: integrated schools that served as models of both material equality and civic inclusion. These struggles for equality represent much more than a brief detour on the road to *Brown*. The equalization battle itself had long entailed a goal that was greater than the measurable parity of school resources, as African Americans routinely yoked calls for school equality to assertions of citizenship. That politicized equalization campaign persisted well into the 1960s, mobilized black communities, narrowed material disparities between black and white schools, fostered black school pride, and profoundly shaped the eventual struggle for desegregation. The remarkable achievements of equalization activism, however, should not obscure the inherent limitations of any fight for equality in a deeply segregated society. In fact, the stories that follow ultimately point to the inextricable connections linking educational equality, racial inclusiveness, and the achievement of first-class citizenship.

This book draws on a rich body of literature that has explored the emergence and early decades of segregated schooling in the South as well as the dramatic years of school desegregation and court-ordered busing.[4] Yet if the system of segregation did not "reach its perfection" until the 1930s, as historian C. Vann Woodward once argued, we still need a fuller understanding of the period between Jim Crow's origins and its de jure demise. During this middle period, segregated education received its fullest institutional expression and largest investments from southern state governments. At the same time, African Americans developed deep loyalties to their schools, teacher organizations, and parent associations, even as they mounted ever-stronger challenges to the notion that equality and segregation could coexist. As historian James Anderson has argued, a closer examination of localized grassroots struggles in the years leading up to desegregation "will contribute much to our understanding of how and why *Brown* has gone from transformative vision to troubled legacy." Or as Jacquelyn Dowd Hall has put it, we need to situate the dramatic changes of the 1960s within the context of a "long civil rights movement" that began a generation before *Brown* and extended for more than a generation beyond.[5]

Greater Than Equal also seeks to reconcile two somewhat competing accounts of the prelude to desegregation. On one hand, viewed from the vantage point of the National Association for the Advancement of Colored People (NAACP) and the allied NAACP Legal Defense and Education Fund (LDF), efforts to equalize the segregated schools appear to be a relatively fleeting experiment in a failed strategy. In the 1930s and early 1940s, the NAACP labored tirelessly to equalize teacher salaries and to pave the way for the integration of higher education, but for both practical and philosophical reasons, it never invested significant resources in equalizing primary and secondary school facilities. By 1950 the NAACP's legal team had turned its full attention to a direct and unequivocal attack on Jim Crow.[6] On the other hand, as case studies by David Cecelski and Vanessa Siddle Walker have shown, African Americans developed abiding school loyalties during the last generation of legalized segregation, loyalties that freighted the process of desegregation with considerable ambivalence and in some cases overt protests against the closing of black schools.[7] Taking a statewide look at these stories, this book demonstrates that both impulses— LDF's desire for a quick transition to integration and enduring grassroots interest in strengthening and preserving historically black schools—were simultaneously at play. Individual communities often included a wide spectrum of black opinion about which approach should predominate.

This book also highlights one of the more compelling "what if" questions within contemporary educational policy studies. Many scholars have wrestled with the merits of the roads not taken in 1954. Derrick Bell, for example, contended that given the political landscape of the 1950s, black children would have been better served at that time by the strict enforcement of *Plessy*'s separate but equal doctrine. This book, in one sense, puts that hypothetical question to the test by grounding it within the political and economic circumstances of individual southern communities. Those localized stories emphasize the entrenched white resistance to complete equalization, which certainly would have stymied attempts at *Plessy*'s strict enforcement; these stories also emphasize blacks' increasing recognition of educational equalization as an uncertain path to full citizenship. Nonetheless, Bell's argument invites important consideration of how *Brown*'s focus on questions of racial separation muted earlier concerns for material equality of the schools. As Risa Goluboff has more broadly argued, *Brown*'s focus on race failed to reflect the fact that many African Americans held a "multivalent" vision of civil rights that combined questions of race and class.[8] More than hypothetical musings, these "what if" questions are critical for charting future policies that will build on *Brown*'s merits and correct its shortcomings.

North Carolina offers a particularly important case study for this reckoning, as it loomed large in regional discussions of school equalization. It was the only southern state where the NAACP failed to convince black teachers to litigate for salary equalization and thus offers a salient example of the fault lines that developed across the South between local and national black leaders. Its somewhat narrower racial spending gaps in education earned North Carolina a reputation as one of the more progressive southern states, though North Carolina's commitment to Jim Crow was no less solid. Indeed, state officials believed that by "modernizing" segregation, they would ensure its survival.

This story's roots extend back at least as far as September 1865, when a statewide gathering of 117 black leaders, most of them former slaves, took place in Raleigh. Despite their newly free status, none of them would be able to claim citizenship until 1868, when Congress adopted the Fourteenth Amendment. Though they lacked formal political power, these men submitted a statement to a nearby group of white lawmakers who were revising the state constitution. While conciliatory in tone, this statement included a list of requests: protection of property and person, assistance in reuniting families, and the removal of racially discriminatory statutes from the state's law books. Situated among these entreaties was an appeal for "education for our children." Black North Carolinians, they suggested, held the right of public education to be a fundamental entitlement of free citizens.[9]

In putting public education on the state's agenda, black freed people were not simply staking claim to well-established privileges in white society. They were revising the meaning of citizenship in the South. The defining rights of American citizenship historically rested on a base of civil and political privileges and protections. During the antebellum years, the rights of citizenship in the North also came to include access to certain social institutions, of which public education figured most prominently. These rights of "social citizenship" developed more slowly in the South. On the eve of the Civil War, about half of North Carolina's white school-aged youth attended publicly supported common schools, but the state did not require local districts to provide any such facilities. Not surprisingly, most early southern public schools offered only a rudimentary education.[10] In calling for the state to embrace public education as a basic right of free citizens, former slaves were proposing significant alterations in the relationship between the southern people and the state.

White lawmakers largely ignored those demands in 1865, but African Americans soon seized another chance to put schooling on the public agenda when Congress required the southern states to hold new constitutional conventions and honor the voting rights of black men. In North Carolina, 15 of the 120 delegates to the 1868 Constitutional Convention were African Americans. These men joined forces with white Republicans in penning constitutional guarantees of male suffrage, state-supported schooling, and the election (rather than appointment) of county officials. In another triumph for black political power, the 1868 statewide elections brought 20 black men to the state legislature. These men helped to write a law mandating a four-month public school term for all children, regardless of race. This legislature also appointed James Walker Hood, a black bishop in the African Methodist Episcopal Zion church, to the office of assistant state superintendent of public schools. Only three years after the end of the Civil War, African Americans were using the rights of political citizenship to secure the privileges of education for their children and grandchildren.[11]

This new school system hewed in practice to southern society's increasingly institutionalized color line, although lawmakers did not add an amendment requiring school segregation to the state constitution until

1875. That amendment stipulated that there "be no discrimination made in favor of, or to the prejudice of, either race," but white officials largely disregarded that nod to equality. Many black leaders both chafed against rising white demands for segregation and saw reason to support the creation of black schools. Hood, for example, had warned that the legal mandate of racial separation would legitimate the rankest sort of discrimination in favor of the white schools, but he also believed that black children would receive better treatment from black teachers. He therefore supported the creation of black schools by "mutual consent and the law of interest." Whites held even fewer doubts about what was best for their children and firmly demanded that the races be schooled separately. State school superintendent Alexander McIver judged in 1874 that many North Carolinians would have preferred "no public schools" to "mixed" ones.[12]

These debates over school segregation soon took a backseat to urgent questions of political control. The possibilities for black leverage in school politics appeared increasingly grim in the late 1870s and 1880s, when white Democrats "redeemed" the legislature and revised the state constitution so that it gave them control over the appointment of local public officials. In 1883, the General Assembly demonstrated its growing hostility to black education by passing the Dortch Act, which allowed local districts to tax each race separately for its schools according to the property values held by each race. That measure promised to shortchange African Americans, who held far less property than their white neighbors. The state courts overturned the measure in 1886, but two years later, the General Assembly gave local school boards near-total control over the distribution of state school funds. Not surprisingly, funding disparities between black and white schools began to widen.[13]

Despite these setbacks, African Americans continued to vote in significant numbers, and a small number of black men held onto seats in the state legislature.[14] Moreover, in 1881, black educators had formed the North Carolina Teachers Association (NCTA), which gave them a forum for promoting public education. The NCTA spoke out passionately against the Dortch Act and continued to work to protect black North Carolinians' educational interests through the decade, as white political power was on the upswing and black schools increasingly came under attack. Black educators could therefore write with guarded confidence in 1888 that although blacks' "educational development" might be "temporarily retarded by unconstitutional and unchristian legislation," their citizenship was a "fixture."[15]

In the early 1890s, African Americans found new opportunities for using that "fixture" of citizenship rights to advocate for public schooling. Plummeting agricultural prices brought hard times to North Carolinians across racial lines and inspired many white farmers to subordinate racial prejudices to concerns of class. Their hostility to the landowning elites who controlled the Democratic Party reached a fever pitch by mid-decade. In 1894, a biracial coalition of Populists and Republicans offered a combined slate of candidates and handed the Democrats a stunning defeat. Winning a legislative majority in 1894 and electing a Republican governor in 1896, these black and white "fusionists" set about enacting democratic reforms, including dramatically increased spending on public education. They also allowed for the direct election of local officials, thereby facilitating an increase in the number of black officeholders.[16]

By the turn of the twentieth century, however, black citizenship rights would fall victim to a legal and political assault on black freedom. In its 1896 *Plessy v. Ferguson* decision, the U.S. Supreme Court legitimized Jim Crow with the dubious qualification that segregated facilities be "separate but equal." Two years later, North Carolina's white Democratic elites waged a vicious propaganda campaign against "Negro rule" and imprinted those admonitions with images of the black male rapist. That campaign eventually turned violent. In Wilmington, white Democrats led a deadly coup d'état that forced hundreds of blacks to flee the city. Combined with rampant election fraud, the 1898 campaign of terror gave Democrats a legislative majority. To prevent future biracial coalitions, the Democrats penned a new constitutional amendment that imposed poll taxes and suffrage restrictions based on voter literacy. In practice, these tests barred black voting, as election officials devised loopholes for white voters and trumped-up restrictions for blacks. Voters passed this disfranchisement amendment in 1900 by popular referendum. Effectively stripped of the vote, African Americans would not sit in the state legislature again until 1969. The General Assembly then enacted a series of segregation statutes that codified racial exclusion and separation in most public places. In both law and custom, first-class citizenship now had a white face.[17]

Plessy—as well as the state constitution—had held up equality as the legal accompaniment to segregation, but neither document provided reliable yardsticks for measuring "equality." In *Hooker v. Town of Greenville* (1902), the North Carolina Supreme Court, still occupied by judges appointed prior to the white supremacy campaigns, made a fleeting attempt to add teeth to the vague school laws, ruling that local boards of education should distribute school funds on an equal per capita basis. Only three years later, however, a newly appointed court of Democratic judges reversed that ruling, arguing that equal funds did not matter as long as local districts provided each race with "equal facilities." The court cited only two markers of equal facilities: length of school terms and a "sufficient number of teachers." In the years to come, local officials found ways of circumventing even those weak requirements. By the 1910s, disfranchisement's devastating effects on black public education were clear. In the words of Louis Harlan, "After 1900 the Negroes could no longer bargain votes for schools in the legitimate manner of political man. . . . The Republicans became as Lily White as the Democrats, and the Negro was helpless to protect the public schools of his children." As subsequent historians have shown, African Americans were not as "helpless" as Harlan suggested. They sustained poorly funded public schools through institutions of self-help and philanthropy. Nonetheless, Harlan rightly pointed to dramatic changes in the relative position of blacks within southern public education. In 1900, blacks constituted about one-third of the state's population and received just over 28 percent of state school funds; by 1915, their share had dropped to 13 percent, an unprecedented low. The absence of full citizenship rights unquestionably compromised blacks' ability to secure access to the privileges of public education.[18]

For African Americans, the political upheavals of the 1890s dramatically redefined the meaning of citizenship and invested new significance in the privileges of public education. Black citizenship no longer included a solid base of civil and political rights on which the more derivative privileges of social citizenship, such as education, rested. Jim Crow turned that model on its head. For African Americans in the segregated South, the institutions of social citizenship often had to function as a substitute for rather than an extension of those more fundamental civil and political rights.[19] Black North Carolinians looked to public education as their way back to the civic foundations of American life. The perceived inseparability between education and citizenship inspired an almost religious reverence for schooling among southern blacks, but it also raised some difficult questions: How were African Americans, as second-class citizens, going to create an equitable public school system? To what extent could equal but segregated education help them to reclaim the privileges of first-class citizenship? In making those questions central to this study, I have charted the changing strategies that blacks used to secure a system of public education that facilitated first-class citizenship, and the system of racial management that whites created in response.

This book opens in the turbulent years that followed World War I, when African Americans embraced new opportunities to put education on the public agenda. Chapter 1 shows how black leaders used postwar social dislocations as leverage in bargaining for expanded access to public schooling. State officials made some concessions to those calls for educational equality but at the same time held high expectations regarding black "self-help" in building schools. The state also institutionalized white management of black schooling by creating the Division of Negro Education, a supervisory agency charged with cultivating "the right kind of citizenship" among African Americans. The bureaucratization of black schooling stimulated new efforts to define educational equality and prompted African American teachers and parents to pursue that goal as clients of the state. While African Americans routinely pledged loyalty to their new white "guardians" of black education, such pledges must be read alongside evidence of black experimentation with strategies for self-determination.

Chapter 2 considers one of the first victories that African American leaders scored in the battle for school equality: state approval of the same basic curriculum for black and white public high schools. This chapter considers why state school officials were willing to make this concession toward educational equality and why this achievement, in the context of the state's early black public high school development, was initially more symbolic than substantive. Chapter 2 also looks at two additional reform movements that further laid bare the limits of curricular equalization in the Jim Crow South. Inspired by the black history movement of the 1920s, some black educators began to argue not simply for equal access to white-authored curricula but also for the power to shape what students learn about their collective past. Only then, black educators argued, would school curricula offer black youth a full sense of cultural citizenship. During the depression years, the relationship between schooling and economic citizenship took on new urgency, prompting black educators to press for equalized vocational programs that would offer students alternatives to "Negro jobs." By the 1940s and 1950s, however, black reformers facing enduring income gaps and impossibly narrow employment options were asking whether even the best vocational training would liberate black youth from the oppression of a highly segregated labor market.

Chapter 3 turns to higher education and the complex career of James E. Shepard, arguably the most prominent black educator in North Carolina during Jim Crow and one of equalization's most ardent champions. A remarkable politician, Shepard goaded the state into incorporating the South's first publicly supported black liberal arts college in 1925 and later pressed for the development of North Carolina College for Negroes into a full-fledged university. Shepard insisted that white officials pay the "high price" of segregation by expanding his school's offerings, but the state in many ways paid the lesser costs of Shepard's bid for equalization. In seeking white patronage, Shepard actively blocked early NAACP-backed efforts to integrate the University of North Carolina. This chapter looks at those early pioneers of higher education desegregation and considers the conflicted role that Shepard—and, more broadly, his generation of black institution builders—played in the emerging civil rights movement.

Generational fault lines as well as the tensions between the imperatives of local black leadership and the goals of the national NAACP's educational litigation campaign also take center stage in chapter 4, which centers on North Carolina's struggle for teacher salary equalization. In 1933, national NAACP representatives rallied thousands of black teachers in the state behind the goal of salary equalization, but senior leaders in the black teachers association refused to cooperate with the NAACP's plans for litigation. They instead sought to retain some measure of negotiating power with local officials by joining them in a cooperative project to keep "outside agitators" at bay. While these educators could be cast as unapologetic accommodationists, their choices reflect their ambivalent efforts to reclaim black citizenship through local leadership and leverage. In 1944, the state implemented a unitary salary schedule, a victory that white officials often cited in diverting attention from an overall picture of egregious educational inequalities.

The task of exposing equalization's formidable unfinished business fell to grassroots organizers following World War II. Chapter 5 looks at the men, women, and youth who rejected the NCTA's more cautious approach and led an extraordinary fight for school facilities equalization. At the center of this chapter is a battle for school equalization that began in Lumberton, North Carolina, in 1946. Inspired by the local NAACP Youth Council, black students in Lumberton went on strike to protest school conditions. When the state and national press illuminated the stark realities of those conditions and when parents filed a school equalization lawsuit, school officials agreed to build two new black schools. This case eventually laid bare strategic differences within the local black community and between national and local civil rights leaders. Under the leadership of Thurgood Marshall, the NAACP's national legal team initially supported the Lumberton case but soon shifted its attention to school desegregation litigation. The Lumberton protest, however, inspired a wave of black-led struggles for equalized facilities and galvanized the state to launch its own movement for equalization. On the eve of *Brown*, then, a battle for ownership of the school equalization movement had emerged. State officials promoted equalization as an alternative to integration, whereas black citizens tended to view it as *Brown*'s ideal accompaniment. In other words, black citizens did not lose interest in improving their schools even as support for the idea of integration grew.

By 1954, significant measurable disparities remained between black and white schools, but the previous decade of equalization activism had narrowed the funding gap and a sizable number of black students greeted *Brown* from within relatively new facilities. Within this context of improving school conditions, chapter 6 considers why many black North Carolinians nonetheless embraced *Brown*. Integration pioneers came from some of the state's most poorly equipped black schools as well as from some of its newest and most modern, an indication that both tangible and intangible factors informed the decision to enter white schools. *Brown* did not, of course, receive an unqualified embrace among black North Carolinians, and prescient voices of caution emerged as early as the 1950s. Black ambivalence about *Brown* in part reflected the fact that the ruling threatened the existence of black schools at what many African Americans saw as a moment of historic institutional ascension. Moreover, *Brown* heightened long-standing concerns about black exclusion from state policymaking. Black leaders insisted with new urgency in the wake of *Brown* that the markers of first-class citizenship included both integrated classrooms and a system of shared educational leadership, where blacks and whites cooperatively managed the training of future citizens.

Fearful of the risks involved with white-authored desegregation plans, many African Americans nonetheless concluded by the 1960s that the struggles for educational equality and racial integration were inextricably linked. Today, as legal backing for integration plans has waned, North Carolinians across the racial spectrum increasingly have prioritized the fight for school equality. In one sense, this book reinforces the importance of that fight. The men and women whose stories are told in this book keenly understood the foundational significance of resources, teacher salaries, and test scores—that is, of equality's measurable evidence. But many of them also insisted that a school's value could not be measured in numbers alone. They imagined the possibilities for schools that were greater than equal, schools that modeled a diverse and inclusive society of first-class citizens. I hope that the pages that follow will help us to do the same.

The Negro people seem to be pathetically desirous of sending their children to school.
—*Biennial Report of the Superintendent of Public Instruction of North Carolina,*
1924–25/1925–26

It is essential that our children should be given the best training and education
possible to qualify them for the responsible duties of citizenship.
—Petition from African American parents in Smithfield to local school officials, 1925

White people in our state are not asked to sweat blood [so] that
their children may be helped through the schools to become good citizens.
—George E. Davis, Rosenwald school supervisor, 1927

CHAPTER ONE

The Price of Equality

Black Loyalty, Self-Help, and the "Right Kind of Citizenship"

"Ho' Stop! Look! Listen!" In the summer of 1919, flyers bearing that head-line circulated around the small town of Ahoskie in North Carolina's north-eastern corner. The black community's Educational League was advertis-ing its "Two in One" celebration, an event billed as both a "Homecoming of our boys, and an Educational Rally." Returning veterans of World War I and the "elder soldiers" of the Civil War were to gather at the Colored Ma-sonic Hall and march down Main Street, followed by a brass band and a procession of schoolchildren waving American flags. After reaching the First Baptist Church, the crowd would listen to remarks from local leaders and enjoy a free dinner. Anticipating a "High Day in Israel," event planners urged, "Come One, Come All!" While the celebration's publicists promised parades and pageantry, they held educational promotion as their "main object." In exchange for food and festivities, the league would collect con-tributions for school improvement projects. Among the invited guests were white officials, including the county superintendent of schools and the state supervisor of Negro rural schools. The celebration of black mili-tary service cloaked a much larger project. Having performed the high-est of patriotic duties by sending men to war, African Americans saw new opportunities to stake claims to education as a fundamental right of loyal citizens. Nearly one thousand people attended the rally. Records do not indicate whether those officials in attendance pledged increased educational appropriations, but the state supervisor of Negro rural schools later noted that the people of Ahoskie were "anxious" to build a new school. At the very least, Ahoskie's black citizens had rallied their way onto the state's radar.[1]

Across the state and nation, the war had freighted questions of racial loyalty with especially heavy import. Many whites had bristled at the sight of black men in uniform and feared the potential for black militancy at home. The war also had opened up northern labor markets to black workers, prompting a new wave of black migration from the South. As the wartime rhetoric of democracy bolstered black calls for racial justice, white concerns regarding black loyalty chafed against a rising spirit of black self-determination. Interracial tensions reached a crescendo in 1919, a year that, according to historians John Hope Franklin and Alfred A. Moss Jr., "ushered in the greatest period of interracial strife the nation had ever witnessed."[2]

Within that context, black leaders employed pledges of loyalty as leverage in postwar campaigns for expanded access to state services, particularly education.[3] They insisted on a reciprocal bond of interracial loyalty that conceded white political privilege but afforded white patronage of black public education. When the state failed to reward black loyalty and demanded a heavy dose of "self-help" in building schools, black leaders demonstrated increased interest in political organization and alliances with "outside agitators." In 1921, betraying its nagging concerns about containing black protest, North Carolina created the Division of Negro Education, which promised to discourage agitation and cultivate among African Americans "the right kind of citizenship." Born out of white fears of black insurgency, this new agency nonetheless opened up space in which blacks could make claims on the state. African Americans ultimately used that space to press for educational equality and to renegotiate the kinds of citizenship that black public education would facilitate.

World War I and the Specter of Black Disloyalty

"No truer American can be found anywhere than among the Negroes of the South," declared Durham educator James E. Shepard in April 1917 to an African American assembly at Raleigh's Odd Fellows Hall. The black man, he insisted, could not be "incited to rebellion" and would not use the war to advance his own agenda. In fact, the black man "forgets his wrongs and limitations and even his rights when duty calls." Earlier that week, duty had called when President Woodrow Wilson asked Congress for a declaration of war against Germany, insisting that the "world must be made safe for democracy." At this early stage of America's involvement, whites took some comfort in the pledged allegiance of Shepard and other black leaders. The day after Shepard's speech, Raleigh's white newspaper hailed him as a model race leader who would "dispel from the minds of those who may have received the poison of German influence, all distorted aims of treason born ambitions." Governor Thomas Bickett similarly affirmed his "abiding faith in the loyalty of the colored population" and nostalgically recalled "the loyalty of black men to white women and children from 1861 to '65 when the white men were at the front." Bickett conveniently failed to mention the seven thousand black North Carolinians who had fought for the Union army during the Civil War.[4]

Race leaders had their own reasons for eliding the complexities of black loyalty and instead emphasizing their patriotic service. As Nan Woodruff has written of black wartime service in the Mississippi Delta, "African Americans understood that in bourgeois democracies the ability to be patriotic and to fight for one's country were the attributes of citizenship."[5] Speaking at the North Carolina Agricultural and Technical College (A&T) in Greensboro in 1917, the school's president, James Benson Dudley, reminded his audience that "in every war and conflict that our country has engaged in, we have as a race been loyal." Dudley warned that the present crisis again demanded loyalty and that it was "not the time to discuss our racial conflicts." To be certain, black North Carolinians gave more than lip service to wartime calls for service. One Kinston mother sent seven sons to the front lines, and more black soldiers trained at A&T than at any other black land-grant college. Moreover, the state's counties with the largest black populations exceeded average collection rates of war savings stamps. Black enthusiasm for wartime service forced Charlotte's white newspaper to admit that it was "about time for all that silly talk about the probable disloyalty of the Negro to be given a back seat—or better still, toted out and given burial."[6]

If black loyalty to the wartime cause was above reproach, black loyalty to the nation's racial order was on increasingly shaky ground. In 1917 A&T history professor D. J. Jordan publicly criticized President Wilson's record on race and, in reference to a race riot in East Saint Louis, Illinois, asked, "Is this the kind of Democracy I am asked to give my fortune and my life to make safe in the world?" Rumors circulated of Governor Bickett's outrage at this lapse in black deference. Race leaders subsequently issued an apology, but the incident had exposed an undercurrent of protest. Ironically, propaganda issued by the State Council of Defense seemed custom-made to incite black rebellion. One recruiting poster screamed, "THE WORLD CANNOT LIVE HALF SLAVE, HALF FREE." As historian William Breen has argued, the state faced a dilemma. It hoped to encourage black service but feared that statewide black mobilization "might come to constitute a threat to the existing political balance and to the doctrine of white supremacy."[7]

State officials ultimately were less concerned about black loyalty to the nation than black disloyalty to the Jim Crow social and political order. The former, they feared, might well inspire the latter. Black political activity was indeed on the rise. In 1916, for example, African Americans in Raleigh formed the Wake County Twentieth Century Voter's Club. While the vast majority of the state's black adults were not registered voters, even small numbers of blacks at the polls alarmed whites. As the *Charlotte Observer* argued, "The negro's lapse into politics would be the very worst thing that could befall the race in this State." Refusing to heed such advice, the Wake County club reemerged in 1919 promoting black candidates for local offices. Those candidates lost, but Raleigh's black leaders had demonstrated their resolve to "lapse into" the forbidden world of politics.[8]

Southern blacks also began cultivating ties to civil rights organizations based in the North, particularly the National Association for the Advancement of Colored People (NAACP). Founded in New York in 1909 by a coalition of white and black Progressives, the NAACP attracted black popular support through its chief spokesman, W. E. B. Du Bois, who edited the NAACP's organ, *The Crisis*. During the war, Du Bois urged readers to "close ranks" and temporarily subordinate the fight for racial justice to the fight for democracy abroad. By war's end, however, Du Bois charged that blacks were "cowards and jackasses" if they were not willing to "fight a sterner, longer, more unbending battle against the forces of hell in our own land." This message of race pride and protest did not fall on deaf ears. Before the war, the South was home to only a small percentage of the NAACP's local branches; by 1919, the region contained well over one-third. In North Carolina, the first three branches formed in Raleigh, Greensboro, and Durham in 1917, with seven more following within two years and statewide membership exceeding one thousand by 1920.[9]

The Crisis's power rested not only on its critiques of the South but also on its stories of the North, where black southerners turned for opportunity, including better schools. Du Bois admitted that the North was "no paradise," but he judged the South to be "at best a system of caste and insult and at worst a Hell." The war hastened the Great Migration, which brought more than half a million southern blacks to the Midwest and

North between 1916 and 1919. The combined effects of wartime industrial production and immigration restrictions prompted northern industrialists to recruit black southern labor. The promise of better schools further lured southern blacks. As one migrant said of her fellow southern expatriates, "The first reason they give for coming North is to educate their children."[10] Charles Clinton Spaulding, the president of Durham's black insurance company, North Carolina Mutual, relayed a similar tale to the mayor of Rocky Mount in 1921. As a consequence of the lack of schools, Spaulding warned, "two of your best citizens are now planning to sell out and go North." Many migrants would be disillusioned by the extent of northern discrimination, but their hopes for equal opportunity sparked a generation-long exodus from the Jim Crow South.[11]

Southern whites most feared blacks who sought to reshape rather than escape the South. As Russia's Bolshevik Revolution stoked diffuse fears of radicalism, whites looked on any sign of black insurgency with heightened alarm. Most blacks, of course, had far less reason to concern themselves with communist Reds than with the red of blood. Ominously referring to the late-nineteenth-century terrorist leagues that violently restored white Democrats to power, Governor Bickett cautioned black North Carolinians in 1919, "Make a drive for political domination and the Red Shirts will again take to the saddle."[12]

The Red Shirts did not formally reorganize, but predictions of bloodshed soon came true. During the infamous Red Summer of 1919, race riots broke out across the nation. By year's end, mobs had lynched seventy-seven black men, up from sixty-four lynchings in 1918 and forty-four in 1917. Whites lynched four black men in North Carolina in 1919, a small number compared to figures elsewhere but more than enough to bring home the threat of mob violence. That summer, Governor Bickett condemned the increasingly popular Ku Klux Klan as "a very foolish and a very wicked order," but in the same breath he affirmed that "it [was] the unalterable determination of the whites to keep in their own hands the reins of government." The state, he suggested, would make few concessions to the postwar "New Negro." At the height of the Red Summer, Greensboro educator Charles H. Moore lamented the increasing number of whites "to whom the sight of an intelligent, self-respecting, aspiring and well-to-do Negro man is more obnoxious than one of the opposite kind."[13] At no time since the 1890s had the South—and the rest of the nation—seemed so close to racial war.

Against the backdrop of the Red Summer, Shepard's wartime assurances of black loyalty gave way to urgent calls for interracial dialogue. In an August 1919 letter to southern governors, he insisted, "Something must be done and done quickly to re-assure both races." Shepard proposed that the governors convene a region-wide interracial conference. State neglect, he warned, would invite "distrust, depression, gloom and perhaps bloodshed." Still quick to assure whites of black loyalty, Shepard condemned those black leaders who engaged in "agitation" and "intermeddling by foreign organizations." But he also made demands: "kind treatment" for returning black soldiers, representation on juries, and the franchise for "all who are qualified to vote."[14] Couched within the deferential language of black loyalty, here was a call for the fundamental privileges of citizenship.

Possibly inspired by Shepard's proposal, state superintendent of schools Eugene Brooks seized on the call for interracial dialogue.[15] Since becoming superintendent in 1918, Brooks had received considerable correspondence from black leaders. Durham physician Aaron Moore wrote to Brooks on behalf of the black North Carolina Teachers Association (NCTA), charging that the state was "unjustly discriminating in their appropriations for the work of Negro education." He noted that the last legislature had appropriated only thirty-five thousand dollars to the state's black normal schools—a tiny fraction of its total four-million-dollar education budget—on the flimsy "pretext" that black schools were "not doing the work required of them." Brooks forthrightly acknowledged that appropriations had "fallen short" of what black schools "rightly need and justly deserve" and promised to "strive earnestly to see that justice is done." Several months later, Brooks explained in the *New York Times* that the South could no longer ignore the duty of black education. "If his education is not directed by us," he warned, "others that do not understand our social structure, that are ignorant of the nature and needs of the negro and have false notions of his relation to the white race in the South, will take charge of it." Brooks requested that Shepard convene race leaders to discuss "the distrust that seems to be in evidence here and there in the state" and to set about launching race relations in a "new direction." Brooks and Shepard invited approximately sixty black leaders to Raleigh on 26 September, with Brooks noting in the invitation letter that the state's "new educational program" required "the wisest leadership possible."[16]

The idea for such interracial dialogues had recent precedent. In January 1919, a group of white ministers and businessmen met in Atlanta and founded the Commission on Interracial Cooperation (CIC), a regional task force designed to foster education and dialogue about race relations. Local CIC branches soon formed across the South and sponsored interracial gatherings. In a "declaration of principles," the CIC urged on its members a spirit of Christian cooperation. The CIC set out to tackle some of Jim Crow's most egregious inequalities, but over the next twenty-five years, the group never challenged segregation itself. Moreover, while the CIC opened interracial dialogue, it also tended to reinforce the notion that whites should serve as the chief architects of southern race relations. Brooks had the CIC model in mind when he planned his interracial meeting.[17] He drafted a statement of principles, which he intended black representatives to use as the basis for an official "platform." While Brooks planned to give the attendees a chance to debate and revise this statement, he insisted that the Department of Education "would be unable to carry out very broad plans unless there can be some common ground of safety upon which the leaders of both races may stand." He suggested that educational progress demanded consensus with a white-authored vision for progress.[18]

On the morning of 26 September, forty people gathered in the Hall of the House of Representatives at the State Capitol in Raleigh. The group included thirty-six black men, two black women, and two white men. Approximately three-quarters of the African Americans in attendance were educators, including several private school principals and the presidents of the four state-supported black normal schools. The remaining black representatives included journalists, ministers, businessmen, the state director for Negroes of the Bureau of Tuberculosis, and the custodian of the Raleigh Post Office. The two whites included Superintendent Brooks and Nathan Carter Newbold, the state's Negro rural school supervisor. After a full day of discussion, the black representatives unanimously adopted Brooks's statement, which the state then published as "A Declaration of Principles by Representative Negroes of North Carolina."[19]

On the surface, the strong black support for the statement appeared to be an exercise in self-subordination. While the statement denounced mob violence, it also repeatedly cautioned against "agitation." Blacks were to avoid the "labor agitator" who "recounts the iniquities of the white man" and "entices" blacks to leave the South. Moreover, they were to disavow "this continual harping on the injustices of the white man to the Negro" and publicize "what the white race is really trying to do for the Negroes." The declaration entirely avoided the issue of black voting, instead suggesting that blacks should voice grievances by "appealing to right and justice before the proper authorities and by building up a wider friendship with right-thinking men of both races." Most important, blacks were to dismiss any notions of "social equality." Anyone who advocated "intermingling of the races on terms of social equality" did "great harm to the Negro."

If black and white were "to live together" in happiness, each race should protect the sanctity of "its own social life." Blacks, then, were left with a curious dilemma. They were to supplant politics with private appeals between white patrons and black clients, but they could never approach their white "friends" as social equals. If much of the statement spelled out limits on black action, the section on "Educational Advantages" hinted at potential rewards for toeing the line. Admitting that black schools suffered from insufficient funds, the document declared, "There never was a time in North Carolina when the State was so ready to give adequate educational opportunities to the Negroes." It outlined a new plan for black education that included county training schools, increased teacher salaries, improved buildings, expanded normal schools, and the establishment of public high schools. Lest any doubts remained, however, the document asserted that school improvements would not come "if the Negro is led unwisely and race friction increases."[20] Black educational advancement hinged on keeping black "agitation" at bay.

The Declaration of Principles received considerable white support. The press hailed it primarily for its affirmation of racial order rather than its promises to improve black education. The *Raleigh News and Observer* reprinted it on the front page and judged that it "deserves the widest sort of circulation," particularly since it "deprecates the appeal to force about which so much is heard in the radical negro press." Durham's paper also gave it front-page coverage and held it up as proof that "the colored people of this state are as sensible as they have been credited with being." The Greensboro and Salisbury papers contrasted the "sane" and "wholesome" thought of black North Carolinians with the supposed radicalism of blacks elsewhere. The *Charlotte Observer* found "especially commendable" the warnings against "intermingling of the races on terms of social equality." The white teachers association "urged all teachers and school officials of the white race to co-operate with the negroes, and give aid to their leaders in their attempts to raise the intellectual and moral level of the negro children." To be sure, the declaration had its white critics. South Carolina's state school superintendent worried that appeals to interracial cooperation invited thoughts of social or political equality. The former notion "would mean a degradation of the race and is unthinkable"; the latter idea "would mean a return to the time of carpetbaggers and scalawags." He felt certain that racial management in South Carolina, where blacks constituted a majority of the population, required "a different solution."[21] Skeptics aside, many white leaders believed that the declaration appropriately encouraged black uplift without violating the basic mores of the Jim Crow South.

Numerous black leaders also endorsed the Declaration of Principles. Aaron Moore felt "more proud than ever" and pledged, "We shall always stand by the splendid work being done by those in authority." Spaulding offered Brooks his "personal thanks and appreciation for the profound interest you manifested in the welfare of our people." Goldsboro principal Clarence Dillard judged the declaration to be a work of "Divine inspiration," while Fayetteville State Normal School president Ezekiel Smith suggested that the meeting had sparked nothing short of a spiritual revival. When Smith explained at a Baptist gathering that both Governor Bickett and Superintendent Brooks endorsed the declaration, the congregation spontaneously sang "Praise God from Whom All Blessings Flow."[22]

After collectively raising their voices with encomiums to the state, black leaders demonstrated that forbidden strategies for citizenship lay just below the surface of professed loyalties. A number of key men who had endorsed the Declaration of Principles spearheaded a campaign in the 1920 gubernatorial primary against Republican Party candidate John J. Parker, who courted white voters with promises of black political exclusion. Holding the reins of the anti-Parker political machine was educator and self-proclaimed political naysayer Charles Hunter. While he had not attended the 1919 meeting in Raleigh, Hunter had sent state officials personal endorsements of the declaration. He reaffirmed his loyalty to white leadership and reminded them that he had long discouraged blacks from the "blind pursuit of political will-o' the wisps." Hunter's legacy was, in fact, far more complex than he claimed. Born a slave to a prominent Raleigh family in the early 1850s, he came of age during Reconstruction and established connections to the city's black political vanguard. As black political fortunes dimmed, Hunter advocated black uplift through educational and economic pursuits, but he did not completely abandon "agitation." In addition to organizing the anti-Parker movement, he played a large role in planning Raleigh's 1919 Emancipation Day Celebration, at which thousands of blacks denounced Jim Crow. As Hunter biographer John Haley has noted, many black men had an undeniable "Janus-faced character" in simultaneously proscribing and practicing politics.[23]

Hunter and other leading black men were also instrumental in organizing the South's new NAACP chapters. Hunter not only helped to charter Raleigh's branch but also served as a delegate to the 1917 national meeting. Likewise, five black men from Raleigh who helped found that city's

NAACP chapter in 1917 signed the Declaration of Principles two years later. The Durham NAACP branch included "loyal" leaders Aaron Moore and C. C. Spaulding, high school principal William G. Pearson, and, for a time, James Shepard. When NAACP secretary James Weldon Johnson toured the state in 1924, he concluded, "North Carolina is a Southern State in which the program of the N.A.A.C.P. can be carried out with great success."[24]

The prospects for the NAACP's success were not uniformly bright, however. Black educators who relied most directly on the good graces of white officials trod cautiously into the postwar ferment. As the leader of a state-supported school, A&T president James Benson Dudley alternately pushed the boundaries of black protest and sought white goodwill. Active in Republican politics in the late nineteenth century, he turned to educational leadership after disfranchisement and for the rest of his career carefully weighed his interest in racial protest with his need for white approval. In the 1910s, he spoke out passionately against the inequalities of residential segregation and Jim Crow railway cars, but during the war he muted such protests. At war's end, Dudley returned to the center of agitation when he stood up to a "prominent white citizen" who objected to advertisements for A&T in *The Crisis*. Dudley's fellow Greensboro educator, Bennett College president Frank Trigg, forbade the circulation of *The Crisis* on his campus, but in 1920 Dudley was "holding his ground well," suggesting that he would not follow Trigg's accommodating lead. Before the year was out, however, Dudley again retreated. He condemned black women's suffrage activism, and ads for A&T disappeared from *The Crisis* in 1921 and did not reappear until the summer of 1924. Dudley even went so far as to state publicly in the early 1920s that most blacks had few racial grievances.[25] By the time of his death in 1925, Dudley's career had been marked by moments of courageous protest as well as conflicted concessions to white rule.

Whites primarily expressed the need for assurances of loyalty from black men, not their wives and sisters, who presumably posed fewer threats to the racial order. Only two black women had been present at the 1919 meeting in Raleigh, a relative absence that belied their central role in black civic life. Especially in the wake of disfranchisement's eviscerating effects on black male political power, black women became vital interracial diplomats. As Glenda Gilmore has explained, white women "lobbied to obtain services *from* their husbands, brothers, and sons"; in contrast, black women "lobbied to obtain services *for* their husbands, brothers, and sons."[26] Many whites saw such female government clientage as safely within the acceptable parameters of black activity.

The minimal representation of women at the 1919 meeting meant that the state had, in fact, missed an opportunity to affirm the loyalty of leading black "agitators." When Charlotte educator and clubwoman Mary Mc-Crorey received an invitation from Superintendent Brooks to attend, she deferred to her husband, Biddle College president Henry Lawrence Mc-Crorey. His presence, she assured Brooks, would "be of more value to the conference than mine." McCrorey's self-effacing reply masked her significant civic influence. In 1919, she was among the organizers of the campaign for ratification of the woman suffrage amendment. Moreover, she was among a growing number of black leaders who read *The Crisis* with rapt interest, and in 1918 she arranged for Du Bois to speak in Charlotte. McCrorey's modesty may not have fooled Governor Bickett. In 1919, when he addressed the Colored Auxiliary of Charlotte's Associated Charities—a group founded by McCrorey—he pointedly warned against the dangerous influence of "whisperers," northern firebrands, and "the fellow a thousand miles away who sits at a roll-top desk and writes editorials."[27]

Few black women advocated more passionately for both political involvement and educational equality than McCrorey's fellow educator and clubwoman Charlotte Hawkins Brown, the founder of Palmer Memorial Institute in Sedalia. As president of North Carolina's Association of Colored Women's Clubs, Brown organized on behalf of women's suffrage and, in cooperation with the NAACP, led a voter registration movement. At the same time, she cloaked much of her advocacy for black youth in the language of black loyalty and white guardianship. In her 1919 novella, *Mammy*, Brown depicted a former slave who cared for a neglectful and unappreciative white family with unwavering devotion. *Mammy* was both a celebration of black loyalty and a sentimental reminder to whites of their paternalistic obligations. In a similar vein, Brown proposed to state officials in 1919 the establishment of a school for black juvenile delinquents by arguing, "While the average colored mother watches over the families of the white race, her own children are growing up in the streets neglected and uncared for."[28] Black women's guardianship of white children, she suggested, demanded reciprocal state protection of black youth.

In the early 1920s, carefully crafted pledges of loyalty from both black women and black men seemed more likely to reap rewards than did radical agitation. The 1920 fall elections had brought disappointing results. While Hunter's faction could take pleasure in knowing that Parker lost in the Republican gubernatorial primary, the election's ultimate victor, Democrat Cameron Morrison, won on a white supremacy platform. In another defeat for black politics, black women tested their right to vote in large numbers, but trumped-up literacy restrictions stymied their efforts. On the final scorecard, black leaders' strategic experimentation won some critical points. The state's NAACP branches remained small in the 1920s but gained ground in the 1930s and 1940s. And even if few African Americans successfully exercised the right to vote, black suffragists limited the strategies that whites could use to maintain white supremacy. In Gilmore's words, black women who ventured to the polls "dared whites to use violence and won the dare."[29] The refusal of black men and women to relinquish their right to "agitation" signaled to state officials that black loyalty could not be assumed. This realization did not result in a radical reordering of politics, but it did usher in a new era of state interest in black public education.

"The Right Kind of Educational Leadership . . . Will Insure the Right Kind of Citizenship"

In his last months in office, Governor Bickett explained to the state legislature that in "deny[ing] to the negro any participation in the making of the laws," whites had created a "peculiar obligation to protect the negro in his life and property, and to help and encourage him in the pursuit of happiness." Bickett had once compared this "peculiar obligation" to "the relation of guardian and ward." The southern statesman was either "to foster and protect the welfare of his ward" or to face the consequences of his neglect. If the South did not provide schools, Bickett warned, blacks would move to the North, an experience that would "unfit them to be useful citizens in the South." In southern schools, blacks would "absorb southern ideals" and "transmit these ideals to the youth under their charge." Paternalistic duty and the exigencies of black unrest demanded that whites acknowledge black educational aspirations. Bickett appointed three whites and two blacks to the five-member Commission on Negro Legislation, which pronounced the state's program for black education "entirely inadequate" and proposed the establishment of "a Division of Negro Education."[30]

This new agency was to serve two purposes: supervision and publicity. Supervision would prevent blacks from looking outside the state for guidance. "In safety to itself the State should no longer neglect this duty," a report from Newbold's office warned. Black teachers were an especially vulnerable "soil for the planting of any doctrine." The division would also serve as the state's mouthpiece, countering pervasive "misinformation" with "reliable" facts. The report asked, "To whom now do agitators go for information about race conditions and educational advantages of the Negro race?" The state had left such matters in the hands "of those who have not always desired race harmony." The new division would employ the "ablest and sanest Negroes in the State in whom both races have confidence." Securing "the right kind of educational leadership" promised to "insure the right kind of citizenship" among African Americans, "regardless of what agitators out[side] of the State may do."[31]

In searching for ways to manage black education, the state institutionalized a decade-old initiative of the General Education Board (GEB), a New York–based umbrella agency for educational philanthropies. In 1910, the GEB had begun providing funding for a "Negro school agent" for each southern state and tasked these agents with working in cooperation with public school officials. Virginia state superintendent Jackson Davis became the first such agent, and by 1919, all of the former Confederate states had Negro school agents—all of whom were white men. GEB officials debated the merits of securing black agents but concluded that blacks lacked sufficient influence in politics. Nonetheless, the GEB insisted that its state agents were not paternalistic standard-bearers of the Old South but disciples of the New South's enlightened racial management.[32]

As their chief "guardian" for North Carolina's black schools, GEB officials chose Nathan Carter Newbold, who had presided with Superintendent Brooks at the 1919 meeting in Raleigh.[33] As historian James Leloudis has suggested, Newbold's path to interracial work contained a number of detours that could be read as efforts to reconcile a divided identity. Born in 1871 and raised in the home of his paternal grandfather, a sheriff and former slave owner in Pasquotank County, Newbold also came under the influence of his mother's family, whose Quaker and abolitionist roots taught him an appreciation for social nonconformity. Having inherited paths to both the South's white establishment and its antiestablishment conscience, the young Newbold sought a middle road. After graduating from Trinity College in Durham, he chose to become an educator, a profession he believed held opportunities for political and social influence. In less than a decade, Newbold had distinguished himself as an efficient school superintendent, holding positions in Asheboro, Roxboro, and Washington, North Carolina. He was among a network of educational officials who were transforming one-room country schools into modern graded institutions and holding new influence in state politics. After attending an elegant reception at the governor's mansion in Raleigh, he wrote to his wife, "The teacher is coming into his own. . . . Prominent people will now vie with each other to do honor to those who train children."[34]

Nathan Carter Newbold served as director of the North Carolina Division of Negro Education from 1921 until his retirement in 1950. (Courtesy of Nathan Carter Newbold Papers, box 5, David M. Rubenstein Rare Book and Manuscript Library, Duke University)

Prominent people soon were vying for Newbold, but in ways that at first seemed to threaten rather than enhance his public standing. In 1912, GEB representatives invited him to their headquarters, where they laid out for him a "vision of service and usefulness" as North Carolina's first agent for Negro schools.[35] Upon receiving this offer, Newbold hesitated. And when his local school board offered him more money to stay, he declined the GEB's offer. But when the same opportunity arose again the next year, Newbold took this second chance, albeit with lingering hesitation. By all accounts, he had sought to serve both blacks and whites as superintendent.[36] All the same, he clearly felt uncomfortable with the notion of serving solely black children. Betraying this unease, he specified that his new title would be "state superintendent of rural schools," even though his main responsibilities rested with black schools. Newbold's hometown newspaper announced his new job as "superintendent of elementary schools for the state," but such obfuscation did not shield him for long. When one white colleague expressed dismay at his new focus on black schools, Newbold insisted that he would "render greater service to my own people in North Carolina than to Negroes." In uplifting blacks, he would "add to the dignity, the self respect and the humanity of the State as a whole." Behind this public confidence lay enduring misgivings. "Why should I give up [my current job]," he asked himself, "to enter a new and untried field—one, which to a native Southerner might prove on many occasions to be most embarrassing and difficult?"[37] He confided that his "chief reason" for taking the job was to escape the humidity of the coast, although the salary increase provided further enticement.[38] While the state abounded with black men who would have readily advocated for their schools, the politics of Jim Crow demanded a white man, and the man selected initially accepted the task with ambivalence.

Newbold quickly drew inspiration and direction from precisely the people he was supposed to lead. He toured the state, talking with black parents and teachers, an experience he found "interesting, sometimes almost thrilling." He felt at times like he was at an "old-time camp meeting," as African Americans expressed their educational ambitions with an almost religious fervor. In his early years as state agent, Newbold primarily championed the basics: adequate buildings, certified teachers, and consistent school attendance. He encouraged black educators to teach the fundamentals of reading and writing alongside simple home industries. If his initial program was narrow in scope, Newbold's advocacy of black education marked a significant departure from the norm of state neglect. Charlotte Hawkins Brown pointed to this general absence of white allies for black schools when she told him, "I do not want to call on you for everything, but we have learned to look to you in the state of North Carolina as a friend interested in the welfare of Negro youth." Keenly aware that Newbold might harbor doubts about his new position, Aaron Moore reminded him that black communities "appreciate the embarrassment that you find in putting over this work."[39] While Newbold still occasionally employed the race-neutral title "state agent for rural schools," both blacks and whites understood that he was the man to see with appeals for black schools.[40]

The Division of Negro Education (DNE) offered blacks a channel for redress in matters of education and new—if circumscribed—opportunities for representation in policymaking. During its first year of operation, the DNE employed three white educators—Newbold (director), Guerrant H. Ferguson (assistant director), and Taylor B. Attmore (director of the Rosenwald school building program). The division also employed three black educators—William A. Robinson (supervisor of Negro high schools), George E. Davis (supervisor of Rosenwald school buildings), and Annie W. Holland (supervisor of Negro elementary schools). Newbold explained the logic behind a biracial staff: the white supervisors could "speak with more force and authority to white school boards and white superintendents," while the black supervisors could "speak with more force and effectiveness to the Negro people."[41] Southern state bureaucracies rarely offered such opportunities for black professional inclusion, but the DNE marked only a partial departure from regional conventions. The DNE's black employees received lower salaries than their white counterparts, and for the four decades that the agency existed, its black employees worked in privately owned offices in Raleigh's black business district, whereas Newbold and his white colleagues occupied offices in the headquarters of the Department of Public Instruction. Shortly after his new position became official, Newbold spoke before the NCTA and made explicit the boundaries of black inclusion. Blacks, he advised, should avoid two "red flags": politics and social equality.[42] These warnings suggested that Newbold initially did not plan to use his new position to disrupt the prevailing racial order but instead saw himself as reinforcing the well-worn idea that whites knew what was best for blacks.

If Newbold adhered in many ways to the mores of the Jim Crow South, he nonetheless won black praise. At the meeting where he had sounded warnings against the "two red flags," Greenville educator Charles M. Eppes passed a resolution of thanks to Newbold and other state officials. James Shepard extended personal congratulations and noted, "We know our interests are safe in your hands." James Dudley declared on behalf of the NCTA, "We heartily endorse the work of Prof. Newbold and pledge to him our unstinted support and loyalty." Superintendent Brooks pointed to such accolades as evidence that the DNE was proving an effective tool for racial management, reporting at the end of the agency's first year of existence, "The fact that the negroes had representation in the government . . . gave them a new loyalty to the state. . . . As a result of this supervision the negroes complain considerably less."[43]

These pledges of loyalty, like those voiced in 1919, merit more than a cynical nod. Not only had the DNE opened doors to black representation within an otherwise lily-white world of state politics, but Newbold's insistence on interracial discourse and civility also signaled a significant change from the turbulent 1890s, when white mob leaders and statesmen blurred into one.[44] His appointment provided evidence that the state would consider black education a part—if not an equal part—of its overall responsibility. As a black doctoral student wrote in the mid-1920s, "Previous [to the formation of the DNE] it is no secret that the supervision of public schools for Negroes had either been neglected by the State authorities or had largely been left in the hands of outside agencies."[45]

Black leaders, however, were hardly willing to rest their fate exclusively in the hands of their new white guardians. When a writer for the *South*

Table 1.1. Public School Enrollment in North Carolina, by Race, 1919–1960

Year	White	Black	Total	Black Percentage of Total
1919–20	478,189	213,060	691,249	30.8
1929–30	607,344	259,595	866,939	29.9
1939–40	619,767	270,962	890,729	30.4
1949–50	625,167	268,578	893,745	30.1
1959–60	777,172	328,240	1,105,412	29.7

Sources: *Biennial Report*, 1920–21/1921–22, pt. 2, 50; *Biennial Report*, 1946–47/1947–48, pt. 1, 20; *Biennial Report*, 1962–63/1963–64, pt. 1, 38.

Atlantic Quarterly canvassed North Carolina in the early 1920s, he found that most black leaders still held a "keen interest" in politics and "considered disfranchisement of their masses as a temporary matter." What most rankled them was "the failure of the whites to treat the negroes fairly in such matters as schools and charities, as they had promised negro leaders in return for not contesting disfranchisement." Moreover, black leaders still proved willing to hold white officials publicly accountable for their promises, as demonstrated in 1921 when Newbold and Brooks invited more than two hundred black and white leaders to the first in a series of annual interracial conferences. As Newbold later explained, "It seemed to us wise to ask the leaders of the Negro people to meet in a conference where we might give them direct information about the State's long step forward in Negro education." The "long step" was the General Assembly's 1921 appropriation of nearly one million dollars for black education, the largest such appropriation ever, as well as increased appropriations at the local level for new black school construction. Whites, Newbold insisted, were ready to give blacks a "fair deal." This celebration of progress suddenly halted, however, when Salisbury educator J. H. Johnson asked a seemingly straightforward question: Why did officials not divide public funds among blacks and whites on an equal per capita basis? The basis for Johnson's query could not be denied. Despite constituting nearly one-third of the population (table 1.1), blacks received less than 10 percent of what the General Assembly appropriated in 1921 for permanent improvements at institutions of higher learning. Similar disparities were evident in the distribution of local funds. In response to Johnson's question, Newbold hesitated and appeared "confused," likely stunned by the boldness of the inquiry. He acknowledged the inequities but failed to explain them away.[46]

Fully aware of the limits of white guardianship of black schools, many blacks nonetheless used the language of paternalism in goading whites to action. Shortly after his public rebuke in Raleigh, Newbold crossed paths with Lizzie Targinton, a black teacher from Pasquotank County whose brothers had been "bond to" Newbold's grandfather. Upon Newbold's request, Targinton later sent him a "little history of the family, our family" in which she wove their overlapping life stories into a larger narrative about race. "Your grandfather used to say to my mother, I wish the colored people had the advantage of School," she recalled. Emphasizing Newbold's duty to fulfill his grandfather's wish, she added, "Like Elisha and Elijah the mantle has fallen on you from your grandfather. [Y]ou did not ask for it but you inherited [it]. . . . God has stirred up the wills of the white people through you to do this great work." Targinton traced for Newbold a lineage of white paternalism to which he could lay claim. In truth, however, white paternalism was not the most significant continuity that emerged from her family history. She also told of her family's resilient desire to acquire education, well before the state took an interest in black schooling. During the Civil War, Targinton's family moved to New Bern so that she could attend school. She later enrolled in St. Augustine's College in Raleigh, where she trained to become a teacher. Her commitment to education endured even as the white supremacy campaigns of the 1890s diminished public expenditures for black schools. At the time she wrote her letter, she was attending a reading circle twenty miles from her home and teaching a class of more than sixty children. "I am trying to lift my race as I am lifted," she wrote. Targinton passed on a desire for education to her daughter, who graduated from Howard University in Washington, D.C. While Targinton staked new hope for educational improvements on Newbold, her generation had found ways to learn without reliable state advocates. Denied the privileges of first-class citizens, they had looked first to their own communities and secondarily to the benevolence of white patrons to feed their poor, heal their sick, and school their children. In the coming years, Newbold and other officials relied heavily on these traditions of self-help in laying the foundations of black schools.[47]

"Sweating Blood" for School Equality

In the early 1920s, the state judged its schoolhouses—for both races—to be "still mainly poor," but a wide racial disparity exacerbated those conditions. The average rural white school was valued at $1,290, while the same for blacks was a mere $350. A 1921 report offered a glimpse inside such schoolhouses: consisting of only one room, these structures had "weatherbeaten exteriors" that offered a "cheerless" picture. The potbellied stove in the center of the room heated unevenly, leaving the children "half hot and half cold." Students sat for "six weary hours a day" on homemade benches, a feature "particularly common in colored schools." Many schools lacked "adequate provisions for drinking water" and relied on outhouses that were "dilapidated, disreputable, and filthy beyond belief." Such conditions obviously threatened students' health and safety, but even more was at stake. Testing found that pupils from one-room schools also tended to trail academically behind those from larger consolidated facilities. Poor conditions also discouraged students from staying in school, contributing to black illiteracy rates that in 1920 were three times higher than those for white North Carolinians.[48]

In the mid-1920s, the state undertook a "school building boom" to reduce the number of small and inadequate schoolhouses. From 1921 to 1927, the General Assembly allocated more than $17.5 million for a school building loan program as a stimulus for increased local educational spending, but only a small percentage of those funds reached black schools. Newbold once estimated that North Carolina officials spent ten times as much on white school buildings during the 1920s as they did on black schools. In 1919–20, white per pupil property values were four times greater than black values; in 1929–30, white values were still 3.7 times greater (see table 5.2).[49]

Inequalities in school spending patterns meant that self-help was vital to black educational progress. Historians have shown how black self-help initiatives under Jim Crow functioned as both a strategy and a substitute for citizenship. August Meier has argued that African Americans formed institutions for economic and moral betterment with the hope that they would "gain the respect of white men and thus be accorded their rights as citizens." Walter Weare has similarly claimed that the "overweening zeal" that blacks held for such programs "suggest[ed] a surrogate for politics and a platform to counter the racist doomsayers who predicted the extinction of the Negro race within fifty years." If self-help programs unquestionably carried many promises, it is less clear what they delivered. According to James Anderson, self-help activity "said much about blacks' desire for education and their willingness to sacrifice for it, but it also said much about their powerlessness, their taxation without representation, and their oppression."[50]

Some of the most ardent disciples of the black self-help philosophy were the so-called Jeanes teachers. The Jeanes program began as the philanthropic initiative of Anna T. Jeanes, a white Quaker heiress from Philadelphia, who died in 1907 and willed one million dollars for the improvement of black rural education in the South. Jeanes designated Hollis

Burke Frissell and Booker T. Washington, the presidents of Hampton Institute and Tuskegee Institute, respectively, to be trustees of the Negro Rural School Fund, later renamed the Anna T. Jeanes Fund. Washington and Frissell selected James Hardy Dillard, a white educator and dean at Tulane University, for the fund's presidency. Under Dillard, the fund hired black women to work as "industrial supervisors," overseeing the teaching in black rural schools and particularly encouraging the instruction of cooking, gardening, and handicrafts. Another chief function of Jeanes teachers was "organizing the people of the community into associations for self-help." The board's prototype was Virginia Estelle Randolph, who became the first Jeanes teacher in 1908. The daughter of former slaves, Randolph ran a one-room school in Virginia, where she promoted the fund's values by organizing students into "Willing Workers Clubs." Fund official Jackson Davis praised her model program as "a discipline in self-help and in the responsibility of citizenship in the highest value."[51]

The first Jeanes teacher in North Carolina began work in 1909, and state officials enthusiastically expanded the program in the postwar years. Between 1919 and 1921, the state arranged through a combination of private and public funds to more than double the average Jeanes salary. Newbold explained that the state was undertaking nothing "more vital and more far reaching" than its Jeanes work.[52] White officials embraced the Jeanes program partly for its economic dividends. Jeanes teachers raised private donations for black schools, thus easing the need for public appropriations. Jeanes teachers also judiciously oversaw the spending of public funds. Newbold judged that "the State's money going into counties for public schools will be better, more effectively and more economically used where supervisors are employed than where there is no supervision." Moreover, he found that Jeanes teachers raised far more money for their districts than the districts contributed to their salaries. As one superintendent put it, Jeanes teachers were "a most economical arrangement for any county."[53] In selecting individuals to uphold the Jeanes gospel of interracial diplomacy and self-help, officials preferred women, who seemingly posed less threat to the political establishment than did male supervisors. The program eventually employed some male teachers, but Newbold continued to believe that the ideal Jeanes teacher was a woman of "sound education," good health, "unimpeachable character," and "a pleasing personal appearance." He believed that Jeanes work required a "mother attitude and instinct" that few men possessed.[54]

No woman modeled Jeanes ideals better than Annie Welthy Holland. Born around 1871 on land that adjoined the Virginia plantations worked by

Jeanes supervisor Annie W. Holland founded the North Carolina Congress of Colored Parents and Teachers in 1927 and served as the state supervisor of Negro elementary schools from 1921 until her death in 1934. (From Nathan C. Newbold, ed., *Five North Carolina Negro Educators* [Chapel Hill: University of North Carolina Press, 1939])

her enslaved ancestors, Holland knew what it meant to sacrifice for schooling. Having exhausted her county's educational offerings at age twelve, she began work on a college degree at Hampton Institute, but financial circumstances prevented her from completing it. She set out to earn a living teaching in the state's rural schools, where she helped organize agricultural cooperatives among black families. After nearly two decades of work in Virginia, Holland became a Jeanes teacher in North Carolina in 1911 and quickly distinguished herself. In 1915, the NCTA raised money to employ her in conjunction with the Jeanes Fund as the state's chief home demonstration agent for African Americans. When the state created the DNE in 1921, Newbold hired Holland to serve as the state supervisor of Negro elementary schools, a position whose duties included Jeanes oversight. Integral to the state's program for black schools, Holland's professional status nonetheless reflected the double burdens of race and gender. As the DNE's only black female employee, Holland's salary fell below that of her two black male colleagues, whose salaries fell below those of their white male counterparts.[55] Holland's income belied the vital role she played in both black and white communities. She worked closely with many white home demonstration agents, who drew on her "intimate knowledge of the negro homes." Local school officials also routinely called on her to stamp out fires. "She was a peacemaker and organizer of real ability," recalled Newbold. "Frequently superintendents would write when there was some difficulty in a school and request that we send Mrs. Holland to iron out these difficulties."[56]

Lauded as an interracial diplomat, Holland nonetheless encouraged blacks to pull together for better schools rather than depend on white goodwill. Her emphasis on self-help found lasting expression in her 1927 organization of the North Carolina Congress of Colored Parents and Teachers (often referred to as the "Colored PTA"). Prior to the organization of a statewide black PTA, Holland had urged Jeanes teachers to organize local associations. By 1929, the state had 953 local black PTAs with a collective membership of 17,597. A 1933 study concluded that those associations had done more for black child welfare than any state agency, building schools, purchasing equipment, providing hot lunches, lengthening school terms, supplementing teacher salaries, and sponsoring health clinics. These projects fostered a shared sense of investment in schools. In 1927, the Lincoln County PTA had built new schools "where teachers had formerly taught in shacks," increased student attendance by as much as 50 percent, and converted erstwhile "indifferent" parents into mothers and fathers who took "great pride in sending their children to school, neat and tidy with well prepared lessons and all the necessary school books."[57] PTAs transformed black schools from symbolic representations of second-class citizenship into material demonstrations of black respectability.

Like the Jeanes Fund and PTA activities, the Rosenwald Fund opened up space for black self-help organization. The brainchild of Tuskegee Institute founder Booker T. Washington, the Rosenwald program reflected what Meier has described as Washington's insistence that "while whites had some responsibility, the most important part in the Negro's progress was to be played by the Negro himself." When black migration to the North escalated in the years before his death in 1915, Washington launched a crusade for black schooling that combined strategies of self-help with new appeals for outside assistance. He suggested to several benefactors that the expansion of black public education in the South could stabilize the agricultural labor on which both southern planters and northern industrialists depended. One of those philanthropists was Julius Rosenwald, a Chicago businessman of German Jewish heritage and president of Sears, Roebuck, and Company. In 1917, Rosenwald incorporated a foundation that would provide grants to southern communities to build black elementary schools on the condition that black citizens raised matching funds. The Rosenwald grants and matching funds were to cover half the cost of the schools, while public funds were to supply the rest. The public contribution was important to Rosenwald, who argued that charities alone could not sustain vital social services in the modern age. While this goal of public accountability signaled a new phase in black education, the Rosenwald program nonetheless perpetuated expectations of black sacrifice. Since African Americans already paid taxes earmarked for public education, the burden of raising matching funds amounted to what Anderson has termed "double taxation." The Rosenwald Fund provided welcome assistance even as it entailed a heavy dose of black self-help.[58]

Black communities welcomed the Rosenwald program despite its demands. In 1915, when the initiative was still in its infancy, the NCTA hired Charles H. Moore, chair of A&T's English department, to work with state officials in promoting Rosenwald work. Even before the fund's 1917 incorporation, African Americans in Chowan County raised $486 for an experimental Rosenwald school, far more than the $300 provided by the fund.[59] News of the program spread like wildfire. In 1919, Newbold "frequently receive[d] letters from Negro teachers asking for help on new buildings." He planned to oversee the building of 100 such schools that year alone. By the mid-1920s, North Carolina led the South with 412 Rosenwald schools.[60]

The Rosenwald campaign, Newbold noted in 1919, "had enabled us to get a hearing from certain county school officials which nothing else has so far." Whites had several reasons to give the program a "hearing." Some officials claimed that the program yielded a more docile and less restless black population. Moreover, the Rosenwald Fund rewarded black self-help with white paternalism but discouraged notions of black entitlement. A lawyer and school board member from Yanceyville reported his eagerness to reward the "darkies" of his community who "pulled the money out of their pockets" to cover school expenditures for their Rosenwald school. Believing that such acts of black sacrifice deserved "encouragement," he convinced the county board of education to offer the school more funding.[61] Even Newbold, who was more willing to accept notions of black entitlement than were most white officials, similarly couched his advocacy of Rosenwald work in the familiar language of white patronage. He saw black schools as "a disgrace to an independent, civilized people," evidencing "injustice, inhumanity and neglect on the part of our white people." Nonetheless, he believed that it was "only fair to the white people of the state" for blacks to raise contributions to repay their long dependence on whites. He told whites that they had a "legal and moral obligation" to help blacks, but he also suggested that blacks should earn white noblesse oblige in measured degrees. He assured white officials that "the colored people do not expect that as much money shall be spent on their school as is spent on the white school." The Rosenwald Fund also conformed to southern mores by giving whites authority. Blacks were responsible for raising matching funds, but only the local superintendent could submit an application for aid. Upon approval of the proposal, the fund would deposit money with the state, which then disbursed it to local officials. Finally, the fund stipulated that Rosenwald schools constituted "the property of the public school authorities."[62] Thus, schools built with black hands and partly from private black contributions remained under the official control of southern whites.

African Americans worked within the fund's limitations, using it to stimulate both black self-help and white investment. Charles Moore tirelessly "endeavored to commit our people to the policy of self-help" while laboring to stimulate public accountability. In 1916, for example, he wrote to the *Charlotte Observer* to expose the shortcomings of the local schools. Moore's spirited independence in goading local officials eventually rankled Newbold. In 1919 he essentially demoted Moore and hired a white assistant, Taylor B. Attmore, as "supervisor of the Rosenwald Fund." Moore, who became "supervisor of Rosenwald buildings," came under Attmore's supervision. When Moore continued to rile local officials, Newbold pushed for his resignation.[63]

Moore's replacement, George E. Davis, similarly expected white officials to provide the rightful funds owed to black schools, but he practiced greater deference and carefully framed his appeals to whites as beneficial investments in the South's "chief laboring class." Born in Wilmington and educated at the Biddle Institute in Charlotte, Davis briefly pursued a medical degree at Howard University before returning to Charlotte to teach.[64] Pitching the Rosenwald Fund to that "laboring class" required Davis to collect money among cash-strapped families. Under his guidance, teachers raised funds through plays and concerts, rallies complete with box lunches, and subscription programs. One teacher reported that school events "brought out a large number of parents anxious for better conditions for the education of their children." Students also participated. One girl collected fifty-four dollars in pennies, nickels, and dimes, which she proudly brought in a shot bag to a community rally.[65] Monetary donations fluctuated along with cotton and tobacco prices. In 1922, Davis found that people "came in from the cotton fields" and put cash on the table, but when a drought and hailstorms destroyed crops several years later, the cash flow slowed. Robeson County's black community was "continually holding entertainments . . . to try to raise money," but most folks had little to spare. When their coffers came up empty, black communities offered labor. Anderson has estimated that black labor "probably constituted an even larger share than cash donations" to the Rosenwald schools. The black community at Snow Hill, for example, painted and "ceiled" its Rosenwald school building, purchased a range for the cooking room and a sewing machine for the domestic science room, paid the domestic science teacher's salary, donated additional land for the school site, and hosted a three-day conference for the county's black teachers. In short, they stood "ready to help in anything that [would] make [their school] a better one."[66]

That readiness to help spoke to the desperate circumstances found in many black school communities. A typical request for Rosenwald aid came from the Merry Hill community in Bertie County, where a three-room school housed more than two hundred children, with three or four children squeezed onto benches made for two. In contrast to these bleak conditions, Rosenwald schools were, in the words of historian Thomas Hanchett, based on "the most up-to-date designs in American rural school architecture." The fund required that the schools be solidly constructed and "embody the most modern principles of school hygiene and sanitation." The fund also recommended that each school be built on "two acres of well drained land, located, if possible, on a public highway." The surrounding soil was to be "suitable for [a] playground and school garden," and there was to be a nearby supply of "pure drinking water." Each school was to have at least "two sanitary toilets, approved by the State Board of Health," and each classroom was to include large windows that provided plenty of light. These facilities often represented an almost miraculous improvement over previous conditions. As a student who attended a Rosenwald school in Stokes County in the 1930s put it, Julius Rosenwald "was amazing grace to us at that time."[67]

Whites sometimes misread black enthusiasm for the Rosenwald program as evidence that blacks needed white stimulation to appreciate education. The state superintendent reported in the mid-1920s that the Rosenwald Fund had rendered a "very salutary effect upon the feeling and attitude of the whole race." Building schools "satisfies, to some extent, the instinct of ownership—the desire of possession. The parent can say in some measure at least: 'This is mine and for me.'" This feeling of "ownership," the report continued, translated into more enthusiastic school attendance: "Public education is no longer something that is being imposed on him from without and against his will. It is something to be ardently desired. He no longer sends his child to school at the bidding of the law; he accepts the opportunity as an inestimable privilege."[68] That reading of Rosenwald participation correctly perceived black desires for institutional ownership but ignored the fact that blacks had "ardently desired" to at-

This five-room Rosenwald School at Stewart's Creek (ca. 1922–23) in Harnett County juxta-posed with the structure that it replaced shows the marked improvement over past con-ditions afforded by the combined efforts of the Rosenwald program and black self-help activity. (Courtesy of The North Carolina State Archives, Raleigh)

tend school long before either the "bidding of the law" had required them to do so or the Rosenwald program had provided them with a place to go.

Black pride in Rosenwald projects intensified black anger when whites failed to reciprocate their investments. Rosenwald supervisor George Davis's trademark equanimity once gave way to rage after inspecting a new Rosenwald school in the town of Marion in McDowell County. He found no central heating system, no indoor toilets, and no seats in the audito-rium. Davis also learned that the school was to operate under a six-month school term, while the county's whites attended school for nine months. Davis asked William F. Credle, the state's white Rosenwald supervisor, to delay further payments to county superintendent N. F. Steppe until he cor-rected the school's shortcomings. "I am in [the] position to know that [the Negroes] have been put upon in this matter," confided Davis. The forty families served by the school had raised more than two thousand dollars, a "great sacrifice." Davis believed that "they should not be pressed any more. *They are extremely poor* and have their pastors and churches to sup-port." The whites had justified their double standards for white and black children by creating "shoe-stringed" town limits, effectively segregating all the African Americans into a separate school system. "That's cow-ardly," Davis charged. "That's contrary to Anglo-Saxon claims to *fair play!*" Credle tried to reassure Davis that Steppe would remedy "some of the little things you mentioned," and less than a week later, Davis backed down and secured some discarded auditorium seats from the white school. He told Credle that he did not wish to stir up any "bitter feeling" and would exercise "diplomacy."[69]

Davis faced a similar dilemma after visiting Combstown, a rural community near Mt. Airy in Surry County. Fearing that "one should not write a letter when in the state of mind I am," he nonetheless struck while the iron was hot and penned a letter to Newbold. He had put "considerable effort" into securing a school "in place of the little unfurnished dog kennel" currently in use. For two years, the superintendent had promised a new building as long as Combstown residents raised nine hundred dollars. The black community already had collected five hundred dollars when the superintendent retreated from his promise of twenty-four hundred dollars in public funds. Davis drove to Combstown "in a blinding rain" to attend a school board meeting. He waited his turn to speak, standing for more than an hour while the board discussed appropriations for white schools. Finally, when a board member made a motion for budget approval, Davis spoke up and broached the "Combstown matter." The superintendent stalled and left the room, only to return and explain that the county commissioners would not approve the appropriation. Davis told Newbold, "If I were a white man, I would be ashamed of and for my group." He implored his supervisor "to throw the weight of [his] influence into the scales for the Negro." The black citizens of Combstown requested "mere crumbs, upon which they pay a tax, while they stretch hands bearing gifts." Blacks alone, he added, bore such heavy demands of sacrifice. "White people in our state," he insisted, "are not asked to sweat blood [so] that their children may be helped through the schools to become good citizens." Several days later, Davis again tried to explain away his reaction, telling Newbold that the "blue devils of fatigue may have directed my thoughts." Newbold assured Davis that he wanted to hear the "exact conditions" as he found them, but he added, "You may not find it necessary to feel yourself so discouraged as you did."[70] Newbold's optimism may have reflected his relative detachment from the realities of black life. In traveling the state and working in the trenches with fellow African Americans, Davis had come to understand black poverty and educational disadvantage in deeply personal terms.

Davis nonetheless believed that the Rosenwald program provided an important chance to demonstrate black fitness for citizenship. After attending a school dedication in Pender County, he happily reported that whites had been at the ceremony and banquet. "I was born within thirty miles of this place and I have known the time that white people would have lost their social prestige among their fellows had they been courageous enough to come out and dine 'with publicans and sinners,'" Davis recalled. He noted that "a special table" had been provided for the whites, but only out of "social custom," not because the whites had demanded it. Davis hoped that such events were bringing together a biracial "aristocracy of brains" that would roll back the layers of misunderstanding and prejudice that divided the South's citizens.[71] In the 1920s, others in the field of southern black education shared Davis's hopes. By decade's end, however, buoyant spirits gave way to the racial politics of economic retrenchment.

A "Golden Period of Negro Education"?

At a gathering on black education at Shaw University in 1923, Newbold relayed an ominous report from the U.S. Department of Justice. The Russian government was rumored to have sent four hundred thousand dollars "to convert the Negro people of America" to Bolshevism and recruit them for the Third International. Newbold quickly assured his audience that Lenin and Trotsky had scant chance of finding converts in North Carolina, where wise educational management had kept "racial friction" at bay. "Instead of fearing that its Negro population may prove disloyal," Newbold explained, "North Carolina is consciously, with its eyes fully open to all the facts, going resolutely ahead with plans for giving its Negro people better and still better educational opportunities." This sort of state-sponsored self-congratulation persisted throughout the 1920s, as public officials widely broadcast North Carolina's new program for black education, including increased appropriations for black higher education and teacher training, participation in the Rosenwald program, beginning efforts toward providing black secondary education, and greater supervision through the DNE. In 1928, Newbold judged the past decade to have been one of "remarkable development."[72]

Local boosterism reached a transregional audience in 1926, when the country celebrated its sesquicentennial with an international exposition in Philadelphia. The exposition's Committee on Negro Activities chose to feature an exhibit on North Carolina, which was "generally considered to be in the van-guard" of black education. Newbold's office assembled an exhibit that focused on the state's largest black public high schools and its black colleges and normal schools. It also featured the governors and superintendents who had presided over the recent growth in black pub-

Included in a display at the nation's sesquicentennial celebration in 1926 in Philadelphia, this photograph of Washington High School in Raleigh was used by state officials as evidence of North Carolina's progress in black education. While the number of black high schools was increasing, many black North Carolinians still lacked access to public high schools. (Courtesy of The North Carolina State Archives, Raleigh)

lic education, men whom Newbold regarded as "largely responsible for any progress that has been made in Negro education." Tributes to northern philanthropies, including the Jeanes and Rosenwald Funds, rounded out the exhibit. After its stint in Philadelphia, the exhibit spent time at Winston-Salem's black teachers college and its white high school before finally appearing in the ballroom of Raleigh's Sir Walter Hotel.[73] Shortly thereafter, a representative from the U.S. Bureau of Education addressed the NCTA and hailed the state's rapid advancement in black education. Playing on regional rivalries, he told of a northern friend who declared that North Carolina was so progressive that it had ceased to be southern.[74] North Carolina received further accolades in 1928, when Julius Rosenwald came to the town of Method in Wake County for the dedication of the South's four-thousandth Rosenwald school. Speakers heaped praise on North Carolina for building more Rosenwald schools than any other state, and Rosenwald recalled the event as "a continuous triumphal march." By 1930, Newbold was predicting that within five years, North Carolina could offer "a program [of black education] which is far-reaching and fairly comprehensive."[75]

In the wake of postwar anticolonial movements in Asia and Africa, North Carolina's achievements also received attention from a broad range of educators, reformers, philanthropists, and European colonial officials who wished to adopt the tools of white racial management found in the American South. As one philanthropic official put it in 1919, colonial administrators were particularly interested in how the South's pioneering use of industrial curricula might prove valuable "in dealing with a new problem—the post-war demands of colonized peoples for self-determination." In 1925, the state hosted visitors from South Africa, Rhodesia, Uganda, Kenya, Nyasaland, and India. The following year, British and Belgian colonial officials ranked North Carolina, Hampton Institute in Virginia, and Tuskegee Institute in Alabama as the key places to see in the United States. North Carolina had become "a sort of laboratory for training people who are to direct Negro education." This endless "stream of visitors" proved to Newbold that "North Carolina is, in a very real sense, a way-station in the journey of these caravans seeking light and hope to take back to the land which has been known as the 'Dark Continent.'"[76]

Much of this boosterism touted—and exaggerated—the role that white paternalism had played in building North Carolina's black schools. At the 1925 Negro State Fair, Governor Angus McLean declared that the state was "spending millions" on black education and that "practically all of this money [was] furnished by the white people." Four years later, Governor O. Max Gardner held educational progress as evidence of the state's "extraordinarily cordial" race relations. He further boasted that "there is nothing finer in Anglo-Saxon history than the modern concern of the white man in his North Carolina attitude towards the North Carolina Negro."[77] In these whitewashed narratives, black self-help activities played little role. The state's reputation instead pivoted on the enlightened leadership of white philanthropists and state officials.

Privately, some white officials admitted that such self-congratulation was premature. A state auditor confided in 1926 that he "felt positively ashamed of his State" and its paltry appropriations to black schools. Moreover, whites were insisting with increased resolve in the mid-1920s that "retrenchment begins with the colored schools." Newbold noted a "peculiar type of psychology" among local officials, who "seem to have the idea that it will not be possible to do anything in the matter of providing respectable school buildings for Negroes until they have provided a good school building of standard type for every white school district in the county." To be sure, Newbold was not yet pressing local officials to build fully equal facilities. In a case from Lenoir County, he balked when officials drew up elaborate plans for the white schools and completely ignored the black schools. Newbold feared such egregious neglect would invite outsiders to ask, "Where is your boasted interest in Negro education?" Even so, he did not demand that the county draw up equal plans and suggested a "very much less pretentious" goal for the black schools.[78]

In the face of enduring discrimination, African Americans continued to employ strategies for school improvement other than self-help and patient appeals to white officials. Raleigh, Durham, and Greensboro each had at least several hundred registered black voters by the mid-1920s.[79] These small enfranchised coalitions occasionally pressured school boards on matters of equality. When Raleigh's school board planned to allot only one-thirteenth of a $1.3 million school bond for black schools in 1926, African Americans cried foul, since blacks constituted one-third of the city's population. The school board quietly agreed to increase its appropriation to the black schools after black leaders registered one thousand voters and threatened to defeat the bond referendum.[80]

In 1925, black parents from Smithfield experimented with legal recourse after becoming "very much aroused" when the school board threatened to cut the school term for the Johnston County Training School from eight to six months while keeping the local white schools at eight months. The Smithfield parents turned the logic of prevailing self-help programs on its head. While both the Jeanes and Rosenwald Funds implicitly asked blacks to prove their fitness for citizenship by providing for their educational needs, Smithfield's black parents suggested that African Americans would not be able to perform the duties of responsible citizens without first having adequate schools. "It is essential that our children should be given the best training and education possible to qualify them for the responsible duties of citizenship," they wrote. The parents hired a white attorney, who drew up a complaint alleging that unequal terms meant that blacks would be paying taxes for services denied to them. Newbold traveled to Smithfield and found that "the facts gathered by the attorney are very convincing." The litigants apparently had a favorable outcome. A year later, Newbold reported that the Smithfield story "has reached many Negro communities and they know that respectable white lawyers can be secured to champion their cause and that Superior Court judges will stand for a fair administration of the law." Newbold backed the Smithfield parents, but the possibility of future litigation privately alarmed him. He urged black communities to "work out with their local school authorities these problems without going to court about them," and he cautioned white officials against complacency. When black parents in Duplin County voiced dissatisfaction with school conditions two years later, Newbold warned the local superintendent that African Americans "know more about the law . . . than many of us give them credit for knowing. I mean to say that they are far beyond what many of our people think."[81]

Indeed, African Americans across the state were studying up on school law. Chowan County minister C. C. Drew hoped that such knowledge would liberate his community from unrealistic expectations of self-help. His local school board had told him "time and again" to raise funds to replace the existing black school, whose roof was "about to fall in." In 1928, he requested from the state board of education a copy of the school laws so that he could "be informed [along] these lines and [determine] if as taxpayers we must aside from that raise money to build public schools." Drew expressed his faith that North Carolina held more regard for its citizens "than to allow the humblest to have to suffer." Had Drew pressed his case with formal litigation, he most likely would have encountered formidable obstacles. In the 1925 Smithfield case, the litigants at least had pushed an issue (school terms) with reasonably clear—if often circumvented—legal standards. Drew was raising the issue of facilities, where the law allowed impossibly broad interpretations. Moreover, the Smithfield parents had employed the services of a sympathetic white attorney, a rare find in much of the state. Many black communities at this time also lacked access to black legal counsel, especially after the state's only black law school, at Shaw University, closed in 1914.[82]

The practical barriers to and justifications for legal and political agitation only increased at decade's end as the hardships of the Great Depression took their toll. While the depression increased the need for self-help activity, it also drained the resources for redress of school inequalities. In the first jolting years of hard times, black communities looked to Jeanes teachers as virtual relief workers. "This month for the most part has been spent in getting or begging charity donations," reported one Jeanes teacher in 1930. "Our aim is to clothe the children in order that they may attend school." In 1933, Alice Rayford of Granville County taught reading, math, and geography; settled disputes among parents; purchased schoolbooks; held PTA events; supervised industrial work; attended teachers meetings; arranged hot lunches for students; and delivered food to "poverty stricken families." Black educator Ambrose Caliver of the U.S. Department of Education gave Jeanes teachers a tall order in 1931: Keep "a stiff upper lip" and "find new avenues of employment for these millions who will be thrown out of employment."[83] By some measures, Jeanes teachers made a dent in that enormous task. The fund's president noted in 1932 that Jeanes teachers had encouraged black cotton farmers to diversify and grow foodstuffs, thereby reducing "actual want in rural sections of the South." Moreover, Jeanes teachers continued to raise money for the schools. In 1930–31, North Carolina's Jeanes teachers raised more than $25,000. In 1932–33, black donations remained steady at $24,563.63.[84]

Despite Jeanes teachers' heroic achievements, their fund-raising and social welfare work stretched them thin. "Perhaps the largest proportion of supervisors' time is consumed in raising money for new schoolhouses, school equipment, and extension of the school term," a 1933 report concluded. The Jeanes teacher had become the "'maid of all work' of the Negro school system," noted a similar study four years later.[85] In some ways, self-sacrificing Jeanes teachers unintentionally reinforced patterns of white neglect. A 1926 survey indicated that superintendents channeled the time they gained from Jeanes teachers into the white schools. In 1931, noting the wide-ranging burdens assumed by many Jeanes teachers, one Rosenwald official urged them to remember that "the specific purpose is that the children shall learn . . . no matter how many toothpaste exercises are given, or how many outside wells are moved or souls saved."[86] Such advice, however well intentioned, obscured the obligation that Jeanes teachers felt to compensate for the inequalities of the Jim Crow South.

Just as state budgets tightened, the philanthropies that blacks had embraced in the 1920s began to scale back appropriations. In 1932, the Rosenwald Fund ended its rural school building program. Fund officials recognized that black children still were "not yet receiving anywhere near their share of school money," but they feared that whites were "rely[ing] too heavily on outside aid" and needed to take "full responsibility" for black education.[87] The Jeanes Fund also decreased its appropriations in the 1930s, urging the southern states to assume the financial responsibility of school supervision. Contrary to characterizations of northern philanthropists as heavy-handed reformers of the South, the GEB-affiliated philanthropies began planning for their own obsolescence. Jeanes Fund president James Dillard explained in 1927 that it was "most desirable to get Negro education out of the idea of its being a missionary work . . . to get the education of the Negro children thought of as part of the regular job of States and counties." Dillard further believed that "the more any of the Funds can sink themselves from view the better." The following year, a GEB agent proposed "to throw upon the state, county, or community the whole responsibility for carrying on the work of public education."[88] The GEB continued to fund the Negro state agents throughout the 1940s but reduced overall appropriations to black education in the South. North

Carolina already covered nearly three-quarters of its Jeanes salaries, but Newbold feared that a decline in private funding would encourage whites to abandon the program.[89] The Jeanes program managed to survive the depression, but public retrenchment required each supervisor to work full-time as a regular teacher or principal and to perform her supervisory tasks on the side.[90]

In the midst of the Great Depression, strategies of self-help seemed more disconnected from the promise of black citizenship than ever before. As Anderson put it, "What rural blacks did during the period 1914 to 1932 could not be done during the Great Depression. . . . Their behavior of self-help and practice of double taxation, though not extinguished completely, became much less substantial than in the preceding decades." In the early 1930s, Newbold was forced to admit that the heady optimism of the preceding decade had faded, and he feared that the state was losing ground in its program for black education and thereby forfeiting its claims to progressive leadership of the South.[91]

In addition to the material burdens imposed by black self-help programs, whites continued to hold blacks to a double standard for "help" in school affairs. Blacks were to help themselves in matters of school resources, but they were to request white help when it came to questions of school leadership and decision-making. As the president of the state's white PTA organization noted approvingly of her work with black PTA leaders in 1938, "One of the most hopeful signs is that they are not too cocksure and are asking for help in organizing." According to the logic of white paternalism, then, blacks were to be both remarkably resourceful and hopelessly helpless.[92]

Given the black exploitation that marked the self-help initiatives of the 1920s and 1930s, it would be easy to dismiss state claims that the era saw remarkable achievements. Nevertheless, a black educator reportedly dubbed the 1920s a "Golden Period of Negro Education," and others later invoked that slogan.[93] Black pride in the decade's accomplishments had an undeniable material basis. North Carolinians had built 813 Rosenwald Schools, more than any other state. Blacks raised $666,736 for these buildings, a sum nearly equal to the $717,426 contributed by the Rosenwald Fund. Blacks could similarly take satisfaction in the thousands of hot lunches, jars of canned produce, school plays, and tidy schoolyards that bore the unmistakable mark of resourceful Jeanes teachers and PTAs. This era of self-help, in fact, continues to loom large in black popular discourse. As Kevin Gaines has noted, some "middle-class African American media spokespersons," lamenting what they see as the fragmentation of contemporary black communities, look with "apparent nostalgia" on the Jim Crow era as a "golden age," when blacks pulled together for the greater good.[94]

As Gaines adds, this nostalgia relies on a "shortsighted racial reckoning." The segregated past does offer powerful evidence of black community strength, but that strength was in many ways born of oppression. The oppressive side to black education's "golden age" was no less a reality in North Carolina than elsewhere, despite the state's progressive reputation. In a 1927 survey of black educational conditions in several southern states, Du Bois argued that North Carolina was "without doubt the best," but he was quick to qualify the state's exceptionalism. "It is only by contrast with the unreconstructed South," he wrote, that North Carolina "shines."[95] Similarly aware of the limits to North Carolina's progressivism, black parents and educators in the coming years would lead a series of educational equalization campaigns, insisting with increasing force that a new era of black entitlement and first-class citizenship must follow the "golden period" of self-help.

[It was once believed] that Negroes should have industrial education. The classics would spoil him by causing him to aspire to places designed for whites only. If our association had done nothing else within the past thirty years except to participate in changing this philosophy, it would have justified its existence and support.
—North Carolina Teachers Association president Oliver R. Pope, 1934

We didn't call it black history, as such then, but we just encouraged the children [to think] that, "You can do something, too."
—Former state supervisor of Negro elementary schools Ruth Woodson, 2002

Where formerly there was more or less an aversion on the part of the Negroes themselves to having vocational and industrial courses in their high schools, they are now rather keen that such courses be offered for their children.
—State agent Nathan C. Newbold, 1935

CHAPTER TWO

Lessons in Citizenship

Confronting the Limits of Curricular Equalization

in the Jim Crow South

In fighting for curricular equality, African Americans first had to challenge popularly held white assumptions of black intellectual inferiority, assumptions that endured even at the state's center of white progressivism. Historian Guion Griffis Johnson recalled that when she was acquiring her doctorate during the 1920s at the University of North Carolina in Chapel Hill, esteemed southern historian J. G. de Roulhac Hamilton argued, "As a child, the Negro is very bright and seems to give promise of development, but his mind freezes at the age of twelve. And he never develops beyond the age of twelve."[1] While many whites would continue to believe throughout the Jim Crow period that blacks were best suited for a less academic and more "practical" course of study, state school officials in the 1920s were increasingly willing—for both philosophical and pragmatic reasons—to offer tacit approval for black high schools with the same curriculum found in white schools. By the end of the 1920s, then, the storied industrial/classical fault lines were fading at the level of school policy.

The achievement of nominal curricular equalization, however, raised as many questions as it answered. Many black schools lacked the resources or local administrative backing necessary to implement the state's standard curriculum. For example, even though state law technically required local districts to hold equal-length terms for black and white schools, as late as the early 1930s, it was not uncommon to find officials in rural areas operating longer terms for the white schools. Even in cases where black and white schools operated for equal terms, the economic circumstances of black farming families, especially those who answered to white landowners, often meant that black children had difficulty taking full advantage of school offerings. "It was sad to see school buses filled with white children going to the schools, while truck and wagon loads of Negro children were going to the cotton and tobacco fields," recalled one Jeanes supervisor. By the 1940s, most districts operated equal terms, but white privilege could still be found in the distribution of curricular resources. Noting the lack of supplemental readers in black elementary schools, black educator and state board of education member Harold Trigg lamented in 1956, "The Negro college student of today has had a one-reader education."[2] The links between resource allocation and curricular parameters were particularly evident in the state's early black public high schools, where coursework was more likely to require expensive equipment and facilities than was the case in elementary schools.

While much black interest in school curricula centered on the basic equalization of course offerings, two reform movements addressed broader questions about the role of curricula in preparing students for full citizenship. As historian Carter G. Woodson's black history movement gained ground in the 1920s, some black educators argued that true curricular equality entailed not just access to white-authored courses of study and equal resources but also the right to influence how and what students learned. Lessons in black history, they argued, imparted a kind of cultural citizenship that functioned as a necessary antidote to white assumptions of black inferiority. By the depression era, curricular interest shifted with new urgency to the fundamental relationship between schooling and the achievement of full economic citizenship. In reaction to the narrow range of employment options available to black high school graduates, African Americans pressed for the more diverse vocational programs found at some white high schools and colleges. Many African Americans ultimately questioned whether even the most modern vocational training—or curricular reform of any sort in a segregated context—could empower students to overcome the challenges of a racially ordered labor market.

Staking Claim to the "People's College"

In the 1920s South, the idea of race-specific school curricula had roots that extended back more than half a century. During Reconstruction, white entrepreneurs and reformers in both the North and South sought ways of molding black children into obedient agricultural laborers who would stabilize the southern economy and, in turn, shore up northern manufacturing. At Hampton Institute in Virginia, Samuel Chapman Armstrong, a white educator and former Union army officer, pioneered a modified industrial curriculum that primarily prepared future black educators to teach neither technical skills nor advanced training in the liberal arts but rather the educational fundamentals as well as a white-approved work ethic and moral code. Hampton's curricular incorporation of manual labor served as a platform not for black employment diversification but instead for socialization within Jim Crow's racially ordered labor market. When Booker T. Washington founded Tuskegee Institute in 1881 on the Hampton model, northern philanthropists found a key ally. The Anna T. Jeanes Fund and the Rosenwald Fund also played critical roles in spreading the industrial philosophy. Jeanes teachers supervised industrial work, while the Rosenwald Fund required its schools to include facilities for such activities. To be sure, educators touted "practical" or hands-on training for white children as well. A 1921 state report urged a more "diversified" curriculum for white rural schools, noting that classes in cooking, sewing, and manual training were typically found only in black schools, especially those supervised by Jeanes teachers.[3] Yet while whites tended to view industrial training as a supplement to their curriculum, many held it as the ideal linchpin of black schooling. As North Carolina governor Angus McLean argued in 1925, black schools overemphasized education "along academic and theoretical lines." He advocated a more "practical" focus, particularly agricultural instruction modeled on the curriculum at Hampton and Tuskegee Institutes.[4]

Black educators resisted an exclusive focus on industrial lessons and had long advocated curricular equality between the races, but they also had reasons for at least selectively adopting the industrial model. Washington, for example, did not oppose black higher education, but he believed that the majority of blacks needed schooling oriented toward the realities of the southern labor market. Moreover, in its promise of more efficient domestic and agricultural laborers, industrial work held the added benefit of currying white favor. When a white farmer and employer of black laborers observed a class in hygiene at the Wake County Training

Cooking class at Wake County Training School, 1915. This school's industrial courses curried favor with local whites, who approved of training blacks for domestic service in white homes. (Courtesy of Jackson Davis Papers, 1906–47, Accession #3072, #3072–a, Special Collections Department, University of Virginia Library, Charlottesville)

School, he suddenly became convinced that the school was "helping me and my family" and donated money and land.[5]

Industrial lessons also taught students to prepare food and clothing for their families. In cash-strapped tenant and sharecropping families, Jeanes teachers schooled children in cooking, sewing, gardening, chair caning, basketry, shuck mat making, cobbling, housekeeping, pine straw work, rug making, embroidery, and flower arrangement. In encouraging these skills, many Jeanes teachers organized Home-Makers' Clubs, where children worked to grow corn, can produce, raise chickens and pigs, and make pickles and jellies. Teachers also encouraged cleanliness, making sure that all dwellings and outhouses were painted, whitewashed, and tidy.[6] Mary Holliday, a longtime Jeanes teacher in Iredell County, learned how such humble activities could transform lives. Holliday began her career boarding with a family of two adults and eleven children in a two-room cabin. Among the family's few possessions was an abundance of corn shucks and white oak branches. Holliday taught the family to transform their modest commodities into mats, baskets, and chair bottoms. At the end of the school term, the family members displayed their handiwork, and Holliday "swell[ed] with pride" when a representative from a cotton-packing company promptly ordered one hundred of their five-bushel baskets.[7]

Industrial activities also demonstrated black respectability and readiness for citizenship. In 1931 Mary McLeod Bethune noted that communities with Jeanes supervisors bore distinctive marks: "There will be sewing circles, neat little yards, gardens of flowers, cupboards of jellies and jams, clubs for older people as well as the young." Far from superficial enhancements, these projects were "demonstrating that the time has come when Negroes can and will reach down and lift up and help their people to higher planes of living and thinking." Jeanes teachers made sure that their students' work caught white notice. When the Wake County Jeanes supervisor organized a "Keep-Clean Contest" in 1923, she secured the county health nurse to inspect black schools and grade them on ventilation, "care of toilets," wood boxes, and grounds appearance. In arranging to feature the cleanest school in local newspapers, this teacher challenged white stereotypes of black life and presented an image of self-respecting citizens.[8]

Despite the merits of industrial activities, Jeanes teachers shared other black educators' concerns about equalizing academic instruction. While equipping students to live more productively off the land, Jeanes teachers did not intend for students to content themselves with minimal aspirations. One teacher visited forty-seven homes in a single month in 1924 in an effort to convince parents to send their children to the local high school. By the late 1920s, in fact, academic supervision took center stage among Jeanes duties. When state supervisor Annie Holland created a "suggestive outline" of work in 1927, she held teachers to high academic standards. They were to ask superintendents for standardized tests in math and reading. If the superintendents claimed to have no money for these exams, the teachers were to raise the money. Jeanes supervisors also were to make sure each school had a library, urge students to form book clubs over the summer, and encourage teachers to be model learners by participating in reading circles, summer schools, and extension courses.[9]

Some whites misread black interest in academics as a naive preoccupation with the trappings of literacy. In 1931, Jeanes Fund president James Hardy Dillard urged black teachers not to abandon "plain, humble handiwork" and to teach academics selectively. "It is a mighty good thing," he said, "to get children to have their attention focused on a thing instead of words. They study words too much, and words cause thoughts and thoughts are what is troubling the world today—the trouble has come from regard concerning words when one knew not what they meant." Another fund official likewise noted with disapproval that blacks "thought of education in terms of books and symbols and not in terms of successful living and performance of the common tasks of everyday life in the home and on the farm."[10]

What to whites seemed like an impractical pursuit of "books and symbols" was in fact black recognition of literacy's real and symbolic power. One British observer of Jeanes work argued that blacks believed "that to depart from a purely academic curriculum would be to admit racial inferiority." Literacy indeed promised to counter white assumptions of black intellectual weakness and to qualify blacks for political citizenship. Many election officials, of course, subjected blacks to literacy tests that had little to do with actual reading ability; nonetheless, in the Jim Crow South, the ability to read and write functioned as a badge of enfranchisement.[11]

Black teachers sometimes had more mundane reasons for choosing "books and symbols" over industrial lessons. As Glenda Elizabeth Gilmore has noted, it was "more expensive to build a bookcase than to explain an algebra problem on a broken piece of slate."[12] Black educators, therefore, offered a curriculum that reflected state guidelines, their own pedagogical convictions, and the material realities of resource-starved schools.

The issue of curricular equality took center stage among black educators during the 1920s, when a new movement for black public secondary education gathered momentum. White high school enrollment more than doubled in the first half of the decade, from 29,294 in 1920 to 67,707 just four years later.[13] Rural whites still often lacked access to the secondary grades, but many of the state's cities boasted of impressive new white high schools. In 1919, Asheville dedicated a new white high school valued at $300,000. A stately building in the Gothic style, Asheville High included an auditorium that seated 850, three science laboratories, a library, a lunchroom, a gymnasium, and departments of manual training and home economics. As superintendent of the Person County Schools, Nathan C. Newbold had proposed the building of a white high school as early as 1906. In listing the school's objectives, he prioritized "a strong literary course intended for students who desire to enter college or university." Vocational courses, such as "manual training," were to be added "as demand for them grew." By the mid-1930s, urban and rural whites alike expected the public high school to serve as the "people's college."[14]

Well into the 1920s, the state almost totally excluded black youth from the privilege of attending high school. As North Carolina Teachers Association (NCTA) president Oliver R. Pope recalled, most whites believed that the liberal arts would "spoil [the Negro] by causing him to aspire to places designed for whites only." In 1919, the state had accredited only seven black high schools, and four of them were private institutions. All of the early black high schools operated as extensions of the state normal schools and private colleges. Throughout the early 1920s, the majority of state-accredited black high schools were private institutions, and most had been established by church and missionary organizations that approved of liberal arts training for African Americans. Similar patterns prevailed across the South. In 1916 approximately 95 percent of the region's black high school students attended private schools.[15] As late as 1925–26, North Carolina had forty-nine accredited black high schools, twenty-five of which were private; whites had 494 such institutions, only forty-one of which were private. The lack of black public high schools created a striking disparity in enrollment patterns. In 1923–24, the percentages of white and black school-age youth enrolled in the public schools was roughly equal—86.6 and 84.9, respectively—but black students disproportionately occupied the lower grades. While 9.3 percent of white school-age youth attended public high schools in 1923–24, a mere 1.6 percent of black youth did so.[16]

The state's first tentative foray into black secondary education came in the 1910s, when the major industrial philanthropies attempted to yoke black desires for advanced training to the Hampton-Tuskegee model of industrial learning. In 1911, the General Education Board–affiliated John F. Slater Fund inaugurated its "county training school" movement. These schools, built with a combination of private and public funds, were to offer the elementary grades and three years of secondary normal and industrial training. The Slater Fund designed its schools to function as "industrial boarding schools," where future black teachers would live, take teacher-preparation courses, and acquire experience by teaching the elementary grades. The Slater Fund also intended to help disseminate the Hampton-Tuskegee model across the rural South. North Carolina first used Slater Fund money to build county training schools in 1914 and by the end of the 1920s had built forty-three such schools. As late as the early 1920s, however, none of these schools functioned as true high schools; instead, they offered elementary-level work and a smattering of normal and industrial courses. By the 1930s, many county training schools evolved into public high schools, but they often retained the self-effacing "training school" designation, a label that squared well with white distaste for black academic ambition. Throughout the Jim Crow period, these institutions dotted the rural southern landscape.[17]

At the same time that African Americans could not look to the industrial philanthropies and their early county training schools for access to true secondary institutions, they were also losing financial support from northern church and missionary philanthropies. The latter group historically had been more open to black liberal arts education, but in the 1920s they decreased their appropriations to southern black schools. In the early 1900s, for example, the American Missionary Association (AMA) supported forty black secondary schools in the South; by 1950, that number had dropped to one. In the face of diminishing philanthropic funds, black private school presidents had little choice but to seek state funding. By the mid-1920s, Newbold observed "a decided drift on the part of the private schools to get into the public school fold."[18]

T. S. Inborden understood the challenges of sustaining a private school. In 1895, he used AMA money to found the Joseph Keasly Brick Agricultural, Industrial, and Normal School in the tiny community of Bricks, in Edgecombe County. Initially offering basic elementary and industrial coursework, the school was by 1922 one of only fourteen state-accredited black high schools. By 1926, however, declining appropriations from the AMA left Inborden facing a choice between shutting down and seeking state takeover. He opted for the latter. Assuring Newbold of his desire to cooperate with state officials, Inborden nonetheless held a strong sense of ownership over his school. "I have worked night and day to put the school on the map and I have done a piece of work that is fine," he explained. "It is as much mine as Tuskegee is Booker Washington's or as Hampton is Armstrong's." Such feelings of institutional ownership notwithstanding, black educators cast the move from private to public as part of a larger project for civic inclusion. State supervisor of Negro high schools Harold Trigg urged his colleagues to remember their debts to the small private high schools as well as to recognize that the future of black education lay elsewhere. "Education for citizenship," he argued, "must be supported, controlled and administered by that same government which has its being in the hearts and minds of the citizens who give it governmental powers."[19]

Black mobilization for public secondary schools was strongest in the urban South. "There is such a great demand for higher training for the Negro boys and girls in the larger cities and towns," Newbold reported in 1919. That demand partly reflected demographic trends. The region's cities experienced tremendous black in-migration in the 1920s, as falling agricultural prices deepened black disillusionment with the plantation economy. In convincing whites of the need for black high schools, African American educators played on fears of unrest. William A. Robinson, a former high school teacher from Kentucky and a stepson of Durham educator James E. Shepard, began work for the state in 1921 as inspector of high schools. Once described as "the shock troop in the struggle for tax supported secondary education for Negroes in North Carolina," Robinson exposed the state's lack of black high schools in *The Crisis*, published by the National Association for the Advancement of Colored People (NAACP), and routinely warned of the social consequences of such exclusion. School inequalities, he charged, were "inevitably creating in the South a vast, defenseless, exploitable group; a social cesspool of ignorance, disease and crime, and social problems of all kinds." Such warnings inspired a new white receptiveness to black high schools as an institution for social management.[20]

The NCTA threw its support behind the public high school movement and coupled that fight to renewed calls for curricular equality. In 1924, the association ranked as its top priority "a larger and more liberal support of High Schools [with] curricula similar in content in the High Schools of both races." Black high schools, NCTA leaders insisted, should function as "people's colleges," much like their white counterparts. The National Association of Teachers in Colored Schools (later renamed the American Teachers Association) similarly demanded that all schools be held to the same standards and accredited by the same agencies.[21]

Many whites scoffed at these demands for advanced black instruction and felt vindicated in their opinions by new "scientific evidence" of black intellectual inferiority. The results of U.S. Army intelligence tests of World War I recruits seemingly offered proof of a racial and ethnic hierarchy of mental aptitude, with white northern Europeans at the top and African Americans at the bottom. Those tests, whose validity social scientists later rejected, reinforced what many white southerners already held to be true. A survey conducted in the late 1920s indicated that the majority of North Carolina's school superintendents believed that black children had a smaller "capacity to learn" than their white counterparts and thus required a less rigorous curriculum.[22] The State Board of Charities and Public Welfare further documented entrenched resistance to curricular equality in a 1933 survey of racial attitudes among county officials. While a number of those interviewed noted that the black children in their jurisdictions embraced schooling with more enthusiasm than did white children, only a quarter of the interviewees favored equal educational opportunities for blacks and whites. Most allowed for some cultural training for exceptionally talented African Americans, but 13 of the 109 officials favored no education at all for blacks. Nearly 15 percent thought that blacks should not go beyond the third or fourth grade, and 27.5 percent disapproved of black education beyond the seventh grade. Twenty-eight percent favored giving blacks industrial training only. In explaining their views, the superintendents revealed the unfiltered racism that infused the minds of many white southerners. "The negro is born inferior to the white man and does not need the cultural education given a white child," opined the Pamlico County superintendent. "Look at the average negro," suggested the Haywood County superintendent, "and it is easy to see from the shape of his head that there is little above the eyes." According to the Martin County superintendent, "The white child has years of civilization behind him as the basis for the education he receives. The negro has nothing." By extension, education was to fit blacks for their place as a "servant class."[23]

Challenging these popular white assumptions of black intellectual inferiority, a new generation of black and white social scientists offered alternative theories of racial difference. As early as the late nineteenth century, black sociologist and historian W. E. B. Du Bois had recast the racial divide as primarily a matter of mutable cultural differences. In 1911, with the publication of *The Mind of Primitive Man*, white anthropologist Franz Boas similarly argued that while American black culture was in some respects less advanced than white culture, its deficiencies were attributable to the damage imposed by slavery and discrimination. The African culture from which slaves derived, he insisted, bore all the marks of an advanced society. "In short," Boas wrote, "there is every reason to believe that the negro when given facility and opportunity will be perfectly able to fulfill the duties of citizenship as well as his white neighbor." By the 1920s, some white southern intellectuals—most notably, those who studied under sociologist Howard Odum at the University of North Carolina—likewise advanced cultural explanations of racial difference.[24]

As state agent, Newbold eventually found himself influenced by this intellectual ferment and favorably disposed to the idea of equalized school curricula. In 1922, he admitted that while he had once been an advocate of race-based curricular differences, he was beginning to see "the fallacy of this point of view." He was grappling with the work of leading social scientists, including Boas. He was also digesting a discussion of the army intelligence tests in the *Atlantic Monthly*, which had suggested that blacks and other low-scoring groups should largely be denied publicly funded higher education. Newbold sought a middle ground between such exclusionism and full educational equalization. While he had begun to imagine the possibilities for complete equality, he did see a racial difference "in degree or rate of progress." His racial worldview included "an ascending scale" demarcated by three points of progress. "The whites as a whole may have reached *two* on this scale while the negroes are still struggling with *one*," he explained. This developmental divide promised eventual equality, even if it justified white guidance of gradual black advancement. If Newbold's musings left him a guarded proponent of black potential, he nonetheless told a 1922 audience at Shaw University that he found "no sound reason" why black high schools should not be "organized on the same basis as our other high schools."[25]

By 1924, Newbold had translated his changing convictions about racial difference into policy recommendations. When Raleigh was making plans for its first black public high school, the city's superintendent requested state curricular guidelines. Newbold replied that "the State Department of Public Instruction takes the position that the courses of study in Negro high schools should be identical with those for the whites." About the same time, Newbold announced that the state "believes that there should be one standard for teachers not two," prompting Virginia's leading black newspaper to hail his pronouncement as "the most revolutionary and progressive utterance on the race question that ever came from a Southern white man."[26] North Carolina was not the only southern state at this time to offer only one curriculum for its schools, although state officials in several one-standard states actually favored race-specific standards, suggesting that their unitary curriculum was more a reflection of practical concerns than of convictions of equality.[27] To be sure, many local officials in North Carolina did not share Newbold's views, but few actively attempted to resist the new state guidelines. As sociologist Charles S. Johnson put it in 1930, white supervision of black schools was often "meager and indifferent," which meant that black educators frequently were most limited by poor resources rather than heavy-handed white supervision. One superintendent, for example, stated in the early 1930s that although he wanted to implement an industrial curriculum at the black high school, he offered the standard course of study because the state had provided no alternative. Greensboro principal John Tarpley discovered when he took over at Dudley High that "it was left to the principal, in many respects, to devise his own curriculum" based on the resources available.[28]

In 1934, the NCTA's Pope reflected on the organization's push for public high schools with standard curricula and concluded that no other achievement had been more influential in shaping white attitudes. Those schools, he suggested, stood as symbolic challenges to white doubts about black intellectual capacity. In fact, he added, "If our association had done nothing else within the past thirty years except to participate in changing this philosophy [of black inferiority], it would have justified its existence." Newbold similarly noted in 1930, "The establishment of the principle of one course of study for high schools in North Carolina, as well as higher institutions, has meant as much or more in the way of encouragement and stimulation for the Negroes of North Carolina than perhaps anything else we have done."[29]

A closer look inside one of the state's early black high schools, however, reveals that this historic achievement represented the beginning rather than the culmination of a larger battle for equality. Few North Carolina schools illustrated both the promise and limits of early black public high schools better than Durham's Hillside High. Its longtime principal, William Gaston Pearson, embodied the possibilities for achievement in the Jim Crow South. Born on the eve of the Civil War, Pearson acquired his education through skillful diplomacy. In the 1880s, he befriended a white businessman, who paid his expenses at Shaw University. Pearson began teaching in 1886 at James A. Whitted School in Durham while helping to found the North Carolina Mutual Insurance Company, the Mechanics and Farmers Bank, and the Fraternal Bank and Trust Company, three of Durham's leading black-owned businesses. A builder and seller of houses, Pearson was at one time rumored to own more than one hundred rental properties and to employ a chauffeur. He also attended several national conventions of the Republican Party, suggesting his desire to empower his race both politically and economically.[30]

Pearson's hard-nosed business and political instincts served him well when he became principal at Whitted School and later at Hillside. The first public graded school for blacks in Durham County, Whitted also ranked as one of the first black public schools in the state to add secondary grades. Pearson quickly expanded the school's academic program while keeping visible the school's industrial work in barbering, laundering, and shoemaking. The Durham paper reported approvingly on a 1915 industrial arts display at Whitted and praised Pearson's priorities: "It has been said by some, that negroes, given a slight taste of the liberal arts, learn to look with disgust upon the industrial arts, but the teaching of Professor Pearson has neither encouraged nor tolerated such thoughts, as he holds that the moral effect of industry is that it promotes self-respect and self-reliance."[31] Pearson ultimately made sure that his students got more than a "taste of the liberal arts." When the Whitted School burned in 1921—a fire that the local paper blamed on dilapidation and rat infestation but that may in fact have been started by blacks desperate for better facilities— local white banker and tobacco manufacturer John Sprunt Hill donated land for a new building. Named Hillside Park High School in his honor (and renamed Hillside High School in 1950 when it changed locations), the building's thirty-one classrooms marked a significant improvement over the old facility. Early reports indicated that Hillside students were taking courses in English, history, math, general science, biology, Latin, Spanish, music, home economics, commercial arts, and manual training. By the early 1930s, the school had added courses in chemistry, physics, and public speaking. In 1923, the school was one of the first four public black high schools to receive state accreditation.[32]

A large part of Hillside's success rested with its faculty, most of whom held four-year college degrees. The same was true at many of the South's other early black high schools. At Raleigh's Washington High School in 1927, for example, all but one of its seventeen faculty members held a four-year degree, with their alma maters including not only the local Shaw University but also Howard University in Washington, D.C.; Talladega College in Alabama; and Fisk University in Tennessee.[33] In 1928–29, 85 percent of the teachers and principals at the state's black public high schools held four-year college degrees. Moreover, more than three-quarters of those degrees were in the liberal arts, rather than in home economics or agriculture. Even though at this time black teachers on the whole had less training than white educators, the elite ranks of black educators at the South's black public high schools typically had just as much training—and often more years of experience—than their white counterparts. Noted civil rights activist Pauli Murray, who graduated from Hillside High in 1926, remembered her school's educators as well-trained men and women "who brought with them advanced ideas which helped to raise our sights."[34]

Hillside faculty indeed held students to high academic and personal standards. Remembered as a "strict disciplinarian," Pearson demanded proper deportment and hard work. According to one of Pearson's colleagues, principal L. S. Cozart of Raleigh's Washington High, strict discipline was not meant to train students for lives as deferential cogs in the wheel of the Jim Crow South; instead, such discipline was intended to remind students they were "citizen[s] of a small democracy, and that good citizenship demands that [they] obey the rules." High schools, in other words, were to give students a taste of both the duties and privileges of citizenship.[35]

Hillside pupils practiced the rules of democratic participation through extracurricular activities. Teachers organized students into debating societies (a Du Bois Forensic Club for boys and a Phillis Wheatley Debating Club for girls), a Book Lovers Club, a Historical Research Club, a Commercial Club, a drama club, and popular hall-monitoring societies. Sports teams included football, baseball, track, and basketball.[36] Black teachers considered such activities essential components of the "training for

Pauli Murray's graduating class at Hillside High School in Durham, 1926. Murray is at the far right on the front row. As was particularly true at black high schools at this time, female graduates outnumbered males. (Courtesy of the Schlesinger Library, Radcliffe Institute, Harvard University)

citizenship." As one teacher put it, in clubs and teams, students began to understand such abstract notions as group "rights and duties, obligations and privileges." While the same was true of white schools, opportunities for group belonging held added meaning for black youth who faced daily lessons in social exclusion. In addition to graduating first in her class in 1926, Pauli Murray played basketball, edited the school newspaper, and held forth on the debate team, activities that brought her and her peers into lively competition with other black schools. "These modest advances," she later recalled, "sustained our hope and gave us a sense of achievement at a time when the prevailing view that Negroes were inherently inferior remained unchallenged."[37]

As Murray discovered shortly after graduation, however, Hillside was both an exception to and a reflection of North Carolina's unequal educational opportunities. At the same time that Durham built the new Hillside High in 1922 for approximately $125,000, it was building a new white school, Durham High, at a projected cost of $325,000. Hillside had a broader curriculum than was offered to most black—and many rural white—students in the state in the 1920s, but Hillside's offerings were not enough to win Murray entrance into Hunter College in New York. During the year she spent completing her college entrance requirements at a predominantly white high school in New York, she was dismayed to find herself poorly prepared in a number of subjects. She ultimately graduated with honors and entered Hunter, but her eyes had been opened wider to the injustices of Jim Crow.[38]

Hillside's inadequacies were not lost on the folks back home. Durham's black newspaper, the *Carolina Times*, routinely lamented the school's second-rate facilities and underpaid faculty. Editor Louis Austin drew attention to the fact that the local white schools had gymnasiums but Hillside did not. He also judged Hillside's laboratories a "joke" compared to those at white schools. "No one but a deliberate liar would say that the Hillside High School comes any ways near being the equal of" the white school, he charged. He pointed out the irony that the state had accredited Hillside as an A-grade institution, a measure he chalked up to white dissemblance. Enraging Austin even more were conditions at East Durham Elementary School. That building, designed to hold 140 pupils, housed 225. The school had no cafeteria and only one drinking fountain. In the school's two restrooms, the faucets lacked sinks and emptied into tin cans on the floor. Worn-out blackboards, peeling paint, and potbellied stoves added to the dismal picture. Austin found such conditions especially deplorable at a time when the Durham Board of Education had appropriated money for gyms at local white schools. The needs of Durham's black schools, Austin contended, stood as dramatic evidence of the "educational rape of Negroes."[39]

When Durham officials refused to add a twelfth grade at Hillside in the mid-1930s despite the fact that the local white high school had twelve grades, black parents sought legal counsel. Most high schools in the South in the 1920s stopped at the eleventh grade, but by the mid-1930s the state was promoting the addition of a twelfth grade as the means of creating a more "intelligent citizenship." Austin contacted NAACP executive secretary Walter White for help with "a move on foot" to bring suit against the school board. He had approached several lawyers about the case, but "they all seem afraid." White contacted NAACP assistant special counsel Thurgood Marshall, who promised "to cooperate to the fullest extent." Shortly before Marshall's planned visit to Durham, however, parents received a "favorable response" from local officials and suspended legal action.[40]

Its shortcomings aside, Hillside far outstripped what many North Carolina communities offered to black students. Though they comprised nearly a third of the state's school-age population in 1930, African Americans had access to only 10 percent of the state's public high schools. While more than 40 percent of whites of high school age were enrolled in high school, the same held true for only 13 percent of blacks. Moreover, North Carolina spent more than fifty dollars on teacher salaries for each white high school student but only twenty-eight dollars for each black high school pupil. Total operational and maintenance costs for white high schools in 1930 exceeded two million dollars; for black high schools, such costs barely topped three hundred thousand dollars.[41]

Black high schools suffered from minimal library and laboratory facilities, worn furnishings, and castoff textbooks. The practice of giving black schools discarded books from white schools technically violated a 1935 state law that prohibited any exchange of schoolbooks between the races. Countless memories of black school alumni, however, suggest that the law's main intent was to prevent the use of "colored" books in white schools rather than the reverse. The law came about when the state shifted from a system where students purchased most of their books to one where the state provided free basal texts to the elementary grades and oversaw a textbook rental system for the upper grades. Since local officials handed out books to the schools, textbook distribution practices varied somewhat from district to district. Some local officials may have waived rental fees for black students in exchange for the dubious privilege of using outdated books. One mid-1960s study found that southern black students were somewhat more likely than their white peers to attend schools with free books but that their texts tended to be older and in shorter supply. Other local officials no doubt charged black students standard fees for substandard books.[42]

Limited resources constricted early black high school curricula. One survey concluded that most black high schools in North Carolina in the 1920s offered few courses beyond basic requirements and rarely offered classes in music, public speaking, the commercial arts, physical education, and the modern languages. The same was true across the region. From his new post as principal of Austin High School in Knoxville, Tennessee, former North Carolina state supervisor William Robinson took a sobering look at the South's black high schools in 1930. As a result of deficient labs, "chemistry is still taught more or less like fiction in many of our Negro high schools," he wrote. And even though whites waxed eloquent about blacks' natural musical talent, few black schools at that time enjoyed full musical programs. Given the inadequate resources, Robinson concluded that "for a Negro to do high school teaching . . . he must be impelled by extreme missionary zeal or else he is forced into it because he is not capable of doing anything else."[43]

From its position of relative privilege among black schools, Hillside produced more than its share of race leaders. Murray once noted that despite "the handicaps of segregated education" in Durham, her generation "contribute[d] some stalwart recruits to the cause of racial advancement and to the never-ending struggle for survival with dignity." Hillside alumni indeed played a disproportionately large role in breaking down racial barriers in education. In 1933, Thomas Hocutt became the first African American to attempt to integrate the University of North Carolina. Murray gave UNC its second test in 1938. In 1955, three more Hillside alumni—John Brandon, Ralph Frazier, and Leroy Frazier—became the university's first black undergraduates. In reflecting on her own path to civil rights activism, Murray recalled lessons in race consciousness and pride at Hillside High, as when teachers asked students to recite poems by Paul Laurence Dunbar. Growing up in segregated Durham, Murray experienced oppression and humiliation, but she also acquired "a sense of identity and a sense of racial pride, fragile though they might be." Reflecting back fifty years later, she believed that at least in that respect, she possessed something for which the post–civil rights generation was still looking. "To those of my generation reared in the South," she wrote, "it has always been somewhat bewildering to observe young blacks seeking an identity that we already had half a century earlier."[44] That culture of affirmation stemmed in part from black educators' efforts to adapt rather than simply adopt white-authored courses of study. In fact, while black teachers welcomed the movement for curricular standardization, they cautioned against an uncritical embrace of white-authored courses of study.

History Lessons and the Battle for Curricular Ownership

One of the first issues around which the NCTA mobilized was the General Assembly's 1881 decision to throw out public school textbooks written by regional outsiders or those hostile to white southern perspectives. Black educators charged that they had the right to control which textbooks their students used. That early effort at curricular influence reflected a nascent national movement for the study and promotion of black culture and history. Booker T. Washington and other turn-of-the-century black leaders coupled appeals for economic self-help and solidarity with allied calls for black cultural pride. After visiting the folk schools of Denmark, where students studied Danish history, language, and culture to the near exclusion of classical studies, Washington concluded that comparable programs would benefit American blacks far more than would studying Greek or Latin.[45]

In planning lessons in the culture and history of their race, black teachers found little of use in conventional textbooks. A 1926 survey of history and civics books used in the South found that most discussions of blacks dealt exclusively with the period of slavery. Almost no mention was made of black participation in either the Spanish-American War or World War I. Moreover, the texts used "derogatory or unfair statements in referring to the Negro." Civic texts similarly ignored the African American experience. Courses in American civics and citizenship gained popularity in the late nineteenth century, and North Carolina approved such a course in the mid-1890s. As historian Julie Reuben has pointed out, school authorities designed these courses not as a way to politicize youth but as a way of emphasizing the duties and responsibilities of citizenship. In her words, "Upright behavior, not political participation, became the defining mark of a good citizen." Indeed, North Carolina's original civics curriculum said very little about the political process and had much to say about moral obligations. Nowhere was mention made of the ways in which race imprinted southern citizenship.[46] Early twentieth-century black teachers, then, had to step outside the formal curriculum if they wanted their students to learn about black triumphs and struggles both past and present.

Historian Carter G. Woodson did more than any other individual to offer black educators alternatives to the racial distortions of conventional school curricula. Born in Virginia in 1875, Woodson earned a doctorate in history, the only child of former slaves to do so. By the time of his death in 1950, Woodson was often referred to as the Father of Negro History. He founded the Association for the Study of Negro Life and History (ASNLH) in 1915, the *Journal of Negro History* in 1916, and Negro History Week in 1926. At the time he founded the ASNLH, the film *Birth of a Nation* was popularizing a version of southern history that left little room for positive stories of black achievement. Woodson reasoned that to counter such propaganda, blacks needed to tell their history themselves. This new story was important for whites to hear but was fundamental for blacks, as it would enable them to construct an affirming self-image. A revised historical consciousness, Woodson explained in 1921, promised political empowerment: "If you will read the history of Africa, the history of your ancestors—people of whom you should feel proud—you will realize that they have a history that is worthwhile. They have traditions . . . of which you can boast and upon which you can base a claim for a right to share in the blessings of democracy."[47]

Beginning in the mid-1920s, Woodson recruited black teachers to spread that message throughout the South, and North Carolina figured prominently in that campaign. The ASNLH convened its 1925 annual meeting in Durham, where Woodson invited Newbold to speak. In return, Newbold invited Woodson to speak to the state's summer schools for black teachers.[48] In 1926, Woodson returned to the state and addressed the NCTA, which pledged seventy-five dollars to the ASNLH and resolved to encourage the teaching of black history. Some black educators took up that call by adding formal courses in black history to the curriculum. In the late 1920s and early 1930s, students at the Berry O'Kelly County Training School in Method and Dillard High School in Goldsboro took black history courses that used textbooks written by black historian Benjamin Brawley. Shepard added a similar course in the "History of the Negro Race" at North Carolina College for Negroes in 1927. The college catalog noted "there ha[d] been a steady demand by students in Negro schools for a broader knowledge of the past of their own people." The recent development of "adequate historical material" had made it possible to meet this "long felt need."[49]

The economic hardships of the depression era stymied the growth of the black history movement, which depended in part on student purchases of supplemental texts. One study from Durham found very little formal instruction in black history and noted that students simply could not afford to pay for books outside the basic curriculum. In 1930, when ASNLH field-worker Lorenzo Greene urged the state to add two books on black history to its supplementary list, Newbold said he would do so if the prices were reduced "to accommodate cash-strapped black families." The following year, only about 2 percent of the state's black high schools offered courses in black history. Separate courses were somewhat more common in the Deep South states, where a larger number of majority-black communities had engendered a heightened sense of group identity.[50] Nonetheless, a region-wide survey conducted by the U.S. Bureau of Education in 1932 concluded that "despite the fact that there seems to be a growing interest among Negro schools in studying Negro history, the offering in this subject is extremely meager." Woodson admonished African Americans for regarding black history as a dispensable luxury. Speaking at Johnson C. Smith University in Charlotte, he called for a new era of curricular creativity that would respond to the needs of black students.

With the 1933 publication of *The Mis-Education of the Negro*, Woodson echoed that appeal. To liberate themselves from white-authored narratives of the past, black teachers needed to engage in curricular innovation rather than uncritical duplication. The "chief difficulty with the education of the Negro," he wrote, "is that it has been largely imitation resulting in the enslavement of his mind."[51]

Southern state officials met Woodson halfway in his goal of transforming historical education. On one hand, state officials had few problems with adding a token work of black history to its recommended textbook lists. As early as the turn of the century, North Carolina approved books by and about African Americans for supplemental use in the social studies curriculum, and the Department of Public Instruction granted teachers extension credit for taking courses in black history.[52] Other states also cooperated with Woodson's efforts to distribute black history materials, with the ASNLH reporting similar success across the region.[53]

On the other hand, state officials did little to encourage white schools to use the available black history materials, and they generally kept blacks at arm's length in making substantive curriculum decisions that might have transformed how all races learned history. The state included a few black educators on committees working to revise the standard course of study in the mid-1930s, but Newbold admitted that these representatives did not have "full and complete opportunity" to direct the committee's work.[54] In the early 1930s, the national NAACP urged members to challenge negative portrayals of African Americans in standard history texts, but revising entrenched historical interpretations proved a daunting task. Most conventional American history books continued either to depict African Americans in stereotyped images or to omit them altogether, thus imparting the impression that black contributions to history were negligible. A 1935 survey of school texts used in the South concluded, "The student inevitably gets the impression from these books that the Negro has figured in American life only as a semi-savage slave and as a dangerous freedman, unprepared for citizenship and a menace to civilization."[55] In the mid-1950s, three-quarters of a century after organizing around the racial politics of textbook selections, the NCTA was still working for the inclusion of African Americans on the State Textbook Commission and urging the elimination of textbooks that "either omit the Negro as a contributing factor in our civilization or present him in a biased fashion."[56]

Given the paucity of state-provided black history materials, some black teachers turned to the *Negro History Bulletin*, a magazine that Woodson began publishing in 1937, with nine issues released each year, in correspondence with the school calendar. Each issue contained material that teachers could integrate into lesson plans: stories, poems, illustrations, lists of books on black history, articles with study questions, and a monthly list of "Persons and Achievements to Be Remembered." The *Bulletin* urged teachers to familiarize students with the important pioneers in their communities—the first black doctors, lawyers, and so forth—and advised them to establish student governments that would pattern the national system of party conventions, campaigns, and elections, thereby impressing students with the importance "of being a full-fledged citizen." In addition to its curricular recommendations, the *Bulletin* carried a "School News" column that spotlighted teachers who modeled ASNLH ideals.[57]

Such supplemental resources helped to sustain the black history movement even as the number of formal black history courses diminished in the postwar period. In the early 1940s, 20 of the state's 250 black public high schools offered a class in black history; by 1950, only 4 of the 228 black high schools did so. The state supervisor of Negro high schools judged in 1955 that classes in "Negro History have been almost eliminated from the program of studies." According to historian Jonathan Zimmerman, such separate black history courses temporarily fell out of fashion as the integrationist impulse of the early civil rights movement took hold.[58]

Nevertheless, many black teachers throughout the Jim Crow period found ways to impart lessons in race pride outside of formal coursework. ASNLH publications often carried stories of Negro History Week observances in North Carolina, commemorations that included plays and pageants as well as the decoration of school facilities with pictures of notable African Americans. In 1950, the Jeanes teacher in Granville County arranged for all thirty-two schools in her district to have speakers during Negro History Week. State supervisor Ruth Woodson urged such activities on teachers. "We didn't call it black history as such, then," she recalled, "but we just encouraged the children [to think] that, 'You can do something, too.'" New Bern teacher Arlestus Attmore did research in the library after school hours to add to his textbook's meager "smattering of people of the black race." Georgia Sutton, who began teaching in the 1950s, similarly recalled, "The only way you would [teach black history,] you'd have to sneak that in. It was just never included in textbooks." Such compensatory efforts, as one educator noted in 1934, "created within the Negro a new feeling of his importance which has changed his sense of social debt to one of social contribution." Daily rituals further reinforced that message. Louise Jones, who attended Juniper Level Elementary School in Wake County in the 1930s and 1940s, remembers that her teachers began

A lesson in American civics at Annie Holland School in Rocky Mount in the 1950s or 1960s. (Courtesy of the Charles S. Killebrew Collection, Braswell Memorial Library, Rocky Mount, N.C.)

each day with the singing of "Lift Ev'ry Voice and Sing." Written in 1900 by James Weldon Johnson and adopted in the 1930s by the NAACP as the "Negro National Anthem," the hymn celebrated the African American triumph over slavery. Jones recalled, "We knew all the words. The song was a part of us. We relished it. It made me feel like I was somebody, too."[59]

Perhaps the ultimate shortcoming of the black history movement was its failure to permeate white schools, where students were left with the impression that blacks had made few contributions to history. As one Chapel Hill High ninth-grader put it in 1943, "The Negro has come a long way up from savagery in two hundred years. The white people have the Roman and Greek cultures and many more behind and after them." Governor R. Gregg Cherry similarly commented in 1945 that despite the horrors of slavery, black Americans could feel grateful that their transport out of Africa had offered them "the right and privilege of a ready-built civilization." Carter Woodson was quick to warn that such assumptions of black cultural dependence perpetuated racial oppression. After all, he asked, "Why not exploit or enslave a class that everybody is taught to regard as inferior?" Woodson never intended for blacks to be the exclusive beneficiaries of the black history movement, instead dreaming of the day when both classrooms and textbooks would reflect the nation's rich racial and ethnic diversity. At the time of his death in 1950, however, that dream still seemed remote.[60]

The civil rights activism of the 1960s eventually breathed new life into the black history movement. Inspired by that era's emphasis on racial solidarity and pride, black youth figured prominently among a new generation of advocates for curricular inclusiveness. Coinciding with the integration of southern schools, that revitalized black history movement also held unprecedented potential for reaching the white historical consciousness.[61]

Vocational Education and the Struggle for Economic Citizenship

Just as segregation had weakened the interracial capacity of the early black history movement, Jim Crow fundamentally constrained a concurrent campaign for vocational education. That movement's leaders eventually asked whether arming black students with even the best vocational training would shield them against the indignities and limited opportunities of a rigidly segregated job market.

In 1930, Governor O. Max Gardner kicked off a Live-at-Home campaign by inviting black and white students to enter an essay contest centered on farm life. State officials designed the campaign to encourage the raising of foodstuffs and to lessen the population's dependence on cash crops, whose prices had plummeted during the 1920s. They further aimed to curb a rising tide of rural migration to cities by demonstrating how farm families could "*have without buying* most of the goods for which they spend the most money." While both races were assigned roles in this plan, Gardner suggested that blacks in particular belonged on the land. In fact, he happily noted, blacks' "splendid response" to the Live-at-Home movement bore "out Booker T. Washington's assertion that the Negro is naturally a farmer and is at his best when he is in close contact with the soil." When the essay contest concluded in June, a large crowd gathered at the State House of Representatives for what by all accounts was an unusual awards ceremony. According to a correspondent for *Time*, whites and blacks sat "crowded cheek to jowl." Journalists commented "with astonishment upon the sudden evaporation of race prejudice." Even more remarkable was the fact that "Negroes spoke from the same rostrum as Governor Gardner about the 'recovery of their race's self-respect.'" The journalist also captured what seemed like a southern anomaly. There stood young

Governor O. Max Gardner poses on Capitol Square in Raleigh with the winners of the Live-at-Home Essay Contest in 1930. On his right is Ophelia Holley of Windsor, and on his left is Leroy Sossamon of Cabarrus County. (Courtesy of The North Carolina State Archives, Raleigh)

"Leroy Sossamon, blond and blue-eyed," and "Ophelia Holley, chocolate brown," each holding equally large silver cups on the same platform with a southern governor. Newbold also later pointed to the event's novelty by emphasizing that Holley was in fact "a real Negro." When the press went to snap a picture of this scene, the governor's cronies appeared "suddenly apprehensive" and "reminded him that no southern Governor had ever had his picture taken publicly with a Negro." Such a picture, they added, "would be used against him in future campaigns." Gardner appeared "un-daunted" and "ordered the photographer to proceed." Two weeks later, *Time* featured a picture and story of the event. It portrayed a South that held a racially undifferentiated vision for how its youth should live and prosper.[62]

In practice, however, the contours of southern schooling in the 1930s hewed to a different sort of vision. As the South's plantation economy declined and opportunities even for black tenancy decreased, southern white school officials resisted the diversification of vocational training for a generation of black youth who would not find it possible to eke out a living on the farm. In what became a self-perpetuating argument, officials often reserved the newest and most sophisticated vocational training programs for white schools by explaining that students should prepare for the jobs that were readily available for their race. Blacks therefore lacked access to the vocational programs that at least in theory promised opportunities to both "live at home" and prosper.

Historians have tended either to ignore the vocational movement in relation to black schools or to conflate it with the Hampton-Tuskegee philosophy of industrial education.[63] While many black educators questioned the latter's seeming complicity with the socioeconomic status quo, the vocational curriculum of the 1930s and 1940s promised to pave the way to middle-class prosperity. In hindsight, it would be easy to dismiss the vocational curriculum as a chimera that carried more promises than it delivered.[64] By many accounts, it did not guarantee economic mobility to working-class students, and it cheapened the task of learning by inextricably linking schools to the demands of the marketplace. The relative absence of this flawed curriculum in black schools arguably constitutes a story of negligible importance. Moreover, a first-rate vocational education would not have compensated for white unwillingness to hire blacks for well-paying jobs. As Adam Fairclough has argued, the "fundamental weakness" of all phases of school equalization was the decidedly unequal job market that black graduates faced.[65] Yet even if vocational education failed to live up to its promises, the interest that it sparked is important for understanding how education figured into a larger black vision for economic citizenship.

The vocational movement originated in the early twentieth century, when high schools in the North took on a new mission of training students for jobs. By the 1920s, according to historian Harvey Kantor, that new mission "had become a primary rationale for education and had stimulated a flurry of reforms to integrate the school more closely with the economy." Industrialization and the mechanization of skilled trades drove that change. As northern workers resisted the attenuation of their autonomy by joining unions and organizing strikes, an unlikely coalition of social reformers, industrialists, and labor leaders viewed vocational education as the solution to society's ills. Labor leaders and social workers hoped that this approach would replicate the apprenticeship system, refashion industrial labor as skilled labor, and stem the tide of child labor. Industrialists, by contrast, looked to vocational education to instill in youth a work ethic that privileged cooperation over resistance.[66]

Originating in the industrialized North, the vocational movement attracted increased southern interest in 1917 when Congress passed the Smith-Hughes Act, which provided grants to the states on a matching fund basis for vocational training in public high schools. Prior to the measure's enactment, southern laggardness in vocational education was partly explained by delayed industrialization as well as by the region's underfunded public schools. Two southern congressmen sponsored the Smith-Hughes Act, and it generally won regional approval as a way to channel federal funds to impoverished schools and integrate youth into a modern economy. In 1917, North Carolina appointed a director of vocational education and began hiring high school vocational teachers; by the 1920s, the state superintendent insisted that vocational training was a valuable addition to high school curricula and to adult education. In 1926, 115 high schools employed at least one vocational teacher offering the federally approved vocational curriculum. Ten years later, statewide enrollment in vocational programs had increased dramatically. In agricultural classes, for example, enrollment in both high school and adult classes increased from 323 in 1918–19 to 20,328 in 1935–36.[67]

The state followed Smith-Hughes guidelines in developing vocational courses in three areas: agriculture, industrial arts, and home economics. The agricultural curriculum was meant to teach boys the practices of modern farming, with lessons in soil conservation, livestock breeding, pest control, crop diversification, and product marketing. Designed to develop skills for a range of trades as well as careers in engineering and design, the industrial arts included instruction in art metalwork, auto mechanics, concrete construction, electricity, general metalwork, mechanical drawing, pottery, printing, sheet metalwork, textiles, and woodworking. Home economics courses covered such topics as nutrition, hygiene, and clothing and applied the ideas of domestic science to the demands of home and family management. While home economics courses had relevance for future paid domestic workers, some parts of the curriculum resonated more closely with the lives of middle-class housewives, who, for example, could more easily afford to ponder the "careful selection of accessories." In addition to the core Smith-Hughes curriculum, high school vocational departments eventually included career counseling and courses in the commercial arts (stenography, bookkeeping, and typing). The state superintendent explained in the mid-1930s that vocational courses sought not only "to teach people how to live, but how to make a living as well." The state was producing "efficient earners" who could "maintain a higher standard of living."[68]

In extending the vocational curriculum to black schools, whites initially aimed to reinforce rather than diversify blacks' existing employment choices. In the late 1920s, for example, the Julius Rosenwald Fund, which had helped build hundreds of black schools across the rural South, experimented with the idea of building black urban high schools that would offer a vocational curriculum modeled on the Hampton-Tuskegee philosophy of industrial education. When high school supervisor William Robinson learned of these plans, he fired off a letter to fund official Alfred K. Stern and challenged the notion that blacks should be schooled for their "inevitable lot": "Would it not be more in keeping with American ideals [of] democracy and human justice to put into play certain influences which would tend to equalize economic and industrial opportunity rather than merely admit the existence of an unjust, un-American situation and provide for its permanence?" Robinson pledged to support "a serious effort at vocational training" but saw no need to replicate the "anemic type of industrial work [currently] done in the small schools." Stern insisted that he wanted not to create an "industrial caste group" but rather to equip black youth "to best face actual conditions of life."[69]

The Rosenwald Fund's vision for black vocational training temporarily won out. Robinson left his post in 1928, and the fund charted plans for a new black high school in Winston-Salem that would tailor its training to the types of industrial jobs that blacks typically held. Newbold embraced the Rosenwald efforts, believing that they "constitute[d] a distinct innovation in high school education for Negroes in the South." The state agent generally believed that there should be "one basic curricula . . . in all public schools for whites and Negroes alike," but he agreed with fund officials that it was acceptable to adapt the vocational curriculum to fit the "special type of manufacturing or industrial work" available to blacks. In truth, most of the black industrial jobs in Winston-Salem—menial positions in tobacco factories—required very few skills. Thus, the vocational program at the new Atkins High School ultimately offered very little innovation. Boys could take courses in auto mechanics, barbering, carpentry, chauffeuring, and janitorial service. By contrast, boys at the nearby white Reynolds High School could take classes in mechanical drawing, sheet metalwork, cotton mill mathematics, tobacco manufacturing, and electricity. The differences between the girls' classes were less stark but nevertheless tinged by race. Both races took cooking, dressmaking, nursing, cosmetology, household management, stenography, and typing. Yet white girls had the additional option of taking a class in dietetics, while black girls had classes in "maid service."[70] In using the job market as a model for its vocational curriculum, the Rosenwald Fund had replicated existing patterns of first- and second-class economic citizenship.

Winston-Salem's uneven development of vocational programs reflected statewide patterns. Most black high schools in the 1930s lacked full-fledged vocational programs and offered courses that required the least expensive materials. For example, a 1930–31 survey of 1,405 black schools found that 1,130 taught sewing, 400 taught manual training, and only 195 taught cooking. At most rural black schools, it was far easier to secure access to thread and needle than to a fully equipped kitchen or mechanics shop. To be sure, many white high schools also lacked advanced vocational programs, but white pupils on the whole received a disproportionate share of the available vocational resources. In 1934–35, only 44 of the state's 409 vocational teachers worked in black schools. Newbold admitted, "For colored youth little has been done in training for vocations except in teaching." A 1937 state report similarly found that even though blacks comprised 29 percent of the state's school population, only between 10 and 15 percent of the total federal, state, and local funds spent on vocational instruction went to black schools. Unequal spending patterns often resulted from the "failure of local officials to make reasonable appropriations to match state and federal funds." In one county, officials refused to provide matching vocational funds to even the largest black high school despite having allocated such funds to all the white schools, explaining, "If we give to that school we will have to do the same for every other colored school in the county." The officials instead suggested that black parents raise private funds for vocational education. Newbold estimated in 1938 that vocational training reached only one-sixth as many black students as white students, even though whites had urged nonacademic courses on blacks "ever since the days of Booker T. Washington."[71] Vocational training had acquired the imprint of white privilege, just as the liberal arts had a generation earlier.

To the extent that available resources allowed, black educators resisted exclusion from the vocational movement. As early as the mid-1920s, a survey of black high school curricula found a "decreased emphasis upon Latin and [an] increased emphasis upon subjects of a more practical nature." In the mid-1930s, the NCTA included vocational education among its ten recommendations for the improvement of black schools. Many black educators agreed with Greensboro principal John Tarpley's contention that "too many of our high schools are purely college preparatory in nature." As Newbold observed, "Where formerly there was more or less an aversion on the part of the Negroes themselves to having vocational and industrial courses in their high schools, they are now rather keen that such courses be offered for their children." In his travels across the region in the early 1930s, black educator Horace Mann Bond noted "one of the choicest bits of irony": Whereas blacks had once "bitterly opposed" nonacademic instruction, now they actively sought vocational education. Whites, who once had imposed industrial training on blacks, now refused to fund advanced vocational instruction. Bond found most industrial courses hopelessly outmoded. "The apparatus for teaching shoemaking in the typical Negro school [was] as antiquated as that of a medieval cobbler," he wrote. "The Negro high school may have Latin, Greek, or any other subject which it wishes that calls for no equipment or expensive construction; but the large appropriations for the installation of machinery go to the white schools."[72]

Black educators did not completely oppose the idea of race-specific vocational programs, but they tended to favor differentiation in the form of special guidance programs that would raise the confidence of black youth and prepare them to challenge a hostile job market. They most resisted the notion that they should be steering black students exclusively into "black jobs." As the editor of the *Journal of Negro Education* wrote in 1935, preparing blacks exclusively for black jobs "is tenable only if one accepts the assumption that Negroes should have a special 'place' in our national economy such as existed during slavery." North Carolina's Trigg advocated an expanded vocational guidance program as a way to help black youth imagine new employment possibilities. He feared that the average black student "looks at occupations in America, but he does not see them." Black young people's ability to see themselves in a full range of occupations was "obscured in the fog of conflicting philosophies of the Negro's relation to American life."[73]

Rather than prepare black youth to enter and refashion a biracial labor market, some black scholars advocated economic separatism and racial collectivism. Du Bois became the most prominent spokesman for these ideas when he broke ranks with the NAACP in 1934, insisting that the group's focus on legal equality ignored the more pressing issue of black economic dependence on whites. Du Bois doubted whether blacks could ever enter American industry on their own terms. Instead, he urged blacks to "work for [them]selves" by creating an all-black labor market. "We can consume mainly what we ourselves produce," he wrote, "and produce as large a proportion as possible of that which we consume." Speaking to the NCTA in 1935, Du Bois urged black teachers to organize small agricultural cooperatives, like those found in Scandinavia. He extolled, "Two generations ago 42 per cent of the Danes were tenants, today 90 per cent own their land." Du Bois predicted that only a fundamental "social reorganization" would liberate blacks from the chains of economic dependence.[74]

Many leading black educators shared Du Bois's hopes for economic empowerment and his concerns about the limits of schooling to achieve it, but they cautioned that plans for "self-sufficiency" were nothing more than a flight of fancy. Especially during the depression, some took the approach that even a "black job" was better than no job at all. When Ambrose Caliver of the U.S. Bureau of Education published a 1938 report on the "Vocational Education and Guidance of Negroes," he recommended that black teachers counsel students frankly about their limited job prospects. He also advocated that black schools prioritize home economics, which would help blacks cope with the "disorganization of their family life during slavery" and prepare the 62 percent of black women who held jobs in domestic service. The bureau encouraged black educators not only to push for equal vocational training but also to help students cope with existing conditions. Some black teachers adopted this pragmatic approach and couched appeals for vocational funding within acknowledgments of the racial order. Principal J. W. Groves Jr. of the Chatham County Training School requested a domestic science department in 1933, arguing that most students would "go directly into service for their white neighbors or housekeeping for themselves." Shepard similarly promoted his school by asserting, "A trained person makes a better servant."[75]

For their part, black students were disinclined to accommodate the southern labor market. One survey among black high school students in North Carolina in the early 1930s found that very few aspired to jobs in agriculture and domestic service. Only 15 of 393 boys planned to take up work on the farm or in personal service for white families. Fully three-quarters of all the students surveyed wanted professional careers. These ambitions seemed to invite dashed hopes, as most of the South's black adults held nonprofessional jobs. Concluded the survey's author, "Most of the Negroes attending public secondary schools in North Carolina entertain vocational aims which they will never attain." Black students expressed openness to vocational training in agriculture and skilled trades as long as it involved skills that allowed for upward mobility. In the absence of programs for economic advancement, many black youth set their sights firmly on professional careers.[76]

By some accounts, limited vocational training cast many black youth— especially boys—adrift. Black males constituted only 37.6 percent of the black high school population in the mid-1930s, a reflection of their disproportionate representation among high school dropouts. A committee of black educators concluded in 1937 that more black males would stay in school if they had "sufficient vocational educational opportunities."[77] A series of profound shifts in southern agriculture compounded the black male vocational dilemma. The proportion of black-owned farms had been declining since the 1910s, thereby dimming what were already uncertain hopes of escaping a life of tenancy or sharecropping. A sharp drop in agricultural commodity prices in the 1920s accelerated the generation-long exodus of rural blacks to cities both within and outside the region. The introduction of New Deal agricultural relief programs in the 1930s unintentionally gave blacks added reason to abandon farming. In requiring landowners to divide benefit payments among tenants on a proportionate basis, the federal government indirectly encouraged white landowners to reduce their reliance on tenancy and hire wage laborers. Labor shortages during World War II hastened black rural out-migration. Even when the urban job market constricted during the postwar years, blacks continued to leave the rural South in search of greater economic opportunity. At the same time, many landowners increasingly mechanized their operations, thereby further reducing the need for farm labor. By 1955, John Larkins of the North Carolina Department of Public Welfare concluded, "The farm, once the bulwark of the economy of the Negro, no longer serves as a haven for those unable to adjust to urban living."[78] While the South's plantation economy had ensnared many blacks within a lifetime of poverty, its demise "liberated" blacks to enter a segregated and punishing urban labor market.

In the 1930s, when the full impact of these economic and demographic changes was still unclear, many black educators held out hope that armed with the right training, black rural youth could find economic salvation. Principal Milton Calloway of the Rosenwald High School in rural Camden County believed that a well-developed vocational program would curb the tide of boys leaving farms for cities. "The governmental reorganization of agriculture demands that the Negro be taught modern agriculture as a means of keeping him satisfied on the farm and to enable him to make a decent living at that which he is best fitted," Calloway wrote in 1939. He feared that black vocational training often had "been ignored by the proponents of training for culture." Many Jeanes teachers similarly argued that the rural South offered blacks at least the possibility of self-sufficiency, if not prosperity. In 1936, one Jeanes teacher found considerable interest among black leaders in a "back to the farm" movement and argued that many problems afflicting blacks could be "wholly solved by

In the 1930s and 1940s, black educators pushed for more opportunities for their students to receive vocational training. Of particular concern were vocational opportunities for boys, who tended to leave high school before graduating. In this undated photograph, a student at Stephens-Lee High School in Asheville is learning to weld. (Courtesy of Heritage of Black Highlanders Collection, D. H. Ramsey Library Special Collections, University of North Carolina, Asheville)

the return of more Negroes to the farms, and more of our younger people becoming more interested in rural home life, gardening, cattle raising, poultry farming, nurseries, flowers and flower shops." Some older Jeanes teachers complained that younger educators were not taking a true interest in rural communities. Regional supervisor Shellie Northcutt lamented in 1941 that "everybody had the big idea that we must have liberal arts and that unless you are trained for [becoming] a doctor . . . you are going back to the days of slavery."[79]

These debates walked a fine line between recognition of rural life's merits and complacency about its limitations. Jeanes Fund president Arthur Wright felt certain that black students needed to "learn to utilize those things which easily come to hand in order to get the most out of life on the financial level on which many are bound to live." Jeanes teachers were therefore to remain disciples of "work and [the] simple virtues of life." State Jeanes supervisor Marie McIver also hoped to teach youth to make the most of their current circumstances, but she wanted them to visualize a world beyond the realities of rural poverty. She raised that concern when offering an advance review of *Tobe*, a 1939 picture book by Stella Gentry Sharpe that portrayed the life of a sixteen-year-old boy and his family on a tenant farm in eastern North Carolina. One black reviewer for the NCTA's journal praised the book for "portray[ing] Negro life as it is" and its avoidance of racial stereotyping. McIver, however, worried that the book would encourage black children to set their sights on narrow horizons by "tend[ing] to make *farm tenancy* ideal." She noted that the book portrayed "a happy home of ten individuals" despite the fact that they were living in modest circumstances. She commented, "Some youngsters will certainly want to know why this family does not have a better place in which to live, since they 'work and work and work.'" McIver wanted books for black children that would "inspire in them a desire to live better lives."[80]

By the 1940s, many observers concluded that black schools had done far too little to offer such inspiration. In his 1944 landmark study of American race relations, Swedish economist Gunnar Myrdal argued that Jeanes teachers had made "heroic attempts" to ease the "extreme poverty and cultural backwardness of the Southern rural community," but these teachers ultimately constituted a "remarkable and pathetic figure in the history of Negro education." Myrdal further charged, "In spite of all the talk about it, no effective industrial training was ever given the Negroes in the Southern public schools, except training for cooking and menial service. The expensive vocational training, which conflicted so harshly with the interests of the white workers, has never become more than a slogan." Myrdal too quickly dismissed the important function that Jeanes teachers had played in empowering rural communities, but his overall assessment of black vocational education pointed to hard truths. The numbers of black vocational students and teachers had increased in the early 1940s—in 1939-40, only 14 percent of the state's vocational teachers were black, a figure that grew to 24 percent by 1944-45—yet black vocational opportunities remained limited, especially in the poorest rural areas, where black youth most desired to escape the labor patterns of their parents. In rural Sampson County, none of the four black high schools offered any vocational programs beyond one or two home economics courses and one course in business training. Agricultural and industrial training courses were "entirely lacking." Out of seventy-eight rural black high schools surveyed in 1948-49, more than one-third offered no vocational training.[81]

While many educators had particularly feared the impact of weak vocational programs on future male breadwinners, the postwar years gave rise to a particularly striking gap in one growing area of female employment. High school commercial classes in typewriting, bookkeeping, and shorthand increased substantially after the war, along with the number of women in clerical jobs, but white high schools were far more likely to offer such courses. In 1945-46, nearly half of all white high schools already offered a course in typewriting, more than triple the 13 percent figure for

Commercial education classes grew in demand among black students in the 1940s and 1950s, although white high schools tended to offer a broader variety of such courses. In connection with his 1951 film, *The Tar Heel Family*, documentarian George Stoney visited a typing class at this unidentified school. (Courtesy of The North Carolina State Archives, Raleigh)

black high schools. Nearly one-fifth of white high schools offered book-keeping, while not quite 2 percent of black high schools did so. This gap in commercial education no doubt reflected and perpetuated white employers' refusal to hire black secretaries.[82] The differentials in certain male-oriented training programs were actually less stark, partly because offerings were minimal for both races. In what was largely still a rural state, educational officials overall had placed little priority for both races on the industrial arts. In the mid-1940s, the demand for such courses had grown, but fewer than one-fifth of all North Carolina high schools had industrial arts classes.[83]

Black youth of both genders, of course, had to face the unique double

Black rural youth had misgivings about following their parents into farming but none-theless took advantage of the agricultural training their schools offered. Here, a Future Farmers of America gathering inspects tractors in Pitt County in 1958. (Courtesy of *Daily Reflector* Negative Collection [#741], East Carolina Manuscript Collection, J. Y. Joyner Library, East Carolina University, Greenville, N.C.)

burden of limited training programs and employment discrimination. It was no wonder, then, that at John Chavis School in Cherryville, princi-pal W. H. Green believed that a curriculum of "straight academic work" had failed his students. He observed that many graduates despaired when they realized that they were "no better prepared to make a living for them-selves than before going to high school."[84] Uncertain about how to make a living, black youth grew ever more resolute about how not to spend their working lives. A 1948 study of ten rural black high schools in eastern North Carolina found that while more than 90 percent of the students' parents farmed, only 2 percent of the students were planning to become farmers. Their top three occupational choices—teaching, business, and nursing—all required advanced schooling. Given that three-fourths of these stu-dents were raised on tenant farms, it was not surprising that few wished to follow in their parents' footsteps. Nevertheless, many lacked the money for college and well over half reported never having received any voca-tional guidance at school.[85]

Even for the college-bound, the links between schooling and economic citizenship remained tenuous. The state's black land-grant college, North Carolina A&T, had long carried the promise of training students for diverse vocations. The southern states had embraced that mission at white land-grant colleges but had inadequately equipped black institutions. In the early twentieth century, students at those schools could either take a traditional slate of liberal arts courses or prepare for careers in small-scale farming or basic trades such as tailoring, shoemaking, carpentry, and auto repair. Faced with those choices, many students eschewed the "agricultural and technical" track and opted for teaching certification. In 1932, 4,059 of the 5,698 students in the South's black land-grant colleges were studying to become teachers.[86]

The general drift of A&T students toward teaching alarmed F. D. Bluford, who served as the school's president from 1925 to 1955. He insisted in 1929 that "something should be done to make the Negroes more business and industrial minded" and to "counteract the professional tendency among them." President D. K. Cherry of Kittrell College agreed, noting that the two or three professional fields open to blacks had reached a saturation point. He believed that "business, agriculture, and skilled labor have been seriously neglected by college trained Negroes." Faced with limited funds for advanced technical courses and the realities of job discrimination, however, Bluford had little choice but to build the liberal arts track. As Shepard noted disapprovingly in 1936, "A. & T. College is purely a liberal arts college."[87] Other black leaders joined the chorus of criticism. Durham's *Carolina Times* scolded Bluford and insisted that blacks needed a place "to develop farmers, tailors, carpenters, brick masons, shoemakers, cooks, plumbers, steamfitters, etc." In fact, the paper argued, "North Carolina Negroes need the type of education for which A. and T. was chartered, more than they need the type of education offered by any other school in the state." Newbold similarly expressed dismay that A&T was not achieving the same results found at its white counterpart in Raleigh, which offered "a fine example of what such an institution can do for agricultural and engineering education." He felt certain that A&T "could likewise render a similar service to the Negroes of this whole State if it would intelligently, definitely and consistently promote agricultural and rural life education."[88]

In criticizing A&T administrators for straying from the school's "agricultural and technical" mission, blacks and whites alike seemed to be looking for an easy scapegoat for the deep-seated problem of employment discrimination. Newbold admitted as much when he asked in 1929, "If Negro men educated at A. & T. College do not go to work for General Electric,

General Motors, or Bell Telephone Company, are there no other fields of useful endeavor which may be substituted for such corporation employment?" Alternatives to the white professional world were indeed limited. Historian James Anderson has pointed out that black land-grant colleges faced two choices: "They could train teachers for the segregated black elementary and secondary schools, or they could prepare blacks to be good agricultural and domestic laborers and thus reproduce the mostly unskilled, dead-end occupational structure that locked blacks in poverty."[89]

Many A&T students therefore continued to see teaching as their best chance for economic security. A&T graduate James W. Turner understood the perils of that strategy. Having graduated in 1938 with an A-grade high school teaching certificate and degrees in English and history, all he could find was a year's position at an elementary school, followed by two years of teaching at A&T. After serving in the armed forces during World War II, Turner returned to North Carolina hoping to find a permanent teaching job. In 1949, the thirty-three-year-old husband and father still had not found a regular position and wrote in despair to Newbold to explain that his "whole heart is wrapped up in teaching." Newbold regretted that Turner's dilemma was "very familiar," as the state had "a considerable surplus of well-trained Negro teachers," especially at the high school level. The state's equalization of teacher salaries in 1944 only had added to the profession's appeal. "I am sorry," Newbold added, "that I cannot offer you more encouraging information."[90]

Spurred by the demands of the Sputnik generation for more training in technical fields as well as by white hopes for curbing the integration of higher education, the state expanded A&T's offerings, including those in engineering, during the 1950s and 1960s.[91] But throughout the Jim Crow period, black college graduates in the South faced an exceedingly narrow employment market. "The teaching profession has largely been the ladder on which Negroes of lower social and economic classes have moved into upper class status," wrote John Larkins, the North Carolina Department of Public Welfare's director of Negro work, in 1955. In fact, the only two professions where blacks held proportionate representation at the time were teaching and the ministry, and the proportion of blacks in some skilled trades had decreased in the 1930s and 1940s. The lack of black employment diversification contributed to wide income gaps. In 1949, the state's median white family income was $2,215, 2.1 times higher than the $1,056 that a nonwhite family earned; a decade later, the median white family income was 2.3 times greater than the median nonwhite family income. State patterns mirrored regional trends. Robert Margo has found that the southern labor market was more starkly segregated in 1950 than in 1900. As the region grew more industrialized and prosperous, whites so disproportionately reaped the employment benefits that labor disparities widened. "Segregationist ideology, like slavery," explains Margo, "was not incompatible with economic growth or structural change."[92]

Those labor market realities forced fully half of the class of 1959 at St. Augustine's College in Raleigh to head north after graduation. "It hurts to lose these students," President J. A. Boyer lamented, "but if they can't get teaching jobs or positions in the post office or in social work, they have to become janitors and porters to stay in the state." This hemorrhaging of educated blacks contributed to an overall decline in the state's black population. Whereas blacks comprised 33 percent of the population in 1900, that figure had dropped to 25.4 percent by 1960.[93]

Black college graduates had reason to feel betrayed by education's promise, as did students at the educational and socioeconomic margins. Of those black youth who started first grade in North Carolina in 1949, only 27.5 percent graduated from high school in 1961, just over half the number of whites from the same cohort.[94] The segregated labor market certainly offered black students few incentives to finish school. Patterns of discrimination internal to black schools may also have played a role. At Durham's Hillside High—the school that had inspired Pauli Murray and many others to high aspirations—some graduates later recalled that faculty gave light-skinned and middle-class pupils preferential support. One student who received little encouragement to attend college internalized a painful message: "I'm not light and bright."[95]

Intraracial class and color distinctions aside, Jim Crow's last generation of black students collectively experienced basic curricular parity yet somewhat circumscribed choices at the level of high school electives (table 2.1). Exact comparisons are difficult to make, as state data relied on principal reports and course nomenclature varied across schools. But the evidence suggests that white schools were more likely to offer courses in upper-level mathematics, languages other than French, and specialized commercial education subjects. White schools were also more likely to offer upper-level agriculture courses, although actual black student enrollment in those courses was comparatively high and therefore generally matched black representation in the high school population. A slightly greater percentage of black high schools had a fourth year of home economics, and black enrollment in such courses exceeded their representation in the student population. In the absence of commercial education courses, black female students may have been more likely than their white counterparts

Table 2.1. Select Curricular Offerings at Black and White High Schools in
North Carolina, 1963–1964

Course	Percentage of White Schools Offering	Percentage of Black Schools Offering
Advanced algebra	54	14
Trigonometry	46	31
Sociology	57	79
Geography	66	38
Industrial arts	66	50
Trades and industries	29	42
Distributive education I	17	3
Spanish I	35	14
Latin I	38	4
French II	80	92
French III	16	11
Chorus and choir	53	68
Basic business	45	52
Typewriting II	87	69
Shorthand I	74	46
Shorthand II	28	6
Bookkeeping I	84	38
Business arithmetic	45	21
Office practice and management	35	15
Agriculture III	73	57
Agriculture IV	65	42
Home economics IV	13	22

Source: Biennial Report, 1962–63/1963–64, pt. 1, 33, 57–58.

Note: The number of schools offering these electives was compared to the total number of schools for each race that offered through grade twelve. In 1963–64, there were 499 such schools for whites and 226 for blacks.

to opt for an additional year of home economics. White schools were slightly more likely to have "industrial arts" courses, and black schools were somewhat more likely to have "trades and industries" courses. The distinctions between these two categories were blurry, although the former often included such skills as woodworking and mechanical drawing, while the latter typically included auto mechanics, bricklaying, and machine shop. Not all differentials worked in favor of whites—it appears that by the 1960s a greater share of black schools offered separate courses in music and some social sciences. Nonetheless, the typical white high school offered an overall broader selection of courses.

Twin hopes for equal curricula and equal job prospects stoked interest in school integration. In rural Person County in 1952, one of the state's earliest suits for desegregation alleged that "of the many flagrant discriminatory practices" on the part of local officials, "the most serious" was that "in a highly agricultural area," all of the allotment for agricultural training went to white schools. A broader challenge to curricular inequality came around the same time from Topeka, Kansas, where one of *Brown*'s component cases advanced the point that curricular parity entailed more than equalizing formal course offerings. As one witness for the plaintiffs explained, if segregated schools "denied the experience in school of associating with white children, who represent 90 percent of our national society . . . then the colored child's curriculum is being greatly curtailed." North Carolina NAACP president Kelly Alexander similarly concluded in 1956, "Segregated schools cannot educate for an integrated world."[96]

Before *Brown*, most black North Carolinians limited their demands to equal curricular opportunity within the segregated context. When students boycotted Adkin High in Kinston in 1951, their demands included a vocational building, a facility that local white high school students already enjoyed. "Adkin students need the building in order to prepare themselves for later life," the protesters argued.[97] Such demands hinged on the hope that equalized black schools could prepare students for the demands of "later life" and by extension weaken larger racial barriers to opportunity. The ultimate test of that vision was James E. Shepard's embattled bid for a black counterpart to the University of North Carolina.

To you who are discouraged, citizenship is not in constitutions but in the mind.
—North Carolina Central University founder James E. Shepard, 1903

It seems to me that our struggle is two-fold: against those whites who
would deny us our rights, and against the "handkerchief heads" within our own group.
—Civil rights activist Pauli Murray, on her frustrated attempts to integrate the
University of North Carolina, 1939

He was asking [for] money to complete a great negro university. . . . He admitted
the high cost of it all, but asserted the higher cost of denying it or delaying it.
—*Greensboro Daily News* columnist W. T. Bost, on James Shepard's appeal to
state legislators, 1941

CHAPTER THREE

The High Cost of It All

James E. Shepard and Higher Education Equalization

If state officials had an Achilles heel in their efforts to uphold segregation, it was higher education. Many white elementary and secondary schools in the state dated back to only the late nineteenth or early twentieth centuries. Thus, in the mid-twentieth century, creating a parallel system of black elementary and secondary schools entailed matching a public investment of several decades. To be sure, this was an enormous task, and the state never fully embraced it and certainly never accomplished it. Yet arguably even more Herculean was the task of replicating in a short span of time the University of North Carolina at Chapel Hill, the state's flagship public university, which in the mid-twentieth century had already been well over a century in the making. Chartered in 1789, UNC remained small throughout much of the nineteenth century but experienced considerable expansion in the first half of the twentieth century, especially in the area of graduate and professional education. As the numbers of black high school graduates increased dramatically in the 1940s, so did black demand for higher education. Creating a comparable black university in time to meet that demand would have required a rapid and concentrated investment of money. It stood to reason, then, that the legal arm of the National Association for the Advancement of Colored People (NAACP) focused much of its early educational litigation on higher education, particularly graduate and professional education, where it was believed the southern states would have little chance of living up to the "separate but equal" requirement.[1]

Efforts to equalize public higher education placed Durham's North Carolina College for Negroes at the center of debate. Founded in 1910 by James Edward Shepard as the privately funded National Religious Training School and Chautauqua for the Colored Race, Shepard's college was incorporated by the state in 1923 as the Durham State Normal School. Two years later, it was reincorporated as the North Carolina College for Negroes (renamed North Carolina College at Durham in 1947 and North Carolina Central University in 1969). The school was the South's first publicly supported four-year liberal arts college for African Americans.[2] For decades, whites had opposed a liberal arts education for blacks, but the state's adoption of a single curriculum for its high schools, along with the incorporation of North Carolina College (NCC), indicated that by the mid-1920s, white southerners were willing to make at least tacit curricular concessions to black demands for educational equality. At the same time, white officials advocated the slow and gradual development of a black college program, and only in the wake of desegregation litigation did the state even consider a more ambitious vision. Shepard, by contrast, had hoped from the beginning to create a school that was equal in all respects to white institutions.

Shepard's story and the history of NCC comprise only one piece of black higher education history in North Carolina. In addition to the other black public colleges, the historically black private colleges played an enormous role in postsecondary training of black North Carolinians.[3] NCC, however, looms particularly large in this broader story. Positioned as the black counterpart to the University of North Carolina, NCC served as a crucial yardstick for measuring how well the state was living up to its legal obligations of separate but equal educational facilities.

NCC's central role in debates about higher education equalization also brings into focus questions about the politics of black school ownership in the Jim Crow South. On one hand, it would be easy to dismiss Shepard's mission to create a "Negro university" as a deeply flawed departure from the integrationist impulse of the black freedom movement. Indeed, Shepard often has played an antagonistic role in narratives of the early civil rights movement. In what arguably were cowardly acts of self-preservation, he opposed black efforts to litigate for admission to the state's flagship white university and instead sought the expansion of his own school. In so doing, Shepard found himself publicly allied with Negro education director Nathan Newbold and other state officials. On the other hand, Shepard's career could also be read as a protest against the indignities of segregation. He upheld the color line but resisted white efforts to maintain it on the cheap. After some members of the North Carolina General Assembly balked at his budget requests, Shepard told them, "The price of segregation comes high, gentlemen." Moreover, Shepard's behind-the-scenes relationship with Newbold reveals a long history of conflict and mutual distrust. Shepard deeply resented white paternalistic control of his school and on more than one occasion resisted Newbold's guidance. As Durham editor and frequent Shepard critic Louis Austin conceded, Shepard was the only black educator who "was able to outmaneuver or circumvent Dr. Newbold's strangle hold on Negro education in North Carolina." Historian John Hope Franklin, who taught at NCC in the 1940s, similarly recalled Shepard as a "strange man . . . a conservative by day, and a kind of radical by night." Despite Shepard's famed conservatism, Franklin remembered him as "very anti-segregation." In blurring the lines between strategies of protest and accommodation, Shepard's story reflects the dilemma of a generation of black leaders who deplored the injustices of Jim Crow yet sought at any cost—both to the state budget and, more tragically, to the emerging integration movement—to protect and expand black institutions.[4]

Cultivating a "Citizenship of the Mind" at the National Religious Training School

As elsewhere in the South, early black college life in North Carolina drew its vitality almost exclusively from a network of private schools established by southern freedpeople and northern church and missionary foundations. The first black liberal arts college in the state—and the entire South—was Shaw University, founded as Raleigh Institute in 1865 by the American Baptist Home Mission Society. Two years later, the mission board of the Presbyterian Church founded Biddle Institute (the precursor to Johnson C. Smith University) in Charlotte, and the Episcopal Church founded Saint Augustine's College in Raleigh. A host of smaller schools followed in the 1870s and 1880s. Established in 1879 by the African Methodist Episcopal Zion Church, Salisbury's Livingstone College prided itself on its relative independence from white benevolent organizations and stood as a testament to the financial resourcefulness of post-Emancipation black communities. Even the schools that drew much of their funding from northern white missionaries also leaned heavily on local black support. In return, the graduates provided local communities with doctors, ministers, teachers, and entrepreneurs. Students at early black colleges took courses similar to those at white colleges: literature, history, math, science, philosophy, theology, and both classical and modern languages. In addition, Shaw University established some of the South's earliest black schools of pharmacy, medicine, and law. These curricular parallels with white institutions said much about the faith that black college founders and students possessed in the possibilities for cultural assimilation. Black college graduates were to demonstrate that racial differences were, in fact, only skin-deep.[5]

Southern whites historically had resisted this sort of parallelism in black higher education. When North Carolina established its first black normal schools in the late nineteenth century, it did so on the Hampton-Tuskegee model, which included heavy doses of domestic and industrial courses, tinged with lessons in moral uplift.[6] By 1905, the state had consolidated its black normal training at three sites: the State Colored Normal School at Fayetteville, the State Colored Normal School at Elizabeth City, and Slater Normal School in Winston-Salem.[7] Spurred on by the Second Morrill Act of 1890, the state used federal land-grant money to establish Greensboro's North Carolina Agricultural and Mechanical College for the Colored Race in 1891 (renamed the Agricultural and Technical College of North Carolina [A&T] in 1915).[8] In regional terms, North Carolina stood out for having a black land-grant college and three black state-supported normal schools. In most southern states at the turn of the century, the black land-grant colleges provided the only institutions of public higher education. All the same, North Carolina's black public colleges suffered from paltry appropriations and offered a limited slate of courses. In 1905, state superintendent Charles Coon remarked, "These schools are not colleges." In their early days, the normal schools primarily offered a "high-school course" that would train teachers in domestic science, agriculture, and the academic basics. At A&T, which until 1926 was open only to men, the early curriculum emphasized courses in agriculture, bricklaying, shoemaking, and tanning leather.[9]

Weak from the beginning, state funding for black higher education waned further in the wake of disfranchisement (table 3.1), prompting some blacks to shun cash-starved state schools.[10] By 1920, of the 1,675 students enrolled at the state normal schools, only 496 were taking coursework above the seventh grade, and even they mainly focused on high-school-level work. In the early part of the decade, A&T offered only two years of college courses, and President James Dudley faced perennial budget woes. In 1919 he confided to a colleague who was quitting his teaching job,

Table 3.1. Biennial State Appropriations at All North Carolina Public Colleges and Universities, by Race, 1885–1941

Biennium Beginning	White	Non-White[a]	Total	Non-White Percentage of Total
1885	$48,000	$8,000	$56,000	14.3
1895	93,000	26,000	119,000	21.8[b]
1905	230,000	44,000	274,000	16.1
1915	745,000	67,500	812,500	8.3
1925	3,665,000	473,500	4,138,500	11.4
1933	1,828,685	216,493	2,045,178	10.6
1935	2,844,605	390,187	3,234,792	12.1
1937	3,561,713	538,269	4,099,982	13.1
1939	3,343,226	643,801	3,987,027	16.1
1941	3,819,592	693,822	4,413,414	15.7

Source: N. C. Newbold, "Financial History of State Institutions of Higher Education for Negroes in North Carolina," 27.

Note: Appropriations for instructional and maintenance costs, not permanent improvements.

[a]Includes appropriations to Pembroke State College for Native Americans.

[b]Original source incorrectly reported this percentage as 24.4.

"I think you are fortunate yourself in getting out of the school work, for it is quite discouraging."[11]

Confronting that entrenched system of inequality would require interracial diplomacy and keen political instincts, skills that James Shepard acquired as a young man. Born in Raleigh in 1875, Shepard came into a world where black southerners still talked about slavery not as a distant social memory but as part of their lived experience. When Shepard's parents, Hattie Whitted Shepard and prominent Baptist minister Augustus Shepard, told such stories to their firstborn son, he would have learned that his ancestors served as slaves to Governor Charles Manly. If the bonds of slavery offered Shepard conflicted links to a lineage of state leaders, education offered his generation hope of staking its own claims to power and influence. As a boy, Shepard attended local primary schools and graduated in 1894 with a pharmacy degree from nearby Shaw University. After college, he briefly practiced pharmacy in Durham and Charlotte. A tireless entrepreneur, he was one of the first investors in Durham's North Carolina Mutual Life Insurance Company. Founded in 1898, North Carolina Mutual eventually became the South's largest black-owned business.

James Edward Shepard works at his desk around 1925, when his school was incorporated as the North Carolina College for Negroes. (Courtesy of the Durham County Library Historic Photographic Archives)

Shepard's role in North Carolina Mutual declined after several years, but he remained a lifelong partner with company executives in the general business of racial uplift. In 1895, Shepard extended his ties to a tradition of black entrepreneurship and leadership by marrying Annie Day Robinson, the granddaughter of Thomas Day, who as a free black cabinetmaker had carved out the most prosperous furniture business in antebellum North Carolina.[12] Both family and professional ties linked the young James Shepard to the builders of a black middle class.

Shepard's early career also included participation in the insurgent world of late nineteenth-century black politics. Shepard took a dim view of the Fusionist black Republicans who joined forces with the swelling ranks of the Populist Party in the 1890s, an indication of his conviction that the "better classes" from both races should lead the people, rather than the other way around. By some accounts, his political ambitions smacked of opportunism, as he briefly toyed with the idea of joining the Democratic Party long before most African Americans would have considered doing so. He ultimately rejected that plan and staked his hopes for political power on a biracial coalition of reformers in the Republican Party. Shepard won two political appointments at the turn of the century: a clerkship in the Recorder of Deeds Office in Washington, D.C., in 1898 and Raleigh's deputy collector for the Internal Revenue Service in 1899. When the Democratic Party began its campaign to remove blacks from politics in the late 1890s, Shepard did not submit peacefully but reportedly "stumped the state" in defense of black rights.[13]

For Shepard, well on his way to a political career, the turn-of-the century white supremacy campaigns would have dealt an especially devastating blow. In their immediate aftermath, however, he fared better than most black politicians, retaining his IRS appointment until it expired in 1905. As historian Helen Edmonds has noted, Shepard's diplomacy guaranteed that "he, alone, escaped the Democratic abuse leveled at Negro officeholders." Yet with future political appointments unlikely and with two young daughters (Marjorie Augusta and Annie Day) at home to support, he soon conformed to a world more rigidly determined by race than the one in which he was born. In 1903, Shepard foreshadowed his new path before an African American assembly in Charlotte: "To you who are discouraged, citizenship is not in constitutions but in the mind. That man is free and has liberty who can curb passions and evil desires. My mind, my soul, and my virtue are ever free. Let us teach our children lessons of sobriety and truth, let us live at peace with all mankind, let us stay in the Southland and work out our destiny."[14] Here was a call that was to become the hallmark of his career. Shepard urged blacks to reclaim their citizenship through moral and educational development rather than through public agitation, northern migration, or legal recourse.

In depoliticizing his public pronouncements, Shepard modeled other black Progressive-era reformers who, in the words of Kevin Gaines, carried the hope "that rights and freedom would accrue to those who had achieved the status of respectability." Many southern whites, however, imagined no political rewards for black cultural refinement. With characteristic invective, Governor James Vardaman of Mississippi declared, "I am just as opposed to Booker Washington as a voter, with all his Anglo-Saxon reinforcements, as I am to the cocoanut-headed, chocolate-colored, typical little coon . . . who blacks my shoes every morning. Neither is fit to perform the supreme function of citizenship." In the context of such virulent racism, Shepard's self-transformation might be read as either a hopelessly naive test of white goodwill or as a truckling surrender to the rules of Jim Crow. Indeed, his post-disfranchisement reinvention has led historian Glenda Gilmore to conclude that this erstwhile politician was "retreating behind a landscape of accommodation." Shepard certainly redirected his career into spheres of white-approved activity, but he nonetheless resists easy categorization. Over the next half century, the pace at which he wanted to develop black higher education routinely outstripped the incremental progress that whites imagined for blacks. His purported accommodationism, in other words, competed with his desire to challenge white visions for black progress. Moreover, his relentless negotiations with white officials for power and control suggest that he never fully relinquished the political mantle he had assumed in the 1890s. Like other black leaders of his generation, he at strategic moments discouraged agitation among the black masses, but he never surrendered politics for his own purposes, and he continually fought for the return of black voting rights.[15]

In searching for new arenas for leadership, Shepard first looked to the church. From 1905 to 1909, he served as a field superintendent for the International Sunday School Association, a nondenominational agency. In 1907, that work brought him to Rome, where he was the only African American speaker to address the World Sunday School Convention.[16] As the son of a Baptist minister, Shepard likely felt well suited for church work, but his experiences with white religious leaders firmed his resolve to create his own institution for uplift. As W. E. B. Du Bois later wrote, Shepard "formerly worked as secretary for a great Christian organization, but dissatisfied at a peculiarly un-Christian drawing of the color line, he determined to erect at Durham a kind of training school for ministers and social workers which would be 'different.'" In reaction against a world that increasingly scorned the ambitions of black men, Shepard hoped to create a space that would keep alive the possibilities for black leadership. He returned to Durham, and in 1910, with backing from several local white elites, he founded the National Religious Training School and Chautauqua for the Colored Race. The school initially held institutes primarily for ministers but eventually began training both male and female teachers. It cultivated black leadership within the twin arenas of white-approved uplift, teaching and preaching. Not long after the school opened, both Du Bois and Booker T. Washington toured the campus. Shepard was soon receiving national attention as one of the South's rising black educational leaders.[17]

If any place in the South seemed capable of meeting Shepard's restless ambition, Durham surely was. Durham blacks certainly suffered the same discrimination and indignities that southern blacks everywhere endured, but black leaders across the nation nevertheless hailed the city as the "Capital of the Black Middle Class" for its rare opportunities to learn and earn. By 1922, Durham blacks enjoyed access to Hillside High, one of the state's leading black public secondary schools. Moreover, Durham included its own Wall Street of black-owned businesses, among them the North Carolina Mutual Life Insurance Company and the Mechanics and Farmers Bank. While the city's famed tobacco factories offered blacks only the dirtiest and least remunerative work within tobacco manufacturing, black migrants to the city welcomed those jobs at a time when most southern industries adhered to lily-white hiring policies. As out-migration from the South escalated, Durham's "whirl of Negro business and industry" offered blacks hope that the region still might offer possibilities for upward mobility.[18]

Shepard's early appeals for his school suggested that he would accommodate white desires for a black population of contented workers, not politicized leaders. "Religion, Industrial Training and Literary Training must go hand in hand," touted one pamphlet. Within that curricular trinity, Shepard pledged to privilege moral instruction. As one article put it, Shepard "feels, and rightly so, that the education of the Negro, whether industrial or collegiate, must be based upon a moral and religious foundation, if it is to cause the real betterment of the Negro race." He further assured supporters that he was finding "practical channels" for the emotionalism of his race and would produce "earnest steadfast citizens and reliable workmen." Even the school's name, which employed the preferred white designation for black secondary schools, strategically avoided academic pretension.[19] Shepard's carefully crafted appeals won endorsements from President Theodore Roosevelt and North Carolina governor Robert B. Glenn. When the school ran into such severe debt that it went up for auction, the wife of philanthropist Russell Sage bought it in 1916 and returned it to Shepard. He renamed it the National Training School and formalized its teacher-training component. He continuously courted favor with prominent local white citizens, who donated land, money, and supplies.[20] In his self-styled project for humble uplift, Shepard had found a winning formula for white approval.

If Shepard employed obsequious promotional platitudes, his enterprise nonetheless won admiration from leaders across the storied Du Bois–Washington divide. After visiting the Durham campus in 1912, Du Bois described how the school's "four neat white buildings" emblematized black self-reliance and solidarity. "The whole thing," he wrote, "had been built in four months by colored contractors after plans made by a colored architect, out of lumber from the colored planing mill and ironwork largely from the colored foundry." Students "slept on mattresses from the colored factory and listened to colored instructors from New York, Florida, Georgia, Virginia, Pennsylvania, New Jersey, and North Carolina." Despite Shepard's initial emphasis on blending moral, literary, and industrial instruction, by the mid-1910s, the school's faculty bore all the markings of a liberal arts college. In 1916, the school employed two faculty to train future teachers, two to train future ministers, two to instruct in the domestic sciences, and no fewer than eleven to teach the "literary branches," whose courses enrolled the majority of the students. By the mid-1910s, the school included the elementary grades; an academy (high school), with courses in domestic science, Latin, ancient world history, physiology, algebra, and German; a college of arts and sciences, with courses in trigonometry, English literature, French, Greek, Latin, and logic; and departments of commerce, teacher training, ministerial preparation, music, and domestic science.[21] Shepard's curriculum troubled representatives from the General Education Board (GEB), who repeatedly rejected his requests for financial aid in the 1910s. The GEB found Shepard "untrustworthy" and deemed his proposals not "practicable." While some of the GEB's objections centered on the school's financial woes, Shepard's curricular ambitions also raised eyebrows. Noting in 1921 that the school's curriculum adhered to the "old line classical type, Latin, Mathematics, Greek, and English," one GEB representative frowned on Shepard's "pretentious array of schools and departments."[22]

Unable directly to court the industrial philanthropies yet desperate for funding, Shepard turned in 1920 to the state's Department of Public Instruction and proposed that the state take over his school as a public institution. He no doubt made this move with considerable ambivalence. Financial need aside, he had cultivated a sense of autonomy and institutional ownership that ill suited him for the deference required of black presidents of state schools. Shepard also had to convince state officials that he possessed something they needed. While black liberal arts colleges were not yet on the state's agenda, black normal schools were. Thus, Shepard insisted that with state money he could offer a "well equipped Teacher Training Department," leaving unclear the extent to which he would scale back his liberal arts program.[23]

By the early 1920s, then, Shepard found himself at both the nadir and height of his career. On one hand, his school faced the most severe financial crisis in its history. Shepard's wife, Annie, who oversaw the dining room during the school's early years, later recalled, "There were times when we had no heat, no light, and often not enough food." On the other hand, in the midst of this hardship, Shepard's talent for institution building had won him recognition from national black leaders across the ideological spectrum. Moreover, holding stints in the 1920s as grand master of the Prince Hall Free and Accepted Masons of North Carolina and as president of the North Carolina Teachers Association (NCTA), Shepard wielded considerable local influence. Despite the accommodating language he used when courting whites, blacks had come to view Shepard as someone who refused to act like a second-class citizen. North Carolina Mutual executive Asa T. Spaulding, who attended the National Religious Training School in the late 1910s, recalled that the school "was kept spotlessly clean and well manicured, and all shrubbery well trimmed at all times. Dr. Shepard believed in the best possible in environment, and in the quality and beauty in everything." Shepard's personal appearance, Spaulding recalled, similarly commanded respect. "A tall slender man" whose "figure was so erect that his broad shoulders and large head leaned slightly backward," Shepard "bowed his head to NO man as a superior."[24] In the nadir years of the Jim Crow South, Shepard was cultivating for himself and his students a citizenship of the mind that belied their second-class status.

Courting State Funds, Managing State Control at the North Carolina College for Negroes

Shepard's proposal for state incorporation came at a time when North Carolina was looking for ways to fill its new black public high schools with locally trained teachers. The existing state normal schools did not offer four-year degrees that would certify high school teachers or principals. For a time, Newbold explored how the state might work more closely in this regard with North Carolina's private black colleges.[25] Those schools desperately needed money in the early 1920s, as many of the Reconstruction-era missionary philanthropies had begun to scale back their programs. Black private school faculty, however, increasingly resisted white control. At Shaw University in Raleigh, for example, that sentiment forced the resignation of the school's last white president in 1931.[26] Many blacks read overtures of state cooperation as thinly veiled attempts at white domination. For a time, the state tried to goad Hampton Institute in Virginia into serving as its supplier of high school teachers. State officials saw Hampton as having two advantages: hearty support from the GEB and a reputation for training blacks in white-approved political sensibilities. But GEB officials worried that in creating an expanded "college course" at Hampton, the school might lose its moorings in industrial training. At all costs, one official warned, Hampton should avoid the designation of "college," as it would encourage the teaching of "Latin, Greek, and other subjects not calculated to advance real education." There were great "potentialities for mischief contained in the word, 'college,' when it is applied to Negro schools." These concerns notwithstanding, Newbold saw greater danger in hiring teachers "about whose training we know nothing." He felt sure that "the best Negro leaders in our State agree with the best White leaders that the Hampton type *is* what we want."[27]

North Carolina officials continued to negotiate with Hampton Institute in the 1920s, but they also became ever more convinced that they needed to develop a school where blacks could receive four-year degrees. As one official argued, "It seems to me as a matter of self-preservation, and for the continued peaceful relations between the races, that it is incumbent upon the State to provide a place so these teachers who are to hold the most important positions in colored schools can be trained at home." State officials were not proposing the development of a black counterpart to the University of North Carolina. Instead, they envisioned an institution devoted to the training of high school teachers. "The educational system for the white people was built from the top down," noted the state superintendent of schools. "I am suggesting that we build for the Negroes from the bottom up." To create this system, Newbold saw room for as many as five state-supported black normal schools, one of which would "be raised to a four-year standard" for the training of high school teachers. Newbold hoped to convert Slater Normal School in Winston-Salem into the four-year school, most likely because of his affection for its president, Simon G. Atkins. Newbold once described Atkins as "the type of man who has had no political aspirations and has not ever been allied with any group or organization which had selfish ends." In Newbold's mind, Shepard's spirited independence better suited him for a less critical role, such as heading up one of the normal schools that trained elementary teachers.[28] Ironically, Atkins may have been more successful than Shepard in conveying a deferential spirit to white officials, but his educational aspirations differed little from those of his Durham colleague. As Adam Fairclough has shown, Atkins strategically promoted his school's industrial work while simultaneously building a full college curriculum that surpassed the Hampton-Tuskegee model.[29] Atkins and Shepard's shared convictions of educational equality made them competitors for white backing in a world that placed little value on black collegiate ambition.

Shepard did not share Newbold's modest vision for his school, but with approximately fifty thousand dollars worth of debt, he had little choice but to seek the support of his skeptics. When the fall semester opened in 1923, the state took over the National Training School, and it became the Durham State Normal School, a transition that must have required Shepard to swallow his pride. His new board of trustees—initially composed of four white men, including Newbold—specified that Shepard use the title of "principal," a seeming demotion from his presidency of the National Training School. The board also seemed intent on monitoring Shepard, specifying that he was to "spend his time on the grounds of the School." He was to keep "in satisfactory touch with the public—a dual public," phrasing that suggested that he was required to make his activities known to both whites and blacks. In what was perhaps another attempt to rein Shepard in, the board requested that he resign his position as grand master of the Masons. In response, Shepard reportedly quipped, "I would rather give up the school than to give up the position as Grand Master of the Masons." While the board did not press that matter, Shepard did apparently agree to suspend college-level work that fell outside the state's two-year normal curriculum—no Latin, no advanced science or mathematics, and more home economics.[30] This curriculum resembled that found at the small white normal schools, but it fell short of Shepard's plans for a full-fledged college. The state, for its part, assumed the school's debt as well as its twenty-five acres of land, eight buildings, and equipment—a total property value of $135,000. While the school needed many facility upgrades, it nonetheless provided the state with an attractive addition to its modest constellation of black colleges. A 1921 visitor to the school described it as a charming campus marked by walkways lined with trees and flowers and clean, freshly painted buildings.[31] Shepard's meticulously groomed campus reflected his ambitions for a training ground for first-class citizens.

When the new version of the school opened in the fall of 1923, Shepard found his promise to implement the state's two-year normal school curriculum a "deep source of regret." Defying his agreement with state officials, Shepard allowed four men to continue taking the school's former standard course of study, a decision that "astonished" Newbold, who reminded Shepard that the state had "no intention at the present time of undertaking college work in the Durham State Normal School." Already vexed by Shepard's insistence on Masonic involvement, Newbold chafed against Shepard's unwillingness to comply with state directives. Shepard at first responded deferentially, explaining that he had not forced the four students in question to leave because the faculty seemed perfectly willing to accommodate their former slate of courses. Nonetheless, he promised to eliminate the college course of study. One black educator later noted of this controversy, "Shepard, always the astute politician that he was, diplomatically and graciously condescended to Newbold's requests."[32]

In truth, Shepard's flair for diplomacy masked his impulse for resistance. Only a couple of weeks after promising to comply with the state's request, Shepard unloaded the "fullness of [his] own heart" in a lengthy epistle to Newbold. Shepard noted a flurry of rumors alleging Newbold's anger over his defiance and confessed, "It had been my dream to be president of a college"; before state incorporation of his school, he had "had this dream realized." The National Training School had been a true college, he argued, with graduates including school principals, ministers, and North Carolina Mutual Life Insurance executives. College work, Shepard insisted, "is nothing new to me." Shepard remained somewhat diplomatic, assuring Newbold that he had always tried to cooperate with the state and reminding the state agent that he had initiated the 1919 Raleigh meeting between black educators and state officials. Some northern blacks, he added, had accused him of "represent[ing] the Southern white people." Shepard hoped that his credentials of loyalty would convince the state to develop a four-year college at Durham, especially since his school already possessed the "college spirit." Shepard concluded by noting firmly that regardless of state imperatives, he could not be convinced "to do anything which I believe is not for the best interest of my race." Along those lines, Shepard stated his intention to continue his work as grand master of the Masons, adding, "I think I am entitled to claim some leadership in the State." Newbold responded directly to Shepard's confessional letter with little fanfare, but he privately reasserted his opinion to GEB officials that the state should not establish a four-year black college at Durham. Slater Normal School at Winston-Salem remained his first choice for curricular expansion.[33]

Of all the points of disagreement between Newbold and Shepard, the recurring question of Shepard's Masonic work is most puzzling. Newbold later claimed that his objection concerned a simple conflict of interest. Shepard received a salary for his Masonic work and, according to Newbold, spent considerable time meeting his Masonic responsibilities. Newbold very reasonably insisted that he would raise the same objections to a white college president with conflicting outside activities. The politics of Jim Crow, however, distorted such comparisons. While white men certainly valued their lodges, Masonic work afforded black men a sphere of quasi-political activity at a time when they lacked access to formal politics. Within fraternal orders, black men could escape expectations of deference to white rule and act as free voting members of a democratic body. Membership in fraternal orders soared at the turn of the century, just as black men experienced political exclusion. Moreover, the Masons had groomed for leadership a proud lineage of black educators. The founder of North Carolina's Grand Lodge of Prince Hall Masons was James Walker

Hood, the Reconstruction-era assistant state superintendent of schools. Shepard's refusal, then, to accommodate Newbold's wishes spoke to the racially ordered opportunities for male leadership in the South. Newbold's unease also may have reflected his awareness of a shift in the nature of black Masonic activity. While black Masons in the wake of disfranchisement eschewed political involvement and instead focused on humanitarian work and moral uplift, by the 1920s, many lodges advocated black political activity. By the postwar period, many would support the work of the NAACP.[34]

Temporarily setting aside his personal grudges, Newbold advocated increased appropriations at all of the state black normal schools and "begged" five thousand dollars from the GEB for the physical plant at the Durham campus. Such advocacy did not always endear him to other white officials. At a 1924 state board of education meeting, the governor questioned Newbold's appeal for the black schools, leaving him feeling "hurt, humiliated, [and] embarrassed." African Americans understood the challenges that Newbold faced in advocating on behalf of their schools, but this recognition did not diminish their expectations. At the NCTA's 1924 annual meeting, members called for "the establishment of an A Grade College for the training of Negro youth for larger usefulness and more complete living." Newbold agreed with the need for a "Four-Year Standard Liberal Arts College" and believed that Shepard's school eventually would serve that purpose, but he predicted that it might take "two to four years" before the school's physical plant could house a true college.[35]

Newbold's prediction came true more quickly than he anticipated. After consulting with representatives from the GEB, Newbold and state superintendent of public instruction Arch T. Allen planned to submit two bills to the January 1925 legislature that would "raise the standards" of both Atkins's Slater Normal School and Shepard's school to four-year teacher colleges. The former would train elementary school teachers; the latter would train high school educators and offer some liberal arts courses, but not a full-fledged liberal arts curriculum. Before Newbold and Allen could submit their bills, Shepard hired a Durham lawyer to author competing legislation that would establish his school as both an institution for training high school teachers and a liberal arts college. Shepard's bill also omitted a stipulation that Newbold and Allen had included requiring Shepard to raise at least $150,000 "from outside sources."[36]

Newbold had underestimated Shepard's ability to cultivate white allies for his plan. In October 1924, Durham's white newspaper endorsed the creation of a black liberal arts college in the city, arguing that if blacks had to go outside the state, they would "naturally take on habits and methods that are suitable to the surroundings of their school and sometimes not suitable to North Carolina." When Shepard employed his considerable oratorical talents before a legislative committee, the political pendulum swayed even further his way.[37] Representatives' emotional appeals for this bill drew on familiar notions of white paternalism and black loyalty. Several members of the legislature shared sentimental recollections of loyal black mammies who had nurtured them as children. The bill's legislative sponsor fondly recalled black slaves who "stayed at home and protected the hearthstones of our fathers, while they were away at the front fighting." Whites, he added, could not "afford to break faith" with the state's black population and invite their disloyalty. The bill passed the House with only one dissenting vote, and on February 20, 1925, after Senate approval of the measure, the Durham State Normal School became the North Carolina College for Negroes. The new school was to train high school teachers and principals and to satisfy the "growing desire among negroes for a liberal college education." As was customary, the bill authorized the governor and state superintendent to appoint the school's president and twelve-member board of trustees, and also in keeping with custom, the school's early board was composed of white men. The rewards of black loyalty would lie safely within white hands.[38]

The white press cast the legislature's action as evidence of prudent white management of race relations. The *Charlotte Observer*, for example, asserted that blacks deserved one such college since "they have made intelligent and appreciative use of the privileges so provided." Having carefully erased Shepard's role in pushing for the school, the press suggested that whites were rewarding blacks for good behavior by bestowing on them a token institution for cultural advancement. Newbold—one of the few whites who understood that NCC had not emerged from a carefully scripted act of white-bestowed patronage—admitted surprise at Shepard's "good scheming." Even though his ultimate vision for the school may not have differed radically from Shepard's, Newbold clearly was annoyed with Shepard's insistence on control. In Newbold's eyes, Shepard had erred not so much by seeking a liberal arts college but by violating the rules of black deference. Still committed to rewarding his favored institution at Winston-Salem, Newbold and Allen pushed through another bill turning Slater Normal School into the Winston-Salem Teachers College, a four-year school for training elementary teachers and principals. Unlike the Durham school, the one at Winston-Salem would not offer a full liberal arts curriculum but instead would certify elementary educators at the highest level. This move reflected Newbold's desire to expand the Winston-Salem school as well as his interest in balancing Shepard's power with men Newbold perceived as more cooperative.[39]

Anyone who had ever closely observed Shepard at work should not have been surprised by his skillful maneuvering. The same man whom Newbold had found so uncooperative could court white approval with obsequious flair when doing so suited his strategic objectives. For example, he ingratiated himself with state legislators by sending them Christmas gifts each year. At the same time, however, he only selectively complied with the etiquette of Jim Crow. When he visited the State Capitol in Raleigh on his many lobbying ventures, he refused to ride the freight elevator reserved for blacks. Likewise, when white men visited his office, he politely denied them the white privilege of discourtesy. Shepard told one such visitor who failed to remove his hat, "Well, now, let's go outdoors and talk, because I don't want to embarrass you and ask you to take your hat off, and I think you'll be more comfortable on the outside."[40]

Shepard's battle for institutional autonomy was only beginning. Over the next two years, he and Newbold wrangled over issues that on the surface seemed trivial yet bore all the markings of a racially infused battle for control. In March 1925, an anonymous letter to the Greensboro newspaper alleged that Newbold's bill to expand the normal school at Winston-Salem reflected the insecurities of a man who "feels that some power has slipped from his grasp." Newbold never accused Shepard of writing this letter, and Shepard flatly denied any role in it, but the incident increased suspicion between the two men. An unsigned report in Newbold's papers documented a laundry list of perceived problems with Shepard's leadership: the school's history of debt, his Masonic activity, his failure to seek the board's permission before advertising his school in *The Crisis*, and his hiring of a black attorney to work as a "lobbyist." In short, the report painted a picture of an untrustworthy leader who violated the accepted bonds of loyalty between white patrons and black clients.[41] When further questions about Shepard's leadership and Masonic involvement surfaced, the school's board of trustees voted to keep him as head only on the condition "that he give up the things which he has been doing heretofore outside the educational field and devote his whole time to the college." One month later, a GEB official noted his belief that "there is a widespread feeling among those interested in North Carolina Negro education that Mr. Shepard is not altogether reliable, or the man who can really make this a genuine state college for Negroes."[42]

Despite the infighting, NCC opened its doors for classes on September 17, 1925. Filled to capacity, the school had to turn students away. Shepard then turned his attention to pressing matters of resources, as his school did not yet meet the state's requirements for an A-grade four-year college.[43] The following year, the GEB judged Shepard's school a "paper institution" that lacked the necessary faculty, equipment, and facilities for its stated course of study. When the U.S. Bureau of Education inspected the school, it recommended that the college's income "must be substantially increased." The library suffered from a "great lack of suitable books for students of college grade," and the science equipment was "lacking in many details."[44] Having once stood at the mercy of philanthropists, Shepard now stood at the mercy of the state legislature.

In 1926, the Durham Negro Business League published a pamphlet that sought to shore up Shepard's bargaining power. It included a letter from Shepard that took issue with Governor Angus W. McLean's proposed budget allocation of $325,000 for all of the state's black colleges, a small fraction of the total appropriations to white schools. Shepard asserted that his school alone needed $500,000 for new buildings. The pamphlet also included endorsements from a sampling of the state's white college presidents and school superintendents. Shepard's ability to win those endorsements may have rested in part with residual white fears of northern-trained black teachers. Shepard strategically noted that only 85 of the state's 385 black high school teachers had received their training in the state. The state responded to Shepard's appeal with conditional aid. In 1927, the legislature pledged $200,000 to NCC, contingent on the school raising $100,000 in matching funds. Local tobacco and textile magnate Benjamin N. Duke gave the school $42,000, and Shepard raised an additional $8,000. Having raised half of its required matching funds, NCC could expect half of the state's appropriation.[45] To receive the remaining half, Shepard approached the GEB with appeals that had the solid backing of McLean and several members of the school's board of trustees. Newbold and Superintendent Allen also added their reluctant endorsements. Sensing Newbold and Allen's lukewarm support, the GEB delayed action. One GEB associate judged NCC to be a "well managed school" that deserved support, but others expressed doubts regarding whether "all of the educational forces in North Carolina had complete confidence in the administration of the college at Durham." In the fall of 1927, Newbold withdrew his support from NCC's grant appeals, restating his familiar objections to Shepard's Masonic work. Undeterred, Shepard rallied his allies, including the state attorney general.[46] Allen urged Shepard to resign from his Masonic post, a move that Allen believed would guarantee Newbold's support. Shepard stood firm. As this feud persisted, state reports continued to document NCC's desperate lack of resources—particularly its meager library, inadequate labs, and overtaxed faculty—and recommended that the school eliminate its premedical track, which required expensive upper-level science courses, and focus on its original mission of training high school teachers. "The institution will serve itself best by doing a few things well," one report concluded.[47]

Unwilling to scale back ambitions for his school, Shepard ultimately ended his long standoff with Newbold in the spring of 1928 and resigned as grand master of the Masons. Having won this concession from his erstwhile foe, Newbold immediately threw his support behind Shepard's GEB application, joining with Allen to request that the school receive a $100,000 grant. Newbold's endorsement cleared the way for GEB approval. Fund official James Dillard noted, "We all know, to speak out plainly, that Mr. Newbold's opposition to the president of the institution was the real cause for turning down one of the most encouraging and notable propositions ever put before the General Education Board in the cause of Negro education." Jackson Davis of the GEB found the NCC ordeal "one of the most perplexing situations" he had ever encountered. He found it difficult to believe that a southern state would support a black liberal arts college, in addition to four other black colleges and normal schools. Newbold's intransigence with regard to Shepard did not square with the state's commitment to an expanding constellation of black colleges. This paradoxical situation, in fact, pointed to the highly personal nature of southern race relations. Even though Newbold and other moderate white southerners had accepted the need for black higher education, he had developed a familiarity with Shepard that left him feeling personally betrayed by Shepard's recusancy. Only after Shepard deferred could Newbold salvage those fragile ties of paternalism that bound together blacks and whites. As NCC prepared to graduate its first class in the spring of 1929, the GEB finally granted the school $45,000.[48]

The GEB's gift was still not quite enough to earn the long-promised $100,000 from the state, but the 1929 legislature granted the school $145,000 anyway. When NCC's 1929 budget came before the legislature, one lawmaker objected to the idea of a "Negro University," but the majority dismissed his objections and passed the budget. That same winter, when a legislative proposal arose that would have consolidated NCC with A&T as a cost-saving measure, a swift public outcry came to the school's rescue. With the school's future seemingly secured, Durham's black newspaper declared, "As a result of the twenty-year struggle there has come to

Durham the distinction of being the home of the only state-owned Negro college of liberal arts."[49]

No one, of course, could point with more pride to that distinction than Shepard, but the battle to establish the school had come at costs to his pride and independence. Newbold told a colleague shortly after Shepard resigned his Masonic office, "Certain Negro leaders have used their lodges of one kind and another to push themselves forward. That in turn has given them a chance to get before certain white political leaders. . . . I think we have finally disposed of that, which means a more wholesome leadership." Shepard reassumed his position as grand master in 1936 and retained the office until his death in 1947.[50] By the mid-1930s, however, Shepard's Masonic involvement was the least of Newbold's concerns.

"The High Cost of It All": Shepard's University Ambitions

On 23 October 1929, at a conference on "Negro Education in North Carolina," Newbold outlined the unique roles that each of the state's black colleges was filling. Shepard was no doubt pleased when Newbold affirmed that North Carolina College for Negroes was "working towards the goals set up at" the University of North Carolina at Chapel Hill. The prospects for reaching those goals, however, dimmed the following day, when the stock market suffered the first in a series of dramatic crashes that marked the beginning of the Great Depression. In addition to the usual patterns of racial discrimination in educational funding, Shepard now faced what would turn into a decade of state retrenchment that made his dream of a black public university all the more remote. By 1931, he grimly reported, "We have cut all expenses to the bone. I have put my own personal resources into the school to keep it going."[51]

In terms of total appropriations to higher education during the early depression years, North Carolina compared favorably to many other southern states. Most of those states, however, were supporting only one public institution of black higher education, whereas North Carolina was supporting five. The state's black college presidents, then, had to be exceptionally resourceful to survive. John Henry Bias of the Elizabeth City State Normal School reported in the mid-1930s that to compensate for his school's "reduced revenue," administrators had "wisely used the school's eighteen acres of land" to grow thousands of quarts of vegetables and raise enough hogs for twenty-six hundred pounds of pork.[52]

In this context of stretched budgets and weak white commitment to black higher education, state legislators likely would have indefinitely deferred the expansion of Shepard's school if not for the NAACP's regional campaign to integrate graduate and professional education. The NAACP's first foray along these lines unfolded in North Carolina in 1933. At this time, the South had virtually no graduate or professional programs available to blacks.[53] That gross inequality posed a problem for Thomas Raymond Hocutt, a graduate of Durham's Hillside High and an NCC student. Hocutt hoped to become a pharmacist—the same career that Shepard had pursued. By Hocutt's day, however, Shepard's alma mater, Shaw University, had closed its pharmacy school as well as its medical and law schools as a consequence of declining philanthropic funds. Thus, aspiring black pharmacists had to go outside North Carolina for training, while white students could attend UNC's undergraduate pharmacy school. Hocutt's dilemma presented an opportunity for Durham attorneys Conrad Pearson and Cecil McCoy, who had been searching for someone willing to test the state's segregation laws. Pearson, a nephew of Hillside High principal William Gaston Pearson, had deep links to an older generation of local black institution builders. Those roots in the black establishment might have disinclined him to disrupt the status quo, but as a law student at Howard University, Pearson had come under the tutelage of pioneering civil rights attorney Charles Hamilton Houston, one of the leading architects of the NAACP's legal fight against segregated education. Pearson and McCoy consulted with NAACP executive secretary Walter White about the possibilities for testing North Carolina's Jim Crow laws and had convinced the twenty-four-year old Hocutt to apply to UNC. Here was a clear-cut case of the state not living up to its constitutional guarantees of separate but equal educational opportunities.[54]

Shepard might have been expected to give at least tacit support to this effort. He was listed as a member of the Durham NAACP in 1927 and 1931, had advertised his school in *The Crisis* in the 1920s, and had invited Du Bois to speak on more than occasion. Shepard nonetheless offered other signs of an imminent break with the NAACP. In 1930, he spoke out against the organization's efforts to defeat Herbert Hoover's Supreme Court nomination of John J. Parker, a Republican judge from North Carolina who sat on the Fourth Circuit Court of Appeals. The NAACP's objections stemmed from comments Parker made during a 1920 gubernatorial race in which he endorsed the removal of blacks from politics. The NAACP won its battle but did so with no help from Shepard, who insisted that Parker had been unfairly maligned.[55]

If the Parker case foreshadowed Shepard's antagonistic relationship with NAACP organizers, the Hocutt case left little doubt that the association would not be able to count on Shepard for backing. In fact, Shepard actively impeded the Hocutt effort by leaking details of the case to the press and state officials and by assuring the latter that he was working to "hold this matter in check." Joining Shepard in his public opposition to the case was Durham's most prominent black businessman, North Carolina Mutual president Charles Clinton Spaulding. Hocutt and his backers persisted, visiting UNC on 13 March 1933 in an attempt to register. When the registrar rejected his application, Hocutt's lawyers filed a writ of mandamus with the Durham County Superior Court.[56]

The dogged persistence by Hocutt's legal team flabbergasted white officials. Newbold simply could not understand why the "responsible Negro leadership" would want to embarrass UNC, an institution that had "probably done more to promote the interests and well-being of the Negro race than any institution in the South—perhaps in the entire country." His panic abated only slightly when Shepard privately assured him that he and at least fifty other black leaders opposed the suit. For Newbold, a broader question loomed: "Whether our upstanding Negro leaders in North Carolina are going to work out their salvation here on North Carolina soil with the aid and cooperation of our thousands of right-minded white people . . . or will they depend in the future upon the courts and a few irresponsible individuals and outside organizations, which apparently care nothing for peace and harmony in North Carolina?"[57]

Hocutt's court hearing did little to reassure Newbold. More than five hundred African Americans gathered at the courthouse on opening day. Black bystanders cheered, "Don't give in! Don't give in!" NAACP attorney William Hastie telegraphed Walter White, "Capacity crowd. . . . Town agog." Hastie drew much of the public's attention, displaying an eloquence and professionalism that stood in marked contrast to the state's lead attorney, Dennis G. Brummitt, who referred to Hocutt as "this Nigra" and accused him of "want[ing] to associate with white people." Not only did Hastie calmly win an objection to these reactionary charges, but Brummitt's exaggerated appeals to white racism provoked laughter from some black attendants. Hastie had managed a remarkable feat: a public vindication of black dignity in a southern courtroom. Historian Jerry Gershenhorn has judged the Hocutt trial a "transcendent moment" for young blacks in Durham.[58]

Hastie's mesmerizing performance, however, was not enough to win the case. The judge ruled that while the court could have forced UNC to disregard race-based admission criteria, it did not have authority to force UNC to admit particular students, as the writ of mandamus had requested. The judge added that Hocutt's failure to provide a college transcript would have doomed the case regardless. Hocutt had not sent his college grades because Shepard had refused to release them. White later lamented that Shepard's intransigence represented "the moral effect on some Negro educators of segregation." The NAACP initially planned to appeal the ruling but ultimately decided that Hocutt's average academic record, along with the opposition of Shepard and other older black leaders in Durham, would present liabilities in future court cases. Hocutt's unexceptional grades, however, stood in contrast to his peerless courage. After his lawyers searched in vain for another local student to serve in a second test of UNC, they were forced to admit, "There aren't many Hocutts."[59]

At the very least, the Hocutt case temporarily allowed both blacks and whites to imagine an eroded color line, a vision that inspired hope in many blacks and even quiet acceptance among some whites. A poll in UNC's student newspaper indicated considerable approval of Hocutt's efforts, prompting the NAACP's White to conclude, "Although we lost the case legally, we won it in extraordinary fashion in the court of public opinion." Moreover, Hocutt paved the way for the NAACP's future legal challenges of Jim Crow. As Journal of Negro Education editor Charles Thompson wrote, the case stood as powerful evidence that "Negroes have everything to gain and very little if anything to lose by resorting to the courts."[60]

As the NAACP continued its fight to integrate southern universities, Shepard and some of the state's other leading black educators seized on southern state officials' anxiety to push for the establishment of black graduate programs. In 1934, Shepard asked UNC president Frank Porter Graham whether the time was "opportune" for a law and pharmacy school at his college. Two years later, NCTA president Charlotte Hawkins Brown similarly proposed the extension of Shepard's college into "a full graduate school."[61]

In 1936, as black school leaders vied for institutional expansion, the Maryland Court of Appeals offered another model for black graduate education when it ruled that the University of Maryland had to admit Donald Murray to its law school. Because that decision came from a state rather than federal court, it failed to spark much notice in North Carolina. In fact, the failure of the Hocutt case had invited complacency on the part of state officials. While they had begun to discuss the possibilities for black graduate and professional education in the mid-1930s, their appropriations to black higher education remained inadequate to sustain first-rate undergraduate colleges, much less universities. The black proportion of higher education operating appropriations still remained below pre-disfranchisement levels (table 3.1). Meager operating funds meant that black college faculty shouldered a much heavier teacher load than their white counterparts. In 1937–38, the average enrollment per instructor at the state's white colleges and universities was 14.1, while for black schools, it was 27.[62]

In 1936, NCC's poor library facilities, low level of faculty training, and low faculty salaries caused the Southern Association of Colleges and Secondary Schools to deny the college an A rating. As late as 1938, only one faculty member at Shepard's school held a doctoral degree. A&T, which had seven faculty members with doctorates in 1938, had won an A rating in 1936, but overall conditions at the school remained unsatisfactory.[63] A&T students struck in 1936 to demand better food and medical care, and the struggle to maintain even basic services at the black colleges led some faculty to conclude that any rush to establish graduate education was premature. In 1938, John W. Mitchell, an agricultural extension agent based at A&T, found "the prevailing opinion to be a unanimous expression of hope that there will be no make-shift set up of providing graduate and professional training for the Negro youth of North Carolina." Most of his colleagues believed that "what we need first in the State were some good Negro colleges adequately provided for."[64]

The mid-1930s witnessed a significant amount of construction at the black public colleges, but the state was greatly aided in these efforts by grants from the federal government's New Deal agencies. President Franklin Roosevelt offered little direct support to the emerging assault against Jim Crow, but his administration took an interest in supporting black institutions. Furthermore, First Lady Eleanor Roosevelt routinely extended personal encouragement to southern blacks, as evidenced by her inclusion of NCC in her June 1934 tour of Durham and Raleigh. Shepard embraced the new spirit of inclusion in Washington and traveled there along with C. C. Spaulding to lobby U.S. senator Josiah Bailey of North Carolina and Secretary of the Interior Harold Ickes on behalf of the state's black schools. Between 1935 and 1939, New Deal agency grants helped build a gymnasium, an auditorium, a library, dormitories, and a science building at NCC as well as similar facilities at North Carolina's other black colleges.[65]

As a result of campus upgrades and rising levels of faculty training, NCC won an A rating from the Southern Association in April 1938, but the state still lacked any publicly supported graduate and professional programs for blacks.[66] That glaring inequality returned to the headlines later that year when another Hillside High graduate organized a second test of segregation at UNC. After finishing high school in 1926, Pauli Murray was determined to leave the Jim Crow South. She later recalled thinking, "No more segregation for me. I was fifteen, but that I knew." She left North Carolina to attend Hunter College in New York City and stayed there after graduation, working a series of jobs. By the mid-1930s, feeling family pressure to return home and help care for her aging aunt, she decided to return to North Carolina, but only on her own terms. Having read about Hocutt, who had graduated from Hillside one year after her, and his attempt to gain admission to UNC, she contemplated a similar battle. In November 1938, knowing that her academic record, unlike Hocutt's, would not prove to be a stumbling block, Murray applied to UNC's esteemed sociology department. She hoped to study under Howard Odum and Guy Benton Johnson, two leading experts in the field of southern race relations. In response to Murray's application, dean W. W. Pierson replied, "Under the laws of North Carolina, and under the resolutions of the Board of Trustees of the University of North Carolina, members of your race are not admitted to the University." He added that he expected the legislature to appropriate funds for separate black graduate facilities in early 1939, thereby suggesting that Murray need not anticipate segregation's imminent demise.[67]

Despite its confident tone, Pierson's response to Murray was likely penned with a heightened sense of vulnerability. Two days earlier, the U.S. Supreme Court had ruled in favor of Lloyd Gaines, a graduate of Missouri's Lincoln University who had been denied admission to the University of Missouri's law school on the basis of his race. Chief Justice Charles Evans Hughes ruled that Missouri had a legal obligation to offer Gaines equal educational facilities within the state. In response, Missouri officials scrambled to establish a segregated law school at Lincoln University. The NAACP planned to challenge Lincoln's second-class law school, but the case fizzled when Gaines disappeared. The case nonetheless sent a wake-up call across the South.[68]

With the highest court in the land on her side, Murray pushed further. She wrote to UNC's president and entreated, "How much longer, Dr. Graham, is the South going to withhold elementary human rights from its black citizens?" She added that Graham could score "a victory for liberal thought in the South" if he were to admit her rather than "forcing [her] to carry the issue to the courts." Pierson replied in Graham's absence and reiterated that the state legislature would soon act on the question of black graduate education. As a matter of formality, however, he suggested that Murray go ahead and send her transcript and proof of citizenship to his office. With characteristic flair, Murray promptly replied, "With regard to citizenship, I am an American Citizen (ahem!)." She provided Pierson with the information he requested and stated again that she was reluctant—but willing—to wage a legal battle. Secure in her sense of citizenship, Murray stood firm. In December she wrote to President Roosevelt, who had recently visited UNC and hailed the school for its liberalism. She asked him as one of his "fellow-citizens" to explain what his "recent speech mean[t] for Negro Americans." Did it mean that the university was "ready to open its doors to Negro students seeking enlightenment on the social and economic problems which the South faces?" Murray never received a personal letter from the president, although Eleanor Roosevelt wrote to express sympathy with Murray's frustrations and urge patience.[69]

The story broke in the southern press on 5 January. The same day, Governor Clyde R. Hoey addressed the General Assembly and suggested that the state was committed to expanding black educational opportunities, but only within a segregated context. "North Carolina does not believe in social equality between the races," he declared, "and will not tolerate mixed schools for the races, but we do believe in equality of opportunity in their respective fields of service." White opinion in Chapel Hill divided on Murray's action. Murray received some expressions of support from the university's faculty and graduate students. However, despite his leadership in the interracial movement of the 1920s, Odum withheld support. Moreover, Graham, whose liberalism on the race issue surpassed Odum's, deferred to the state legislature. He explained to Murray his fear that immediate integration would prompt a swift white backlash. "We must not be unwise in the present critical situation and cause a throwback to a darker time with losses all along the line," he insisted. Graham had some reason to anticipate such conflict, as a group of UNC students had threatened violent protests if the school integrated. Nonetheless, the university's caution unquestionably tarnished Chapel Hill's fabled liberalism.[70]

While white inaction angered Murray, she was "even more disheartened" by critics within her own race. In particular, she had hoped to win at least a private endorsement from Shepard despite his hopes for graduate courses at his institution. Shortly after applying to UNC, Murray reminded Shepard that he had long held a "traditional place of respect" within her family, who knew him personally. She hastened to add that she was "not opposed to the establishment of Negro universities per se." Yet, she wondered, "Do you not think it is high time that we as Negroes and citizens of North Carolina begin to demand that our students be admitted to graduate work at Duke University and at the University of North Carolina?" Shepard responded with stony silence. Three weeks later, Murray wrote again, asking, "Am I to take it from your silence that my letter was not important enough to answer?" After Murray's fight broke in the press, Shepard publicly stated that blacks fared better at black schools. While Murray knew that many other local blacks supported her cause, Shepard's public disavowal dealt a particularly harsh blow. She confided to another black student contemplating a court challenge of segregation at UNC that his struggle would be "twofold: against those whites who would deny us our rights, and against the 'handkerchief heads' within our group."[71]

Murray lost her fight against both opponents. In the wake of *Gaines*, the 1939 legislature read the handwriting on the wall and took measures to establish graduate programs in law, library science, and the liberal arts at NCC and in agricultural and technical fields at A&T. It also voted to establish a system of out-of-state aid, known as the Murphy Bill, whereby black students who wished to obtain graduate degrees offered at UNC but not at NCC or A&T could apply for state scholarships to pursue those programs elsewhere. In the fall of 1939, a small number of students began master's programs at NCC. The following fall, seven students began training for law degrees there. By 1941, NCC and A&T had each granted at least one master's degree. At the same time, Shepard was making his university ambitions known to legislators, "telling his white friends that nothing short of a state university for his race can meet the issue." He acknowledged that such a school carried "a high cost" but was quick to remind them of the "higher cost of denying it, or delaying it."[72]

Murray still held out hope of taking the university to court, but she lacked both the necessary legal fees and NAACP support. The organization told her that their concerns were of a technical nature: Murray was living in New York and would thus have difficulty proving North Carolina residency. At least privately, however, NAACP executives also worried about what they judged to be Murray's undiplomatic aggressiveness in correspondence with UNC officials, as well as the potentially more explosive questions of her past communist associations and her experimentation with a lesbian and transgendered lifestyle.[73]

Shepard, Murray later recalled, gloated in his victory. "He told me smugly," she wrote, "that the situation was settled as far as North Carolina was concerned and that while he did not think a court case would do any harm, he believed it would be useless." In one sense, Shepard had profited from Murray's misfortune. As Durham newspaper editor and Murray ally Louis Austin quipped, "Every time Pauli Murray writes a letter to the University of North Carolina they get a new building at the Negro college in Durham." Indeed, state and federal funds for permanent improve-

Table 3.2. Per Capita State Appropriations for Public Colleges and Universities in North Carolina, by Race, 1937–1938 and 1939–1940

Institutions	1937–38	1939–40
WHITE		
University of North Carolina	$197.00	$168.00
State College of Agriculture and Engineering	153.00	124.00
North Carolina College for Women	166.00	128.00
East Carolina Teachers College	100.00	95.00
Western Carolina Teachers College	139.00	141.00
Appalachian State Teachers College	85.00	129.00
Average white per capita appropriation	140.00	130.83
BLACK		
North Carolina College for Negroes	$92.00	$191.00
N.C. Agricultural and Technical College	69.00	69.00
Winston-Salem State Teachers College	52.00	68.00
Fayetteville State Teachers College	49.00	30.00
Elizabeth City State Teachers College	53.00	54.00
Average black per capita appropriation	63.00	82.00

Source: Nelson H. Harris, "The Present Status of Higher Education among Negroes in North Carolina," 42–44.

Note: Appropriations for instructional and maintenance costs, not permanent improvements.

ments had yielded several new buildings at the school in the late 1930s. Moreover, appropriations to Shepard's school for operating expenses temporarily spiked, a trend not seen at the other black public colleges (table 3.2). One of the ironies of Murray's rejection by UNC was that her family already had well-established connections to the school. Murray was a light-skinned woman of mixed-race heritage, and her great-great-grandfather had sat on the school's board of trustees. His descendants included prominent graduates of and donors to UNC. In refusing to admit Murray, then, UNC had in fact rejected one of its own. Four decades after denying Murray admission, UNC offered her an honorary degree. At the time, however, Murray felt that the school had still not done enough to erase all vestiges of segregation in its sixteen-campus system. In a final act of resistance, Murray politely declined.[74]

No one in 1939 could have predicted Murray's ultimate vindication, as Shepard seemed to have triumphed. Early signs indicated, however, that Shepard's victory was by no means complete. Murray continued to do some "sleuthing" in North Carolina in 1940 and determined that the faculty at Shepard's school at least privately did not endorse his plans to establish separate graduate facilities. They complained that the school's library, for example, could not sustain serious graduate study. "Some members of the faculty," Murray confided to NAACP special counsel Thurgood Marshall, "realize the graduate school is only a farce." For his part, Shepard privately acknowledged that NCC's graduate program was inadequate. "I am constantly being made ashamed that we are trying to run a graduate school on the small amount of money which has been appropriated," he once lamented. Nevertheless, he remained committed to the expansion of black graduate offerings and in 1941 approached GEB officials about the possibility of establishing a medical school at NCC. His "great fear" was that the state would establish a black medical school that would be a "second rate affair." The prospect of such mediocrity conflicted with his dream of true parallelism. As he put it, "I don't want anybody in passing to be able to tell this school from a white school."[75]

Shepard was not alone among blacks in the late 1930s and early 1940s in supporting the equalization of higher education but having reservations about white commitment to true parity. At the time of North Carolina's decision to provide graduate work at NCC and A&T, even Durham's *Carolina Times*, a strong supporter of integrating UNC, did not completely condemn the idea of expanding offerings at black schools. The paper asked, "Shall we rejoice or grieve?" If the state had "at last realized the injustice which its Negro citizens have suffered under the unequal educational system . . . then it is time to rejoice." But if the state planned to offer "makeshift graduate courses," then grief was in order. Similar attitudes prevailed across the region. As late as 1947, a poll found that black Texans supported by an eight to five margin the establishment of a black university over the desegregation of the University of Texas.[76]

Only a fine line existed, of course, between supporting higher education equalization for the sake of building black institutions and doing so out of the paternalistic belief that blacks were not ready for integration. In one sense, Shepard's famed authoritarian style of management lent credence to the latter notion. Expecting both students and faculty to be models of decorum at all times both on and off campus, he upheld strict dress codes and kept close watch over everyone's comings and goings. Campus rules forbid students from swearing, "dancing between the sexes," drinking, playing "games of chance," leaving campus without permission, and—ironically, at a school built in part with tobacco money—using "tobacco in any form." "Nothing pleased him better [than] to see a punctual, business-like student," the campus newspaper eulogized after his death. By extension, nothing distressed him more than a student or faculty member who refused to show deference to the rules. When novelist Zora Neale Hurston arrived at NCC in 1939 to establish its drama department, she soon learned that the college offered little room for free spirits. Her unconventional manner of dress, as well as her decision to live alone in a remote cabin some distance from the watchful eye of the president, chafed against Shepard's need for order and propriety. Such rules could be found at many black—and white—colleges at that time, but Shepard's discipline reflected an evolutionary view of racial uplift that informed his opposition to early integration activism.[77] In explaining the famously strict discipline at his school, Shepard once noted, "A race just fifty years removed from slavery needs perhaps an iron hand for its development to whip it into line and to mold it into ideals until the race has really found itself." As one black educator put it after his death, Shepard felt the need to be a "dictator" and uphold "Victorian" mores to prepare a race that he regarded as "not quite ready for complete equality." To be sure, Shepard's paternalism had a benevolent side that manifested itself in acts of legendary kindness. He offered countless cash-strapped students personal loans and campus jobs. Yet in extending his paternalistic reach into behind-the-scenes management of the Hocutt and Murray cases, Shepard presumed to speak for the race in directing the pace of change.[78]

By World War II, Shepard's pace fell behind that of a younger generation of African Americans who saw such gradualism as an outmoded strategy for citizenship. At a time when civil rights leaders were urging a home front fight for democracy, Shepard saw the war as "no more a time for personal quarrels than it is for group agitation."[79] In a widely broadcast 1944 NBC radio debate against poet Langston Hughes, Shepard asserted that blacks did not desire "unqualified freedom." A year later in Boston, Shepard further suggested that many blacks had not proven themselves ready for total equality with whites. Only after more education and social development, he predicted, would whites be ready to accept black men as equals. Such comments prompted the Harlem-based newspaper *The People's Voice*, edited by Congressman Adam Clayton Powell Jr., to give Shepard a dubious place of honor in its "We Ain't Ready Dept" and to bestow on him the unflattering title of "Minister of Apology in the Department of Propaganda for the Southern States and Their Sympathizers Who Believe in Racial Discrimination Predicated on the Legal and Systematic Repression of Negroes."[80]

Shepard may have privately sympathized with the wartime spirit of defiance as long as it did not threaten his institutional ambitions. He sent contributions to the national office of the NAACP in the 1940s, praised White's "fine work," and permitted chapters of the NAACP Youth Council at his school.[81] But Shepard was willing to concede to the changing times only so far. In 1947, when several NCC law students formed a committee to investigate their institution's shortcomings, they crossed the line into Shepard's protected turf. Rumors of a pending integration suit circulated, leading Shepard to seize control and disparage their concerns. "The students who are making the most progress in the school are not inclined to grumble or complain," he explained to Newbold, adding that there were "no grounds for a law suit at present."[82]

In the last years of his life, Shepard intensified his trademark lobbying efforts, sending Governor Gregg Cherry dozens of gifts, including neckties, boxes of fruit, "very fine cigars," a ham, and a silver tray. Interspersed with the arrival of these presents were appeals for NCC. At one point after presenting his proposed budget for the year, Shepard entreated, "There is not one item in that budget that ought to be reduced. It represents the minimum amount out of which a great college can emerge, to support in the future perhaps a University for the Negroes of North Carolina." In further keeping with Shepard's dream of having his college indistinguishable from white institutions, he proposed in 1946 that "for Negroes" be dropped from the school's name, leaving it just North Carolina College, a request that the legislature honored shortly before his death. Shepard's impassioned appeals were not limited to his own school. In the last weeks of his life, he went before the Durham City School Board and characteristically coupled a bid for black representation with a pledge of black loyalty. Requesting that blacks be appointed to the board, Shepard implored Durham's white officials: "The sands in my hour glass are fast running out. . . . I have left my sick bed and come here to ask you gentlemen to grant [blacks] representation on the Board of Education. I shall probably never appear before you again, gentlemen, but I am pleading with you on this occasion to grant my people this request and with it I pledge you their loyalty and their faithfulness." The board denied his request.[83]

His health rapidly declining, Shepard ignored his doctor's orders to rest when the school opened in 1947. Later that fall, he suffered a stroke while working in his office, and he died on 6 October 1947 at the age of seventy-one. A "damp-eyed throng" of friends, family, educators, and government officials packed NCC's auditorium for a memorial service. The Reverend Miles Mark Fisher of White Rock Baptist Church in Durham eulogized Shepard as one of the greatest black educators in history. Mourners later gathered at a local cemetery, where the Prince Hall Free and Accepted Masons oversaw Shepard's burial.[84] It is easy to imagine Shepard, who had fought at nearly all costs to protect his Masonic leadership, taking particular delight in being encircled by his fraternal comrades.

Hailed by dozens of prominent state and regional white leaders, Shepard quickly assumed his role in history as the state's "loyal son."[85] Southern whites undertook the business of memory-making and refashioned Shepard into someone who, in the words of his erstwhile adversary, Newbold, "was not excitable nor easily disturbed by the occasional, nor even the frequent, unbalance in race relations." Former UNC president Frank Porter Graham, who had gone on to become a U.S. senator, dubbed Shepard a "North Carolina Moses of a modern Israel." John Temple Graves of the *Birmingham Post* attributed to Shepard's "faith and spirit and works" the fact that "North Carolina has today the best race relations in the country and the most genuinely advanced colored people." When the state's General Assembly lauded Shepard in a formal resolution, it noted how he had resisted "agitation or ill-conceived demands" and followed a "practical, well-considered and consistent program of racial progress."[86] White legislators recalled Shepard as "the best politician ever to come before them," but they failed to consider that he would have preferred direct representation over the politics of patronage.[87] White memory constructed Shepard as someone who selflessly assumed the role of racial liberator and unerringly walked a steady course of white-approved black uplift.

These reflections were correct in many respects, but Shepard's public persona frequently masked his private resentment of the deferential role that his position as a black state college president required him to play. As a public figure, Shepard often chose accommodation over agitation, but white memories elided the inner conflicts that accompanied his choices. Whites seemed reluctant to entertain the notion that many black southern leaders chose conciliation less as a matter of political conviction than for reasons of expediency. In their own reminiscences, fellow African American leaders offered more clues to the complex aspects of Shepard's legacy. Morehouse College president Benjamin Mays confessed that he "did not always agree with what [Shepard] did and said," but he "certainly did like him." Shepard "took the position," Mays explained, "that if education in North Carolina had to be segregated, the segregated North Carolina College at Durham would have to be so good that no one would be able to label it as a Negro institution." Conrad Pearson, one of Hocutt's attorneys, similarly admitted that he "admired" Shepard, believing that "he did more good than harm." If Shepard had been white, Pearson reflected, "he would have been governor of this state." Black associates, in other words, saw both the limits and achievements of Shepard's career. As historian Walter Weare has put it, "The old-guard black radicals, who stood at the polar extreme politically from Shepard, refused to call him a conservative or an 'Uncle Tom' without considerable qualification and ambivalent admiration for his cleverness in dealing with white political leaders."[88]

From Equalization to Integration in Higher Education

When the members of the class of 1951 arrived at North Carolina College, they had little reason to anticipate that their cohort would be the last to graduate from a completely segregated state system of higher education. Yet by the summer of 1951, a federal court ruling led to the integration of the UNC Law School; four years later, the first black undergraduates arrived on the Chapel Hill campus. The numbers of black students at historically white colleges remained small for some time—and the numbers of white students at historically black colleges far smaller still—but NCC's students of the late 1940s came of age at a critical time in the black freedom movement. One member of NCC's class of 1951 experienced those shifting sands from a unique vantage point. Shepard's granddaughter, New Bern native Carolyn Smith Green, had spent many summer days during her childhood playing at the college president's home in Durham. She was "crazy about" her doting grandfather and never considered attending college anywhere but NCC. Her devotion to her alma mater and to her grandfather's memory endured as she ventured in both space and spirit beyond her grandfather's world. As a graduate student at Boston University in the 1950s, Green met the young Martin Luther King Jr. on the eve of his emergence as a national civil rights leader. She and her husband, James Preston Green Sr., did their part to break down the walls of segregation in Henderson, North Carolina, he at the hospitals where he worked as a physician, she as the first black member of the local guild of physicians' wives and as a leader in the newly integrated parent-teacher organization at her children's school.[89] Within less than a generation, Green's graduating cohort had encountered—and helped to create—a world that her grandfather barely would have recognized and in certain respects had resisted.

The legal foundations of the world Shepard had known began to crumble just months after his death. In January 1948, the U.S. Supreme Court reinforced the *Gaines* decision by ordering Oklahoma to provide equal facilities to Ada Sipuel, an honors student who had been denied admission to the University of Oklahoma's law school on racial grounds. Oklahoma attempted to satisfy the courts by establishing a separate black law school, but in 1949, under pressure from additional litigation, the state's flagship university admitted George McLaurin to its graduate program in education and Sipuel to its law school. Admission, of course, was not the same thing as true integration, and the university at first forced McLaurin and Sipuel to sit separately from their white classmates in specially designated "colored" areas. Only after another Supreme Court case in 1950 did the University of Oklahoma abandon this practice.[90]

In a last-ditch attempt to maintain segregated universities, fifteen of the region's governors voted in 1948 to establish regional black graduate and professional schools that the southern states would cooperatively support and manage. That plan had the strong backing of both Newbold and North Carolina's state superintendent of public instruction, Clyde Erwin, who served as vice chair of the plan's organizing committee, but it soon faced a barrage of criticism from both blacks and white progressives. The NCTA, which under Shepard's leadership in the 1930s had acquired a reputation for caution and conservatism, resolved to "condemn the regional school idea," labeling it "un-American in its intent" and designed for "the perpetuation of the inefficient and unjustifiably expensive 'separate but equal' school system." The plan was also roundly condemned in the black press. Durham's *Carolina Times* saw it as a futile effort to delay the inevitable. "Regional Schools, the Ku Klux Klan, dishonest college presidents who will agree to anything to feather their own nests, combined with all the powers of hell cannot save segregation," the paper predicted.[91] According to a poll conducted by the Southern Conference Educational Fund in the fall of 1948, even the majority of the faculty at seven of the South's flagship public universities—including the University of North Carolina—favored removing the color line in graduate and professional education.[92]

Most state officials did not at least publicly share this willingness to break the color line at the highest levels of education, but they also proved unwilling to appropriate anything close to the sort of funds that would have evened the playing field at the state's universities. Setting aside the larger question of intangible inequalities intrinsic to any segregated facilities, the state had only begun to address the enormous measurable differences between its white and black colleges and universities. In the late 1940s, the state appropriated funds for the first major permanent improvements at its black colleges since the late 1930s. NCC and A&T, for example, received more than two million dollars each from the 1947 legislature. Between 1950 and 1952, those and later appropriations helped facilitate the dedication at NCC of a new science building, music building, classroom building, library, gymnasium, and residence hall. That largesse, however, must be viewed within the context of concurrent and larger increases in funds for the white schools. In fact, in 1947, the University of North Carolina at Chapel Hill alone received more money for permanent improvements (more than eight million dollars) than A&T and NCC combined. The white schools certainly had a much larger total student enrollment than the black schools, a fact that whites routinely emphasized. "There is very little discrimination," claimed the *Asheville Citizen* in 1950, under the logic that white and black per pupil appropriations for higher education permanent improvements had been roughly comparable for the preceding couple of years. Such arguments ignored the fact that to compensate for decades of gross discrimination, the black schools needed to receive much larger appropriations than the white schools received. Moreover, in the decade leading up to the *Brown* decision, blacks' share of higher education operating expenses fluctuated between 12 and 16 percent, a proportion that was not even equal to black representation in the student population.[93]

In 1950, as state efforts to prop up segregated higher education limped along, white officials anxiously awaited the Supreme Court's decision in a case involving a black mail carrier, Heman Sweatt, who sought admission to the law school at the University of Texas. Fearing that "the results could be tragic" if *Sweatt* opened the door to widespread desegregation, Newbold confided to Graham that "this matter takes on the proportions of nothing short of a crisis." Newbold envisioned black children rushing to gain entrance to already crowded white schools, thousands of black teachers losing their jobs, and "perhaps hundreds of miniature civil war conflicts."[94]

As Newbold had feared, the Supreme Court ordered the University of Texas to admit Sweatt in June 1950, although the ruling did not spark the revolutionary change he had imagined. It did, however, buttress the efforts of black North Carolinians who for nearly a decade had criticized unequal conditions at NCC's law school. In March 1949, a group of NCC law students picketed the State Capitol, demanding improvements. Student protester Floyd McKissick recalled of the law school in Durham, "Didn't have enough books. Didn't have enough space. Didn't have enough facilities." That protest, along with rumors of an impending lawsuit, prompted state officials in the fall of 1949 to appropriate twenty thousand dollars from an emergency and contingency fund, which NCC then used to make

In 1949, students from North Carolina College's law school picketed the State Capitol to protest unequal facilities. (Courtesy of The North Carolina State Archives, Raleigh)

some hasty repairs to "an old condemned auditorium" that could expand the law school's facilities. Undeterred by these modest gestures toward equalization, two NCC law students, Harold Epps and Robert Davis Glass, sued for entry into UNC. Epps and Glass completed their degrees at NCC before that case reached resolution, but new plaintiffs kept the case alive. UNC appealed the desegregation of its law school all the way to the U.S. Supreme Court, but in June 1951, the justices ordered the school to admit its first black students. That summer, McKissick, Kenneth Lee, James Lassiter, James Walker, and Harvey Beech became the university's first black law students. That same summer, UNC's graduate school also admitted its first black student, although officials did not realize they had done so until Gwendolyn Harrison showed up for her first graduate-level Spanish class. Officials then attempted to revoke her admission but eventually relented in the face of litigation. In the meantime, UNC also faced legal pressure to integrate its medical school. Since NCC had no such facilities, the trustees abandoned that fight without a court order, and Edward O. Diggs began his medical education at UNC in September 1951.[95]

Throughout the civil rights era, most of the South's black college students continued to attend historically black institutions, where they faced more limited facilities and a more narrow range of degree options than white schools typically offered. In 1950, NCC offered undergraduate degrees in twenty-two areas, whereas UNC did so in thirty; at the master's level, NCC had thirteen degree options and UNC thirty-six; most egregiously, NCC offered no doctoral degrees, while UNC offered twenty-five. A dozen years later, the facilities at the state's black colleges were, in the words of one state official, still "no where near equal" to those at white schools. Not surprisingly, many black students still traveled out of state to pursue education beyond college. Between 1939 and 1956, an estimated twenty-five hundred black students received money from the state to attend graduate and professional programs not available to them in North Carolina.[96] State officials continued to promote the expansion of graduate and professional options at NCC as an alternative to increased integration. Shepard's successor as NCC's president, Alfonso Elder, however, looked far more skeptically than Shepard had on these efforts to create a parallel system of segregated black graduate and professional education. In fact, the state disregarded Elder's opposition when it created a doctoral program in education at NCC in 1951. UNC integrated at the undergraduate level in the fall of 1955, when John L. Brandon, Ralph Frazier, and Leroy Frazier—all graduates of Durham's Hillside High—received admission.[97] With the color line broken at every level of public higher education, Shepard's dream of a "Negro university" arguably seemed out of step with the ambitions of the civil rights generation.

NCC achieved university status in 1969, in part a testament to the fact that many black students continued to choose historically black institutions on their own merits rather than as alternatives to white schools. The Black Power movement had inspired some black youth to question the goals of integration and to seek empowerment exclusively from within black institutions.[98] An even more common impulse was to support the goals of integration while drawing on the strengths of historically black institutions. Future civil rights attorney James Ferguson felt tugs in both directions while growing up in Asheville in the late 1950s. While in high school, he helped found the Asheville Student Committee on Racial Equality, whose mission was to desegregate Asheville's business district. When it came time to choose a college, however, Ferguson deliberated with his parents and decided to attend NCC rather than the recently integrated UNC. He later reflected on his college years as "one of the best experiences" of his life. He "felt fully at home," and his teachers took "an interest in me and my personal development." He also got a taste of politics through his involvement in student government, an experience he doubted he would have had at UNC. Ferguson believed that he had "de-

In 1957, North Carolina College unveiled a statue of James E. Shepard that continues to serve as a point of pride for students. Presiding at the ceremony were NCC professor and alumnus James T. Taylor and Carolyn Smith Green, Shepard's granddaughter and a member of NCC's Class of 1951. (Courtesy of The North Carolina State Archives, Raleigh)

veloped in some ways [at NCC] . . . that I would not have had I gone to the University of North Carolina." Those lessons in leadership served Ferguson well as he later litigated high-profile school integration cases. Somewhat ironically, then, despite his conflicted relationship with the emerging black freedom movement, Shepard had created an environment that nurtured many of the state's civil rights vanguard. Clarence Lightner, who studied at NCC in the late 1930s and early 1940s and in 1973 became the first black mayor of Raleigh, once explained that he and his fellow students "got something instilled in us which I would like to call the North Carolina College spirit. We were instilled with the attitude that if anybody could make it, we could make it."[99]

That spirit and an almost protective reverence for Shepard's memory live on among the members of the post–civil rights generation at North Carolina Central University. When the school recently celebrated its centennial, student body president Dwayne Johnson remarked in reference to the campus's large statue of its founder, "If anyone steps on . . . Dr. Shepard, the students are going to get upset. . . . We take great pride in Dr. Shepard."[100] As the beneficiaries of both Shepard's generation of institution-builders and the generation that opposed him in breaking down segregation in higher education, today's students are the inheritors of a complex South marked by competing black visions for first-class citizenship.

At the same time that Shepard's vision for black equality was first coming under challenge from a younger generation in the 1930s, a battle for teacher salary equalization was exposing similar fault lines in civil rights strategy. That battle resulted in a "most spectacular" victory, if also a great deal of uncertainty about its ultimate victors.

Donning the toga of teachers does not decitizenize.
We are citizens first, teachers afterwards.
—Editorial in the *North Carolina Teachers Record*, the organ of the
North Carolina Teachers Association, 1933

We cannot afford to dis-establish the direct channel of contact which we
have at all times had with those in authority in North Carolina. If this channel is diverted
from the North Carolina Negro to the New York Negro and then back to North Carolina,
the wayside station in New York might not last as long as our problems.
—North Carolina Teachers Association president Oliver R. Pope, 1933

This effort by the state to achieve this goal in equality of
opportunity in public education has been the most spectacular as well as
the most satisfactory in the long series of attempts North Carolina has made
to give every child of every race an equal chance for education.
—State superintendent of public instruction Clyde Erwin,
on teacher salary equalization, 1948

CHAPTER FOUR

A "Most Spectacular" Victory?

Teacher Salary Equalization and the Dilemma of Local Leadership

When poet Langston Hughes visited North Carolina in the early 1930s, he discovered what he perceived as an intolerable degree of complacency among black educators. After receiving from a local black leader a letter of introduction to Nathan Newbold, Hughes paid a visit to the Raleigh headquarters of the Division of Negro Education (DNE). There he observed the office's seeming conformity with the racial etiquette of the Jim Crow South. Upon Hughes's arrival, Newbold's white secretary gave him "a casual glance and went on with what she was doing." As Hughes later recounted in *The Crisis*, the secretary afforded white guests a very different sort of reception: "She dropped her work near the window and came over to them, spoke to them most pleasantly, and ignored me entirely. The white people, after several minutes of how-are-you's and did-you-enjoy-yo'self-at-the-outing-last-week, said that they wished to see Mr. Newbold. Whereupon, having arrived first and having not yet been noticed by the secretary, I turned and walked out." Outraged by the secretary's disregard, Hughes was most troubled by the apparent African American reluctance to hold Newbold accountable for the racial climate of his own office. Hughes wrote, "When I told some Negro teachers of the incident, they said, 'But Mr. Newbold's not like that.' 'Why then,' I asked, 'does he have that kind of secretary?' Nobody seemed to know."[1] Hughes's visit left him with the impression that southern black educators had accepted their own subordination and were patiently waiting in the wings for white recognition.

The accuracy of Hughes's impression of North Carolina's black teaching force was put to the test in 1933 when representatives from the New York headquarters of the National Association for the Advancement of Colored People (NAACP) visited the state, hoping to rally support for a campaign to equalize teachers' salaries. The NAACP had begun testing litigation as a strategy for educational equality, but it had not yet filed any suits to that end. North Carolina seemed like the perfect venue for such a test case. Its black teaching force was one of the best trained in the South and had developed a strong professional identity through the North Carolina Teachers Association (NCTA). To add to the state's attractiveness, North Carolina was home to a growing number of local NAACP chapters. And while salary inequalities in North Carolina were somewhat less egregious than those found in the Deep South, the state's salary scale still clearly bore the mark of disfranchisement. In 1890, the state's black teachers had received an average of 98 percent of white salaries; by 1910, that figure had dropped to only 53 percent. In 1933–34, black salaries were beginning to recover lost ground but still constituted only 65 percent of white salaries. Moreover, black teachers typically taught larger classes than their white counterparts. The racial gap in pupil-teacher ratios narrowed during the depression, but in part because all teachers took on more students during those years (table 4.1).[2] In pitching its legal strategy, the NAACP emphasized notions of professional entitlement, suggesting that black teachers should not be required to assume the lives of selfless servants. African Americans, the NAACP insisted, could be both teachers and first-class citizens.[3]

Despite that promise of liberation, the NCTA's leadership rejected the NAACP's 1933 litigation campaign and effectively thwarted subsequent salary equalization lawsuits in the state.[4] In fact, North Carolina was the only southern state where black teachers did not file salary equalization lawsuits between 1938 and 1948.[5] To be sure, the NAACP's proposed litigation won support from many of the NCTA's rank-and-file members. As Leslie Brown has found in her study of Durham, black teachers, the majority of them women, joined the NAACP in large numbers in the wake of

Table 4.1. Number of Pupils in Average Daily Attendance per Teacher Employed in North Carolina, by Race, 1923–1964

Year	Black Students	White Students
1923–24	32.2	25.0
1929–30	31.7	27.8
1934–35	34.8	33.9
1939–40	32.9	31.9
1944–45	29.5	28.9
1949–50	31.8	29.7
1954–55	29.4	27.4
1959–60	28.1	26.5
1963–64	25.9	24.6

Sources: *Biennial Report*, 1922–23/1923–24, pt. 1, 40; *Biennial Report*, 1962–63/1963–64, pt. 1, 50.

the organization's campaign, thereby foreshadowing the NAACP's post-war success in recruiting North Carolinians (including many educators).[6] Prior to that time, however, NCTA leaders chose to negotiate directly with white officials and implement a state-controlled program of slow and measured salary increases that did not equalize teacher pay until 1944. No single factor explains why the NCTA leadership refused to join forces with the NAACP. Perhaps most significant was the fact that all of the NCTA presidents during those years directly relied on the good graces of white officials. From 1930 to 1944, six men and two women held the NCTA presidency; all but one were state employees. Rank-and-file teachers were also employees of the state, but the NCTA's presidents were principals, college presidents, and state supervisors, positions that involved direct accountability to white officials. NCTA leaders' caution also likely had a generational component. All but one of the presidents from 1930 to 1944 had been born during the 1860s, 1870s, and 1880s. These men and women could therefore remember the racial violence of the disfranchisement era, a period that signified the ultimate perils of contesting white authority.[7]

The NCTA's strategy suggested that North Carolina's black teachers desired the salaries of first-class citizens but did not want to risk their professional status and privileges for the sake of a larger struggle for black entitlement. Their position seemed to herald the assessment of sociologist E. Franklin Frazier, who lamented in his 1957 study, *Black Bourgeoisie*, that "many Negro teachers refuse identification with the Negro masses and look upon teaching primarily as a source of income." He judged their concerns to be primarily "social status and economic security." Historians have offered alternatives to Frazier's judgment but no clear consensus on the role of educators in the black freedom struggle. Some have found black teachers acting as selfless foot soldiers for black equality, while others have cast teachers as conservative standard-bearers of the black middle class. In tracing the roots of civil rights activism, scholars have located teachers both on the front lines of action and on the sidelines of passive observation, if not resistant criticism.[8]

If litigation is to serve as the litmus test of civil rights leadership, then North Carolina's most prominent black educators generally failed to pass muster in the 1930s and early 1940s. The NCTA's reluctance to join forces with the NAACP in pursuing salary equalization, however, reflected more of a strategic difference than a fundamental incompatibility of goals. NCTA leaders preferred negotiation rather than litigation as a means of acquiring the privileges of citizenship. While ties to white officials constrained their choices, the state's black educational leaders nonetheless urged their colleagues to take up the cause of equality as "citizens first, teachers afterwards." Black educators chose to retain some measure of leverage with state leaders by joining them in a cooperative project to keep "outside agitators" at bay. This strategy reflected the constricted parameters of black leadership in the South, where black public figures routinely felt trapped between the political deference demanded of them by the state and the political militancy demanded by outside activists. In an ambivalent response to those choices, the leaders of the NCTA sought instead a middle ground of self-determination.

A Seemingly Natural Alliance: The NAACP and the NCTA

In the mid-1920s, a cooperative equalization campaign launched by the NCTA and the NAACP might have seemed in the offing. In the published minutes of its 1924 annual meeting, the NCTA carried an advertisement for *The Crisis* that recommended that the magazine "be in the hands of every Negro pupil and every Negro teacher." At least some black teachers took that message to heart. One pupil recalled from his elementary school days in Raleigh in the late 1920s and early 1930s that the teachers sold "twenty-five cent memberships" in the NAACP. "You were almost an outcast if you didn't have one of those twenty-five cent cards in your pocket," he remembered. The NCTA also made financial contributions to the NAACP and even appeared one step ahead of the New York–based civil rights organization in recommending in 1926 "that the salary schedule for Negro teachers be revised looking forward to an equalization of all teachers' salaries."[9]

Negro school agent Nathan Newbold (right) and Simon Green Atkins, president of the Slater Normal School (later Winston-Salem Teachers College) and head of the NCTA in the late 1920s, confer in 1922. In his dependence on the good graces of white state officials, Atkins typified the dilemma of a generation of association leaders. (Courtesy of Jackson Davis Papers, 1906–47, Accession #3072, #3072-a, Special Collections Department, University of Virginia Library, Charlottesville)

While drawing strength and inspiration from the NAACP, southern black educators could not ignore the political realities of a fight for equality at home. In collaborating with *Crisis* editor W. E. B. Du Bois in the mid-1920s, state supervisor of Negro high schools William A. Robinson gently reminded him, "Remember that up there in New York you are a long way from our problems which we are face to face with every day and you do not know the delicate mechanism with which progress advances in the South and how easily this may be thrown out of gear."[10] The "delicate mechanisms" for progress were laid bare at the 1927 NCTA annual meeting, when Newbold urged the group to study key points of educational inequality, including teacher salaries, and present its findings to the State Budget Commission. Yet he discouraged any "resort to the law," a strategy that he argued would lead to "pessimism" among blacks and "resentment" among whites. NCTA president Simon Atkins, who as head of the Winston-Salem Teachers College depended heavily on the good graces of white officials, was in no position to challenge Newbold on that score. In fact, Atkins praised Newbold at that meeting for winning the "unlimited confidence" of black educators.[11]

As outside civil rights leaders and local white officials vied for influence among the state's black teaching force, the NCTA was quickly becoming a powerful force in its own right. By 1929, NCTA membership had swelled to more than thirty-five hundred, or approximately 60 percent of the active black teaching force. In the NCTA's new monthly journal, the *North Carolina Teachers Record*, group leaders pledged in 1930 never to "lose sight of our common problems, such as those concerned with getting better salaries, better buildings and longer school terms." The increasing politicization of the NCTA was further evident at the group's annual meeting the same year. The gathering opened with the obligatory greetings from white state officials, but the tone soon shifted when Benjamin Brawley, a prominent writer and professor at Shaw University, took to the podium. Brawley disabused the lieutenant governor of the common white assumption "that the Negro had no concern with politics." Brawley further explained why African Americans "*have* to be concerned with politics." There was "nothing more cruel," he asserted "than to teach Negro boys and girls American history, to instruct them in the Declaration of Independence and in the part played by their brother in the World War, and then to deny them the full promise of American life." Such blatant hypocrisies required political redress, he suggested. Leaving little doubt about the falseness of the popular notion of the apolitical Negro, Brawley added, "Mr. Governor, if ever a Negro tells you that the Negro has no interest in politics, we want you to watch your pockets, for he wants something out of them." With undeniable clarity, Brawley had unraveled the ties of loyalty and deference that bound blacks to white authority. He perhaps possessed an unusual degree of candor, but the NCTA as a whole upheld a spirit of entitlement, even at the height of the Great Depression. In 1931, the group's journal argued that "in the midst of depression and debt," black teachers should "renew [their] fight for better salaries, better teachers, and better school facilities."[12]

As the NCTA was paving the way for greater influence in state politics, the NAACP's national office was exploring the possibilities for testing its legal campaign in North Carolina. Newbold first learned of the NAACP's plans while visiting Teachers College, Columbia University, in New York in the 1920s. Future NAACP executive director Walter White, then an assistant secretary of the group's New York office, invited Newbold to his office for a conference, during which White mentioned the possibility of educational litigation. Shocked by this news, Newbold exclaimed, "My Lord, if you do that, you will break the plan of salvation in the South, for Negroes as well as for whites." Newbold was relieved that for a time White "desisted" in his plan.[13]

For his part, White remained convinced that the South's salvation would be found in the courtroom, not in promises of white goodwill. By 1930, the national NAACP office had reason to believe that the time was ripe for litigation in North Carolina. Earlier that spring, it had spearheaded a successful effort to defeat Herbert Hoover's Supreme Court nomination of John J. Parker, a Republican judge from North Carolina who in 1920 had employed well-publicized race-baiting tactics in campaigning for governor. No doubt encouraged by Parker's rejection, White contacted Newbold again in the fall of 1930 and indicated his intent to campaign for educational equality in the state. As if timed to reinforce the impact of White's message, that same day two black citizens from the small town of Enfield visited Newbold's office to discuss troubling questions about the legality of racially unequal teacher salary scales. Newbold feared that the NAACP had a real chance for "making a show even in our good State of North Carolina." That possibility baffled Newbold, as he believed that the state had tried "to give the Negroes a reasonably square deal in education." He admitted that "exact justice ha[d] not been done," but he had "tried to keep ahead of just the sort of thing which Walter White is talking about." He suspected that the "Judge Parker affair" had stoked the NAACP with "a greater keenness and ambition to push matters further." Now he feared that the state might be on the losing side of a contest for credibility on matters of school equality. He confided to state superintendent of schools Arch T. Allen that in some communities, the NAACP "might, through local Negroes, employ white lawyers, go into court and win a victory for the Negro children." Newbold felt sure that an "invasion" by outside interests would not benefit black children but would mainly give the NAACP "glory and advertising." Moreover, he feared that a court battle would be "exceedingly humiliating and embarrassing to our people" and would allow the NAACP "to advertise themselves as saviors of the poor Negroes in certain communities down South." The state, Newbold argued, must manage black discontent more aggressively, lest blacks believe that their salvation lay with outside agitators. Allen agreed, noting that a NAACP-led campaign would be "almost suicidal for us."[14]

Newbold investigated the state's vulnerability to the NAACP's proposed campaign and uncovered a host of discriminatory practices: black students routinely attended one-room schools despite state recommendations for larger units; many black teachers were not receiving the state's required minimum salary; officials often extended white school terms at the expense of black terms; some school boards divided funds on the basis of how much each race paid in taxes, in violation of an 1886 State Supreme Court ruling prohibiting such race-based allocations. Newbold admitted that some officials held "the premeditated desire and purpose to be unfair," but he took comfort in his belief that most blacks were "devoted to the State's interests." He felt that it would be "easy to keep [blacks] satisfied, contented and happy if the school officials will be reasonably fair and just in dealing with them."[15]

In 1931, firm in their faith that local officials could be convinced to give blacks a fair deal, Newbold and Allen invited leading black educators to Raleigh for a conference at Shaw University. In certain respects, Newbold encouraged black educators to take seriously their rights of legal citizenship. He urged them "to inform themselves on the details of the school law, to study their own local school conditions, [and] to compare these with the opportunities which the school law provides for them." He instructed them, however, to secure their rights by assembling the "sane and sensible leadership of their own race" and conferring with "the friendly school officials." Implied if not directly stated was the folly of going outside these channels for recourse. The black educators pledged their cooperation with the state, suggesting that they would give whites a chance to prove their capacity for fairness.[16]

In the context of this emerging contest for teacher loyalties, Newbold panicked in 1932 when he learned of extensive state cutbacks in school funding. Such retrenchment would make it impossible to "regain the confidence of the colored people all over the State." He warned Allen, "You and I have known dozens of other instances where the colored people could have appealed to the courts and secured improvement in their schools, but they have refrained, partly, I am led to believe, upon our advice and suggestions." When the legislature opened in January 1933, it faced its most severe budget crisis since the stock market crash of 1929. The legislators increased teacher loads at the high school level, cut some Jeanes supervisory positions, and slashed both white and black teachers' salaries by 10 percent.[17] As teacher morale fell, the NAACP seemed perfectly poised for its campaign, but it had yet to secure the firm cooperation of NCTA leaders. That need for backing from leading black educators had stymied Thomas Hocutt's bid to enter the University of North Carolina, which was drawing to an unsuccessful close in the summer of 1933. The greatest challenge that lay ahead, then, was not so much winning the hearts of the NCTA's rank and file but rather convincing its longtime leaders to compromise their carefully forged ties to white officials.

Table 4.2. Average Annual Classroom Teacher Salaries in North Carolina, by Race, 1919–1960

Year	Black Teachers	White Teachers
1919–20	$298.45	$516.15
1924–25	455.41	835.11
1929–30	538.75	954.11
1934–35	415.31	620.93
1939–40	710.63	957.31
1944–45	1,304.46	1,294.34
1949–50	2,628.69	2,535.24
1954–55	3,293.50	3,196.64
1959–60	4,056.01	3,932.81

Sources: Biennial Report, 1948–49/1949–50, pt. 1, 24; *Biennial Report*, 1962–63/1963–64, pt. 1, 48.

Note: Does not include salaries of principals, supervisors, or vocational teachers. Figures include salaries from all funds.

"Citizen-Teachers" and the Dilemma of Litigation

In building their case for salary equalization, the NAACP could point to persistent income differentials at a time when black teachers were dramatically increasing their levels of training. The state, which funded teacher salaries and distributed salary schedules to local districts, held both races to the same certification requirements. To meet those requirements, increasing numbers of black teachers attended summer schools. In 1920, two-thirds of black teachers held less than a high school degree; by 1930, only 17 percent fell into that category, and five years later, most black teachers had two or more years of college. In other words, by 1935 black educators had 86 percent of the training of white teachers but received only 67 percent of the average white salary (tables 4.2 and 4.3).[18] Pitifully low salaries contributed to the rapid feminization of the black teaching force in the early twentieth century. Many male heads of households simply could not afford to teach.[19] Black male educators gravitated toward administrative positions, which typically paid higher, though still low, salaries. Durham's black newspaper judged one such principal who earned seventy-five dollars per month in 1930 either a "philanthropist or a martyr" to work at such low pay. The true martyrs of this era, however, were classroom teachers. The majority-female black teaching force fell victim to both sexist and racist assumptions about the inherent value of southern labor. Sociologists Ira DeA. Reid and Arthur F. Raper wrote of that double burden, "Be she schoolteacher or laundress, factory operative

Table 4.3. Average Scholarship Index of All Teachers and Principals in
North Carolina, by Race, 1921–1946

Year	Black Teachers	White Teachers
1921–22	351.7	492.6
1924–25	395.9	552.4
1929–30	525.7	676.1
1934–35	640.2	741.5
1939–40	752.6	785.7
1944–45	790.6	773.1
1945–46	785.7	767.6

Source: Biennial Report, 1944–45/1945–46, pt. 1, 15.

Note: 400 = 4 years of high school; 800 = 4 years of college.

or cotton picker, the Negro woman is—and always has been—at the bottom of the Southern labor market. The economic and social conditions under which she lives and works represent the cellar of the South."[20]

In addition to the obvious evidence of racial discrimination, any fight for salary parity promised greater support from politically cautious blacks than had the earlier *Hocutt* case. Salary litigation certainly challenged white expectations of black deference, but it posed no overt threat to the color line. In leaving segregation intact, the salary issue could safely be packaged within a larger struggle to reform rather than weaken Jim Crow. No doubt with such considerations in mind, North Carolina Mutual president Charles Clinton Spaulding, who had shied away from the *Hocutt* case, offered critical if largely behind-the-scenes logistical support to NAACP organizers during the early phases of the salary fight.[21]

Furthermore, the salary fight developed at a fortuitous moment, resonating with the spirit of a new administration in Washington. The first phase of Franklin Roosevelt's New Deal legislation included the 1933 creation of the National Recovery Administration (NRA), which attempted to standardize industrial practices by eliminating unfair price controls and wage systems. It also promised workers federal protection of the right to organize and collectively bargain. Although many employers found ways of subverting NRA regulations and the legislation eventually came under legal challenge, its emphasis on wage fairness had begun to legitimate the idea of economic entitlements across racial lines. As historian Robert Korstad has written, "Despite its shortcomings and its brief lifespan, the NRA constituted an opening salvo in the assault on the dual wage structure that made discrimination against black workers the linchpin in the South's separate economy."[22]

Many black teachers raised their level of training by attending summer schools, such as this one held in Asheville in 1922. (Courtesy of Jackson Davis Papers, 1906–47, Accession #3072, #3072–a, Special Collections Department, University of Virginia Library, Charlottesville)

Buttressed by new federal backing, the insurgent labor movement of the 1930s offered further inspiration for the teachers' struggle. The NCTA, like its counterparts across the region, was a professional association, not a union. The only teachers' union that did exist, the American Federation of Teachers, an affiliate of the American Federation of Labor, had organized a small number of southern locals that fought salary discrimination in the mid-1930s. The union did not have a significant presence in North Carolina, but the state's teachers could look to local industrial workers for instructive lessons in the promise and perils of collective action. In 1933 and 1934, a wave of union organizing shocked the southern textile industry. The plight of textile workers, most of them white, differed in important respects from that of black teachers. Even so, the rhetoric that white elites used to repress textile unionization echoed with state criticisms of the NAACP's teacher salary campaign. Critics of both movements railed against the specter of "outside agitation." Moreover, just as black teachers were not of one mind about the merits of an NAACP-affiliated fight for salary equality, textile workers divided into pro- and anti-union factions. In a few places, most notably Durham, textile workers scored remarkable victories during the General Textile Strike of 1934. But in many other locations, efforts to unionize culminated with violent repression by factory owners and lasting divisions among workers. Anti-union textile workers were not naive about the limits of elite paternalism, but they nonetheless feared losing what tenuous privileges and security their loyalty to company management had provided. As one Greenville worker and union opponent wryly observed, "It is true that every textile worker in the south would walk out of the Mill to day if they were not afraid of starvation."[23] An NAACP-backed fight for teacher salary equity would similarly need to reckon with the potential costs of alienating the local power structure.

In the late 1920s, the NCTA had launched a salary crusade with appeals to state officials. The depression had stymied those efforts for a time, but in April 1933, an NCTA delegation visited Governor J. C. B. Ehringhaus and asked him to appoint a committee to study educational inequalities, including salary differentials.[24] The following month, White, the NAACP executive secretary, visited North Carolina and made clear that teacher salaries were squarely on his agenda, too. Speaking at Shaw University, he promised to fight "until the educational inequalities burdened upon the qualified Negro in North Carolina are eliminated." Later that summer, White corresponded with local NAACP leaders about the possibilities for a statewide meeting at which branch presidents would "federate" their organizations into a statewide assembly that could act more forcefully, particularly on the issues of black graduate education and teacher salaries.[25]

Ironically, while the NAACP's nascent campaign stirred up white southerners' fears of radicalism, White's office was busy pursuing its own anti-radical agenda. White felt some urgency in organizing his North Carolina salary campaign out of concern that the communist-affiliated International Labor Defense would beat him to it. While rumors to that effect never materialized, White's worries pointed to the broad spectrum of locals and outsiders who held a stake in the teachers' struggle for equality.[26]

With competing factions poised for action, it remained unclear who would ultimately claim ownership of the fight. When NAACP special counsel William Hastie came to North Carolina in 1933 to investigate teacher salaries, he quickly made enemies by failing to consult local black leaders in advance of meetings with state officials. Questions of leadership also arose within the local black establishment. At about the same time as Hastie's misstep, a group of Durham leaders—including C. C. Spaulding of North Carolina Mutual, James T. Taylor of the North Carolina College for Negroes, and W. G. Pearson of Hillside High—filed a petition with the State School Commission asking for teacher salary equalization as well as the appointment of an African American to the directorship of the DNE. When members of the Greensboro NAACP learned of this move, they balked. Executive committee secretary George Streator complained to White that the Durham group's actions were "ill-timed" and had prompted the commission to obfuscate its intentions with regard to teacher salaries by refusing to publish its teacher salary schedule. Streator further believed that publicity-hungry "interracial racketeers" controlled the Durham branch. These men prided themselves on voicing black grievances but typically accommodated white "pseudo-liberals." Spaulding, Streator insisted, was "not worth in the final analysis a tinkers damn for fighting purposes," and neither was the NCTA. Streator predicted that no black college presidents would support their cause. "The real opposition, brother, is from the white-folks'-N," he concluded. As if to prove Streator correct, in September, James Shepard shared his criticisms of the fledgling salary campaign with Newbold, and throughout that fall, Shepard secretly kept Newbold abreast of the NAACP's plans.[27]

Undaunted by these challenges, White's office worked tirelessly throughout the summer and fall of 1933 to build support for a court battle. Spaulding and fellow North Carolina Mutual executives helped White send out a mailing to nearly all of the state's black teachers, inviting them to a mass meeting in Raleigh on 29 October. Planned as an occasion for organizing a salary suit and a new statewide branch of the NAACP, this meeting promised to help teachers take their fight for equal salaries to its logical next step. The invitational letter insisted that local leaders had used every means available to negotiate with the State School Commission, thus leaving litigation as the only recourse.[28]

In the months leading up to the October rally, NCTA leaders withheld public support for the NAACP's campaign and amplified their own calls for equality. An editorial in the *North Carolina Teachers Record* asserted, "Too long have we been content to believe that our sole duty lay within the four walls of the schoolroom, and that the establishment of school policies was the duty of the administration." In a rejection of the exalted image of black teachers as selfless servants, the *Record* encouraged teachers to try on a new garb of entitled citizenship: "Donning the toga of teachers does not decitizenize. We are citizens first, teachers afterwards. . . . The citizen-teacher owes an obligation to the public to help mold public sentiment as well as to engage in the altruistic pursuits of his calling." Its heady claims of citizenship aside, the *Record* did not endorse litigation as recourse. It urged teachers to educate the public through "constant agitation" and to keep the faith that the state would eventually answer their calls for justice.[29]

The NAACP had won considerable support for its own strategies for black citizenship. On 29 October, a crowd of more than twenty-five hundred, including hundreds of teachers, crowded into Raleigh's Memorial Auditorium for a rally. According to White's office, the gathering occasioned "the greatest enthusiasm seen here since the old days when both races attended political conventions together." The packed audience applauded "militant speeches" by White and Hastie. White castigated Uncle Toms and urged "a clean-out and uncompromising fight against injustice and inequality." The rally coincided with a spirited meeting of the new State Conference of NAACP Branches, which was designed to spearhead the salary fight and monitor other racial concerns. White returned to New York already planning how to channel the "tremendous enthusiasm" evident in the state. The significance of this meeting was not lost on either the white press or state officials. The *Raleigh News and Observer* judged the NAACP head to be a "clever propagandist" and warned that his speeches could inflame blacks who "are not as smart or intelligent as he is." State officials, too, worried about the rally's repercussions. By the end of the week, the State School Commission met to plan how it would respond to salary litigation. NAACP organizers took satisfaction in this white hand-wringing. As Streator later noted, a public gathering of two hundred blacks was enough to alarm white southerners. A gathering of twenty-five hundred blacks, all of them listening to "speakers not always enjoying the approval of white people and their hand-picked colored yeomanry," was nothing short of "miraculous."[30]

Miracles aside, mounting evidence indicated that the state's more conservative black leadership would impede the NAACP's momentum. Shortly after the October rally, Rocky Mount's newspaper published a letter from an unnamed black principal who insisted that the NAACP amounted to little more than a radical fringe movement. "I have seen upheavals before, in 1898," this principal wrote, referring to the Wilmington race riot that ushered in disfranchisement. In a seeming exoneration of the white instigators of that violence, he asserted that the riot "began with the Negro editors and young lawyers." Now, he argued, the younger element was again to blame, along with "a few West Indian Negroes," a likely reference to Dr. George E. Nightengale of High Point, a native of Barbados and president of the state chapter of the NAACP. The principal noted that in 1919, he and other "older Negro men" had "assured" state officials that they would "support our school forces and avoid social equality." This principal added that his loyalty, along with that of "thousands" of other blacks, remained in place. The *Rocky Mount Evening Telegram* seized on this letter as evidence that the salary campaign had little local backing, was "being agitated almost entirely by a group of outsiders," and "does not have the support of the older Negroes." Insiders suspected that the letter had been written by Charles M. Eppes of Greenville, whose conservatism might in part have reflected a generational difference with the emerging leaders of the 1930s. Nightengale was born at the turn of the century, while Eppes was born in the 1850s. Although few black leaders went to such dubious lengths to discredit the NAACP's campaign, there were other voices of caution. Gaston A. Edwards, principal of Lyon Park School in Durham, shared with Newbold his fears of the "undesirable effects which could come from outside interference," insisting that "the teachers are not responsible for the activities of others."[31]

White attempted to stem this tide of naysayers by advising local NAACP leaders "to refuse to dignify Epp[e]s and men of his stripe by attacking them." In addition, White's office issued a public statement denying that the salary campaign was the handiwork of "outside agitation" and insisting that it reflected the frustrations of black North Carolinians who wanted their "full rights as citizens." In a similar vein, Streator wrote an article for *The Crisis*, "The Colored South Speaks for Itself," that cast the state's salary campaign as a homegrown movement.[32]

The "colored South" was indeed speaking for itself, but not in unison. Shepard soon thwarted White's efforts at damage control by organizing a competing homegrown crusade for equality. Two days after the NAACP rally, Shepard assured Ehringhaus, "I want to ask you not to lose your faith and confidence in the masses of Negro people. . . . After all this storm has blown over there will come a calm and I do not believe any court action is going to be taken at the present time to test the validity of salaries." At the request of "several of the colored leaders," Shepard proposed a conference of invited black representatives to devise an agenda that could be negotiated with state officials. When White learned of this plan, he pressed Shepard on his refusal to join forces with the NAACP.[33]

Shepard did not desist in his plan, but the extent to which he could win local backing remained unclear. By his own admission, some local black activists were accusing him of having been "captured" by white officials. One such critic was Livingstone College professor William J. Trent Jr., who judged that Shepard was "again playing his usual role of 'Uncle Tom.'" Born in 1910, Trent chaired the Salisbury chapter of the NAACP and represented a new coterie of black leaders who had little patience for the timidity of the old guard. Yet the men of Trent's generation were not Shepard's only critics. In fact, Trent's father, Livingstone president William Trent Sr., born two years before Shepard in 1873, was an early organizer of the Salisbury NAACP and chastised Shepard for opposing salary litigation.

As employees of a private college, both Trent men were freer than Shepard to compromise their ties to state officials. Nonetheless, if Shepard failed to reckon with the demands of the state's civil rights vanguard, he clearly would face black critics across generational lines.[34]

In what appeared to be an attempt to meet his critics halfway, Shepard's counterconference articulated an agenda that resonated with the NAACP's campaign. His invited spokesmen petitioned the state to allocate salaries purely on the basis of "education, experience, and efficiency." More significantly, they set aside the deferential language of the past and voiced diminished faith in the merits of black loyalty:

> We are disfranchised and told to acquire learning and fitness for citizenship. We undertake the preparation in our inadequate, wretchedly equipped schools. Our children drag through the mud while others ride in busses, we pass the courses required by the state and in most places when we present ourselves for registration we are denied that right and lose our votes. Our teachers, disadvantaged by disfranchisement, by lack of the means to prepare themselves, nevertheless do meet the high and exacting standards of the best white institutions of the country, and then armed with the state's highest certificate[s] go into the employment of a commonwealth which reduces their wages to the level of janitors and hod carriers. We are informed that it is best for us if we stay out of politics. We have stayed out and this is what we have. . . . We do not expect our white friends to feel as we do about these injustices. . . . But we do expect that our public men who have written the statutes guaranteeing us our political and civil rights, as a matter of fidelity to their better selves[,] will demand a scrupulous observation of the law as it is written.

Rather than an obsequious call for patience and cooperation, here was an indictment of the white South that was crafted in the rights-oriented language of legal citizenship. On the specific question of litigation, Shepard's original draft had added an extra note of caution, stating that "the courts of the land are the last place to which we would go for alleviation of these social ills." But a professor from Shaw University objected, and the assembly voted unanimously to excise that statement. It did urge that "the ballot" serve as a "first means of defense," a more subtle rejection of litigation as a strategy for equality. All told, however, this statement had made significant concessions to the legitimacy of the NAACP's agenda.[35]

As evidence of the fluidity between rival factions of the state's leading black men and women, several signers of the petition included officers in the state NAACP: Julia Delany of St. Augustine's College in Raleigh, Winston-Salem social worker and civic leader Irma Neal Henry, and even Nightengale. Nightengale later confided to White that the meeting had rankled him considerably. Not only had Shepard apparently barred leading civil rights attorneys Cecil McCoy and Conrad Pearson from attending, but Nightengale was frustrated by many of the older participants— including the alleged Judas of the group, Eppes. Nightengale thought that many of those present were "pussyfooting" around the issues at hand. He addressed the group, giving them "devil for not being men." Nonetheless, after hearing their statement, Nightengale "saw the possibility of [it] being an aid to us." White agreed. His office issued a response declaring that "North Carolinians of all factions are uniting behind the militant program outlined by the N.A.A.C.P."[36]

Later that month, however, NAACP fieldworker Daisy Lampkin offered a different assessment. Lampkin had toured North Carolina's major cities, informally polling the state's black teachers. She found a considerable spectrum of opinion. In High Point, where Nightengale carried influence, she found "fine interest [and] courageous teachers." In Salisbury, the teachers association voted unanimously to join the NAACP and contribute money. In Charlotte, Lampkin "got almost 100% membership from teachers," but caution nonetheless prevailed on the question of litigation. The Winston-Salem teachers were clearly "afraid to be identified with [the] N.A.A.C.P.," a sentiment that Lampkin speculated reflected their fears of repercussions from Atkins, an NCTA stalwart. In Asheville, the situation was completely "hopeless," as the principal of the local black high school pressured teachers not to join. Lampkin concluded, "If the N.A.A.C.P. decides to make this fight they must expect to do it with very little help from the teachers of the state, and with plenty of opposition." Many of North Carolina's "citizen-teachers," Lampkin suggested, had surrendered in the fight for equality.[37]

In certain respects, Lampkin spoke too soon. After the dust settled, many black educators set out quietly to build up local NAACP branches. In Asheville, where Lampkin had found little overt support for a salary suit, teacher Leila B. Michael quadrupled local NAACP membership between 1938 and 1945. Lampkin was right, however, in her prediction that many leading black educators in 1933 were simply not willing to yoke their fates to an unpredictable court fight. In December, NCTA president Oliver R. Pope, a Rocky Mount principal of Shepard's generation, sent a letter to NCTA members that never mentioned the NAACP by name but offered a thinly veiled denunciation of the organization for its paternalism. Teachers "can think for themselves," Pope asserted, and the NCTA "must not permit non-teachers to use our organization." Casting the NAACP as out of touch with the needs of black southern educators, Pope continued, "We cannot afford to dis-establish the direct channel of contact which we have at all times had with those in authority in North Carolina. If this channel is diverted from the North Carolina Negro to the New York Negro and then back to North Carolina, the wayside station in New York might not last as long as our problems." Not everyone in the NCTA agreed with Pope's assessment. He later recalled that he was "maligned by those who opposed my stand." Nonetheless, for the next decade, the NCTA stood firm in its policy of nonlitigation.[38]

"Mov[ing] Forward Like the Shadow on the Dial Plate"

The end of the NAACP's salary litigation campaign in North Carolina in some ways marked the beginning of a more politicized NCTA. Using their loyalty on the salary question as leverage, NCTA leaders demonstrated new resolve in pressing their grievances before state officials. In 1934 the group presented Governor Ehringhaus with a report that ranked teacher salaries among eight issues recommended for state action—the others included school consolidation, teacher training, a minimum eight-month term for all schools, "adequate buildings and equipment," expanded vocational training, and equal opportunities for professional schooling. In response, Ehringhaus appointed a biracial Governor's Commission on the Study of Problems in Negro Education, which consisted of a fifty-four-member advisory committee and a group of fifty consultants divided into eight subcommittees. Newbold chaired the commission, and white officials chaired the subcommittees, but half of the commission's members were black. While not challenging patterns of white management in black education, the commission did suggest that black educators might be rewarded for opposing litigation with increased representation around the state's meeting tables.[39]

In addition to keeping the direct channels of communication open with state officials, the NCTA pushed its members to "unite their forces at the polls." As Pope put it, "No teacher is quite prepared to claim the full right of citizenship who willfully ignores the opportunity to intelligently register at the polls an honest conviction of men and measures." For Pope, political mobilization offered an acceptable means of pressing common interests. "The cleavage within our ranks which was caused by the salary question is most unfortunate," he noted, "since we are all working for the same things."[40]

In suggesting that black teachers vote rather than litigate their way onto the state's agenda, the NCTA was proposing a strategy that was not yet available to many members. In Durham, for example, whites had long conceded the vote to certain handpicked members of the black middle class such as Shepard and Spaulding. In 1935, Spaulding and Shepard were founding members of the Durham Committee on Negro Affairs, a coalition that waged extensive get-out-the-vote campaigns, resulting in more than three thousand registered black voters by 1939. In more rural areas in the state, the barriers to such mobilization were formidable. One poll from the early 1930s indicated that roughly three-quarters of white public officials in North Carolina opposed black voting.[41] Ironically, the logic that Shepard often used to advocate for the ballot—that the most "intelligent" among both races should be allowed to cast votes—played into the hands of hostile white officials, who were free to interpret at will the results of voting literacy tests.[42] In 1934, when two black teachers from Iredell County heeded the NCTA's call to register at the polls, they confronted the limits of voting as a strategy for equality. T. E. Allison and Robert Dockery complied with registrar C. R. Sharpe's request to read and write sections of the state constitution, but Sharpe rejected their applications anyway, simply telling them, "You do not satisfy me." Taking their case to the state supreme court, Allison and Dockery challenged not the registrar's application of the test but the constitutionality of literacy tests themselves. The court upheld the registrar's discretion.[43] Not surprisingly, then, as late as 1962, only a little over one-third of black adults in North Carolina were registered to vote.[44]

In light of the barriers to both litigation and voting as strategies for equality, where were black educators to go for recourse? For Newbold, the answer had not changed. He insisted in 1936 that "reliable" black leaders "must go again and again to officials in charge of public schools and appeal for more money and more attention for their schools, in very much the same way white people have pleaded for their schools for a generation." What surprised many organizers for the NAACP was not that Newbold would persist in giving such advice but that some blacks seemed to take it to heart. Black North Carolinians possessed "an unusual amount of the 'leave-it-to-us-and-our-white-folks' sentiment," lamented NAACP director of branches William Pickens. Durham's *Carolina Times* similarly bemoaned the paralyzing effect of the established leaders, especially three familiar figures: "'Uncle Tom' Eppes"; Newbold, dubbed "the great white father"; and "Cap'n" Howard Odum, the white sociologist at the University of North Carolina who refused to back Pauli Murray's application. These men were "always on the scene to prevent their Negro ward from getting off the right track."[45]

When Charlotte Hawkins Brown and Rose Aggrey assumed the presidency of the NCTA in 1935 and 1939, respectively, the group might have been expected to take a more radical turn. Not only were they the group's first female presidents, but both had participated nearly two decades earlier in an NAACP-allied campaign for women's suffrage.[46] Furthermore, Brown had served on the board of directors of the early State Conference of Branches of the NAACP. Under their leadership, however, the NCTA did not chart a new strategic path. When Aggrey took office, she signaled her solidarity with the "old guard" by praising Shepard for his "tact, wisdom, energy, and planning." Aggrey and Brown likely felt a sense of solidarity with the female teachers who had formed the backbone of the NAACP's membership drive, but they shared the black establishment's generational perspective as well as its practical concerns for maintaining cordial ties with white officials. As a Jeanes supervisor, Aggrey would have communicated frequently with Newbold and local officials. As president of Palmer Memorial Institute, a private preparatory school in Sedalia, Brown theoretically occupied a position of greater independence, but she routinely had sought public funding for her school and in the mid-1930s was making an intensified bid for state incorporation. Questions of gender and generation aside, then, the state's leading black educators found reason to tread gingerly around the recognized white guardians of black education.[47]

The limits of white paternalism, however, became evident as progress toward salary equalization inched along. In 1934, Governor Ehringhaus's commission recommended that the legislature appropriate special funds to reduce teacher salary differentials by 50 percent in 1935 and to eliminate them completely within three to five years. The General Assembly failed to follow through on that plan, and black teacher salaries remained pitifully low. As one Jeanes supervisor determined, the highest-paid black teachers received a weekly salary of $10.37 at the same time that the wage codes of the New Deal's NRA had set a minimum weekly salary of $12.00.[48] Homegrown promises of salary equity appeared increasingly anemic in an era when the federal government modeled new notions of economic entitlement. Moreover, subsequent governors failed to reward the loyalty of black educators with even token gestures of representation. In 1937, the legislature authorized Governor Clyde R. Hoey to appoint another com-

Although president of the private Palmer Memorial Institute, NCTA leader Charlotte Hawkins Brown relied on state officials for endorsements and funding assistance. Governor J. Melville Broughton spoke at Palmer's 1943 graduation exercises. *Bottom row, left to right*: Brown, Broughton, and Palmer chaplain John Brice. (Courtesy of The North Carolina State Archives, Raleigh)

mission to study black education. No blacks were among its five members.[49] Durham newspaper editor Louis Austin cast doubt on whether "a commission composed entirely of white people" could "get at the bottom" of the problems facing black education. Hoey's commission further angered black leaders when it recommended that a governor-appointed committee composed primarily of representatives from white universities oversee future developments in black higher education. Even Shepard questioned "the wisdom of establishing a Commission in which representatives of the white institutions would have control of the work of any institution for Negroes in the State."[50]

Further frustrating NCTA negotiations with school officials were the state's increasing efforts to disguise its discriminatory practices. In the 1920s, the state distributed blatantly separate salary schedules that recommended for each certification level one salary for white teachers and a lower amount for "colored" teachers.[51] By 1937, Durham attorney Hugh Thompson had difficulty acquiring a copy of the state's schedule. State officials, he reported, were "afraid to release it as it is too obvious on its face." Newbold insisted that "custom and habit," rather than actual laws, encoded salary differentials. The head of the State School Commission similarly downplayed state complicity, explaining to Shepard in 1938 that the state salary schedule provided minimum and maximum salaries for each certification level and that local school officials typically paid the recommended minimum to blacks and the maximum to whites. The official laws, he insisted, did not mandate these patterns. Newbold privately admitted that the state had "rather adroitly" written its salary guidelines to mask its role in perpetuating racial differentials. Questions of state culpability aside, some localities ignored even the state's guaranteed minimum salaries. Still others purposely employed uncertified black teachers to justify low wages. When black educator Horace Mann Bond traveled through Union County in the 1930s, he found ten uncertified black teachers who were paid a mere thirty dollars per month, twenty-five dollars less than the state-required minimum. "The authorities here," Bond wrote, "obviously, were saving money for white schools by employing wretchedly trained and utterly incompetent Negro teachers."[52] Such localized patterns of dissemblance ensured that any fight to litigate salary equality would be difficult and protracted.

As black teachers in North Carolina held out for legislative redress, educators in other southern states seized opportunities for court action. Having failed to win sufficient support for a North Carolina test case, the NAACP had not thrown in the towel. In 1936, it began organizing litigation on behalf of teachers in Maryland and Virginia. Winston Douglas, president of the Virginia Teachers Association, offered powerful justification for a direct attack on salary inequalities: "We as clearly as any group see the beauty of the self-sacrificing life of service; but still more clearly we know the gnawing pains of a half filled stomach and the sting of a winter wind against the ill clad body. We know that beyond a certain limit self-sacrifice is rank idealism and merges into insanity." Citizenship, Douglas insisted, did not require abject selflessness.[53]

As the litigation movement in the Upper South took hold, NAACP leaders dismissed North Carolina as the land of missed opportunity. White urged Plummer Bernard Young, a native North Carolinian and editor of the *Norfolk Journal and Guide*, to take North Carolina's black teachers to task, noting with more than a hint of disdain, "While the North Carolina

Teachers' Association is meekly petitioning powers-that-be to do a little something about 'reducing the differential in teachers' salaries . . . ,' Virginia teachers have raised over $5,000 to pay the cost of court action to *equalize*." By 1938, Louis Austin had similarly lost patience with "gutless, spineless, Negroes, who [were] afraid of losing their jobs." To "right a great wrong," teachers needed to be "willing to sacrifice." The following year, he optimistically predicted that North Carolina's teachers would follow the lead of Virginia and Maryland in taking their grievances to court.[54]

No such lawsuit developed. In February 1939, an NCTA delegation appeared before the State School Commission and warned that "groups within the State and outside the State" were urging teachers to file salary litigation. Litigation opponents were under fire, dean James T. Taylor of the North Carolina College for Negroes explained. In fact, every black school principal in North Carolina was being "accused of being a 'white man's Negro.'" Taylor assured state officials that NCTA leaders still wished to avoid the courts. Shepard, who served as president of the NCTA from 1937 to 1939, reiterated that wish in a radio address later that year: "No Negro who covets cordial relations with his white neighbors wishes to rest his civil rights on the courts alone." These assurances notwithstanding, NCTA leaders suggested that "loyal" black leaders were quickly losing credibility in the arena of black public opinion.[55]

With litigation pending elsewhere in the region and renewed interest in the courts in North Carolina, the 1939 General Assembly appropriated $250,000 to reduce the differential between black and white teacher salaries. For the next five years, legislators allocated increasing amounts toward that goal. As late as 1940, however, the average black teacher salary still constituted approximately three-quarters of the average white salary, even though black and white teachers had nearly equal training at that point (see tables 4.2 and 4.3).[56]

In the face of this painfully incremental progress, some black teachers ignored calls for restraint and took more aggressive action. Newbold recalled that in the early 1940s, a group of "young, rather uninformed Negro teachers created a diversion" at the annual meeting of the NCTA in Greensboro. They "march[ed] up and down the aisles" of the meeting room and chanted, "We want our salaries brought up to State standards." Newbold felt certain that this outburst represented an aberration in the generally cooperative attitudes of the state's black teachers. Yet at about the same time, a quieter attempt was being made to subvert the NCTA leadership. Albert H. Anderson, principal of Kimberly Park School in Winston-Salem, wrote to NAACP special counsel Thurgood Marshall in 1941 for advice on how to "speed up the process of equalization," which the teachers of his city believed was "progressing much too slowly." Marshall rejoiced, taking heart that "at least one group of teachers in North Carolina" possessed the "courage" to take action. Anderson's group investigated the possibilities for litigation throughout the early 1940s but never filed suit.[57] At the same time, NCTA leaders were forced to admit that their approach had not produced the rapid results they wanted. "The program for equity still moves forward like the shadow on the dial plate," a 1941 editorial in the NCTA's journal noted with more than a hint of frustration. Nonetheless, the association pledged to hold steady, "ever keeping before the authorities that we are not unmindful of this unjust discrimination."[58]

"When Color and Country Are in Conflict": World War II and Winning Equalization

When the United States entered World War II in December 1941, calls for loyalty initially trumped earlier concerns for educational equalization. Many black leaders, including educators, took measures early in the war to assure whites of their allegiance. The NCTA proclaimed that "citizen-teachers" held an obligation to serve their nation and that even racial discrimination in the armed services would not "abate [their] loyalty." In a similar spirit, the association endorsed the wartime message of Gordon B. Hancock, the black president of Virginia Union College, who wished to disabuse whites of the notion that blacks might harbor sympathies for Japan since it was a "colored" nation. "When color and country are in conflict," he insisted, "I stand by country." As the war dragged on, however, black educators sought a place for racial interests on the regional and national agendas. Hancock, in fact, turned his concern for country more directly toward matters of color in 1942 by inviting seventy-five black professionals to the Southern Conference on Race Relations at Shepard's North Carolina College for Negroes. The conference originated as the brainchild of Jessie Daniel Ames, a white leader in the Commission on Interracial Cooperation, who saw the need for a "sane approach" to race relations. Although the attendees were "fundamentally opposed to the principle and practice of compulsory segregation," they conceded that pragmatism precluded immediate challenges to the existing racial system. Overall, they urged a policy of racial equality, not racial integration. They recommended "considerably more" state funds to equalize education at all levels. They left alone the explosive question of desegregated classrooms, although they did call for black representation on school boards. White liberals and black moderates uniformly endorsed this Durham Manifesto. More militant blacks charged that the statement would do little to jolt southern whites into action.[59]

The critics of the Durham Manifesto were half right. Moderate black leaders were not making radical demands of the white South, but they were employing the wartime rhetoric of freedom and democracy to push for equality while attempting to preserve some measure of local control. James W. Seabrook, president of the Fayetteville State Teachers College and president of the NCTA from 1941 to 1943, expressed his hope to the State School Commission in 1942 that salary differentials would be completely eliminated within two to three years. Seabrook reminded white officials that "the overwhelming majority of the Negro teachers . . . address[ed] their arguments to the consciences of those in authority rather than to the courts." Any gestures toward salary equity, Seabrook added, would "give the Negro confidence that the principles of democracy for which he is being called upon to fight in the four corners of the earth will be applied to him here at home."[60] In early 1943, a committee of black educators representing the NCTA and the North Carolina Negro College Conference addressed the Joint Appropriations Committee of the General Assembly and reiterated Seabrook's plea. Again reminding legislators of the loyalty and "goodwill" of black North Carolinians, this delegation noted that the war had spurred economic growth and a new democratic spirit, both of which warranted salary equalization. Some whites were ready to accept equal salaries for black professionals. Charlotte's leading white newspaper judged that black educators had made "a fair and reasonable request" and represented a "sane and conservative view," noting with approval that the NCTA had not followed the lead of teachers in other states who were taking their grievances to court.[61]

The NCTA's "sane and conservative" approach was winning white accolades, but it had never won universal black support. In 1943, the Charlotte branch of the NAACP considered organizing a "test case" for teacher salary equalization, but NCTA leaders thwarted these efforts in favor of fighting for equal salaries "southern style." Teachers in Winston-Salem also questioned southern codes of behavior that required blacks to put their faith in the promises of white goodwill. They complained that even as the state had narrowed the gap between its black and white salaries, certain local officials continued to distribute salary supplements from local funds on an unequal basis. This practice prompted Albert Anderson, the principal who had contacted the NAACP's Marshall in 1941, to revisit the possibility of a lawsuit in 1943. Anderson and his colleagues hired local lawyer

Hosea V. Price to inform the chair of the school board of their intention to launch a suit if the board did not at least take steps to narrow the differentials in supplements.[62]

Winston-Salem's black teachers did not have to look far to find new models for labor reform. In June 1943, black workers at the city's R. J. Reynolds Tobacco Company walked out to protest low wages, poor working conditions, and their lack of union representation. In teaming up with union and Communist Party organizers, the striking workers spurned the pleas of Winston-Salem's black establishment, who warned that labor agitation would cause irreparable harm to local race relations. Deadly race riots in Detroit that same month no doubt heightened fears of racial revolt. Echoing the wartime anxieties of two decades earlier, Governor J. M. Broughton warned the state's citizens in July that "listening to outside agitators" would never bring racial progress. In a bold rejection of these outworn admonitions, Winston-Salem's black tobacco workers dared to join forces with the national labor movement. Using the leverage of the National Labor Relations Board, they formed Local 22 of the Congress of Industrial Organizations–affiliated Food, Tobacco, Agricultural, and Allied Workers of America. Even though Local 22 eventually fell victim to company repression and postwar anticommunism, its members dramatically strengthened their bargaining power at the plant during the mid-1940s. At least for the moment, the empty promises of white paternalism no longer measured up to the tangible rewards of collective action.[63]

For all of its limitations, the NCTA's "southern style" approach received tacit vindication in 1944 when the General Assembly allotted the remaining funds necessary to raise black teacher salaries to the same level as white salaries. That appropriation set the precedent for a single standard for teacher salaries based solely on training and years of experience. Ironically, members of the NAACP's inner circle had earlier judged the NCTA president who led the final negotiations with state officials for this achievement, Greensboro principal John Tarpley, as a certain ally in the pursuit of litigation: "With Tarpley's sagacity we will rout that conservative, yes, reactionary state Negro teachers association," predicted Streator in 1933. In one sense, Streator's forecast came true. By the time Tarpley took the reins of the NCTA, it was openly encouraging black teachers to "secure membership" in the NAACP. In bringing the saga of salary inequality to a close, however, Tarpley had seen the strategic value of fully exploiting his ties with white officials rather than resorting to litigation.[64]

In the final analysis, it is not immediately clear whether the NCTA's approach or that of the NAACP proved more effective in bringing salary parity to black teachers. By the end of World War II, neither strategy had translated into a total regional victory, as southern black teachers on average still earned only 65 percent of what white teachers did. In the states where the NAACP had organized salary litigation, the results were mixed. In Maryland, where teacher-tenure laws hampered retaliatory firings of litigants, the state legislature equalized salaries by 1941. In Virginia, a federal court in 1940 found the city of Norfolk's salary scale in violation of the Fourteenth Amendment, but litigant Aline Black lost her job in the process, and the court ruling was not binding in other districts. Moreover, when city officials pledged to appeal the court's ruling, local leaders opted to compromise with white officials for a gradual three-year equalization process rather than pursue the immediate victory for which the NAACP had hoped. One of the lead negotiators of that deal was P. B. Young, the Norfolk editor whom Marshall had urged in 1939 to shame North Carolina's teachers for their conciliatory tendencies. In Tampa, Florida, a two-year court battle resulted in not only the plaintiff's job loss but also a court ruling that upheld a cleverly disguised but nonetheless discriminatory salary scale. Equalization was achieved there by the mid-1940s, but only after white teachers found their own reasons to fight for a salary scale based on training and experience. Perhaps most ominous was the outcome of litigation in South Carolina. As an act of retribution for teacher lawsuits, state officials tied salary levels to scores on the National Teachers Examination, a move that kept many black teachers at low pay and by extension made teachers more cautious about giving the NAACP public support during the civil rights years.[65]

In at least temporarily escaping some of these retaliatory measures, North Carolina's teachers arguably came out ahead. No teachers lost their jobs, and equalization was achieved at about the same moment as in places where litigation was used. The dividends of the NCTA's approach, however, are not easily separable from those of the NAACP. In many ways, the NCTA enjoyed the benefits of litigation while escaping its liabilities. North Carolina officials likely would not have eliminated the state's differential had it not felt pressure from lawsuits in other states.[66]

Moreover, North Carolina's victory was neither complete nor without ambivalent legacies. Even though the state after 1944 distributed its teacher salary funds without regard to race, concerns about discrimination persisted in those districts that gave local salary supplements, a practice that was most common in wealthier urban districts. State superintendent Clyde Erwin maintained in 1946 that local supplements "amount[ed] to very little in the total picture" and affected overall salary levels to an "almost negligible degree," although a state report from about the same time identified local supplements as one of seven "areas in public education in which differentials still exist." The NCTA apparently regarded unequal supplements concerning enough to retain the services of Raleigh attorney Herman Taylor in 1948 to explore the possibilities of a "friendly suit." That suit never materialized, although concerns about localized salary discrimination persisted.[67] Furthermore, the new state salary schedule for public school teachers did nothing to equalize the salaries of other state employees. The presidents of black state-supported colleges, for example, received lower salaries than their white counterparts, regardless of the size of their schools.[68]

Moreover, the state in coming years would frequently tout teacher salary equalization as evidence of its commitment to fairness. As Erwin put it in 1948, the state held up salary equalization as "the most spectacular" victory in its larger program for closing racial gaps in education. Salary equalization, therefore, obscured the egregious inequalities in other areas of the state's public school system. The *Raleigh News and Observer* suggested in 1946 that in giving "special emphasis" to its achievement of teacher salary equalization, the state was deflecting attention from the wretched conditions under which many black children attended school. The state's self-congratulations struck a particularly hollow note in the post-*Brown* years, when North Carolina adopted some of the same punitive measures used in salary battles in other states—including the National Teachers Examination—as tools for reducing the state's black teaching force.[69]

Despite its limitations, the NCTA's achievement of salary equalization forced the state to recognize the value of black teachers more fully than it had in decades. Ironically, after the state equalized salaries, black teachers were shown to be worth more than white teachers. As late as 1940, the training of white teachers surpassed that of black teachers, but by the 1944–45 school year, black teachers averaged slightly more training than did white teachers.[70] Moreover, excluded from many professional careers, highly educated African Americans gravitated toward the teaching profession and carved out lifelong careers there. Salary standardization—based on training and years of experience—therefore promised black teachers larger salaries than those awarded to whites. Indeed, black teachers were the state's most highly paid educators throughout the late 1940s and 1950s (see tables 4.2 and 4.3). Salary equalization also provided formal recognition of what many African Americans already knew: In schools that often lacked basic material resources, the teachers modeled the ideals of equality.

Peerless by official state standards, North Carolina's black teaching force continued to hold compromised political credentials in the eyes of local and national civil rights leaders. At least some of that scorn was misplaced. The NCTA leadership did not always reflect the broader attitudes of the organization's rank-and-file members. Moreover, even the NCTA's leaders consistently urged on black teachers a spirit of entitlement and enfranchisement, ideas that mirrored the NAACP's philosophies. The NCTA encouraged its members to regard themselves as "citizens first, teachers afterwards," a charge that suggested that their vision for empowerment extended beyond narrow questions of professional status. NCTA leaders chose negotiation and political empowerment over litigation not as an act of surrender but as an effort to preserve opportunities for local leadership. The NCTA also had demonstrated its commitment to a larger project for equality by serving as early advocates for a more ambitious campaign for school equalization. As that battle extended into the post–World War II years, however, ordinary students and parents eventually assumed the mantle of leadership. They insisted that a battle for first-class citizenship demanded new strategies of public protest and litigation.

There were a lot of people—black people—that said we shouldn't
have done that, but what [are] you going to do?
—Lillian Bullock McQueen, on the Lumberton NAACP Youth Council's
1946 school boycott

The Negroes here are at a point where they are ready to be led out of slavery.
—Attorney Herman Taylor, on filing a school equalization lawsuit in Lumberton, 1947

Shall we now dilly-dally, neglect to do what we ought and can do,
thus forcing Negroes in and outside North Carolina to go into the courts to equalize?
—Nathan Newbold, director of the Division of Negro Education, 1947

CHAPTER FIVE

How Can I Learn When I'm Cold?

A New Generation's Fight for School Facilities Equalization

"I wish every Southern state had done as well as North Carolina with Negro education," remarked *Richmond Times-Dispatch* editor Virginius Dabney. "We would be much farther along the path to something like reasonable equality of opportunity, if the whole South had followed North Carolina's example." *Life* magazine similarly suggested in 1944 that in North Carolina it was possible to glimpse the beginnings of "'parallel civilizations'— complete equality of opportunity for Negro and white, but complete segregation, too." If Jim Crow could work anywhere, so the argument went, it would work in North Carolina. It was true that in the first half of the twentieth century, the racial spending gap in education was generally smaller in North Carolina than in the states of the Deep South. After the war, however, the state would have increasing difficulty holding onto its claim of regional progressivism as black North Carolinians exposed substantial and enduring inequalities in the state's public schools.[1]

More than North Carolina's regional reputation was at stake. During the Cold War, questions of school equality factored into a national and even international discourse about America's claims to global democratic leadership. One American diplomat noted in 1952 after traveling in South Asia that the local people asked him one question more than any other: "Do negroes have equal opportunities for education in the U.S.?"[2] In com-

promising the nation's diplomatic credibility, the South's educational inequities mattered on a much larger stage than ever before.

By the postwar years, state officials expressed new urgency in addressing educational inequality, but they were unprepared for how quickly and
boldly African Americans forced the issue. Even more unexpected was the
fact that this new call to action first came not from the state's recognized
black leaders and educators but from the black youth of Lumberton, who
organized a school strike in the fall of 1946. The Lumberton protest served
as the opening salvo in nearly a decade of black-led school equalization
activity in North Carolina, mostly in the form of petitions and lawsuits.
Other black school boycotts occurred between 1943 and 1953, but most
unfolded in northern and border states. The marches led by Lumberton
students in 1946 were, according to Elliott Rudwick and August Meier, "an
unprecedented tactic for school protests . . . in a small southern town."[3]

Compared to the history of desegregation, this phase of educational
history has received relatively little attention.[4] If viewed from the vantage
point of the national office of the National Association for the Advancement of Colored People (NAACP), which by the late 1940s was shifting
focus from litigation for primary and secondary school equalization to
integration, this story entails a doomed strategy for softening the injustices of Jim Crow, a strategy that whites eventually co-opted as a means
of forestalling integration. Yet without the hindsight of *Brown*, school
equalization efforts appear less like a historical detour than a remarkable achievement in the black freedom struggle. Through the blending
of direct-action protest, litigation, and older forms of patron-client negotiation, black citizens stimulated educational improvements that by the
1960s had in many communities improved—if not equalized—the conditions under which Jim Crow's last generation attended school.

This period also served as a critical dress rehearsal for the activism of
the late 1950s and 1960s, deepening the ties between black southerners
and outside civil rights organizations. Historians have disagreed over the
nature of those ties and the extent to which the national NAACP reflected
rather than directed grassroots concerns. Black communities drew selectively from the national NAACP's program. They looked to the NAACP as a
galvanizing force whose larger goals of political empowerment and citizenship rights offered a critical blueprint for action even if they did not
always mesh perfectly with the parent organization's directives. As historian Peter Lau has aptly put it, the national organization and local branches
acted in "dynamic tension" with each other.[5] Perhaps the NAACP's most

significant contribution to the grassroots equalization movement was its insistence on a new way of interacting with white power brokers. Through voting campaigns, youth council organization, and legal activism, the NAACP legitimized the use of the ballot, direct-action protest, and litigation as necessary alternatives to the patient negotiations of the past. Even when black citizens did not deploy these strategies to the exact ends sanctioned by the national NAACP, they forged new paths for activism that would become hallmarks of the civil rights revolution of the 1960s.

These new protest strategies both fueled and reflected a broader generational shift among educational activists. James Shepard's death in 1947 and Nathan Newbold's retirement in 1950 symbolically heralded a decline in the patron-client style of negotiation that had marked their generation of leaders. By the early 1950s, even the North Carolina Teachers Association (NCTA), once known for its caution and conservatism, lent support to a wave of educational litigation across the state. As it forced the state to reckon with the costs of upholding school segregation, a new guard of leaders was liberating black school politics from the uncertain promises of white paternalism.

The struggle for primary and secondary school equalization presented a far more amorphous problem than the fight for higher education equalization, where entire degree programs were conspicuously absent from the black colleges, and the fight for teacher salary equality, where white salary scales at least offered a clear benchmark for equality. By the mid-1940s, black and white teachers basically earned the same pay, held the same level of training, and taught from the same curriculum guidelines. Many points of inequality remained, but some were more easily observed and measured than others. Those that entailed what twenty-first-century educators would label "student outcomes"—for example, high school graduation rates or achievement test scores—involved clear racial differentials but complex remedies. Much of the fight for school equality therefore focused on material markers of equality: building conditions, school bus availability, and access to current books and equipment. If these factors were not necessarily the ultimate markers of educational equality, they nonetheless played an important role in creating an environment that was conducive to learning. Moreover, they served as powerful symbolic markers of the intended roles that schools were to play. How were students who walked long distances to second-class school buildings to believe that they were being trained for anything but second-class citizenship?

White rural schools obtained buses more quickly than black schools, thereby facilitating school consolidation. Here, children board a school bus in the 1950s in Grimesland in Pitt County. (Courtesy of *Daily Reflector* Negative Collection [#741], East Carolina Manuscript Collection, J. Y. Joyner Library, East Carolina University, Greenville, N.C.)

Taking Stock of School Conditions in the 1940s

Scorned by many whites in the 1960s and 1970s as an unwelcome tool of desegregation, busing once had been a marker of white privilege in the South. Buses had facilitated the consolidation of white one-room schools into larger and more efficient structures. Indeed, the state ballyhooed the school "auto-truck" as the vehicle that would transport schoolchildren into the modern age. In 1936–37, the state provided more than 4,000 buses to transport rural children to school, yet only 361 of those buses carried black children. One superintendent explained that officials in his county "absolutely balk[ed]" at buying buses for black schools. As late as 1945, only 18 percent of the state's buses transported black youth, even though blacks comprised approximately 30 percent of the school-age population.[6]

Inadequate transportation delayed the consolidation of black schools. Newbold argued in 1939 that "the most important" issue in black education remained the small, rural schools, "dozens and even hundreds" of which were "pathetically deficient." Throughout much of the 1930s and 1940s, the number of black schoolhouses was roughly comparable to the

Table 5.1. Number of Schoolhouses in North Carolina, by Race, 1919–1964

Year	White	Black	Total	Black Percentage of Total
1919–20	5,552	2,442	7,994	30.5
1924–25	4,655	2,431	7,086	34.3
1929–30	3,460	2,365	5,825	40.6
1934–35	2,511	2,267	4,778	47.4
1939–40	2,123	2,084	4,207	49.5
1944–45	1,978	1,918	3,896	49.2
1949–50	1,919	1,640	3,559	46.1
1954–55	1,989	1,201	3,190	37.6
1959–60	2,206	996	3,202	31.1
1963–64	2,216	961	3,177	30.2

Source: *Biennial Report*, 1962–63/1963–64, pt. 1, 36.

number of white schools, despite the fact that the black youth constituted only about 30 percent of the school population (table 5.1). This illogical distribution stemmed from the fact that white schools consolidated much more quickly, and a large number of unaccredited one-teacher black schools continued to operate in the 1940s. In 1945, the state had only 38 accredited black elementary schools, compared to 679 for whites; more than 600 one-teacher black elementary schools remained in existence, compared to only 192 for whites. In 1941, state supervisor of Negro elementary schools Marie McIver reported feeling "haunt[ed]" by "the faces of thousands" of children who attended school under wretched conditions. McIver's colleague, William Credle, similarly found many black schools that were "small, poorly built, dilapidated, unfurnished, unsanitary, and in most every way inadequate to serve modern children in an enlightened, progressive commonwealth." Some even posed "a menace to health" and endangered "life and limb."[7]

Black high school availability had markedly improved since the 1920s but still came up short. From 1923 to 1944, the number of state-accredited black high schools had increased from 11 to 186. Even so, as late as 1943, sixteen administrative units had no black high school. The mountain counties, with their small and scattered black populations, rarely had black high schools within easy reach. One survey of Surry and Yadkin Counties found more than one hundred black youth who had finished the seventh grade but had no place to go for further education. Since many rural counties at best had one black high school, buses proved pivotal to secondary education. One Jeanes teacher explained in 1938 that the lack of buses

Table 5.2. Appraised Value of School Property per Pupil Enrolled, by Race, 1919–1964

Year	White Schools	Black Schools	Ratio of White to Black Values
1919–20	$45.32	$11.20	4.0
1924–25	113.40	29.03	3.9
1929–30	162.92	44.20	3.7
1934–35	152.99	44.55	3.4
1939–40	167.36	55.93	3.0
1944–45	203.80	73.08	2.8
1949–50	314.29	127.38	2.5
1954–55	539.70	336.65	1.6
1959–60	709.54	487.10	1.5
1963–64	826.24	565.55	1.5

Source: *Biennial Report*, 1962–63/1963–64, pt. 1, 37.

Note: School property values include the estimated value of school sites, buildings, furniture, equipment, and library books.

prevented most black youth in her county from advancing to high school and that "some poor little conscientious children" were walking four or more miles to school. Inadequate high school availability contributed to low graduation rates. In 1944–45, only 18 percent of the state's high school graduates were black.[8]

Whether in urban high schools or rural elementary schools, black pupils typically attended classes in second-rate buildings furnished with inadequate equipment and supplies. At the end of World War II, the per pupil school property value for each white student was still almost three times the value for each black student (table 5.2). School libraries offered just one example of unequal resources. In 1944–45, black schools held only 16 percent of the state's public school library books.[9] Aside from instructional materials, black schools frequently struggled to obtain even more basic resources. A parent from rural Northampton County reported in 1946 that the local black elementary school had received only one of four shipments of wood that it was due that winter and that the school would possibly close "on account of lack of fuel for warmth." A 1946 memo from the Department of Negro Education (DNE) found that "many of the smaller [black] high schools have very definite shortages in the areas of Science Equipment, Supplies and Instruction, Library and Sanitary Toilet Facilities." On this last matter, the situation was a "disgrace," as "most of the smaller high schools still ha[d] the inadequate, insanitary, out-door surface toilets." Newbold received a detailed report of such disgraceful conditions from the "grade mothers" of the Franklin County Training School. Their children attended school in a frame building that had been condemned nearly a decade earlier. On overcast days, the lack of sunlight kept classrooms nearly in the dark. On rainy days, the roof leaked and the outdoor toilets collected several inches of standing water. On cold days, the antiquated heating system caked the walls with black soot. The only drinking water came from a rusty outdoor pump. The structure of the building was so poor that one teacher had fallen through the floorboards and was "severely injured." Demanding better conditions could be a risky proposition. When a teacher in Gaston County requested improved supplies, local officials fired her, claiming that she "needed too much for a 'Nigger' School."[10]

White neglect of black schools had a contradictory quality. White officials routinely argued that black children possessed low potential but refused to offer the extra resources that "slow" children needed. Noting this inconsistency, James Shepard asked, "Is the assumption that Negro children are so much more capable of learning than whites that with one-fourth of the facilities and often shorter school terms they can achieve the same goal?" Since the late 1920s, social scientists had been refuting the idea of innate racial intelligence differences and emphasizing the importance of environment as a determinative factor for academic success. In 1929, Clark Foreman, a doctoral candidate at Columbia University who went on to serve as Franklin Roosevelt's special adviser on the economic status of Negroes, gave scholastic achievement tests to more than ten thousand black third- and sixth-graders in a sampling of sixteen counties across the South, including four in North Carolina. Foreman's research revealed two main findings: First, urban children generally scored higher than rural ones. Second, Foreman attributed the urban-rural difference to the superior school facilities found in cities. School environment—measured by Foreman in terms of instructional supervision, length of terms, availability of textbooks, training of teachers, and adequacy of schoolhouses—mattered. He concluded, "As the environment of the Negro pupils approaches that of the white children from whom the norms of achievement were derived, the achievement of the Negro pupils approaches the norm." State measurements indicated that race-based achievement differentials increased with each grade level, reinforcing Foreman's theory that blacks and whites began school with similar potential but diverged in achievement when taught in unequal environments. One report from the late 1940s indicated that by the ninth grade, North Carolina's black students were two grade levels behind their white peers in achievement levels. As one black educator concluded in 1949, the state was "los[ing] potential contributions from a sizable fraction of its citizenry in the way of undeveloped human resources."[11]

When the United States entered World War II, a renewed emphasis on sacrifice and retrenchment threatened to overshadow the needs of the South's "undeveloped human resources." North Carolina Congress of Colored Parents and Teachers president Ada Jarnagin reminded members in 1941, "Today our country is calling in loud terms for self sacrifice and service." Black communities answered that call by hosting war bond rallies, purchasing thousands of dollars in war stamps and bonds, planting Victory Gardens, and collecting Red Cross donations. These wartime sacrifices sometimes directly interfered with the cause of school improvement. One county reported that "$1,000 previously raised for [school] consolidation ha[d] been invested in United States War Bonds for the duration."[12]

Ultimately, however, the social ferment of the war years facilitated an invigorated national dialogue about race that fueled the fires of a postwar school equalization movement. In 1944, two widely publicized indictments of Jim Crow drew national attention. Funded by the New York–based Carnegie Foundation and directed by Swedish economist Gunnar Myrdal, *An American Dilemma: The Negro Problem and Modern Democracy* compiled an enormous wealth of research conducted by leading black and white social scientists. It laid nearly all the blame for the race problem at the feet of whites, who had failed to extend the principles of the "American creed"— equal opportunity, freedom, and democracy—to racial minorities. Among the inequalities cataloged by this massive tome, black southern schools figured prominently as tragic evidence of white hypocrisy. That same year, the University of North Carolina Press published an even bolder critique of southern society. *What the Negro Wants*, a collection of fourteen essays edited by Howard University historian Rayford Logan and written by a broad spectrum of black leaders, underscored black impatience with the existing racial order. Most shocking to whites, all of the authors called for an end to segregation. There could be no true equality, they suggested, as long as the color line remained in place.[13]

Newbold was keenly aware of these voices of dissent. He had helped lead Myrdal on a tour of Durham and Chapel Hill, and he reviewed an early copy of *What the Negro Wants* for UNC Press editor William Terry Couch. He initially approved Logan's book, believing it would serve a "useful purpose." After discussing with Couch the book's potential for controversy, however, Newbold suggested that the authors might adopt a more cooperative tone and excise references to such explosive topics as interracial marriage. When the authors refused to back down, Couch countered by penning an introduction to the book that defensively presented the white South's desire for gradual reform. Newbold approved of Couch's introduction since both men were searching for a way to the put the brakes on change. Newbold found himself yearning for a "revival of the philosophy of Booker Washington." He desired "not to keep the Negro down or embarrass him, but to have a realistic situation in which Negroes would understand the common everyday facts that they face here, and work ever upward and onward."[14]

For Newbold and other white officials, school equalization took on new urgency as the means of preserving segregation. "It is not too late, even now, to begin to equalize opportunities and services and to keep on doing so until a reasonable equality has been achieved," he argued in 1943. Newbold predicted that "if a break comes in the matter of segregation," it would be because whites had "failed to live up to the laws they have made." The prospect of that "break" had inspired some white officials to acknowledge more directly than before *Plessy*'s requirement of equality. Newbold noted that legislators had previously shied away from using the word "equalize"; by 1944, however, even the governor "state[ed] very frankly that educational opportunities between the races must be equalized."[15]

Lip service was one thing, of course; funding was quite another. As early as 1929, when philanthropic funds were dwindling, Newbold wrote, "It seems we *ought* and *must* find a way by which *Uncle Sam* can help the South by *leveling up* as it were educational opportunities for its Negroes." When Franklin Roosevelt took office in 1933 and expanded the reach of the federal government, the prospects for such intervention seemed brighter. Nonetheless, New Deal funds for school construction passed through the hands of local officials, many of whom channeled the money exclusively to white schools. In the mid-1930s, Newbold estimated that the state would receive more than twenty million dollars for Public Works Administration school projects, but local officials wanted to "spend practically all the money available for white schools, leaving only small amounts here and there for Negro schools."[16]

The relative scarcity of private and—until the 1960s—federal funds meant that school equalization would largely be a matter of state and local responsibility. Prior to 1933, the majority of education funds in North Carolina came from local property taxes. For three decades, the state had provided supplements from an "equalizing fund" to localities with smaller than average tax bases, but local appropriations far outstripped state expenditures. After the stock market crash in 1929, property values plummeted, leaving most districts in need of state aid. Legislators voted in 1933 for the state to assume the operating expenses—teacher salaries, transportation operating costs, staff and teaching supplies—required for an eight-month term. Beginning in 1943, the state extended that obligation to a nine-month term. Local administrative units, however, were responsible for financing, either through taxes or state loans, all capital outlays for new buildings, new buses, and extras such as school lunches and vocational teachers. Local boards of education supervised these units. While only county boards of commissioners could levy local taxes, the boards of education could recommend new taxes. Moreover, these boards had the power to appoint superintendents, dictate where and when to build new schools, divide state funds among the schools, and appoint for each district a school committee that would make personnel recommendations and oversee the care of school property. In most cases, whites controlled this chain of command, although some districts had both a white school committee and "an advisory Negro committee." Durham's *Carolina Times* explained the consequences of black exclusion from policymaking: "So long as Negroes have no representation on important boards they will always be given the crumbs in education and other public benefits."[17]

That grim prediction was half right, but in 1946 the young people of Lumberton, without the benefit of representation "on important boards," found alternative ways of grabbing powerful officials' attention. Their struggle unveiled to the state and nation just what the "crumbs in education" looked like in one southern town.

"How Can I Learn When I'm Cold?": Lumberton's 1946 School Protest

"How can I learn when I'm cold?" "It Rains on Me." "Down with our School." "I Stay Cold All Day." "We Want a School." On the morning of October 1, 1946, African American students bearing placards with those pointed messages paraded down Lumberton's streets to protest conditions at Redstone Academy and Thompson Institute, the city's two black public schools. Earlier that day, the NAACP Youth Council had sponsored a meeting of approximately three hundred students from those schools. In consultation with a handful of black adults, including Youth Council adviser Gus Bullock and local dentist Clarence Smith, the students discussed their grievances and planned their course of action. At the parade's end,

Youth Council stalwart and Redstone graduate Lillian Bullock McQueen explained the reasons behind the protest on a local radio station. "It wasn't anything about the teachers," she later recalled, but rather the "dangerous" and uncomfortable conditions in which they taught. In a statement to the press, Smith charged that the schools in question were "not worthy for human beings" and that the quality of academic work had suffered. Bullock further explained that he had sent the Robeson County commissioners and Governor R. Gregg Cherry a letter detailing the students' frustrations. He warned that a school strike would develop within ten days unless the county commissioners initiated "a program of improvements at the two Negro school units here." Having fully used the available media to broadcast their frustrations, the protesting students ventured over to the local movie theater to watch the current feature, *Jesse James*. Rebels in their own right, Lumberton's youth now waited for an official response.[18]

By the following week, Cherry simply had thanked Bullock for his letter, and the county commissioners remained silent. Making good on the earlier promise of a strike, the NAACP Youth Council voted to boycott the schools until officials acted. On 7 October, four hundred students left class and marched out en masse, carrying posters that bore messages of a battle for equality: "D-Day" and "V for Victory." Then, in collective defiance of school attendance requirements, the students again "poured into" a local movie theater. For the next nine days, a critical mass of students, especially from Thompson Institute, continued the strike, drawing considerable attention from state officials and the press. While Redstone School remained open, Thompson temporarily closed as a consequence of low attendance. Finally, on 16 October, Bullock announced that county commissioners had promised "immediate improvements" to the existing schools as well as new buildings "as soon as conditions would permit." With that pledge of redress, students returned to class the following day.[19]

The roots of the Lumberton school protest predated the lifetimes of the youth who led it. The social landscape of Robeson County was marked by deep-seated and racially inflected patterns of poverty and government neglect. Home to the state's largest Native American population, the county practiced triracial segregation. In 1930 just under half of the county's citizens were white, one-third were black, and another fifth were Lumbee Indians. (The county also had a fourth, much smaller, group of contested ancestry, known locally as the "Smilings" or "Independent Indians," who attended a separate county-operated school until the 1960s.) White privilege subordinated both Indians and African Americans, although the latter generally held the lowest political and economic status. At the time of black disfranchisement in the early 1900s, the Democratic Party had protected Indian voting rights in exchange for Indian support. Moreover, in 1930, nearly all of the county's black farm families lived as tenants, whereas only 68.5 percent of Indian farm families and 53.1 percent of white farm families were tenants. White per capita wealth amounted to $675.34, compared to $107.87 for Indians and $63.15 for blacks. Robeson County's nonwhite majority generally had not banded together in collective action against white privilege. The cultural dividing lines between blacks and Indians were tinged with nearly as much wariness and suspicion as those that separated whites and blacks. The crazy quilt of race and ethnicity in Robeson County had not opened new possibilities for shared political power but instead had stratified society into first-, second-, and third-class citizens.[20]

The county's schools reflected local social and political hierarchies. Historian Malinda Maynor Lowery has pointed out that African Americans and Indians alike were shortchanged by a school system grounded in notions of white privilege. In the 1930s, for example, the county's highest rates of illiteracy were found among Indians. In terms of facilities, black schools tended to rank slightly below Lumbee schools, which in part may have reflected the fact that blacks had borne the chief effects of disfranchisement. A 1940 study found that 91 percent of Robeson County's white school buildings were in "very good" or "good" condition, while only 62 percent of Indian schools and 54 percent of black schools held that status. Moreover, nine black schools received the study's lowest ranking, "poor," while none of the white or Indian schools did so. The Lumberton city school district, which had no Indian schools and a slim majority of white students (57 percent in the early 1950s), juxtaposed some of the county's most elite white schools and most dilapidated black schools. Government funds had tended either to bypass black schools or to come tethered to self-help programs. Robeson County, for example, was home to fifteen Rosenwald Schools, but black school conditions had stagnated in the city district of Lumberton, the scene of the 1946 strike. Its only two black facilities, Redstone Academy and Thompson Institute, operated as private institutions until the 1930s, when officials converted them to public schools. Even then, the city chose to rent the existing turn-of-the-century buildings rather than build new ones. By contrast, Lumberton had long provided white facilities, including an impressive new high school built in 1924.[21]

By the 1940s, conditions at both Redstone and Thompson had deteriorated dramatically. At Redstone, exposed electrical wiring and frame construction made the school a "firetrap." Though it served both elementary and high school students, Redstone had no cafeteria or gymnasium and very meager vocational facilities. Its home economics room had no running water, and its chief appliance consisted of a "wood cook stove." Rotting boards made adequate heating almost impossible. "One can stand inside the Red Stone school building," one investigator noted, "and see outside without making use of the windows." Thompson was of brick construction but by some accounts was in even worse condition than Redstone. It had no running water, and school authorities only recently had begun to "electrify" the building.[22]

Redstone and Thompson alumni recollections blend memories of those wretched conditions with stories of faculty dedication and student achievement. Elizabeth Kemp, who graduated from Redstone in 1940 and returned to teach there in 1945, recalled the woefully inadequate lighting and heating as well as the meager instructional equipment. Yet she also remembered with pride the students and teachers who were determined to succeed despite the odds stacked against them. "We had two doctors that finished over there," she noted. "We had lots of ministers, lots of schoolteachers . . . from that very ragged school with the potbellied stoves." Lillian Bullock McQueen, who attended the elementary grades at Thompson and graduated from high school at Redstone in 1943, similarly recounted the physical shortcomings of both schools, including dangerously "rickety" staircases, but the faculty stood out as a bright spot against this dreary backdrop of racial privation. "We had the best of teachers," McQueen insisted. "They were very concerned about you learning."[23]

As McQueen's memories suggest, Redstone Academy and Thompson Institute stood as symbols of both white neglect and black resourcefulness. Each school, in fact, owed its existence to an earlier generation's commitment to education through black self-help. The Lumber River Baptist Association, a local black group, had founded Thompson Institute in 1881. Named for Alexander Hill Thompson, a former slave and a Baptist minister, the school received some funding from the white American Baptist Home Mission Society. Nonetheless, as one observer put it, the school was in large part a "monument to the thrift and energy of the Negro Baptists of North Carolina." William H. Knuckles, a native of Warren County and graduate of Shaw University, served as principal from 1912 to 1942 and expanded Thompson Institute into a five-building campus that functioned as an elementary and high school and normal institution.[24]

Redstone Academy had similar roots in mission societies and black self-help initiatives. Established in 1904 with aid from the Board of Missions for Freedmen of the Presbyterian Church of the USA, the school owed much of its success to the leadership of John Henry Hayswood, who served as principal from its founding until 1949. A native of Louisburg, Hayswood was educated at St. Augustine's College in Raleigh and Lincoln University in Pennsylvania. He came to Lumberton in 1903 to serve several black Presbyterian churches in the area and saw Redstone through its difficult, formative years. When the school lost its buildings in a 1915 fire, Hayswood rebuilt in part by cultivating white goodwill. The local white newspaper, the *Robesonian*, deemed the school "a worthy cause," as it aimed to teach "useful things . . . how to clean a room properly, how to cook and make baskets, and put bottoms in chairs." After his first wife died, Hayswood's marriage in 1933 to Robeson Jeanes supervisor Ethel Thompson further solidified his good standing in the white community. Working out of the superintendent's office above the county courthouse, Ethel Hayswood kept the financial books for the white, black, and Indian schools in addition to her supervisory duties. She also was routinely invited to white weddings at a time when such interracial social invitations were rare. Kemp, who lived with the Hayswoods as a young girl, recalled that they "were one of the most respected black families in this area."[25] In protesting conditions at Redstone and Thompson schools, black students would have to walk a fine line between critiquing racial injustice and insulting their elders' long legacies of hard work and sacrifice.

Well in advance of the 1946 school strike, black parents had voiced frustration to the local board of education. The board's minutes from March 1937 documented that "a delegation from the colored schoolmasters' club presented a general request for better buildings, instructional equipment, and school transportation." The following month, three citizens requested "a modern building for the Lumberton colored children." Principal Hayswood visited the board that summer and won approval for a bus to transport his students, and in 1944 the school board pledged "all possible cooperation" with Governor J. Melville Broughton's commission on school equalization. Two years later, the board proposed a "new school building for Negro children in or near Lumberton." Nevertheless, the black school situation remained unchanged in the fall of 1946. Lumberton's negligence had alarmed state officials as early as 1940, when William F. Credle, the state director of schoolhouse planning, recommended that officials secure Works Progress Administration funds to rebuild two rundown white schools as well as Redstone and Thompson. The county followed through with regard to the white schools but left the black schools untouched. One year later, after visiting one of Lumberton's black schools,

Newbold judged it to be "the poorest and most unsatisfactory building for school children that I know in the entire State."[26]

As discontent with school conditions grew, black citizens formed Robeson County's first chapter of the NAACP in 1944. Brick mason and farmer Vasta James Thompson requested an application for organization in February, and by the following month, more than one hundred citizens had signed on as members. Thompson had little formal schooling, according to his son, Angus, but he "was very much interested in civil rights as well as education."[27] Black Lumberton's mobilization mirrored statewide NAACP growth. The war years, notes historian Raymond Gavins, constituted a "watershed" for the organization. It centralized its administration with the 1943 creation of the North Carolina State Conference of NAACP Branches, and its total membership swelled to nearly ten thousand by 1945. During the late 1940s and early 1950s, some branches declined in membership, likely as a consequence of Cold War–era white attempts to cast civil rights organizations as un-American. When membership again rebounded in the post-*Brown* years, the organization built on its earlier broad grassroots base. By 1955, nearly two-thirds of the state's NAACP members lived in rural areas, and in addition to the urban professionals who had previously joined the group, the postwar NAACP included laborers, farmers, and domestic workers. As Gavins put it, "ordinary people comprised the bulk of the membership."[28]

In 1943, Lumberton's young people chartered a chapter of the NAACP Youth Council, which was the outgrowth of a national movement to inspire a new vanguard of civil rights activists. Formed at the national level in 1936, the NAACP's Youth Councils had well over one hundred local and college-affiliated branches across the nation by the early 1940s. In 1940, Howard University professor John Lovell Jr. judged the Youth Councils to be "the most promising thing" in the NAACP, as their members were more inclined toward social revolution and "less humble and conciliatory toward the white philanthropist" than their adult counterparts. The council welcomed members ages twelve to twenty-five. Meetings blended lessons in civic duty, race consciousness, and religion. In March 1947, for example, the Lumberton Youth Council opened with the singing of "America," discussed the Declaration of Independence and U.S. Constitution, read letters from the National Council, and concluded with a Bible study.[29]

Lumberton's Youth Council owed much of its vitality to its adult adviser, Gus Bullock, a thirty-two-year old hospital employee. Though he

NAACP Youth Councils, such as this one in Charlotte pictured in 1942, energized postwar black educational activism. At the far left is Charlotte funeral home owner Kelly Alexander Sr., who in 1948 became president of the North Carolina State Conference of the NAACP. (Courtesy of the Library of Congress, Prints and Photographs Division, Visual Materials from the NAACP Records, LC-USZ62–36657)

had no children, Bullock came to know many of the town's youth through his role as a scoutmaster and his active participation in the Baptist church. His niece, Lillian Bullock McQueen, recalled that many young people came to Bullock as a trusted confidante. "You could talk with him about just anything. . . . He could talk to you more like you would want your father or mother to talk with you." Bullock was known for offering compassion rather than judgment when young people got into trouble. When a teenage girl in the council got pregnant, for example, he "interceded" and convinced the local Baptist elders to let her stay in the church. The Bullock household in South Lumberton, which included Bullock's parents and siblings, became a frequent gathering place for council members, and it was there that the idea for a protest first took shape.[30]

As McQueen recalled, the strike effectively "opened a lot of the parents' eyes" to the severity of school conditions and their children's frustrations, but some elders disapproved of the students' tactics. Many black citizens feared white reprisals: "There were a lot of people—black people—that said we shouldn't have done that, but what [are] you going to do?" In a letter to the *Robesonian*, the Redstone PTA made its disapproval explicit by arguing that "efforts to solve our problems through peaceful pursuits" were preferred over "a resort to radicalism." They further asserted their "faith in the ability of the county, city, and state authorities" to "provid[e] adequate school accommodations for the Negro children of Lumberton." In letters to the newspaper, committees representing the faculty from both schools challenged the charge leveled by Youth Council supporter Clarence Smith that the quality of academic work had suffered. They acknowledged that facilities needed improvement but asked Smith, "Have you in the past, through acceptable channels, tried to help us improve our schools? Have you worked with the P.T.A. to bring about better conditions?" Thompson's principal, G. H. Young, urged parents to end the strike by sending their children to school. Further distancing himself from his students, Young suggested that the strikers were driven more by naive pursuits than by informed opinion. "Some of the children are striking for the novelty of it and don't understand what it is," Young charged. He warned that while "we do have a bad school situation out here . . . radicals are not in [a] position to remedy this, especially radicals who have heretofore not made any attempt to work with individuals who have been striving toward better conditions." Redstone's principal, Hayswood, indirectly signaled his disapproval by praising the "calm and sane advice" offered by the local newspaper, a critic of the students' tactics. In answer to both black and white critics, Bullock insisted at the strike's conclusion that the strikers had "no intention at any time to stir up race strife but only to insist on fair distribution of educational opportunity."[31]

Black reactions to the strike tended to fall along not only generational and professional lines but also geographic ones. While the majority of Lumberton blacks lived in South Lumberton, a smaller black neighborhood was located in East Pines, near the Hayswood residence and Redstone School. The differences between the two neighborhoods were not really defined by income, as some South Lumberton residents had more money than East Pines residents, many of whom were teachers. In East Pines, however, Hayswood carried enormous influence. As Kemp, an East Pines resident, explained, Hayswood was neither an "agitator" nor an "Uncle Tom." He preferred to influence whites behind the scenes rather than through public protest. "He could make you feel ashamed of yourself that you hadn't done what you were supposed to do," she recalled. Kemp observed that South Lumberton residents historically were "much more militant than we are." No doubt aware of these neighborhood distinctions, the strikers paraded past Redstone School, "but they didn't tarry."[32]

Some of the strongest voices of black encouragement for the strike came from outside Lumberton. McQueen corresponded with Ruby Hurley, the youth secretary for the national NAACP office, in the protest's formative stages. McQueen told Hurley midway through the strike, "We are still continuing on with the National Association's Advi[c]e You're not to[o] young . . . to plan . . . to Achieve . . . To Lead." Hurley replied, "I want you to know that the National Office of the Association stands back of you in your efforts and that we will give you all of the help that we can."[33] At least initially, national and local organizers developed a mutually supportive relationship that belied the notion of heavy-handed outside agitators imposing their agenda on black southerners. The national black press also cheered on the protesters. Reporter Alex Rivera Jr., a native North Carolinian, gave the story front-page coverage in the *Pittsburgh Courier*, complete with a damning juxtaposition of photos of the black schools with one of the local white high school. He upbraided the local black principals for failing to support the students and affirmed that conditions were as bad as charged. Visiting Lumberton's white schools after surveying the black schools, he noted, was like "making a sudden jump from the dark ages to the present atomic society."[34]

Encouragement from the NAACP's national office helped to mitigate the negative and in some cases hostile reaction from local whites. At one point during the strike, several shots were fired at the Bullock residence, an action Gus Bullock interpreted as white efforts to intimidate him. The newspaper offered more restrained but nonetheless unwavering disapproval, arguing that "by prolonging their strike the Negro students of Lumberton no doubt will injure their cause far more than they will help." Eight days later, when the strike concluded, the newspaper was even less charitable. It condemned the strike as "unfortunate and ill-advised" and as a source of "undesirable publicity." The paper made clear its distinct disapproval of outside influence in local affairs: "Race relations in Robeson County are and have been harmonious and they will remain so despite outside sinister and pernicious influences which enter peaceful communities only to stir up discord and strife."[35]

But white reaction to the strike was not uniformly critical. In fact, by its end, protesters were receiving considerable support for their cause—if not always their tactics—from the state's highest school officials and leading white newspapers. The *Raleigh News and Observer*, for example, at first expressed disapproval of the students' actions, editorializing that "strikes are never justified until other remedies have been exhausted." But by the fourth day of the strike, the paper backtracked. "Ordinarily student strikers are not to be condoned," an editorial stated. "But in this case the difficulty

The *Raleigh News and Observer* included this photograph of Redstone Academy as part of its extensive coverage of the 1946 student protest in Lumberton. (Courtesy of The North Carolina State Archives, Raleigh, and the *Raleigh News and Observer*)

is not in understanding why the students struck. What is hard to understand is why they ever started to school in such buildings and why they were ever permitted to do so." Lumberton's schools constituted a "disgrace to the state." To imprint that point on readers' minds, the *News and Observer* published an extensive front-page photographic indictment of Thompson and Redstone. The pictures showed weather-beaten buildings with broken windows, leaking roofs, sagging floors and doors, an outdoor toilet and water pump, and classrooms lit only by suspended naked lightbulbs and heated by potbellied stoves. Shocked by the findings of its own investigation, the *News and Observer* concluded, "The more that is known about the intolerable condition of the buildings housing the two Negro schools at Lumberton, the more inexcusable the situation becomes."[36]

As public scrutiny intensified, local and state officials took turns assigning blame. On 12 October, Bullock sent the governor a telegram imploring, "BUILDINGS ARE STILL UNSANITARY WHAT YOU ADVISE THE STRIKING CHILDREN TO DO." The governor replied that school buildings were a local concern and suggested that Bullock "adopt a more co-operative policy toward local officials." State board of education comptroller Paul Reid agreed that local districts, not the state, held responsibility for providing school buildings. Lumberton superintendent B. E. Lohr retorted that his board had no authority to make improvements on the two school buildings, since they were privately owned, a logic that elided the fact that his district long ago could have built new buildings rather than continuing to rent dilapidated ones. Credle admitted in the days after the strike that the conditions were "every bit as bad as depicted" in the press. All the same, he argued, black school conditions reflected the effects of the depression and wartime material shortages, not racial discrimination. Many white schools also lacked modern facilities, he explained, noting that white students in the town of Plymouth had struck for similar reasons. J. Henry Highsmith, director of the Division of Instructional Service, agreed that the conditions found at Lumberton, while shameful, were not uncommon.[37]

Officials' early efforts to deflect blame fell flat as evidence mounted that supported the strikers' cause. In a front-page article on 16 October, the *News and Observer* laid bare sobering statistics. Of the state's 1,645 white public schools in 1946, only 1,020 (62 percent) had the basic facilities required for state accreditation; only about 12 percent (211 of 1,768) of the state's black schools met the same standards. Moreover, by the state's own admission, the standards for accreditation were minimal: a library of at least three hundred volumes, one teacher per grade, adequate space for the students, and a smattering of maps, charts, and science equipment. Furthermore, Redstone School actually had received state accreditation, indicating that dubious state ratings masked egregious deficiencies.[38]

State officials conceded that student grievances were more than justified. Newbold visited Lumberton after the strike's first week and found conditions to be just as bad as the press had claimed. "It would be difficult for the most gifted writer," he reported, "to picture the actual conditions as being worse than they really are." While he believed that the city's black school patrons did "not harbor hate nor any malicious intent," he sensed that they "felt keenly that they had been neglected a long time." When state health officer Carl Reynolds visited Lumberton, he too flinched. "The Negro schools of North Carolina are a disgrace to the State. [They] make you weep to look at them," he charged. Reynolds surmised that the local officials in question "just don't give a darn."[39] As the strike stretched into its second week, Lumberton's black community appeared to be winning an important victory in the arena of white public opinion. In acknowledging the disgraceful conditions in Lumberton, state officials were tacitly admitting the failure of the interracial bargain forged a generation earlier. Black loyalty to white guardians clearly had not resulted in school equality.

When the strike concluded, the *News and Observer* expressed its hope that there would be no future protests and "no justifications for such strikes." It urged the General Assembly to "serve notice" to local districts that the gross inequities found in Lumberton would not be tolerated. Raleigh's black newspaper, the *Carolinian*, applauded the *News and Observer*'s searing coverage and castigated the black principals who attempted to explain away the situation. In addition, the strikers had won considerable admiration from national civil rights leaders. NAACP special counsel Thurgood Marshall later commented that "the strike called by the Youth Council was one of the finest things ever pulled in the NAACP."[40] By late October 1946, Lumberton's protesters had every reason to feel vindicated in their resort to "radicalism."

Legal Leverage and Lumberton's Illusive Promises of Equality

If the only goal of the Lumberton protesters had been simple recognition of their unequal schools and promises of redress, the story would have ended in the fall of 1946. Lumberton blacks, however, were not content to sit back and let whites oversee the improvement of Thompson and Redstone. They instead sought legal leverage that would force officials to make good on their promises. Even before the strike ended, the NAACP's youth secretary Ruby Hurley had suggested to local organizers that they might "secure" a lawyer. When Hurley visited Lumberton and addressed a "mass meeting," she "raised the enthusiasm of the citizens to fever pitch." After the county commissioners agreed to allocate money for new black schools, community interest in litigation did not wane. Apparently worried that local officials would improve but not equalize Lumberton schools, black citizens held another mass meeting in late October and invited Durham attorney Herman L. Taylor to speak. Taylor, a law professor at the North Carolina College for Negroes (NCC), later noted that by the end of the meeting, those in attendance had "dedicated themselves to carry the fight to court." Marshall relayed to Taylor that the NAACP's "National Office is more than happy to cooperate in every way possible." By November, Taylor had filed a petition requesting full "equalization of facilities." For the next three years, he made it his personal mission to ensure that white Lumberton did not forget its promise of equality.[41]

In taking on the Lumberton case, Taylor joined a generation of emerging civil rights leaders who carried no personal memories of Jim Crow's nadir. He would instead have drawn formative lessons about the prospects for change from the war era's "Double V" campaign for democratic victory at home and abroad. Born in 1919 in Virginia, Taylor graduated from Virginia Union University and the law school at New York's Columbia University. While at Columbia, he worked as an office manager at the NAACP's legal offices and came to know Marshall, who had become NAACP chief special counsel in 1938. After completing his law degree, Taylor wrote to thank the NAACP board of directors for his tutelage, which he predicted would "forever remain a bright spot with me."[42]

Taylor came to North Carolina in 1945 to teach at the new law school at the North Carolina College for Negroes, where he soon learned that opponents of civil rights litigation could be found on both sides of the color line. He chafed against James Shepard's expectations of deference and the limited resources at the underfunded law school. In fact, he resorted to doing his research at the nearby University of North Carolina. Reasoning that "the students over at our school didn't know what they were missing," he one day surprised them with an impromptu field trip to Chapel Hill. Following their tour of the state's premier law school, Taylor told his protégés, "I carried you over there for a reason. . . . You all got a right to be going to that school. You all are getting second class training here." Not content simply to expose the inequalities he observed, Taylor grew "rather restless" and began taking outside cases that directly attacked educational disparities. In his second year at NCC, Taylor took the Lumberton case and similar work closer to home. When seven black teachers in Durham sought counsel after being fired for complaining about inadequate supplies, Taylor "began to raise Cain with the Durham school board, and the newspaper played it up blow by blow." After one board member complained about this young upstart at NCC, Shepard wasted no time in requesting a conference with Taylor. Anticipating the president's displeasure, Taylor announced his resignation and explained, "I know why you've called me here. . . . You've got to do what you've got to do, and I've got to do what I've got to do." Making clear that his plans foreclosed the self-censorship demanded by Shepard, Taylor added, "There's a lot of stuff going on right here in North Carolina and nobody's doing a thing in the world about it." In explaining his resignation to NAACP legal assistant Robert Carter, Taylor reflected, "I might as well take the bull by the horns and get out in the raw where I could battle as I saw fit." He was "practical enough to realize" that a career in civil rights litigation could not be pursued "as long as I was a part of Shepard's school."[43]

Freed from the constraints of his affiliation with a state-supported college, Taylor turned his attention to Lumberton, where he saw opportunity for a historic test case for educational equality. He believed that with the exception of a few "Judases," most Lumberton blacks were "quite anxious to get the case underway." He warned the national office, "We cannot expect cooperation from any of the Negroes in the school system, neither principals nor teachers, for they are all afraid of losing their jobs." But he was reassured by the parents who had agreed to serve as plaintiffs. They were "dead earnest," and none worked for the schools. A lawsuit, he reckoned, would prompt "no mild outburst [since] the 'good white folks' in North Carolina have heretofore so effectively thwarted suits of this nature." White North Carolinians believed "it can't happen here," Taylor wrote, but he felt confident that Lumberton blacks were "ready to be led out of slavery."[44]

In July 1947, Taylor and his assistant, Winston-Salem attorney Curtiss Todd, filed suit in Robeson County Superior Court on behalf of Lawrence S. Stephens, Sam Bullock, and Bessie Thompson, all parents of Lumberton schoolchildren. The defendants in the case included the Board of Trustees of the Lumberton City Schools, the Robeson County Board of Education, the Lumberton City schools superintendent, and the Robeson County commissioners. The complaint contended that the black schools in Lumberton were "inadequate and unhealthy . . . overcrowded and . . . dilapidated." The white schools, by contrast, were "modern, safe, sanitary, well-equipped, [and] lighted." According to the suit, those inequalities violated the Equal Protection Clause of the U.S. Constitution's Fourteenth Amendment and Article IX, Section 2, of the North Carolina Constitution, which prohibited racial prejudice in the provision of public school facilities.[45] Buttressed by the egregious conditions found in Lumberton's black schools, here was a test of the "separate but equal" doctrine that seemed destined to succeed.

The case soon garnered widespread attention. The *Pittsburgh Courier* hailed it as "unprecedented in the history of public instruction in North Carolina" and as having "impeccable timing and thunder-clap surprise." Part of the case's significance rested in North Carolina's history of circumventing past legal challenges. State officials routinely pointed to their avoidance of lawsuits in the teacher salary equalization fight as proof that white North Carolinians knew how to manage race relations. The Lumberton case promised to complicate North Carolina's progressive image and thrust the state into a very public battle. As the *Pittsburgh Courier* put it, the case "poignantly forecasts that North Carolina can no longer expect to ride on the courage and litigations of her sister states."[46] The suit also merited notice for the fact that it rested on the grassroots activism of ordinary black citizens. Lawrence S. Stephens was a barber; Samuel

Bullock Jr. (father of Lillian Bullock McQueen) was a truck driver for the Lumberton Ice and Fuel Company; and Bessie Thompson was a domestic worker and wife of a farmer. As historian Thomas Sugrue has noted about school litigation in the North during the same era, these cases indicate that litigation—sometimes critiqued as a "'top-down' approach to social problems"—often represented an organic process, where national organizations and grassroots protesters cooperatively "reshaped public policy, state by state, school district by school district."[47]

That organic process was at times the source of conflict, even among local organizers. When Robeson County NAACP president David Mitchell first learned of Taylor's plans to organize a lawsuit, he "got into it and broke it up," arguing that the suit had support only from the Youth Council and not the "consent of the parent body." The NAACP national office showed no patience for the local old guard, insisting that if Mitchell was "in league with the authorities or afraid to press for [blacks'] democratic rights," then he had "no business being President of the NAACP." If the national office initially saw itself as protecting Lumberton's civil rights vanguard, organizers on the ground soon saw things differently. Less than six months after the strike, Hurley reported to Marshall that the people of Lumberton "are growing impatient and feel that the National Office is letting them down." Clearly annoyed, Marshall confided, "I, personally, get sick and tired of people in our branches who wait 81 years to get to the point of bringing legal action to secure their rights and then want the lawyers to prepare the case, file it, have it decided and have everything straightened out in fifteen minutes."[48]

Local and national organizers were falling out of sync, not only in terms of pace but also in terms of goals. In 1948, an assistant special counsel in the national office raised with Marshall the possibility of introducing into the Lumberton case questions of "general inequality" apart from the "physical facilities." That way, the NAACP could "begin to try out [its] anti-segregation policy on the lower school level." Integration with white schools, rather than the construction of new black schools, was quickly emerging as the national NAACP's chief goal. Only integration, the national office had concluded, could guarantee truly equal schools for black children. One year later, Hurley echoed that call, suggesting to the president of the NAACP's North Carolina chapter, Kelly Alexander, that he investigate Lumberton's usefulness in a broader fight against segregation.[49] Some local organizers may have supported that "broader fight" in spirit, but they nonetheless continued to pursue their case as an equalization suit. After several delays as a consequence of demurrers filed by the defendants, the case finally reached court in January 1948. Taylor was in high spirits and informed the national NAACP office that it should gear up for an extended legal fight. The judge had ruled that the plaintiffs "had a legitimate cause of action" and gave them twenty days to correct some technicalities. In May, the plaintiffs broadened their equalization suit by naming the state board of education and state superintendent of public instruction Clyde Erwin as defendants. That bid ultimately failed, but the attempt signaled the plaintiffs' intention to pursue the case fully.[50]

Despite its apparent momentum, the legal case slowly lost ground over the next two years. The defendants bought more time by filing yet another demurrer in Robeson Superior Court, which the judge sustained in July 1948. Feeling "hopelessly involved in Superior court," Taylor decided to file a new suit in federal court in August. In the meantime, the Robeson County commissioners appropriated money for two new black schools, one in South Lumberton that would replace Thompson Institute and one in Northeast Lumberton that would replace Redstone Academy. The latter, J. H. Hayswood School, was completed by January 1949. That spring, Taylor sensed that the state and national offices of the NAACP had lost interest in his case, which was still pending in the federal courts. Not only were national organizers turning their attention to integration cases, but they also were at odds with Taylor, who felt unfairly compensated for his time. Taylor nevertheless remained committed to winning the case. As he confided to Robert Carter, "I had looked upon the Lumberton Case as an effort on the part of the National Office to get things moving in North Carolina and to start the ball rolling, as the Lumberton Case was good material for this purpose." He was "not prepared to say," however, what effect the two new black schools would have on his chances for success. In September 1950, a little over a year later, Taylor received his answer: The suit was dismissed in U.S. District Court. Asserted the *Robesonian*, "Matter Closed."[51]

For many of Lumberton's African Americans, however, the matter was not closed. While the protest and litigation had prompted local officials to build two new schools, questions of equality endured. One bone of contention concerned the placement of the city's only black high school, J. H. Hayswood School, on the northeast side of town even though the majority of Lumberton's black citizens—and the majority of the leaders of the school protest—lived in South Lumberton. Moreover, that building was completed more than a year before Thompson Institute was replaced in South Lumberton. The privileging of Redstone's replacement likely represented a move by local officials to reward Hayswood for his longtime cooperation in containing black agitation. The head of the county commissioners visited the Hayswood home shortly after the school protest and promised that he would get the high school. Some Lumbertonians also remained concerned about whether either of the city's new black schools truly matched the resources at the white schools. Less than one year after the dedication of the South Lumberton School (Thompson Institute's replacement), the school's PTA complained of its lack of an auditorium and cafeteria. The initial feelings about J. H. Hayswood School (Redstone's replacement) were more positive, especially because for the first time students enjoyed access to a "gymtorium" (a combination gym and auditorium). There, too, however, concerns about overcrowding and needed upgrades emerged within a couple of years.[52]

Despite evidence of lingering differentials, Lumberton whites were eager to declare school equalization fait accompli and direct their attention back to the white schools. In January 1949, the *Robesonian* pointed out that Lumberton would soon have black school facilities that were "among the most modern and adequate in the state" but that the white schools were overcrowded. A 1951 headline similarly boasted, "Negroes First in Improvement for Lumberton." Ironically, the paper also acknowledged that the city had just spent three hundred thousand dollars on the new Rowland-Norment School for whites, a sum that approximately equaled the amount spent on both of the new black schools. At the dedication of the South Lumberton School, the chair of the Lumberton school board seemed to suggest that the city had done its part to insure educational opportunity and that blacks now needed to take advantage of their new resources. "The physical equipment for better education being provided," he observed, "it was up to the people and their leaders to make further progress."[53]

The local black community insisted that local officials must provide more. "The Negroes are 'breathing down our necks,'" Superintendent Lohr privately reported in 1953, adding that it was "imperative" that the black schools receive additional classrooms. Even publicly, Lohr admitted that "the Negro schools are probably in even greater need than the white schools, and they must not be ignored in the building program." Hayswood School needed a cafeteria, laboratory, agriculture shop, and more classrooms and restrooms; South Lumberton needed more classrooms and either an auditorium or a gymnasium.[54]

Lohr's concessions to black grievances notwithstanding, many whites continued to believe that town officials already had leveled the educational playing field. The *Robesonian* emphasized that both black and white schools needed better resources: "Lumberton now finds itself with what might be called equal but inadequate schools." Wade Spearman, a prominent black businessman, refused to let that claim go unchallenged. He reminded the paper's readers that the now overcrowded South Lumberton School was the only school of its size in the city that lacked a gymnasium or auditorium. Equalization, Spearman insisted, was not an accomplished fact. "We definitely have two problems confronting us," he wrote, "meeting the overcrowded conditions as now exist, and equalizing the facilities for all of our children."[55]

Additions to Hayswood, including four new classrooms and a cafeteria, were completed in 1954, but only one year later, a survey determined that the school was "poorly constructed and poorly heated" and needed more classrooms, an agriculture shop, and shower facilities. South Lumberton School was in "good condition" but needed more classrooms and a gymtorium. In 1954–55, the per pupil school property value for each white student in Lumberton was $507.48; for each black student it was $369.85. Nonetheless, many whites could not conceive of integration as a solution to these deficiencies. As the *Robesonian* opined in September 1955, "Each new building or addition is evidence of confidence that somehow public education will be continued. Each one increases the county's investment in the type of school system that it has—a system providing for segregation of races."[56]

The legacies of black Lumberton's equalization battle ultimately were mixed. It had not erased inequality, although it had substantially improved conditions for black students. Such improvements arguably delayed integration, as they made black school conditions more tolerable for African Americans and more defensible for whites. That said, the experience of participating in equalization activism galvanized African Americans in Lumberton and across the state in ways that at least indirectly facilitated the collapse of Jim Crow. In the spring of 1948, when the school suit was still pending, Lumberton Youth Council member Dorothy Leggett attended an NAACP conference in Washington, D.C., and requested an interview with U.S. senator Clyde Hoey. Prefiguring a later generation's willingness to question authority, Leggett forthrightly asked the North Carolina senator to explain his opposition to President Harry S. Truman's proposed civil rights legislation. When Hoey responded that "people in North Carolina are treating Negroes fine," Leggett "pointed out that school buildings for Negroes in her hometown are not adequate or equal to those for white children." After Leggett reported back to the Youth Council about the senator's intransigence, members "began to map plans" to defeat Hoey and other civil rights opponents.[57] Perhaps unrealistic at a moment still marked by high levels of black disfranchisement, those plans nonetheless signified a new spirit of black protest that at least temporarily was jolting educational officials into action across the state.

Lumberton's Larger Legacies

At a 1947 meeting of school superintendents, DNE director Newbold reminded his audience that during the construction boom of the 1920s, white children received "most, or practically all" of the new school buildings. At that time, the Rosenwald Fund helped compensate for state discrimination by building what officials still regarded as some of "the best Negro schools in the state." Since no such "good angel" was poised to rescue the state in the late 1940s, the question before the superintendents was, "Shall we now dilly-dally, neglect to do what we ought and can do, thus forcing Negroes in and outside North Carolina to go into the courts to equalize?"[58] Pender County superintendent T. T. Murphy knew how he would answer that question. His board of education "realized that we had an obligation to the Negro" and had decided to improve the black schools. "Our Board does not crave any such publicity as Lumberton has received," he explained. To be sure, unapologetic white negligence was still easy to find. When African Americans in Henderson complained in 1947 of having no school available to them while whites had access to five, the local superintendent quipped that blacks should "drink more liquor" and thereby increase the alcohol taxes that could be used for the schools. Newbold understood that the racial disparities in facilities were far greater than local funds alone could address, and in 1948 he began pressing for a major infusion of state school construction funds. As he told Governor Cherry, there was a "very urgent need for many new school buildings in North Carolina—some for white children and many for Negro children." Hundreds of schools were "unspeakably poor and inadequate."[59]

In the late 1940s and early 1950s, African Americans from across the state redoubled efforts to bring those poor school conditions to light. North Carolina Mutual president C. C. Spaulding relayed to Newbold in 1947 that black communities were taking a keen interest in the Lumberton case. Ever the politician, Spaulding assured Newbold that he was advising blacks not to press lawsuits but noted that such caution was generating considerable criticism.[60] Even in the absence of formal lawsuits, black communities found ways of exposing inequalities in damning detail. In Charlotte, for example, local NAACP representatives commissioned a study of school conditions that exposed disparities at the high school level "so serious and fundamental as to handicap every Negro child enrolled in these schools." Only one of the city's two black high schools had received approval from the Southern Association of Colleges and Secondary Schools, and extensive curricular differences between the white and black high schools persisted. Neither black high school had a gymnasium, while all of the white high schools did. Both black high schools suffered from overcrowding and large class sizes. Furthermore, the per pupil value of furniture and equipment at the white schools ranged from eighty to thirty-seven dollars; at the two black high schools, the values were twenty and eighteen dollars. The report recommended that "immediate steps" be taken to equalize Charlotte's schools and added, "This will be expensive; but this is the price of segregation." When NAACP representatives presented a petition with those demands to the school board in September, the meeting "grew heated." The board questioned the report's accuracy and insisted that "everything possible is being done to provide equal opportunities." The national office of the NAACP supported the Charlotte branch's equalization efforts but hoped to see that battle evolve into a fight for integration. Marshall worried that the petition might legitimate the idea of "adjustment through separate schools" and reminded Kelly Alexander that "we are dedicated to the policy of insisting on the removal of segregation, and . . . cannot appear to approve segregation in any fashion."[61]

Alexander had not yet announced a direct attack on all levels of educational segregation, but in the fall of 1948, he revealed plans for a protest march that would draw attention to several key issues, including black representation on policymaking bodies, equal educational and employment opportunity, and integration at the level of graduate and professional schools. Alexander called off this impending "March on Raleigh" when W. Kerr Scott took office as the state's new governor and agreed to meet with an NAACP delegation. In the weeks after this unprecedented meeting, Scott took pains to offer white constituents private assurances that while he favored "equal opportunity for economic advancement . . . no question of social equality is to be considered seriously."[62]

Despite what some white constituents may have feared, Alexander hardly had Scott in his pocket, but the new governor did make more concessions to the NAACP's campaign against educational inequality than had his predecessors. In April, he appointed St. Augustine's College president Harold L. Trigg as the first African American member of the state board of education. Trigg's appointment received endorsements from black leaders and progressive whites, although Durham's black newspaper was more skeptical, dubbing Trigg a "pastmaster at producing a possum grin," someone who knew "how to tickle weak white folk's fancy."[63] While some black leaders scoffed at Scott's choice of Trigg, the governor partially redeemed himself by recommending that the state allocate fifty million dollars for school construction, with half of the money coming from a direct legislative appropriation and half from a state bond issue. Scott did not tout the bond plan as a racial equalization measure, but he later urged officials to spend the funds with that goal in mind.[64]

In tethering the goal of black representation to demands for school equalization, the NAACP delegation that visited Governor Scott signaled an important postwar shift in educational politics. African Americans increasingly rejected white guardianship over black school matters and amplified calls for direct participation in policymaking. Durham's *Carolina Times* editorialized in 1950, "Crying on the shoulders of white people about the poor condition of Negro schools . . . will do no good." The "one and only way" to right the wrongs in the public schools was "for every Negro man and woman to register and vote."[65] Black parent and teacher associations similarly encouraged power sharing in school politics. In 1946, the NCTA voted to locate its new permanent headquarters in Raleigh, where the group felt it could forge stronger ties with its white counterpart, the North Carolina Education Association, and "maintain a constant vigilance on legislative matters."[66] NCTA leaders similarly urged members to join the racially integrated National Education Association, and both the NCTA and the North Carolina Congress of Colored Parents and Teachers called for the appointment of at least one black member to all boards overseeing black schools.[67]

By the late 1940s, black North Carolinians had begun making small inroads into state and local politics. In 1947, Kenneth Williams broke new political ground by winning a seat on Winston-Salem's board of aldermen, marking the first time in the twentieth century that an African American defeated a white opponent in a southern municipal election. In 1949, in addition to Trigg's appointment to the state board of education, the Raleigh City Council appointed a black attorney, Fred J. Carnage, to that city's school board, making him the first African American in North Carolina to hold such a seat since the nineteenth century.[68]

Those important milestones aside, African Americans were still largely voiceless around school policymaking tables. That left the courts as a necessary source of leverage in the fight against educational discrimination. As late as February 1949, Newbold asserted that with the exception of the Lumberton case, the state had "been able to keep ahead of the Negroes."

By spring's end, the first in a wave of lawsuits forced Newbold to revise that claim.[69]

In May, Durham parents representing sixty pupils filed suit in the U.S. District Court alleging that local and state officials had practiced racial discrimination in providing school facilities. Alexander billed this action, organized by the Durham Committee on Negro Affairs and litigated by Durham attorneys M. Hugh Thompson and J. H. Wheeler and Richmond attorneys Oliver Hill and Martin A. Martin, as "the 'opening gun' of a state-wide campaign for equal facilities." The plaintiffs petitioned state super-intendent Clyde Erwin to withhold state bond money from school con-struction projects in Durham until the city equalized its facilities, noting that Durham's capital outlays for each white child were $497, versus a mere $194 for each black child. At a 1950 hearing, "a predominantly Negro audience packed the steaming courtroom" and listened to the plaintiffs' legal team present a 135-page report.[70] Held up in litigation until 1951, *Blue v. Durham Public School District* brought the first clear legal victory for elementary and secondary school equalization in North Carolina. Judge Johnson J. Hayes of the Middle District Federal Court ruled that Durham's black schools were more crowded and less modern than white schools and had inferior recreational, music, art, and library resources. Hayes restrained the Durham City Schools from discriminatory spend-ing and ordered the city to pay the plaintiffs' court costs. While Hayes dis-missed the case against state officials and thereby limited the decision's reach to Durham, the ruling nonetheless took whites by surprise. Hayes had a reputation for conservatism, having recently ruled that conditions at North Carolina College's law school were equal to those at UNC. More-over, the case had exposed serious discrimination in the South's "Capital of the Black Middle Class." As the *Raleigh News and Observer* put it, "This decision has to do with a city in which Negroes have had a better chance of fairness than in any other county in this or any other Southern State."[71]

In the wake of the Durham suit, Scott conferred privately with Trigg and Newbold. Both men reportedly criticized the Durham school board's neg-ligence but reassured the governor that the state was giving black schools "due consideration." Trigg later told one reporter that the state was dis-tributing school funds on an "equitable basis." The *Carolina Times* fumed. "TRIGG AND NEWBOLD: UP TO OLD TRICKS," screamed a banner head-line. An editorial further lambasted both men: "When a slick Negro edu-cator of the Harold L. Trigg stripe gets in the bed with a 75-year old white State official of the N. C. Newbold type and both of them pull the cover over their heads, nobody on earth is able to tell what goes on under that cover." Trigg's comments constituted the latest installment in what the *Times* judged to be a "long and unsavory record of appeasement." The *Times*, in fact, had far harsher words for Trigg than for the governor, whom the editors judged to be "honest about his desire to treat Negroes of this state as citizens." Trigg, by contrast, had "lost the opportunity of his life to be a great help in working out a better understanding between the races."[72] Black representation on state boards, the *Times* suggested, mattered only insofar as blacks were willing to tell whites difficult truths.

Kelly Alexander was one black leader who rarely shrank from difficult truths. When the Durham case had opened, he was still lending his endorsement to equalization cases, but by June 1949, he found "no evidence that separate educational facilities will ever provide equal educational advantages." What was needed, he asserted, was a "county by county campaign . . . to fight discrimination and segregation in the educational system of North Carolina." He argued that this campaign should "include court action on the elementary, secondary, and university level," with the uncompromised goal of "an integrated school system." There was, he added, "no place in the NAACP program for complacent Negroes," only those committed to training youth for "first-class citizenship."[73]

Few blacks at this time publicly embraced Alexander's call for school integration, but several new equalization cases developed, especially east of the industrialized Piedmont, in the state's Black Belt.[74] In 1950, black citizens from Plymouth, in Washington County, filed suit when officials laid out plans to spend all of their allocation from the 1949 state bond on white schools. That case failed in court when school authorities promised to build a new black high school that would "be in all respects equal, and in some respects superior" to the white school. The plaintiffs challenged this contention, arguing that the new black school would require many students to travel long distances, thus entailing a new form of discrimination. The court rejected that argument and ruled that any "inconvenience" in transportation would be "more than compensated for by improved and superior educational advantages."[75]

A second 1950 suit came from the town of Wilson, in Wilson County, where the local Negro Citizens' Committee had for several years pressed for improved school conditions. Rumors quickly circulated around town that African Americans were using the equalization suit to pave the way for desegregation litigation. The Citizens' Committee flatly denied these charges in a letter to the newspaper, adding that they had long delayed litigation in hopes that officials would answer their repeated demands for school equality. Instead, officials continued to build additions to the white schools. Newbold expressed to suit organizers his disappointment that they had resorted to litigation, although he conceded that they "owe[d] it to [them]selves" to exhaust all strategies for school improvement. In private correspondence with white officials, Newbold warned of a "creeping paralysis" spreading from the eastern half of the state and suggested that local districts should equalize the schools in short order. The Citizens' Committee dropped its suit when Wilson officials agreed to the requested improvements. At that time, the local paper argued that white citizens had dodged a bullet but that complacency was not in order: "If we want to keep segregation, then, we must bend over backward to see that the facilities are equal."[76]

In times past, white concerns for avoiding litigation would have found at least tacit support from the NCTA, but by 1950, the organization's leaders refused to rule out litigation as a legitimate tool for school improvement. That year, outgoing president Hugh Brown urged members to join the NAACP and to make themselves "heard in the meetings of the local Boards of Education, the State Board of Education, in the Legislature and, if need be, in the courts of the land." Brown admitted that it might "seem strange" to some "that a minority group, armed with so little of the means of working democracy, should dare to tell the world how to make a democracy work." Yet "the means of democracy must be shared," he argued, "if there is to be any democracy at all." Many NCTA members apparently agreed, resolving to support "the growing interest in Civil Rights and First Class Citizenship for every American" and voting to donate five hundred dollars to aid the legal teams handling school equalization suits pending in the federal courts. Furthermore, an antilitigation faction within the group lost its bid for the 1950 presidency. One year later, the NCTA invited Marshall to address the annual meeting. Looking ahead to the demise of segregation, Marshall challenged those in attendance to set aside their fears of employment security and instead recognize the "necessity of being judged on the basis of ability rather than on the basis of color." The theme of that year's meeting—Achieving First-Class Citizenship through Education— further reinforced the group's allied goal of direct representation in school politics. Speakers urged teachers to model the ideals of a participatory democracy in their schools and professional organizations with the goal of paving the way for fuller representation at all levels of society. "Creative participation in policy making forms the essence of First Class Citizenship," reminded the group's journal, "and if this is practiced in the schools it will become a way of life."[77]

The NCTA may have mobilized less cautiously behind school equal-

While fighting for greater influence in educational politics, the NCTA reminded classroom teachers, "Creative participation in policy making forms the essence of First Class Citizenship and if this is practiced in the schools it will become a way of life." Here, students from O. R. Pope School in Rocky Mount portray the members of President Dwight D. Eisenhower's 1953 cabinet. (Courtesy of the Charles S. Killebrew Collection, Braswell Memorial Library, Rocky Mount, N.C.)

ization litigation than had been the case with salary litigation because the former did not require the teachers themselves to serve as litigants. As President Albert H. Anderson told the group in 1951, "I am not proposing that this organization enter into litigation in any instance but I am proposing that we use our resources, financial and otherwise, to back up those who are willing to take such steps." Generational differences may also have played a role. Anderson was born in 1906, while one of his chief opponents, Oliver Pope, was born thirty years earlier. Pope, in fact, had led the antilitigation charge at the height of the salary equalization battle in 1933.[78]

In another sign of generational dislocation, Newbold retired in 1950 at the age of seventy-nine after thirty-seven years in the field of black education. He reflected on his long career as having been guided by a simple philosophy: "that [black] children should have educational opportunities equal to those enjoyed by my own and my neighbors' children." White newspapers lauded the state's longtime white dean of black schools. The Winston-Salem paper hailed him as "one of the finest personalities and best men in the public life of North Carolina." The *Raleigh News and Observer* praised him as the "quiet but effective custodian of North Carolina's faith in equality of opportunity for all children." He had long understood that "equality is the only lasting basis upon which separation can stand." At a time when the color line seemed especially vulnerable to attack, whites almost looked wistfully to Newbold as a venerable sage who had long ago found the right formula for making segregation work. White observers were less quick to recall that Newbold's advocacy of equality had not always found such an enthusiastic embrace. When he began his work, many southern whites chafed at his demands of basic fairness. One white colleague admitted that two decades earlier he had "thought Newbold radical and attempting things which were not then possible in the South." The state, which honored Newbold with a retirement banquet, had played only a small role in recruiting him for his work. That had been the job of the New York–based General Education Board, which paid his salary and professional expenses from 1913 to 1943. Only during the last seven years of his tenure had public monies funded his position.[79] In one sense, Newbold had become a favored native son only once his insistence on racial equality seemed palatable in the face of more radical change.

While some white southerners might have preferred to forget the extent to which Newbold had ever gone against the grain of popular sentiment, African Americans readily remembered him less as a reflection of the white South than as its anomalous conscience. State supervisor of Negro elementary schools Ruth Woodson admired Newbold because she saw that he often "stood alone" while other whites simply "weren't bothered" by the needs of black schools. When Newbold retired, he received a flood of letters from black educators who similarly recalled his willingness to advance unpopular opinions. Two Lincoln County teachers wrote, "Everyone knows that you dedicated the best years of your life to the well being of our group." Another educator recalled how as a boy, he "became inspired" when Newbold visited his school and "told of the possibilities he saw for a better life in North Carolina for all its citizens." Veteran teacher Lucy Herring spoke for her generation when she wrote, "Those of us who are 'old timers' will ever be grateful to him."[80]

An older cohort of African Americans felt gratitude for Newbold's past advocacy, but when the question of Newbold's successor arose, black leaders insisted that the position should simply be abolished or filled with an educator selected by African Americans. Raleigh's black newspaper argued, "As long as there is a dual public education system (and it will continue for many years) an official at the state level to represent the Negro's interest, rights and needs will be in order." That director, however, "should be a Negro," someone who was "acceptable" to both whites and blacks. The state ignored these calls for black leadership and instead appointed G. H. Ferguson to the position. A white educator who had begun his career as a principal and superintendent, Ferguson had served as the DNE's assistant director since 1921. The *Carolina Times* argued that the state simply should have eliminated the position rather than clinging to "that out of date and awful monstrosity known as 'Negro Education.'" In 1952, the NCTA similarly recommended that the state eliminate the DNE and integrate all of its employees into the main offices of the Department of Public Instruction. The DNE, which since its founding in 1921 had segregated its black employees in office buildings in Raleigh's black business district, increasingly seemed out of step with a rising integrationist spirit among black professionals. For years, the physical separation between the DNE's black employees and white officials in the state's main education building had been the source of inconvenience and marginalization. Woodson, who worked for the division as an elementary schools supervisor from 1946 to 1960, recalled how she and the other black employees sometimes found out belatedly about conferences that the white employees were planning to attend. When Woodson learned of one such conference after the registration deadline, Newbold gave his reserved slot to her. Such personal gestures of inclusion may have ameliorated but hardly compensated for the larger humiliations of professional segregation.[81]

The push to integrate educational leadership coincided with the state's first grassroots efforts to integrate the schools. In 1951 and 1952, black North Carolinians filed new equalization lawsuits and petitions, and for the first time several of those actions entailed conditional requests for integration.[82] Of those cases, a 1951 suit from Pamlico County generated the most attention, as it was the first lawsuit filed in the federal courts from North Carolina—and only the second in the South—to raise the possibility of integration.[83] Located on the coast, rural Pamlico County in the early 1950s had approximately ten thousand people, of whom 40 percent were black. A state supervisor found at that time that the county's black teachers and students were "struggling against almost insuperable odds—big classes, very, very poor buildings, limited supplies." At Pamlico County Training School, students and teachers were forced to take shelter in a school bus on windy days because the old frame building rocked back and forth. The total value of all of the county's white school buildings at the time was $585,800; for African Americans, that figure was a mere $31,000. For years, the black community scraped together resources for schools. Longtime resident James Fulcher remembered that he and others assembled a makeshift school bus using a Chevrolet motor and a Pontiac chassis. When the county decided to use the bulk of the revenue from a recent state school bond to build an "ultra-modern $250,000 county-wide high school" for whites, the African American community divided over how to address this egregious discrimination. In the weeks before the lawsuit was filed, a delegation of black parents appeared before the county school board and unanimously declared that they had no interest in sending their children to the white schools. Only a few weeks later, fifty-five black school patrons filed suit in U.S. District Court requesting that their children be allowed to attend white schools if equal facilities were not provided. County officials subsequently moved quickly to raise funds for a new black school. With the help of state bond funds and a local Negro school bond of $100,000, the county built a new Pamlico County Training School. Student Joseph Himbry, who attended classes at both the old and new buildings, recalled, "Every year we got something new. . . . So from where we started to where we finished school, we could see a big, significant change."[84]

Even when black protesters did not broach the subject of integration, the exposure and protest of inequalities thrust black school patrons into historic battles for civic recognition. As the leaders of an equalization suit in Perquimans County noted, they had taken on the work of "loyal fighters for 1st class citizenship." The profound political significance of such efforts was especially evident in Wilmington, in New Hanover County, where half a century earlier white Democrats had organized a bloody coup d'état. When local physician Hubert A. Eaton filed a school equalization lawsuit there in 1951, he realized that he was part of something more radical than the improvement of school facilities. After an initial meeting with the New Hanover County Board of Education, he found himself in the middle of "the first public confrontation between white and Negro since the infamous race riot of 1898." The local superintendent also acknowledged the historic nature of the suit, albeit with no attempt to hide his disapproval. As he recalled it, "The spirit of harmony, developed since the days of [Governor Charles] Aycock, was rudely disrupted by a racketeer group that started an 'equalization' suit.'"[85]

Prior to 1954, most school equalization activity in North Carolina took the form of petitions and lawsuits, but in 1951, the small eastern town of

Kinston was the scene of a second school boycott that was reminiscent of the Lumberton protest. That November, more than seven hundred students walked out of Adkin High School to protest its inferior facilities. The preceding day, five students had presented a list of grievances to the school board. Unconvinced of the board's good faith, senior class leaders organized a walkout. One student recalled being inspired by a discussion in her social studies class of how autoworkers had joined together and gone on strike to achieve their goals. The Kinston school strike lasted less than a week, but that was more than enough time to rankle the white community. Several months earlier, the city's newspaper had boasted, "Kinston can claim without any fear of successful contradiction that practically equal opportunities have been provided for both races here." Not surprisingly, the paper judged the strike to be "ill advised and dangerous." The strike also came under fire from the local superintendent, who reminded students in a radio address: "Power tactics on the part of a minority group has never won an objective from a majority group." In fact, the students' "power tactics," along with a lawsuit filed by Kinston parents and attorney Herman L. Taylor in March 1952, closely preceded a number of significant additions to Adkin High, including a new library, classrooms, a gymnasium, and vocational facilities.[86]

Kinston boycotters had won improved school conditions, but that was not the sort of ultimate victory that national NAACP organizers had in mind. They were more interested in equalization demands as the opening foray to a direct attack on Jim Crow. Several months before the Kinston strike, a similar student-led boycott in Farmville, Virginia, presented that sort of opportunity. Farmville students ended their strike after two weeks but only after joining forces with the national NAACP and agreeing to pursue an integration suit, which went on to become one of the five cases decided in *Brown v. Board of Education*.[87]

The North Carolina NAACP's Alexander privately complained about the lack of such cases in North Carolina, which he judged to be an exceptionally "tough state." "Many of our NAACP people," he lamented, "don't want close national office direction." In 1950, the state organization's legal committee agreed that all of its affiliated attorneys should pursue only cases designed to end segregation, but Alexander anticipated considerable difficulty in enforcing compliance. He cited particular concerns about Taylor, who, in addition to the Lumberton and Kinston cases, was pursuing equalization cases in Chapel Hill and Perquimans County. The worries about Taylor proved unfounded, as he and his partner, Samuel Mitchell, later handled numerous school integration cases.[88] Nonetheless, the early integration movement continued to be hampered by questions of black consensus. In 1951, when twenty-one citizens of Martin County petitioned for either full equality or integration, several local black educators disavowed the call for integration. Raleigh's black newspaper argued that those critics had "been pressed into 'service' by the county and city officials . . . and placed on the radio in an effort to stem the rising tide against segregation in Martin County." Alexander took those "Uncle Toms and pseudo leaders" to task, accusing them of "selling the people short on this matter of first class citizenship."[89] Whites were indeed quick to exploit any sign of black division. Despite the fact that a 1951 Person County suit that opened the door to desegregation had dozens of plaintiffs, local officials attempted to discredit it by noting the "striking" fact "that very few of the substantial and leading negroes of the county" had agreed to participate.[90]

Black reluctance to support integration stemmed in part from fear of white reprisal as well as from the recognition that whites finally were investing in black schools. Between 1940 and 1952, per pupil spending for the state's black students rose by 462 percent, far outstripping the 285 percent increase for whites. Some districts had spent a sizable proportion of their state bond funds as well as local funds on black schools. The *Raleigh News and Observer* predicted in 1951 that "in numerous communities, new centers of high school or intermediate education for Negroes will be superior to the existing buildings for white children built some years ago." The *New York Times* similarly observed in 1952 that across the South, "the improvement of Negro schooling in recent years has been remarkable." It was perhaps no surprise, then, that the recruitment of integration litigants required a certain amount of persuasion. National NAACP organizer Herbert Hill recalled encountering "lots of resistance in the branches because real progress toward equalization was now beginning to be made. . . . The dissidents said, 'You mean that you want us to oppose all this?' And the answer was not only yes but that the new facilities ought to be shut down and that the black community ought to settle for nothing less than integrated facilities only. It was a big lurch."[91]

In making that "lurch," black leaders would point out that the state's schools were still far from equal. In 1953–54, the per pupil school property values were $490.28 for whites and $316.03 for blacks. This differential was considerably smaller than the fourfold difference that had existed a generation earlier, but enduring disparities meant that many black schools still relied heavily on the compensatory efforts of black teachers. In commenting on the "strong points" of black schools, state supervisors invariably noted teacher resourcefulness. "The teachers are doing a mar-

Even within the most modest classrooms, black teachers searched for ways to inspire students. In this classroom at Cary Colored Elementary School in 1953, the teacher posted a reminder, "A man who reads lives many lives; a man who doesn't walks blindfolded." (Courtesy of The North Carolina State Archives, Raleigh)

velous job under adverse circumstances," noted a typical report from the field.[92] Despite the remarkable achievements of the facilities equalization movement, the "human resources" of black schools still constituted their strongest foundation.

On the eve of the *Brown* hearings, Clyde Erwin, state superintendent of public instruction, remained "optimistic" that a "framework of separate but equal schools" could be maintained, but he admitted that much work remained. In 1951, Governor Scott had estimated that at least eighty million dollars was still needed to equalize the state's schools. D. Hiden Ramsey of the state board of education likewise recognized that "despite the activities of the school building committee, many eastern counties will end up with a shocking disparity in school building facilities as between the races." Given such disparities, the *Winston-Salem Journal and Sentinel* came to the "inevitable" conclusion in 1952 that "the money will have to come from somewhere to build better schoolhouses, if we are to maintain our policy of segregation of the races in the public schools of North Carolina."[93]

With that goal in mind, state officials called for a new fifty-million-dollar school construction bond issue in 1953. Some whites expressed reservations about the fact that the 3 October bond referendum would precede a ruling in the *Brown* case pending before the U.S. Supreme Court. Lumberton's newspaper criticized Governor William Umstead for asking citizens to "vote in the dark," not knowing whether the money would support segregated or desegregated schools. African Americans also approached the bond with "caution and coolness," in their case because the state had not outlined how the money would be divided between the races.[94] The press forthrightly acknowledged that a major impetus behind the bond was the growing pressure to equalize the schools, yet the Umstead administration promoted the bond with few references to race, instead emphasizing the fiscal strain created by the first wave of Baby Boomers enrolling in the schools. The bond ultimately passed by a wide margin, and a white attorney from the eastern part of the state reported to Lieutenant Governor Luther Hodges his impression that many voters supported the bond in hopes that "such action might tend to influence the Supreme Court." The black press and civic groups also supported the bond, believing, as one editorial put it, that "should the Supreme Court abolish segregation it is much more desirable to be integrated into schools of high quality than those of poor quality." Just what effect the infusion of more money into segregated black schools would have was still unclear. Soon after the bond's passage, Durham's *Carolina Times* suggested that wise use of the money might at best rehabilitate the state's image in the minds of black citizens: "If all the money is spent on Negro schools, Negro leaders might begin to have faith in the efforts of state officials to equalize educational facilities of white and Negro schools of the state. It will not, however, satisfy. The ultimate goal is absolute equality, and that can only come through integration."[95] The following spring, the Supreme Court came to the same conclusion. At that point, however, the shift from school equalization to integration had only just begun.

Since our parent-teacher Congress is interested in emphasizing [the]
full dimensions of citizenship of children and youth regardless of race, creed, or color,
we commend and support the United States Supreme Court for its inevitable
decision of 1954 outlawing segregation in public education.
—Resolutions of the North Carolina Congress of Colored Parents and Teachers, 1954

If we do not make good on our suggestion . . .
that facilities must be made truly equal, then we are going to have trouble.
—Governor Luther Hodges, 1956

I think I kind of looked forward to getting to know
some white guys and them knowing us. In my heart and mind I wasn't
thinking about getting in a fight with anybody.
—Joseph Holt Jr., on his family's efforts to integrate the Raleigh schools

CHAPTER SIX

From Equalization to Integration

Struggles for Schools and Citizenship in the Age of Brown

In October 1954, the North Carolina Conference of the National Association for the Advancement of Colored People (NAACP) held its eleventh
annual convention in Lumberton, the site of the 1946 protest that had ig-
nited a wave of school equalization activity. Held in the wake of Hurricane Hazel, one of the worst storms to hit North Carolina in the twentieth
century, this conference confronted another storm brewing on the hori-
zon. Five months earlier, the U.S. Supreme Court had declared segregated
schooling unconstitutional in its historic *Brown v. Board of Education* decision. None of the five component cases came from North Carolina, but
the ruling removed the constitutional foundation of Jim Crow from the
entire nation. The unanimous decision meant that, in the eyes of the nation's highest court, the whole notion of equalizing segregated schools
was fundamentally flawed. The Court, in fact, judged that some of the involved schools were either equal or well on their way to being equalized
with regard to "tangible factors." No matter, the court declared. Segregated schools engendered "a feeling of inferiority" in black children that
made such institutions "inherently unequal." Because education constituted "the very foundation of good citizenship," segregated schools de-

prived black children of the Fourteenth Amendment's guarantee of equal protection of the laws. Thurgood Marshall, who had led the NAACP Legal Defense and Educational Fund's litigation efforts that culminated in *Brown*, served as the Lumberton conference's keynote speaker. He advised losing no time in embracing *Brown*, arguing that the "only effective way to accomplish desegregation is to do it at once and firmly."[1]

The South's implementation of *Brown* turned out to be anything but swift and decisive. That is not to say that all southern whites were hell-bent from the beginning on defiance. In fact, as William Chafe has shown, some white North Carolinians initially greeted the decision with at least a resigned willingness to comply. The Greensboro school board voted six to one in favor of compliance, and more than one of the state's major newspapers similarly counseled calm acceptance of the decision. Nonetheless, President Dwight D. Eisenhower never endorsed the ruling; state leaders, both for reasons of perceived political expediency and out of their own segregationist convictions, soon advised against *Brown*'s implementation and created the legislative means of circumventing it. In the absence of resolute state and federal leadership, most southern whites were hardly going to demand integration, especially not "at once," as Marshall had urged. North Carolina escaped the drama of Massive Resistance, but the state's reputation for civility may in part explain its inaction. Even white progressives, as Chafe has explained, privileged "good manners" over "substantial action" and resisted change that could involve conflict.[2]

Regional white resistance and late federal enforcement effectively delayed meaningful levels of southern school desegregation until the late 1960s and early 1970s. North Carolina proved no exception to this regional pattern. In 1954, apart from some federally maintained schools on military bases, no public schools in North Carolina were integrated; by the 1963–64 school year, fewer than one-quarter of the state's school districts had begun desegregation and fewer than 1 percent of black pupils in the state attended school with whites.[3]

During this period of white intransigence, African Americans approved of *Brown* in increasing numbers, but that support came mixed with new and abiding concerns. Many African Americans embraced and took inspiration from *Brown*'s central message that segregation—even in cases of materially equal separate facilities—stigmatized their race and undermined its attainment of first-class citizenship.[4] The fact that early integration cases came not just from the state's least equipped black schools but also from some of its newest and most modern ones offered grassroots backing to *Brown*'s contention that educational equality could not be measured in facilities alone. Black citizens, in other words, collectively hoped for schools that would serve as models of both material equality and civic inclusion.

Yet *Brown* failed to address at least two other fundamental black concerns. First, in deemphasizing questions of material resources, *Brown* ignored the fact that many African Americans still felt deeply invested in historically black schools that served as vital centers of community strength and pride. Moreover, *Brown* threatened the existence of those schools at what for many was a moment of historic progress. Black interest in school equalization therefore persisted beyond *Brown* and evolved alongside early integration cases. Moreover, linear progressions often did not exist between the two strategies, and blacks did not necessarily view them as mutually exclusive.[5]

Brown also overlooked school politics. While the decision had carried the promise of integrated classrooms, it had said nothing about the need to integrate the region's policymaking bodies. To be sure, southern whites in 1954 certainly would have balked at any call for democratizing school politics.[6] Nonetheless, in emphasizing the "feeling of inferiority" that black schools had engendered, *Brown* portrayed southern blacks as damaged victims and thereby implicitly, if unintentionally, cleared the way for whites to take the lead in managing desegregation.[7] Black leaders resisted that reading of the decision and insisted that first-class citizenship entailed a system of shared educational leadership, where blacks and whites cooperatively managed the training of the state's future citizens. In fact, broad concerns regarding citizenship and representation stood at the center of both black hopes for and critiques of *Brown*. Those who embraced the decision believed that it would pave the way for greater black representation in society at all levels; at the same time, many blacks feared that integration would entail a loss of representation and meaningful inclusion in the localized environments of the schools themselves.

Brown, then, was not so much a false reflection of black educational priorities as an incomplete one. With the advantage of hindsight, scholars recently have discerned the ruling's flaws and omissions.[8] Even in *Brown*'s first decade, many black citizens presciently foresaw its shortcomings as well as its enduring truths.

Making Meaning of *Brown*

Brown's announcement exhilarated many black North Carolinians. Durham's *Carolina Times* argued that the decision promised liberation to blacks and whites alike. Whites, in fact, were to be the "greatest benefactors," as Jim Crow had "haunted the consciences of decent white people of the South and forced them to have a secret contempt for their churches, courts, and above all, for themselves." Many black educators also praised *Brown*. The news provoked civil rights veteran Pauli Murray's two aunts, both of whom had taught school for many years, to exclaim, "This is the greatest thing since the Emancipation Proclamation!" Given Murray's long efforts to integrate the University of North Carolina, her family's jubilation was not surprising. Less expected was the approval of Harold Trigg, the state board of education's only black member. Sometimes criticized by other black leaders as a sellout to the white establishment, Trigg nonetheless joined more than fifty fellow educators in signing an unwavering endorsement of *Brown*. At North Carolina College, the student newspaper endorsed the ruling, as did President Alfonso Elder. Drawing a thinly veiled comparison between Elder's politics and those of his predecessor, James Shepard, the *Carolina Times* noted that "no weak, apologizing, compromising Negro college head is capable of inspiring Negro youths for the kind of world they must face today."[9]

Brown's message of racial equality had indeed inspired black youth. A young Julius Chambers, who went on to become North Carolina's most prominent civil rights attorney in the 1960s, "heard the Court in *Brown* saying blacks were now free." The decision, he believed, promised respite from the "terrible" conditions at his high school in Montgomery County. For some students, the increased school construction of the postwar years already had brought some degree of liberation from material inequality. Lumberton had dedicated its new black high school in 1949; Chapel Hill did the same in 1951; Raleigh followed in 1953; Wilmington did so on the day before *Brown* was announced; Charlotte opened a new black high school in the fall of 1954. The newness of those facilities may have tempered initial reactions to the ruling. At Chapel Hill's Lincoln High, parent Frances Hargraves recalled that students were "very pleased with the spaciousness and the equipment and everything at Lincoln High. . . . They had the feeling, 'You owned this. This is ours. Something to be proud of, this is our school.' And I don't think they even at that time thought too much about desegregating. That was in the '50s, that's true. But they weren't hip to that. They had school pride, very strong." Despite desegregation's relative absence from students' collective consciousness, Lincoln High's newspaper praised the *Brown* decision as an opportunity to obtain "equality in schools, better facilities, and opportunities to acquire better knowledge." But better facilities and classroom opportunities were not *Brown*'s only potential gifts. The decision, the paper suggested, would finally give students the chance to demonstrate their fitness for first-class citizenship: "This is our chance, our opportunity to step forward and prove to the world that the Negro is as capable as any human being. Yes girls and boys, it is left up to us to take advantage of this great issue."[10]

Despite *Brown*'s transformative potential, many African Americans worried about whether black children would find meaningful inclusion in white-dominated environments. Nearly two decades before the ruling, W. E. B. Du Bois had wrestled with similar questions and concluded, "Other things being equal, the mixed school is the broader, more natural basis for the education of all youth. It gives wider contacts; it inspires greater self-confidence; and suppresses the inferiority complex. But other things seldom are equal, and in that case, Sympathy, Knowledge, and the Truth, outweigh all that the mixed school can offer."[11] This weighing of integration's merits echoed with early black reactions to the decision. The week after *Brown*'s announcement, CBS's popular *See It Now* news show hosted by Edward R. Murrow visited the Piedmont textile town of Gastonia to gauge popular responses to the ruling. At that time, the city was building a new black high school, a project that the superintendent pledged would continue "as though we had heard nothing from Washington." The promise of this school may have weakened but had not extinguished black enthusiasm for the decision. At the black high school, a teacher and two of the three interviewed students praised *Brown*. One believed that desegregation offered the chance to "get a broader education" and to "advance farther than we have in the past." She also noted that communists would no longer use segregation "as propaganda against the democratic form of government." Another student was "pleased . . . that segregation has ended" but made clear that she "would not like to attend schools with the white children because of the fact that we aren't welcome." Reactions were also mixed at a meeting of the North Carolina Congress of Colored Parents and Teachers. One man believed that *Brown* would help the nation save face in the world, while an older woman insisted, "We want the same schools like [whites] have. . . . [W]e don't want to be in their homes and in their schools; we want schools of our own."[12]

Questions about *Brown*'s implementation similarly divided other black communities. In the fall of 1954, 25 black citizens from the town of Maiden, in Catawba County, petitioned the school board: "We want to keep our school and we want equal facilities, but we don't want integration." At the same time, 130 citizens representing the local NAACP asked for "immediate steps" to comply with *Brown*. Much to the surprise of local whites, many of the pro-integration petitioners sent their children to the recently upgraded Catawba Negro School, locally regarded as "one of the most modern" in the county, while the anti-integration faction represented Maiden Negro Elementary, a school lacking sewer facilities and central heating. A local white paper tried to make sense of this situation: "The fact that a delegation made this move [to delay integration] is not in itself astonishing, but the fact that these Negro parents are from the one spot in the county where their children have not been given anything like equal school facilities is truly unusual—and we might say gratifying." As one of the integration petitioners suggested, however, *Brown* promised something greater than improved facilities. It offered affirmation that "the Negro is a citizen of the United States of America and is entitled to all the rights and privileges of that citizenship."[13]

While blacks greeted *Brown* with varied reactions, all could agree on the need for black representation in future negotiations over school policy. The *Carolina Times* admonished blacks to exercise their right to vote, insisting that "it is almost mandatory that Negroes have representation" on the various boards that would implement the ruling. Likewise, NAACP leaders offered officials "all possible assistance in solving the administrative problems of transference from segregated to integrated schools." In the coming months, state leaders routinely rejected such input. That summer, Governor William B. Umstead announced that he would appoint an Advisory Committee on Education to formulate the state's response to *Brown*. State NAACP president Kelly Alexander urged black inclusion in that group. Nearly a month later, with no response from Raleigh, Alexander charged that the governor was playing "hide and seek" and was devising "some trick" to circumvent *Brown*. He complained that Umstead had "refused to sit down with Negro leaders and work out a sensible solution to segregation problems." Shut out of state planning sessions, Alexander urged NAACP members in July to demand a place at local negotiating tables and laid out an unambiguous agenda for such meetings: "THESE NEGOTIATIONS ARE RESTRICTED SOLELY AS TO HOW AND WHEN THE SCHOOLS SHOULD BE DESEGREGATED."[14] In the fall, parents in several communities took up that charge and submitted petitions to their school boards requesting meetings about *Brown*'s implementation.[15]

Stunned by the determination with which some blacks called for desegregation, whites redoubled efforts to control the state's official response to *Brown*. The *Durham Morning Herald* could "hardly imagine a greater waste of time" than the NAACP's bid to influence local officials. "School Boards have no duty to sit down with NAACP representatives to work out desegregation plans," the paper charged. The *Herald*'s worries about the undue influence of the NAACP proved premature. In August, when Governor Umstead appointed his Advisory Committee on Education, only three of the committee's nineteen members were black: President Ferdinand D. Bluford of A&T, President James W. Seabrook of Fayetteville State, and Hazel Parker, Negro home demonstration agent for Edgecombe County. As public employees, all three depended for their livelihood on the good graces of white officials. Even some white leaders scoffed at the patently exclusive nature of this committee. Episcopal bishop Edwin A. Penick warned, "Token representation by Negroes on the committee can hardly be satisfactory to the Negro citizens."[16]

Had the Advisory Committee included more than a "token representation" of black leaders, it would have been forced to reckon with the swelling tide of black support for *Brown*. The same month that Umstead announced the committee appointments, more than one hundred black principals and supervisors from across the state unanimously endorsed the decision. The North Carolina Congress of Colored Parents and Teachers called for "an action program [for] complete integration," which the group saw as essential for securing "the full dimensions of citizenship." Likewise, the executive committee of the North Carolina Teachers Association (NCTA) insisted that adherence to *Brown* constituted a patriotic duty.[17]

State officials largely ignored *Brown*'s backers and instead took their cues from the decision's critics. The Advisory Committee's chair, Thomas J. Pearsall, a Rocky Mount attorney and former Speaker of the state House, received letters from alarmed white citizens, some of whom claimed to be inclined toward school equality as the only reliable antidote to the bugaboo of social equality. As one man put it, "Expensive as a bi-racial system of education is to maintain, we had rather bear the burdens of heavier taxes than to obtain the status of a gigantic southern Harlem where the races are often indistinguishable." That fall, the state attorney general sent a questionnaire to local school superintendents that offered further fodder for backlash against the ruling. The vast majority predicted that whites would not peacefully accept integration. Hyde County's superintendent anticipated "a possibility of violent reaction to Negroes *attempting* to enroll in 'white' schools." If integration had to happen, he added, it could only happen gradually. "Just as death postponed is better than death now so integration postponed is better than integration now," he wrote. In addition to expectations of conflict, the surveys indicated pervasive white doubts about black academic ability. Eighty-five percent of the superintendents believed that differences "in the average attainments between white and Negro children" would "seriously impair instruction in mixed schools." This last finding carried particular weight for Dallas Herring, chair of the Duplin County Board of Education and member of the Governor's Advisory Committee on Education. He thought that a "testing program" could be used to demonstrate "the substantial difference in mental capabilities between the two races," which, in turn, could be used to justify delayed integration. "The mental differences are so great," he argued, "that they simply will not permit adequate instruction in the same classroom." He concluded, "If we must have integration, there is no hope for public education in this county."[18]

The Governor's Advisory Committee echoed this sentiment, concluding in 1955 that the "mixing of the races forthwith in the public schools throughout the state cannot be accomplished and should not be attempted." In an effort to hold open the possibility of eventual desegregation, black committee member James Seabrook had inserted the term "forthwith." But the committee foreclosed the possibility of rapid desegregation by proposing the Pupil Assignment Act, which transferred authority over pupil assignments from the state to local districts. In decentralizing this process, the state sought to bypass *Brown*. The act spelled out seemingly race-neutral criteria—a child's "best interest," the "effective instruction" of students, and the "orderly and efficient administration of the schools"—by which local officials were to make pupil assignments, but the broad nature of these guidelines promised to accommodate race-based assignment patterns. The NCTA condemned the draft legislation and urged the legislature "to UPHOLD the Constitution rather than UPSET it." A group of black citizens representing various civic organizations similarly argued before the General Assembly that the proposed law would only delay the goal of equal opportunity. Deferred change, of course, was the law's intent. Thus, against a strong undercurrent of black protest, the General Assembly passed the Pupil Assignment Act in the spring of 1955.[19]

Over the next few months, federal and local authorities vied for control of *Brown*'s fate. In May, in what later became known as the *Brown II* decision, the Supreme Court ordered the lower courts to implement the 1954 ruling with "all deliberate speed." Marshall, the NAACP's lead counsel, initially judged *Brown II* to be a "damned good decision" that would force the South "to yield to the Constitution." With similar optimism, Wilmington's black newspaper declared in response to the ruling: "We are no longer subject to second-class citizenship." The editors warned, however, that complacency was ill-advised, as the state might well find ways of circumventing the new ruling.[20]

They were right. *Brown II* facilitated rather than impeded southern white officials' delay tactics. About a month before the decision's announcement, North Carolina's assistant attorney general, I. Beverly Lake, and several other southern state officials had made influential arguments before the Supreme Court that emphasized the limits of federal authority over public school policy. Lake's case for state and local primacy in education cleared the way for North Carolina officials to create a plan for *Brown*'s circumvention. Governor Luther Hodges, who had assumed the governorship when Umstead died in 1954, held a press conference in the summer of 1955 and warned that "mass integration in North Carolina would result in the closing of the public schools." Later that summer, Hodges appointed a new seven-member committee on education. Known as the Pearsall Committee (after its chair, Thomas J. Pearsall), this group had no black members. In a televised address, Hodges urged blacks to accept "voluntary segregation" to preserve the public schools. Black teachers wasted no time in rejecting this audacious request and issued a statement that turned the well-worn logic of black loyalty on its head: "We do not now nor have we ever subscribed to voluntary segregation, but as good citizens we have abided by it because it was the law of the state." Now that the federal judiciary had overruled the laws of the state, "good citizens" could not "advocate voluntary segregation."[21]

State officials soon raised the stakes for those good citizen-educators. In 1955, lawmakers replaced teachers' continuing contracts with annual ones, a move designed to give local districts the legal flexibility needed to reduce black teaching staffs in the event of integration. This threat loomed particularly large in North Carolina, which employed more black teachers than any other southern state. Furthermore, in purported compliance with the color-blind principles of *Brown*, the General Assembly ruled in 1955 that it would appoint school supervisors solely on the basis of the number of teachers in each district, rather than employing a supervisor for each race. In 1954–55, there were eighty-five black supervisors, still known as "Jeanes teachers"; the following year, that number dropped to fifty-five, while the number of white supervisors fell by only seven. By 1960, Division of Negro Education (DNE) director G. H. Ferguson concluded that black schools were not receiving "the supervisory attention which they need and deserve."[22]

In the wake of these threats to their employment security, black educators divided over the desirability of integration. Charlotte teachers openly

Shaw University in Raleigh hosted this regional conference of Jeanes supervisors in April 1952. By mid-decade, some of the first black educators to experience demotions or dismissals in the wake of *Brown* were those in administrative or supervisory positions. (Courtesy of the Southern Education Foundation Records, Atlanta University Center, Robert W. Woodruff Library)

supported *Brown* and did not anticipate the termination of their contracts, a fact attributed to the progressive atmosphere created by the district's liberal superintendent. NCTA secretary William L. Greene commented with similar optimism in the fall of 1955 that black teachers expected some job losses, but most felt "it is a calculated risk that we have to take for the sake of the next generation." That same year, however, an NAACP field-worker reported that black teachers in Yadkinville were "100% opposed" to desegregation. In Lexington and Reidsville, black teachers were "sharply divided," while in Rocky Mount they were "dominated by fear of economic loss." In Raleigh, the city superintendent, who reportedly was "truly a Dixiecrat," had effectively silenced black support for *Brown*.[23]

The reluctance of some black educators to embrace *Brown* was particularly vexing to NAACP leaders, but black ambivalence toward the decision was by no means limited to teachers.[24] Others hesitated to throw their full support behind the NAACP out of fear of white reprisals and concerns about how desegregation would impact the black community. Kelly Alexander admitted in mid-1955 that "many Negroes in and out of the NAACP ... disagree with our program." In his view, those men who failed to support the NAACP's program were fundamentally compromising their claims to leadership if not their claims to manhood. Alexander insisted that the NAACP's agenda would "separate the men from the boys." Alexander's gendered rebuke might simply have reflected the conventional male tendency to disregard the significance of female leadership, or it might have reflected his recognition of the fact that many of *Brown*'s strongest grassroots supporters were black women. Indeed, according to historian Christina Greene, black women's organizations stood at the center of the NAACP's post-*Brown* resurgence.[25]

By 1956, mounting white opposition to *Brown* threatened to drown out embattled black demands for compliance. In March, ninety-six of the South's congressmen signed their names to the Southern Manifesto, which indicted *Brown* as the work of "outside agitators" and resolved to prevent its implementation. All but three of North Carolina's representatives signed it, and two of the nonsigners were defeated in the next primary. Reinforcing this regional pledge of defiance, Governor Hodges's committee announced a set of proposals that became known as the Pearsall Plan. The plan amended the compulsory school attendance law so that students who were assigned against their wishes to an integrated school and had no other school options could be excused from attendance requirements. It also contained a constitutional amendment with two components: (1) the state pledged to pay, upon special application, private school tuition grants to parents whose children were assigned to integrated public schools; (2) a local option clause declared that each school district contained multiple "local option units," roughly corresponding to the territory surrounding any given school. Each of those units, if faced with pressure to integrate, could hold a referendum on whether to close its schools. Finally, the Pearsall Plan included a "resolution of condemnation and protest" against the Supreme Court's "usurpation of power."[26]

Black educators denounced the Pearsall Plan, especially its undemocratic creation. The NCTA charged that the Pearsall Committee was not "representative of the people of the state in that one whole clearly defined segment of the population was ignored in its composition." State officials, the NCTA alleged, had been "act[ing] in secrecy" and "report[ing] their findings and recommendations too late for groups not represented in their composition to be heard." In July 1956, the General Assembly held two days of public hearings on the Pearsall proposals. NCTA representatives reiterated their belief that "the principle of integration in school attendance must be established as official policy," and a small biracial coalition opposed the plan on the grounds that it could bring widespread school closings. But the plan enjoyed broad support. Racial moderates hailed it as a "safety valve" against interracial conflicts, while staunch segregationists believed it an effective barrier to integration. The General Assembly ultimately passed the Pearsall Plan with only two dissenting votes. In a public referendum on 8 September, North Carolinians approved the measure by a margin of four to one, thereby giving local officials the upper hand in directing the pace and circumstances of school desegregation.[27]

It soon became clear that in excluding blacks from educational decision making and refusing to take seriously black priorities for their children, whites were fueling precisely the integration movement they had hoped to contain. In the tiny mountain community of Old Fort, in McDowell County, one of the state's earliest grassroots movements for school integration began not as an effort to enter white schools but rather as a movement to preserve a beloved black school. In 1950, local officials had enraged black citizens by unilaterally deciding to shut down the Old Fort Colored School and bus its seventy-five elementary students to a poorly equipped black school in Marion, fifteen miles away. State officials had worked for many years to consolidate both white and black rural schools, but consolidation in Old Fort promised to exact an unequal burden of distance. Moreover, the black community had purchased the school's land, built its washrooms, graded and landscaped the grounds, and "equipped [its] auditorium with expensive curtains." A state investigator found that "there was not one person interviewed who did not regret the removal of the school from the community." Black citizens shared stories of "mortgaging their homes to buy the school grounds." Faced with losing an institution that represented years of personal investment, school patrons hired a white attorney and collected eighty-six signatures on a petition demanding the school's preservation.[28]

Despite black opposition, officials shut down the Old Fort School in 1952 and built a consolidated black school in Marion. Some parents refused to send their children to the new school and operated an "unapproved private school." Black citizens also hired the Raleigh law firm of Taylor and Mitchell and filed suit, alleging discrimination on the basis that their children had to travel thirty miles round-trip to school, while white children lived within walking distance of their consolidated school. At the time, the parents were not demanding integration but rather reestablishment of a black school at Old Fort as well as injunctive relief against discrimination and a declaratory judgment establishing their rights. By the time a ruling came, *Brown* had altered the legal terrain on which such cases could be adjudicated. In July 1955, Judge Wilson Warlick dismissed the suit, arguing that *Brown* rendered the request for a segregated black school unconstitutional. About a week later, the plaintiffs petitioned for integration, prompting local officials to respond that the white schools were overcrowded.[29] Having reached a dead end, thirty-year-old hospital attendant Albert Joyner resorted to direct action protest. On the first day of school in August 1955, he accompanied five black youth to Old Fort's white elementary school and attempted to enroll them. Earlier that week, word of Joyner's plans had circulated throughout town, and several hundred white spectators gathered that morning. The county superintendent informed Joyner that the school board had not authorized integration but that a committee was studying the issue. Joyner and the children left without incident, although about a week later, a white man assaulted him. In the wake of this violence, Governor Hodges expressed his hope that "the people of North Carolina, 'particularly members of the Negro race,' will understand that integration of the races in public schools cannot be accomplished overnight."[30]

The Old Fort case wound through the court system for another year and exposed the formidable barriers that future integration activists would face. In reviewing the case in late 1955, the U.S. Fourth Circuit Court of Appeals affirmed that *Brown* had indeed "made inappropriate" the establishment of a segregated school as a form of relief, but the judges did not offer easy alternatives. While affirming that the plaintiffs were entitled to have "the discrimination removed and rights declared," the appellate court remanded the case and ruled that the federal courts should not act further until the "administrative remedies" provided by the Pupil Assignment Act had been "exhausted." This interpretation heartened Hodges's advisers, who believed that it demonstrated the effectiveness of the Pupil Assignment Act.[31] Subsequent rulings upheld the argument that the plaintiffs as individuals had to exhaust the Assignment Act's administrative remedies before seeking relief in the federal courts. In 1957, sixty-six African American parents applied to send their children to Old Fort's white schools, but the school board rejected them, arguing that they had incorrectly filled out their applications and that additional enrollment in already crowded white schools posed health and safety risks. The color line in McDowell County's schools remained intact for another seven years.[32]

State legislation had effectively stymied the Old Fort case, but Hodges worried that the work of upholding segregation had only just begun. In

In 1956, the Southport Citizens League sent Governor Luther Hodges this photograph along with several others that exposed inadequate conditions at the Brunswick County Training School. The building on the left was serving as a band room; the building on the right housed classrooms. League members noted at the bottom of this picture, "There is no school auditorium for student body assembly. There are no building facilities for physical education purposes." (Courtesy of The North Carolina State Archives, Raleigh)

October 1956, he congratulated Pearsall on "the magnificent work done by your committee" but added his nagging concern that the passage of the Pearsall Plan "may have lulled [the people] to sleep." Hodges revealed the source of his concern as well as a warning: "I am getting letters from various places about equal facilities for Negroes. If we do not make good on our suggestion . . . that facilities must be made truly equal, then we are going to have trouble."[33]

One of those letters to the governor came from an anonymous constituent who reported that "there isn't an equal school in Western North Carolina for Negroes." A subsequent investigation into these allegations indicated that some western counties had made significant improvements to their black schools, while others had allowed grossly inadequate conditions to persist. The situation was particularly bad in Cherokee County, where the black schools lacked central heat and sanitary facilities and did not go past the tenth grade.[34] Citizens on the other side of the state were also writing to the governor. In the coastal town of Southport, members of the black community were running out of patience with their long struggle to improve conditions at Brunswick County Training School. In 1949, officials had promised that they would receive a new building if the state school bond package passed. That promise prompted the local black Citizens League to take "every registered colored voter to the polls to vote." Seven years later, new classrooms were under construction, but the school still relied on several dilapidated buildings. In October 1956, the Citizens League sent Hodges photos of the obviously worn-out facilities. Citing the governor's earlier calls for "voluntary segregation," they argued that they simply could not imagine that anyone whose children attended school under the conditions found at Brunswick County Training School would ever be "willing to voluntarily accept segregated schools." Hodges replied by explaining that the state board of education had just approved $117,660 for upgrades at their school. The Citizens League's president balked, noting that the new plans did not include a facility for physical education or large assemblies, which he regarded as "one of the most important services of a school."[35]

While Hodges was attempting to contain black discontent in the impoverished mountain and eastern Black Belt counties, a more direct challenge to segregation was developing only a few miles away from the executive mansion in Raleigh. That case, like several other early desegregation cases, centered less on material disparities and more on questions of school location and most significantly the stigma of segregation itself, thereby illustrating the limits of containing integration with facilities equalization alone.

Throwing off the "Shackles of Second-Class Citizenship": Brown's Pioneers in North Carolina

Raleigh officials likely felt that they were doing everything right to preempt challenges to Jim Crow. In 1953, the city completed John W. Ligon Junior-Senior High, the city's only black public high school. Prior to Ligon's opening, black high school students attended Washington School, which was built in 1924 and housed twelve grades.[36] At the time of Ligon's dedication, black citizens recognized the school as a marked improvement over earlier conditions. The city's black newspaper hailed the "magnificent" one-million-dollar campus as "a picture of stupendous architecture [that] adds beauty and charm to all the surrounding area." One student later recalled that Ligon "was so clean and beautiful. It was such a change from Washington."[37]

In building Ligon, however, Raleigh hardly had neglected its white schools. In the years surrounding Brown, the city expanded its main white high school, built six white elementary schools, and completed a white junior

Raleigh school officials inspect the city's new Ligon Junior-Senior High School in August 1953. Among those present was the Raleigh school board's only black member, attorney Fred Carnage. (Courtesy of The North Carolina State Archives, Raleigh, and the *Raleigh News and Observer*)

high.[38] Moreover, from Ligon's opening, signs indicated that its curriculum and facilities would not equal those of the white high schools. The Raleigh Citizens Association, a black civic organization, read those signs and reminded city officials that "nothing short of full equalization would satisfy the needs and the desires of the Negro citizens of Raleigh."[39]

Despite these admonitions, many whites were no doubt surprised when only two years after its opening, Ligon was at the center of Raleigh's first battle for school desegregation. With the backing of the Raleigh Citizens Association, the Raleigh Ministerial Alliance, and the local NAACP, fourteen black citizens petitioned to have their children admitted to white schools. The challenge initially focused on questions of location, as most of the petitioners lived closer to white schools than to Ligon.[40]

Of these initial appeals, the most compelling in terms of distance came from Raleigh's Oberlin section, just northwest of the city center. Begun as a settlement of former slaves after the Civil War, Oberlin Village came to include both white and black homes in relative proximity. That pattern persisted in the 1950s despite the fact that the city's African American population was becoming increasingly concentrated in Raleigh's southeast section. According to historian Karen Benjamin, the school board had for decades contributed to the entrenchment of residential segregation by locating black and white schools in opposite sections of town. The building of Ligon proved no exception, as it was situated just southeast of the city center in a predominantly black section, not far from Chavis Heights, an African American public housing development. Northwest of the city center, in the same vicinity as affluent white suburbs and the new Cameron Village Shopping Center, was Broughton High (the city's only white high school from 1955 to 1962) and Josephus Daniels Junior High, built in 1955. A holdout against this overall whitewashing of West Raleigh, Oberlin Village soon proved a stumbling block in city officials' attempts to keep pupils segregated on opposite sides of town. The city's early school desegregation litigation initially centered on Ligon and Daniels, two schools whose namesakes embodied the deep roots of Raleigh's racial divide. Josephus Daniels was the longtime editor of the *Raleigh News and Observer* who in the late nineteenth century had used his newspaper as a mouthpiece for the Democratic Party's white supremacy campaigns. John W. Ligon was a local black school principal who in 1919 was fired for participating in efforts to elect black candidates to municipal office.[41]

The Raleigh school board rejected the 1955 petitioners, but over the following year, local ministers George A. Fisher and Samuel F. Daly, as well as other members of the Raleigh Citizens Association, appeared several times before the board urging that plans be made for integration. In the summer of 1956, a new group of black applicants from the Oberlin neighborhood requested that their children be sent to Daniels Junior High. Thomasine Farrar, Joseph H. Holt Jr., and Grace Watts had recently completed the eighth grade at Oberlin Elementary and had been assigned to Ligon even though they lived within walking distance of Daniels. The Farrar family soon withdrew its application, and Superintendent Jesse O. Sanderson requested conferences with the two remaining families. Both Joseph Holt Jr.'s mother, Elwyna H. Holt, and Grace Watts's mother,

Lucille Hope Jones Watts, taught in the Wake County Schools, and they represented their families before the superintendent. According to Watts, Sanderson suggested that she might lose her job if she pressed for integration. Sanderson denied this accusation, noting that as superintendent of the city schools he had no power over personnel decisions in the county schools. Nonetheless, Watts withdrew her daughter's application. For whatever reason, Sanderson did not press the matter of job security with Elwyna Holt, but he did interrogate her about why she wanted her son to attend a white school. Holt explained that to attend Ligon, her son would have to catch—and pay for—an early morning city bus, transfer to a second bus, and then walk about a block. Attending Daniels simply involved a short walk. Joe Jr. later recalled that their challenge involved much more than questions of proximity, but his mother judged it unwise to attempt "the difficult task of trying to explain the humiliating impact of racial stigma and exclusion to someone who wouldn't see her point of view anyway." Sanderson rejected the Holt family's application on the grounds that their request for transfer was "too late," even though there was no established deadline. In a token gesture to appease Holt's concerns about the distance her son would travel, Sanderson offered to provide free bus transportation for black students from Oberlin Village as long as she would withdraw her application. Holt told him that he could provide transportation if he wished, but she would not back down.[42]

On the surface, Elwyna H. Holt and Joseph H. Holt Sr. seemed unlikely trailblazers. They were not members of the NAACP. Moreover, they were extremely protective of their only child, affectionately known at home as "Little Joe." Born more than a decade after his parents married in 1932, Joe Jr. enjoyed a "somewhat sheltered and protected" childhood. His first four years of school were spent at Cary Colored Elementary School, where his mother taught fifth, sixth, and seventh grades in one classroom and served as principal. When the time came for Joe Jr. to enter his mother's fifth-grade classroom, she decided to transfer him to the black school in their neighborhood, Oberlin Elementary, to remove any suggestion of partiality. At the time, both Joe Sr. and Elwyna depended on whites for employment. Elwyna worked at the mercy of white superintendents and school boards, and her husband worked in Raleigh as a warehouseman for white-owned businesses. However, Joe Sr. had always dreamed of becoming a doctor and had struggled to pay for two years of college, and he hoped that his son would have greater educational advantages. As an educator, Elwyna similarly wanted her son to have the same opportunities as white children, including the privilege of attending a school that did not

Joseph Holt Jr., along with his parents Joseph Holt Sr. and Elwyna Holt, spent three years attempting to integrate Raleigh's schools. (Courtesy of Joseph Holt Jr. and the Raleigh City Museum)

carry the stigma of racial prejudice. At its core, Joe Holt Jr. recalled, his case was about "cast[ing] off the shackles of second-class citizenship."[43]

When school opened in the fall of 1956, word of the Holts' application had not yet spread. The superintendent quietly arranged for the city bus line (ironically named the White Transportation Company) to pick up the Oberlin children free of charge. Joe Jr. knew his parents were a bit "tense," but he had no idea of the storm that was about to erupt. To young Joe, attending Daniels did not seem like much of a stretch. After all, he did not know the majority of the students at Ligon. The black kids from Oberlin Village were greatly outnumbered at Ligon by the residents of the other side of town. While whites might have assumed that a black student would feel comfortable in any black school, black children in West Raleigh had not grown up in the neighborhoods that largely populated Ligon. In fact, Holt felt a great deal of "nervousness" about going into what seemed like a "very alien environment" where he would feel pressure to "make friends real quick." But he had grown up playing in occasional ball games with white Oberlin boys, and it seemed almost natural that he would sit beside them in a classroom. "I think I kind of looked forward to getting to know some white guys and them knowing us. In my heart and mind I wasn't thinking about getting in a fight with anybody."[44]

Holt's equanimity quickly faded in November 1956 when the white-owned *Raleigh Times* published a picture of his family accompanied by the headline, "Negro Dad May Sue on School Application." Holt remembered, "It was as though we had committed a crime, because the only time usually you saw a black person's photo—a large photo in a local newspaper—was when that person had committed some offense." The press had learned of the Holt case while investigating the school board's secret arrangement for Ligon students to receive free bus transportation. When asked about his son's effort to enter a white school, Joe Holt Sr. remarked that he might take "legal action if necessary." The Holt family soon started receiving threatening phone calls and mail, and Joe Sr. eventually lost his job.[45] The Holts also faced new administrative obstacles. In 1957, the Raleigh School Board created an assignment plan that mandated that all children would attend the same school in 1957–58 as they had the preceding year, and any transfer requests had to be made at least two months prior to the opening of school. In June 1957, the Holts wasted no time in submitting a new application for Joe Jr., by then a rising tenth-grader, to attend Broughton High School. They were the only black family that year to apply to Raleigh's white schools. Their reasons included Broughton's proximity to their home and its "fuller academic and extracurricular program." They also argued that an integrated school provided "the added advantages of removing the illegal stigma of racial segregation from his scholastic endeavor." With only one dissenting vote (cast by black attorney Fred Carnage), the school board rejected the application. Undeterred by this rebuff as well as a telephoned bomb threat against their home, the Holts filed suit in the U.S. Eastern District Court in August. Representing them were Raleigh attorneys Herman L. Taylor and Samuel Mitchell. Taylor later said that he and his partner had tried in vain for "some time" to find someone with "the guts and the nerve to be the plaintiff in a case like that." The Holts "were the only ones we could find" who were brave enough to try.[46]

The Holts drew backing from the local black community. The Raleigh Citizens Association, the Raleigh Ministerial Alliance, and the NAACP provided moral support. And only once did Joe Jr. hear overt criticism at Ligon, when a boy told him that fellow students were saying behind his

The burden for initiating school desegregation fell largely to ordinary black citizens and the state's cadre of black lawyers. *Left to right*: Raleigh attorneys Herman L. Taylor, Samuel S. Mitchell, and George R. Greene around the time of the Holt case. (Courtesy of Joseph Holt Jr. and the Raleigh City Museum)

back, "You think you're better than the rest of us because you're trying to go to school with white kids." Overall, Holt recalled that none of his peers "harassed me, nobody mocked me; I was just another student in there, just another guy, and I appreciate that to this day." Moreover, moments of explicit support occurred. One classmate told Holt that he and his family were courageous. When his case appeared in court, several Ligon students attended the hearings in quiet support. Most students were at least passively supportive, Holt believes, because his admittance "would have meant not just that I got in the door, but now you can't keep the rest of us out of schools or other places."[47]

Despite the collective hopes of the local black community, the Holts fought much of their battle alone. Joe Jr. constantly worried about whether he would live up to everyone's expectations. "I felt like if I went [to a white school], I had to be some kind of a genius," he recalled. "I was going to have to just be an ace in everything or the papers would have said, 'Well, you see, he's a poor student.'"[48]

In the end, Holt never received the chance to prove himself. In September 1958, Judge Edwin M. Stanley declared in U.S. District Court that the Holts had not exhausted the administrative remedies provided by the Pupil Assignment Act. The key point at issue was that the Holts had allowed their attorneys to represent them before the school board rather than appearing in person. The Holts' decision not to appear before the board had, in fact, been made in careful consultation with their attorneys, who worried that board members might try to intimidate them. Even if the Holts had made a personal appearance, the board easily could have found ways to reject them under the Pupil Assignment Act. When Durham rejected dozens of transfer applicants in 1959 regardless of whether they had appeared before the school board, Thurgood Marshall quipped that their only chance would have been to be "neither here nor there." Despite these impossible odds, the judge's ruling haunted Joe Holt Jr. He felt that "the black community interpreted that as us screwing up." The Holts appealed to the U.S. Fourth Circuit Court of Appeals, and when that court upheld the district court ruling, they appealed to the U.S. Supreme Court. In October 1959, the Supreme Court declined to review the case, reflecting its inclination to leave school assignment matters to the lower courts. By that time, Joe Jr. was secretly hoping that he would not have to go to Broughton, since changing schools in the middle of his senior year would have been disruptive. But he kept those thoughts to himself, lest his opponents use his concerns as evidence of "not having demonstrated good faith." In 1960, Joe Holt Jr. graduated from Ligon as salutatorian of his class.[49]

By then, a handful of cities across North Carolina had begun token integration. In the fall of 1957, as the nation's eyes turned to the unfolding drama of the integration of Central High School in Little Rock, Arkansas, eleven students in three Piedmont districts—Charlotte, Winston-Salem, and Greensboro—became North Carolina's first African Americans to attend previously all-white public schools. The token nature of these admissions insured that the state's integration pioneers would not have black peers at school. In Greensboro, Josephine Boyd integrated Greensboro Senior High alone, as did Gwendolyn Bailey at Winston-Salem's Reynolds High. Harold Davis, Brenda Florence, Jimmy Florence, Russell Herring, and Elijah Herring Jr. integrated Greensboro's Gillespie Park School, but opportunities for group support were limited by the fact that they were spread across several grades. In Charlotte, four students integrated four schools: Gustavus Roberts at Central High, Girvaud Roberts at Piedmont Junior High, Delois Huntley at Alexander Graham Junior High, and Dorothy Counts at Harding High.[50]

Each of these students endured a unique struggle, but the ordeal faced by Dorothy Counts became the state's iconic image of school integration. When Counts arrived for her first day at Harding, white onlookers jeered, spat, and threw ice at her. In widely reprinted photographs, Counts's quiet

Coverage of white hostility to Dorothy Counts's 1957 integration of Charlotte's Harding High School produced what became iconic images of *Brown*'s implementation in North Carolina. Less well known are the reasons that the members of the Counts family chose to become integration pioneers. (Photograph by Don Sturkey, © 1957, North Carolina Collection, Louis R. Wilson Library, University of North Carolina, Chapel Hill)

dignity and composure stood in stark contrast to the unrestrained contempt of white protesters. After several more days of this torment, Counts withdrew from Harding High and enrolled in an integrated public school in the suburbs of Philadelphia, where relatives lived. That year went well and renewed her faith in the possibilities for interracial friendship, but she was homesick for North Carolina, so she returned and graduated from Allen High School, a private school for African American girls in Asheville.[51]

While the hostility of Counts's reception at Harding soon became enshrined in popular memory, the lesser-known context behind her family's actions reinforces the point that *Brown*'s pioneers were seeking something greater than better buildings. In the fall of 1957, Counts was slated to attend not one of Charlotte's poorest black schools but in fact one of its finest, West Charlotte High, a school that opened in 1938 but had moved to a new million-dollar facility in the fall of 1954. In recalling the opening of the new West Charlotte High, Dorothy Counts-Scoggins later explained, "For us in this community, it was state-of-the-art." Her older brother had graduated from West Charlotte's original facility, and she knew that the faculty was "very dedicated." And she was looking forward to attending school with her friends. Why, then, did her parents assent to Kelly Alexander's suggestion that they attempt to register their daughter in the white schools? For one thing, they suspected that despite the newness of West Charlotte, a white school might offer a broader curriculum and the most current textbooks. Just as important, they were committed to challenging Jim Crow, quite apart from any material advantages that an integrated school would offer. Counts-Scoggins believes that even if West Charlotte and Harding had been identical in all measurable ways, she and her parents would still have applied to Harding. Her father, Herman Counts, was a minister and professor of philosophy and religion at Johnson C. Smith College, and she had grown up absorbing his lessons in racial equality. First and foremost among them was the basic idea that "separation of the races was morally wrong."[52]

Most African Americans shared those feelings, but the widely publicized scenes of Counts's ordeal, as well as the nationally broadcast struggles of the Little Rock Nine, gave black parents plenty of reason for pause. A study of black mothers in Alamance County in the late 1950s found that fewer than one-third expressed interest in having their children transfer to white schools, and many felt apprehension about how their children would be treated in a predominantly white school. Parents also had good reason to fear employment reprisals such as Joe Holt Sr. had experienced. Not surprisingly, NAACP branch reports from the early 1960s routinely indicated the challenges of convincing parents to volunteer their children for school integration. Alexander lamented this trend, which he saw as evidence of "apathy on the part of our parents." While apathy may have explained the inaction of some, caution was a matter of survival for others. When asked in 1961 to list her branch's achievements, one activist from rural Wake County simply noted, "We think it is an achievement to remain alive and active as N.A.A.C.P. workers in this town and county."[53]

Durham, with its large economically independent black business class, was one of the state's few cities to witness a mass movement for school integration in the mid-1950s. By the end of the decade, the local school board had received more than two hundred applications for cross-racial transfers. Like the Holt family in Raleigh and the Counts family in Charlotte, activists in Durham extended calls for integration beyond questions of facilities and convenience.[54] In July 1955, a petition sponsored by several black civic and labor organizations and signed by more than eight hundred parents announced, "If the talents of the Negro working force are to be used to the maximum advantage, we must learn to live, go to school, and work together." Two years later, the parents of Joycelyn McKissick and Elaine Richardson applied to have their children transferred to white schools. Floyd McKissick, one of the University of North Carolina's first black students in 1951, and his wife Evelyn based their daughter's application on the fact that they lived closer to a white high school. Rachel Richardson's request on behalf of her daughter leveled an even more direct critique of Jim Crow itself. In defying *Brown* and upholding segregation, she argued, the school board was "breeding contempt for the law." Furthermore, a race-based school assignment was "harmful to the child psychologically, and makes the child feel that the state is working against it and it will not have an opportunity to develop into full citizenship, in the community." In 1958, when the school board denied their requests, the McKissick and Richardson families filed suit. One year later, more than two hundred families filed transfer requests; the board granted only eight. Durham's story reflected, albeit on an unusually large scale, statewide patterns of *Brown*-inspired mobilization. As historian Christina Greene has put it, black North Carolinians, particularly women and youth, "clearly were motivated by *Brown*, and their demands signaled a departure from earlier efforts to equalize school facilities."[55]

By the late 1950s, black apprehensions about *Brown* were giving way to mounting support, although the overall number of black applicants to white schools remained relatively small. One early 1956 poll found that only 53 percent of southern blacks approved of *Brown*'s mandate; by December 1957, that figure had risen to 69 percent.[56] Ideological approval of school integration, however, was one thing; volunteering one's children to pave the way was quite another. By one statewide tally, in 1957, there were 153 reported transfer requests in just eight school districts. One year later, that number dropped to 87 requests in five districts. In 1959, 318 African Americans from eleven districts requested transfers, and those numbers steadily rose in the early 1960s. Even if more blacks had sought transfers to white schools in the 1950s, school boards likely would have rejected most of their requests. Moreover, the burden of initiating integration rested exclusively with African Americans. As Davison Douglas has pointed out, as late as 1960, none of the state's interracial school transfers had originated with a local school board.[57]

Raleigh was no exception to this rule. Integration did not reach the state's capital city until 1960, when local NAACP leaders June and Ralph Campbell Sr. requested that three of their children—Ralph Jr., Mildred, and William—be admitted to white schools. The school board refused to admit the older two but permitted seven-year-old Bill to enroll at Murphey Elementary. Joe Holt Jr., then a student at St. Augustine's College in

Raleigh, remembers thinking, "What did they do that we didn't do?" The key difference between the Holt and Campbell cases was timing. In February 1960, the sit-in movement had begun in Greensboro, and in April the Student Nonviolent Coordinating Committee, which became a leading protest organization, was founded in Raleigh. The pressure to begin at least token integration was greater in 1960 than it had been in 1956. Two years earlier, the *Raleigh News and Observer* had warned that delays in the Holt case should not invite white complacency. "North Carolina," the paper argued, "must show some acceptance of the law as laid down by the courts or all its laws in this matter will be swept aside."[58]

In the spring of 1961, the pressure to "show some acceptance of the law" mounted when sixty-six plaintiffs filed suit against the Raleigh school board. Organized by the Raleigh Citizens Association, the local NAACP, and Raleigh attorneys Herman Taylor, Samuel Mitchell, George R. Greene, and Richard E. Ball, *Hunter v. Raleigh City Board of Education* alleged that Raleigh—and, more fundamentally, the state's Pupil Assignment Act—made unconstitutional use of race as its "controlling standard" in making school assignments. The case sought to remove any "racial significance" from pupil assignments and protect each student's "right to public education free of the burdens of racial discrimination and segregation." In an effort to delegitimize the Pupil Assignment Act, none of the plaintiffs made formal transfer requests, as the act required. Mayor and school board chair W. G. Enloe judged the case "ill-advised and ill-timed," while superintendent Jesse Sanderson simply replied, "We have nothing to discuss." While hardly advocating full-scale integration, the *Raleigh News and Observer* took the superintendent to task for his cavalier dismissal of the suit, arguing that if the city hoped to convince the courts of its "compliance with the law," then it "may after seven years need to show more than one Negro child integrated among the 16,436 pupils enrolled in the Raleigh public schools."[59] In January 1961, the pressure for compliance grew when the state's new governor, Terry Sanford, chose to enroll his children in Raleigh's only integrated school, Murphey Elementary, where Bill Campbell was now a third-grader. While Sanford did little to force integration over the next four years, his many visits to black communities had convinced him that the expansion of black opportunity required more substantive change than the attempted equalization of segregation. Sanford's quiet acceptance of the changing racial order provided a sharp contrast to the intransigence of Raleigh officials.[60]

In August 1961, the Raleigh school board announced that it would admit eight students to two white schools. The students included Myrtle Lillian

Terry Sanford's 1961 decision to send his children to Raleigh's only integrated school, along with his many visits to black schools during an education tour the following year, helped to legitimate the changing order, even if Sanford remained reluctant to use state power to force desegregation's implementation. Here, Sanford visits Merrick Moore School in Durham in September 1962. (Courtesy of the Raymond Stone Photograph Collection, The North Carolina State Archives, Raleigh)

Capehart, Dorothy Howard, and Cynthia Williams, rising tenth-graders who were admitted to Broughton High, and Rebecca Bryant, Gloria Hunter, Arnell Jones, Larry Manuel, and Anna Morgan, rising ninth-graders who were admitted to Daniels Junior High. Only four of the eight were plaintiffs in the pending lawsuit; the others were selected through negotiations between black leaders and the school board. For some of those handpicked pioneers, their selection came as a shock. As Lillian Capehart recalled, "I did not choose to be a trailblazer." All eight of the students came from the Oberlin section of Raleigh, demonstrating that the board's selection process partly indicated its desire to avoid opening the door to cross-town transfers to Daniels and Broughton, even if doing so meant recruiting some reluctant students and rejecting volunteers. The school board did not require any of the eight students to appear before it, a requirement deemed essential in Holt's case, yet it denied a transfer to a student who did appear before it that summer. Rose Marie Ellis lived closer to Ligon than Broughton, but she and her parents believed that the latter would offer broader curricular opportunities, especially with regard to business courses. When Ellis's stepfather, John C. Washington, appeared with his daughter before the board, he refused to accept her rejection passively. He pointedly asked school board member and real estate developer J. W. York whether he would hire a graduate of Ligon's business department. York stated that he had never had an applicant from Ligon, to which Washington replied, "You're not answering my question." York ended the conversation by retorting, "It's none of your business." After Ellis and Washington left, York motioned to reject their application, and all but black board member Fred Carnage approved the rejection. One staunch desegregation opponent groused about the changes in the board's handling of integration requests: "The school board fought the Holt case, but now they don't require the Negroes to appear in person before the board before admitting them. . . . Now they do whatever the NAACP demands and require the teachers to make the Negro children feel welcome."[61]

In truth, Raleigh's integration pioneers often felt less than welcome. Despite having a supportive teacher during his first year at Murphey Elementary, Bill Campbell "felt unsafe every day." For five years, he was the only black child at his school. Lillian Capehart found the "social alienation" at Broughton High overwhelming: "It was just, you're there, but you're a nonentity. You are still segregated in this integrated school." The only student who would sit next to her in the lunchroom was a girl with severe cerebral palsy who could barely talk. The other students had shunned this girl, but Capehart "felt so happy to have that body there that I didn't even see" her disabilities. At Daniels Junior High, Gloria Hunter similarly struggled with loneliness. She, her brother Gilbert Jr., and their parents, Hermena and Gilbert Sr., served as lead plaintiffs in the 1961 lawsuit, and the entire family felt committed to playing a role in the battle that the Holts had begun. Yet in entering Daniels, she left the sheltered and orderly environment of St. Monica's School, a black Catholic grade school. Her years at St. Monica's had prepared her for the experience of having white teachers, but nothing could have prepared her for the social isolation. She had no classes with the four other black students, and she became the target of bullying from a group of boys. On several occasions, she found "KKK" scrawled in lipstick on her locker. After administrators intervened and suspended the bullies, the worst of the harassment subsided, but it was not until well into her high school years at Broughton that she began to make friends. Rebecca Bryant Willis recalled later that she experienced less overt harassment at Daniels and was pleasantly surprised by the kindness of some teachers and the principal, but she noticed that white neighborhood children would play with her after school but generally ignored her at school. Larry Manuel, the only black male at Daniels, endured his own unique struggle of heightened scrutiny. "I knew they were watching me," Manuel recalled, "because at that time it was taboo for a black male to be anywhere close to a white female."[62] In paving the way for greater black inclusion in society, the Broughton Three and Daniels Five all paid the ironic price of exclusion at school.

The isolation of black students in white schools promised to lessen as their numbers increased, but as late as 1961, only seven school districts in the state's Piedmont region (Chapel Hill, Charlotte-Mecklenburg, Durham, Greensboro, High Point, Raleigh, and Winston-Salem) had even begun to integrate. The only eastern districts to begin desegregation were Wayne and Craven Counties, where the presence of integrated military bases sped the pace of change. Only two mountain districts—Asheville and Yancey County—had integrated. Even in the cities that had begun integration, progress moved at a snail's pace. The year after the admittance of the Broughton Three and Daniels Five, the Raleigh school board received more than sixty requests for cross-racial transfers and accepted only thirty-seven. In protest, a dozen students picketed the next school board meeting and parents appeared before the board in person to explain why they wanted to send their children to integrated schools. The local paper summed up the delegation's common refrain: "Since the children will soon have to function in an integrated society, the parents said they should be prepared by attending integrated schools."[63]

During this period of incremental progress, many black educators gradually set aside their fears of job loss and backed the integration movement. The NCTA routinely recommended "full compliance" with *Brown*, condemned the Pearsall Plan, and expressed support for the NAACP. Moreover, an early 1960s study of more than four hundred black teachers in North Carolina found that they overwhelmingly supported desegregation. Three-quarters belonged to or contributed to the NAACP, and 95 percent said that if put to a vote by secret ballot, they would opt for "full and immediate desegregation." Among the reasons for their support was a belief that desegregated schools offered interracial understanding and "better preparation for life in the modern world." They called for integration despite the fact that 61 percent expected at least some black teachers to lose their jobs as a result of the end of separate schooling. As sociologist Richard Lamanna has concluded, "The data in this study show a complete rejection of the traditional accommodating pattern by Negro teachers."[64]

Black educators approached the emerging civil rights movement from a variety of vantage points. Some openly participated in the NAACP, while others preferred to keep their distance. Principal Phairlever Pearson in Newton made clear to local NAACP representatives that he would personally negotiate on behalf of his school and "that we would have no litigations for any movements or anything as far as our school is concerned." At Greensboro's Dudley High, principal John Tarpley recalled that many teachers belonged to the NAACP, but "they didn't parade it publicly." Principal J. W. Mask of Hamlet, however, refused to hide his NAACP involvement, a stand that soured relations with the local superintendent. Mask escaped reprisal thanks to a white member of the local school board who backed his right to NAACP membership and thanks to the fact that North Carolina had not systemically suppressed the NAACP to the degree found elsewhere in the South.[65]

Black educators were perhaps most united around the fight for shared educational leadership. That goal, they insisted, remained essential, regardless of the pace with which the schools desegregated. Still confined to cramped and segregated quarters in Raleigh's black business district, the DNE's black employees continued to push for the integration of the Department of Public Instruction. The NCTA backed that demand, arguing that "racial segregation of educational leadership is outmoded." In 1958, Ferguson warned state superintendent of public instruction Charles Carroll that the poor conditions of the DNE's segregated offices could lead to "possible embarrassment"; nevertheless, two more years passed before the state integrated the DNE's black employees into the main education building.[66]

In the same spirit of inclusion, both the NCTA and the North Carolina Congress of Colored Parents and Teachers encouraged interracial cooperation and advocated classroom preparation for first-class citizenship. Teacher Ida Duncan, an NCTA member, urged her colleagues at the group's 1955 meeting to instruct and inspire children so that they would be "satisfied with nothing less than the blessing of democracy and full-fledged citizenship." The NCTA urged teachers to form "Citizenship Committees" to encourage black voter registration. Having maintained an open membership policy since 1949, the NCTA also continued to facilitate dialogue with the white teachers association. The North Carolina Congress of Colored Parents and Teachers did the same by forming the Intergroup Relations Committee, which periodically met with a similar committee from the white PTA. Overall the group reported positive results, but it saw "an important need" for "intergroup programs wherein Negroes are invited by Whites," as typically "the reverse procedure prevails." The Inter-group Relations Committee also called for the celebration of Citizenship Day, when black schools would host local officials for discussions of "the duties, responsibilities, and rights of American citizenship."[67]

Black parent and teacher associations allied themselves with the grow-ing integration movement even as they continued in their founding mis-sions of fund-raising and volunteer work for historically black schools. In theory, building up the resources of segregated black schools and paving the way for school integration were not incompatible goals. Nonetheless, by the mid-1960s, many white-authored plans for integration left little room for combining the two.

"Whose Fame and Honor Ever Mounting": African American Schools in Their Closing Era

Goldsboro principal and longtime NCTA leader Hugh Victor Brown ob-served in the early 1960s, "Any attempt to give a full appraisal of the effect of integration upon public education at this time could hardly be just or fair in consideration of the small numbers involved and the brief period of trial, but there is one result of unmistakable appraisal in the erection of school buildings for Negro children." "Magnificent 'architectural ex-pressions' in Negro school buildings are being erected in every part of the State," he reported, and those buildings were "being adequately equipped with the best of educational facilities." Principal J. W. Mask of Hamlet simi-larly recalled that when he moved to a new high school building in 1954, the school had "more classrooms stocked with new furniture than we had ever had before."[68]

In searching for ways to slow integration, North Carolina was not alone in upgrading black school conditions, although it did so somewhat sooner than did states to the south. North Carolina saw its most dramatic closing of the racial gap in school facilities before *Brown* (see table 5.2). In Mis-sissippi, modest equalization efforts began in the 1950s, but it was not until the 1960s that the state organized its most serious, if ultimately in-adequate, school equalization program. In South Carolina, Governor James Byrnes launched a seventy-five-million-dollar school equalization campaign in the early 1950s. By 1954–55, South Carolina surpassed North Carolina in per pupil school property values for rural black youth (table 6.1). South Carolina's more robust equalization efforts at that time partly reflected the fact that its schools remained completely segregated until 1963. In North Carolina, the white segregationist incentive for equaliza-

Table 6.1. School Property Values per Pupil in the Carolinas, by Race, 1952–1957

	1952–53	1954–55	1956–57
N.C. rural white	$439.39	$444.22	$512.54
N.C. rural black	$176.53	$185.97	$207.79
N.C. rural white-to-black ratio	2.5 to 1	2.4 to 1	2.5 to 1
S.C. rural white	$210.75	$632.25	$516.14
S.C. rural black	$35.79	$308.99	$442.11
S.C. rural white-to-black ratio	5.9 to 1	2.0 to 1	1.2 to 1
N.C. urban white	$572.66	$655.73	$726.94
N.C. urban black	$408.82	$545.60	$579.66
N.C. urban white-to-black ratio	1.4 to 1	1.2 to 1	1.3 to 1
S.C. urban white	$483.92	$533.10	$645.62
S.C. urban black	$207.47	$382.55	$523.43
S.C. urban white-to-black ratio	2.3 to 1	1.4 to 1	1.2 to 1

Source: *Southern Schools: Progress and Problems* (Nashville, Tenn.: Southern Education Reporting Service, 1959), 150, table 60.

tion lost some of its potency when a handful of schools integrated in the late 1950s.[69]

North Carolinians continued to build new black schools throughout the post-*Brown* decade, but those gains must be measured against a concurrent boom in white school construction. White investment in white schools was not simply a question of racial privilege. By the early 1950s, the first wave of Baby Boomers was entering the public schools and straining existing facilities for both races.[70] Demographic challenges aside, whites typically did not abide upgrades to the black schools without paired improvements to white facilities. NAACP Legal Defense and Educational Fund director-counsel Jack Greenberg once aptly noted that *Brown* did as much to stimulate education spending as had Sputnik: "Education was stagnant until 1954. After that, the 'separate but equal' theory caused authorities to upgrade all schools. The white children got better schools riding on the backs of Negroes." In North Carolina, the proportion of the 1949 and 1953 state school bonds that were spent on black schools slightly exceeded the black percentage of the school-age population, but even these infusions failed to make up for decades of underfunding.[71]

If Jim Crow privileged white children in the scramble for school funds, the region's racial politics ultimately shortchanged all southern children. When new proposals for federal aid to education emerged in the 1950s, southern members of Congress dredged up white fears of outside intervention and warned that federal funds would entail unwanted control. In 1957, every North Carolinian in the U.S. House of Representatives voted against a bill for school construction grants.[72]

Because of both their material inadequacy and their symbolic complicity with Jim Crow, the South's belated equalization efforts weakened but failed to destroy black momentum in favor of desegregation in Raleigh, Charlotte, and other communities across the region. When Farmville, Virginia, opened a new black high school in 1953, many black citizens were inclined to drop a pending desegregation suit, which had engendered ambivalence from the start. Yet driven at least in part by the influence of the NAACP's legal team, the litigants ultimately pursued the suit, which became one of the component cases of *Brown*. Clarendon County, South Carolina, another district from which a *Brown* component case emerged, had similarly appropriated equalization funds in an unsuccessful attempt to foil desegregation litigation. Little Rock, Arkansas, built a new black high school just one year before the Little Rock Nine applied to attend Central High.[73]

African Americans refused to allow white officials to purchase their loyalty to segregation with new buildings, but at the same time relatively few black communities actively opposed school upgrades. Full-scale integration seemed like a distant—and potentially frightening—prospect; increased funds for black schools promised immediate benefits for black youth and enhancements for much beloved institutions. Integration and equalization therefore coexisted on many local civil rights agendas. In the late 1950s, for example, the Greensboro NAACP simultaneously backed integration and the addition of a gym to the black high school. Explained NAACP leader Edward Edmonds, "We were carrying on two fights at the same time." Each of those fights, William Chafe has argued, "reinforced the other, and both contributed to the prospect of better education for black children." Moreover, as historian Sonya Ramsey has found in Nashville, Tennessee, some African Americans hoped that school upgrades would incline whites to attend black institutions after desegregation began.[74]

The pairing of equalization and integration struggles promised mutually reinforcing dividends for black communities as well as potential legal complications. Despite *Brown*'s central argument that even equalized facilities were inherently unequal, many local officials continued to suggest that the availability of equalized schools delegitimated integration demands. The black citizens of rural Caswell County put that claim to the test in the mid-1950s. In 1951, local officials finally had acted on years of black demands for better conditions by building a new black high school and replacing several small frame schools with modern facilities. Thanks in large part to the dedication of black parents, students, and teachers, the black high school offered academic and extracurricular opportunities that in some ways exceeded those found at the local white schools. At the time of integration, Vanessa Siddle Walker has found, Caswell County Training School (by then renamed Caswell County High School) was still the county's only public high school approved by the Southern Association of Colleges and Secondary Schools. The improved quality of their schools, along with their desire for caring treatment of their children, disinclined many Caswell parents to seek desegregation. Some, however, continued to worry about the possible perpetuation of resource inequalities as well as their children's lack of preparation for assimilation within white society. With such concerns in mind, the parents of forty-three children sued for integration in December 1956. While that case was pending, the same group of parents filed transfer requests in August 1957. They endured intensive questioning from the members of the school board, who used every possible argument, including the newness of black facilities, to dissuade the petitioners. The applicants focused their formal requests on the proximity of white schools to their homes, but their testimony suggests that broader concerns were also at play. One couple, interrogated for an hour, argued that they were so "bitterly opposed to segregation" that they would send their children to white schools even if whites responded with physical violence. The board rejected these applicants, and it was not until the original lawsuit was revived in the early 1960s that the first black students entered Caswell County's white schools. In 1962, the U.S. Fourth Circuit Court of Appeals concluded that even if, as the evidence suggested in this case, the black schools were equal or superior to the white schools, the plaintiffs "were entitled to prefer" the latter. Moreover, school boards could not hold parents to administrative procedures that were "unnegotiable obstacle courses." In January 1963, the first black students to enter the county's white schools endured relentless harassment. Not surprisingly, a poll that spring indicated that while slightly more than half of local black citizens approved of the court's decision to order school desegregation in the county, only 13 percent of Caswell blacks felt certain that an integrated school would provide a "better education."[75]

Unlike Caswell County, which significantly upgraded black schools around the time of *Brown*, some communities never came close to achieving equalization. In those cases, grossly inadequate equalization efforts often bolstered black support for integration. In Yancey County, where less than 1 percent of the school-age population was African American, the black community had long urged local officials to replace the aging one-room, one-teacher school that served approximately thirty students. By 1953, black parents were rumored to have hired an attorney and to be considering integration "not because they wish to attend white schools" but because school conditions were "so completely unsatisfactory." The school board pledged to build a new black school, but five years later, that promise remained unfulfilled. In the interim, the state judged the county's black school unsafe and ordered it to close. At that point, local officials began busing black students eighty miles round-trip to Asheville. Black parents agreed to this arrangement for one year on the condition that the county would build a new black school by the fall of 1959.[76]

Only when officials again reneged on their promise (partly because they had spent hundreds of thousands of dollars building two white high schools) did the black community resolve to fight for integration. Super-intendent Hubert Justice balked at this move. "We've always treated them decent," he explained. "Why some of them are descendants of slaves my grandparents used to own. They got along fine then and we're still trying to help them. But if they keep up this integration business there's going to be trouble—maybe even another Little Rock." At the state level, officials fumed at the negligence of Yancey County officials and privately acknowledged that black parents had a strong case. State board of education member D. Hiden Ramsey viewed the situation as "the most serious threat yet posed to our state policy of avoiding full integration." When local officials dug in their heels, parents filed a lawsuit with NAACP assistance. The NAACP gave the case national publicity, including an ad in the *New York Times* that pictured an African American girl asleep on a bus. The caption read, "80 MILES & 11 HOURS (that's a long school day for a six-year-old)." Under increased scrutiny, Yancey officials hastily built a new (yet very modest) school in 1960. By then, black parents were committed to integration and refused to back down. In September of that year, a U.S. District Court judge ordered the local white high schools to admit black students. Three more years passed before another court order forced Yancey County to integrate its elementary students.[77]

By the 1960s, equalization battles similarly overlapped with integration struggles in North Carolina's eastern Black Belt.[78] In Greene County, local NAACP leaders had worked throughout the 1950s for school equalization, efforts that violated national NAACP objectives but nevertheless stimulated the consolidation of four black schools. In 1959, when nearly three thousand students boycotted school to protest conditions at Greene County Training School (GCTS), they demanded equalized conditions,

80 MILES & 11 HOURS
(that's a long school day for a six-year-old)

In all of Yancey County, North Carolina, there is not one school where 28 youngsters can get the education they want and deserve. Yancey County has schools of course . . . but for whites only. These, however, refuse to absorb the 21 elementary school children and 7 high school boys and girls who make up the entire Negro school population of the county.

Last year, these children had no choice but to be transported far out of their home county to the nearest segregated schools, all the way to Asheville. Day in, day out, these children rode a bus. 40 miles there, 40 miles back . . . on mountainous, twisting Route 19. High school senior or first grader, it made no difference. They left home in the pre-dawn darkness of 6:30 and returned in the nighttime darkness of 5:30.

This year the children could no longer endure their patient waiting for unsegregated schools. The parents and other concerned citizens of Yancey County, Negro and white alike, have been forced to organize a temporary tutoring system while they push their attack on the basic problem.

The situation in Yancey County has scores of parallels throughout the South. It's been more than 5 long years since the Supreme Court decision of May 17, 1954—and yet the segregated school with its callous long-hauls and its myriad inferiorities continues to cheat Negro children of their right to equal training for life.

The dedicated efforts to break through these barriers to democracy urgently need your support. The struggle is complex and expensive. Won't you send your contribution to:

NATIONAL ASSOCIATION FOR THE ADVANCEMENT
OF COLORED PEOPLE
20 West 40th Street / New York 18, N. Y.
(Please make checks and money orders payable to N.A.A.C.P. or to Alfred Baker Lewis, Treasurer)

The NAACP placed this advertisement in the 1 December 1959 issue of the *New York Times* to draw attention to the Yancey County desegregation struggle. (Courtesy of the National Association for the Advancement of Colored People) not integration. "Most of the parents" claimed to have little interest in school integration, focusing instead on the injustice of the county's recent decision to build a new white high school while GCTS remained inadequate. The local NAACP reported to the national office that it had nothing to do with the boycott, as the equalization position of the strikers "was not an NAACP one." All the same, ideological purity apparently mattered less to some local NAACP members than their desire to back the youth's fight. Branch secretary Dora Mae Farmer "was a participant [in the boycott] throughout" and helped to secure officials' tentative promises of school improvements. At that point, the parents reportedly turned "conciliatory."[79]

Conciliation, however, did not amount to surrender. Only six months after the boycott, Dora Mae Farmer and other parents applied to have five children reassigned from GCTS to the all-white Walstonburg High School. That request indicated the fluidity between equalization and integration activism as well as the fact that many transfer requests involved concerns that transcended questions of facilities. The new white high school was not yet completed, and facilities at Walstonburg offered little measurable improvement over GCTS. In fact, the board rejected all five applications on the grounds that Walstonburg High was "manifestly inferior both in size and curriculum" to GCTS and, therefore, the children's "best interest" demanded that they remain at the black school. Despite the fact that two of the involved fathers were threatened with foreclosures on their farms, the parents filed suit in federal district court. In 1964, with litigation still pending, Farmer applied for her grandson and Lillie M. Edwards applied for her son to be admitted to the white school. By then, the new white high school had been built. Yet when asked by the school board to explain their motivations, the question of facilities did not arise. Both women insisted that they felt good about the quality of instruction at GCTS. Edwards explained that although "the Training School has just as good teachers," she was dissatisfied because "when our children finish [at GCTS] they don't have the same opportunities." Farmer similarly told the board that she wanted her grandson "to have a desegregated education and to be entitled to his Constitutional rights, and for that reason and only that reason we are making this request." In refusing to disparage the quality of the local black schools, Edwards and Farmer insisted that it was possible to both desire integration and appreciate the strengths of black institutions. The school board approved their applications, and in January 1965, Farmer reported that the boys were "doing nicely" in their new school and that she was busy with new concerns, including antipoverty work and the testing of segregation in places of public accommodation. "I been running a long time," she explained, but "I'm not tired yet, and I'm not going to give up."[80]

Similar protests that fused the goals of equalization and integration unfolded in the early 1960s in Northampton, Warren, Granville, Martin, and Franklin Counties. The Franklin County demonstration involved a student boycott to protest the school board's refusal to grant cross-racial transfers and its failure to provide improved facilities at the local black schools.[81] In 1961, students boycotted Warren County's Snow Hill School, an aging Rosenwald building with outdoor toilets and potbellied stoves. Parent Melvin Tunstall, a farmer and carpenter, initially deflected questions about whether desegregation was one of the protesters' goals. "This has nothing to do with integration or segregation," he explained. "It's just to try and get better schools for our children." The *Raleigh News and Observer* argued that Warren County whites should "welcome and be warned" by such protests that still allowed for redress according to "the old 'separate but equal' formula of Southern race relations." The students returned to class after being transferred to a nearby black school with larger facilities, but two years later, at least some of the county's black citizens apparently felt that the old southern formula had run its course: The parents of fifty-three pupils filed a school desegregation lawsuit. Not long thereafter, a second school boycott developed. This time, the leaders of the NAACP Youth Council sought "to dramatize not only their determination to desegregate local schools but their demand for improvements in the physical plant and administration of the Negro county high schools."[82]

By the 1960s, some black leaders attempted, often unsuccessfully, to block school construction projects that threatened to prop up the color line. In 1960, Durham's only black city councilman, Rencher Harris, opposed a local school bond package that failed to include an integration plan. Harris reluctantly challenged the bond, as he understood the need for new facilities, but he felt that the city should not expand its existing system until it had reckoned with how it would fully integrate students.[83] Likewise, when Lumberton officials called for school bond issues in 1962 and 1963, a local NAACP chapter questioned the fact that officials had earmarked the funds for new "white schools," "Negro schools," and "Indian schools." Such racially designated schools, they argued, were wasteful of resources and "contrary to the law of the land."[84] As senior class president at Asheville's Stephens-Lee High School in 1959–60, future civil rights attorney James Ferguson organized a student protest of a "makeshift" addition to his school. He recalled that even then, he and his fellow protesters believed that "our school should be comparable to the white school and, what's more, that we should be permitted to go to the white school if that's what we choose to do."[85]

In demanding integration either in addition to or in lieu of equalization, blacks were certain to arouse white hostility as well as possible opposition from their own communities. When a new black school was built in her hometown, Mississippi civil rights activist Anne Moody recalled, "students, teachers, and principals alike, were bragging about how good the white folks were to give us such a big beautiful school, [and] I was thinking of how dumb we were to accept it." Similar fault lines emerged in North Carolina communities. Wilmington physician Hubert Eaton, who had organized an equalization lawsuit that led to the 1954 construction of a new building for Williston High, filed a second lawsuit in 1964, this time for his daughter's entry into a white school. The later suit engendered far more white hostility than the first, as well as some criticism from blacks who decried the eventual closing of Williston. Eaton shared their concerns, but he ultimately believed that "it was far more important that we, as blacks, move into the mainstream of American life in all ways and at all different levels."[86]

In requesting new or improved black schools, parents often insisted that their demands did not equate to an endorsement of segregation. Even so, it was nearly impossible in the context of escalating racial tensions to make such distinctions heard. In Cabarrus County, the local paper reported the results of a 1963 survey indicating that the vast majority of black citizens desired a new "segregated high school" rather than integration with the white high school. Some of those surveyed quickly protested the paper's use of the word "segregated." "We simply asked for a high school of our own," one parent explained. In their minds, desiring a better school for their children and supporting segregation were not one and the same. Nonetheless, in a visit to Cabarrus County in the summer of 1963, Kelly Alexander of the state NAACP "aimed sharp criticism" at the parents and suggested that their proposal was playing into the hands of segregationists. Some local black citizens apparently agreed. Several months later, the parents of 108 Cabarrus County youth filed a desegregation lawsuit. Among the suit's requests was that the county abolish segregation in new school construction projects.[87]

Black divisions over desegregation partly reflected the fact that *Brown*'s announcement came not at a moment of overall declension for southern black schools but rather at what for many was their institutional apogee. Some of the most glaring educational inequalities had diminished by the mid-1960s. The state had roughly the same per pupil instructional expenditures on black and white students, and many black schools had benefited from physical improvements to their facilities. Between 1919–20 and 1963–64, black per pupil school property values had increased fifty-fold, whereas white values had increased eighteenfold.[88] No attribute of black schools compared more favorably to white schools than the men and women who staffed them. In 1963–64, 27 percent of the state's black educators held graduate-level certificates, whereas about 17 percent of white educators did. In the late 1960s, for example, Raleigh's Ligon High had a higher percentage of teachers with graduate degrees than any of the city's three white high schools. As a consequence of black educators' higher levels of training and experience, their salaries ranked slightly above those of whites.[89] Pupil-to-teacher ratios were nearly equal in the early 1960s, a huge change from four decades earlier, when black teachers averaged seven more students per teacher than their white counterparts (see table 4.1). Moreover, in a generation's time, both blacks and whites had dramatically increased the number of years of schooling they had obtained. In 1940, black North Carolinians age twenty-five and older averaged 5.1 years of school, while whites averaged 7.7 years; by 1970 those figures were 8.5 and 11.2, respectively. While a racial differential remained among older adults, the gap was far smaller among people aged twenty to twenty-four. By 1970, blacks in that cohort had on average completed 12.2 years of school, nearly equal to the white average of 12.6 years.[90] Some points of relative parity—for example, the percentage of students in high schools accredited by the Southern Association of Colleges and Secondary Schools—said as much about the state's low rankings for white students as they did about the state's commitment to racial equality.[91] Nonetheless, in a number of areas, the racial gap in school conditions was not as wide in the 1960s as it had been a generation earlier.

By no means was this period a golden age in the state's educational history, however. Despite the more rapid increase in black per pupil property values, in 1963–64, those values still constituted only 68.4 percent of white values, and the closing of this gap had stalled by the late 1950s (see table 5.2). Curricular differences between black and white high schools also remained evident, primarily at the level of electives (see table 2.1).[92] Moreover, achievement testing indicated that black and white students began their schooling careers with a relatively small gap in reading and mathematical skills, but the gap widened as the children advanced through school.[93] And even though both blacks and whites had increased their overall levels of educational attainment, whites were still more likely to acquire postsecondary schooling. Between 1954 and 1964, the percentage of white high school graduates in the state who advanced the following year into postsecondary institutions (colleges and trade schools) increased from 40.9 percent to 53.8 percent; for blacks, the percentage barely budged from 32.9 percent to 34.0 percent.[94] Most significant, postwar equalization efforts had done nothing to address either the lack of black power in school politics or the larger question of whether even the best-equipped segregated schools could facilitate the attainment of first-class citizenship.

Despite these persistent inequalities, integration nonetheless required African Americans to cede control of deeply revered institutions that only recently had begun to receive anything close to their fair share of resources. The story of Ridgeview School in the Appalachian foothills town of Hickory illustrates why many black communities experienced the *Brown* era as a time of both institutional gain and loss. Established in 1916, Ridgeview School served students of all grades throughout the Jim Crow period and was the town's only black school that offered instruction beyond the elementary grades. Ridgeview High received state accreditation in 1928, although the school lacked many of the facilities found at the newly built and architecturally acclaimed white high school, Claremont Central High School (also known locally as Hickory High). By 1935, the city had erected two new buildings for Ridgeview following a fire that destroyed the original structure. Still, by 1949, the local newspaper concluded that the school was "badly crowded and lacked many facilities." The black community routinely chipped in to meet the school's needs. For example, students funded the purchase of lockers by bringing a "dime apiece weekly." As in all southern communities, blacks in Hickory lacked the political representation necessary for direct influence over the division of education funds. The experience of powerlessness was compounded in foothill and mountain towns by the fact that the black populations there lacked strength in numbers. In Hickory, blacks constituted about 15 percent of the population in 1950, compared to 27 percent statewide. "We did not have a voice," explained longtime community activist Billy Sudderth. Black citizens were at the mercy of "plantation politics."[95]

The racial politics that informed school appropriations meant that not until the early 1950s did Ridgeview see its most intensive period of expansion. In 1952, the city completed a new vocational building, three new classrooms, and a new lunchroom for the school. On the same day that *Brown* was announced, the local paper announced, "Negro Schools Get Priority in County." A state survey team had concluded that four of Catawba County's five schools in most need of upgrades were black schools, and Ridgeview School was in "urgent need" of improvement. The following December, the Hickory school board voted to spend its entire allotment from the 1953 state bond (just over one hundred thousand dollars) on a new building for the high school grades at Ridgeview. The new Ridgeview High, which included a library, home economics room, biology room, business education facility, administrative office, and four classrooms, opened in the fall of 1957. Three years later, Ridgeview received six new elementary classrooms.[96]

Hickory's black citizens were hardly blind to how belated upgrades to southern black schools could serve white interests in preserving segregation, but they welcomed the long-needed educational resources. Ridgeview graduate Billy Sudderth recalled discussion within his family about how the additions to the school were "a window dressing" designed to dampen enthusiasm for integration, but the general "mentality of the local people was that it was a progressive thing." The addition "provided a lot more than we had had in the past," recalled Flossie Waller Saddler, who graduated from Ridgeview in 1960. She particularly enjoyed the new science labs and the expanded curriculum that the additional classrooms made possible.[97]

Physical facilities aside, the part of the Ridgeview experience that most stands out in black memories was the nurturing community that students, parents, and teachers collectively created. As former student Larry Johnson put it, "It wasn't the structure, it was the environment" that made Ridgeview a great school. Most essential to this community were teachers who held "extremely high" expectations for student behavior and academic performance. According to the state's instructional index (based on years of experience and training), black teachers in the Hickory schools in the mid-1950s ranked slightly above white teachers, a pattern commonly found throughout the state. Principal Taft Broome was especially revered in the community. "Everybody looked up to him," recalled Janice Lutz Johnson, a 1966 Ridgeview graduate. "He wasn't a tyrant—he loved us all. But you knew when he said something, it was gospel." The teachers similarly evoked feelings of both reverence and affection. Beloved physical education teacher Dean Patterson, who taught at Ridgeview from 1958 to 1966 and then later at the integrated high school, shepherded hundreds of students through the awkward years of adolescence with the assurance that they "could talk to her about anything." Home economics teacher Janet Thompson "was just the epitome of a lady, and you just wanted to be like her," Johnson remembered. For her part, Thompson recalled that she held young people to first-class expectations despite the second-class treatment that white society often afforded them. Even after moving to the new building, the school received cast-off supplies, she recalled, "but we didn't use that as an excuse. We said, 'Get your lesson. Get your lesson. Learn, learn, learn, learn!'" Such dedication paid off in 1958, when Ridgeview High won approval from the Southern Association of Colleges and Secondary Schools, a more rigorous standard than state accreditation.[98]

The white community rarely bore witness to the classroom dedication of Ridgeview's teachers and students, but athletics occasionally offered a venue for demonstrating the Ridgeview spirit to the white community. Under the leadership of coaches Burrell Brown and Sam Davis, the school's basketball and football teams achieved legendary status. In the 1950s, the football team became known as the Untouchables after its opponents failed to score against them for three years. Friday night games became so popular that they occasionally accommodated large crowds by playing at Lenoir-Rhyne College, a nearby white institution. Hickory High coach Troy Washam said of the Ridgeview games, "Everyone in town would go see them. White and black."[99]

By the 1960s, Ridgeview School was in many ways a stronger institution than ever before, but simultaneous upgrades to the white schools meant that measures of equality were a constantly moving target. In 1952, for example, the same year Ridgeview got sixty thousand dollars in upgrades, the city opened a "million dollar" white junior high and equipped it with "ultramodern school furniture" and "all necessary teaching aids and classroom supplies." Overcrowding at the white high school led to several upgrades there in the 1950s and early 1960s, including a three-story classroom building and additions to the library, shop, and business education facilities. A 1964 study found that all of Hickory's schools had adequate libraries except Ridgeview and East Hickory Elementary (the town's only other black school). The latter school had no library at all. Moreover, the curriculum at Claremont Central included a broader selection of courses, especially in the areas of math, languages, fine arts, and vocational subjects.[100]

The persistence of such inequalities eventually helped to fuel the movement for school desegregation in Hickory. As late as the spring of 1965, Hickory's schools remained completely segregated, but the city faced mounting pressure to comply with Title VI of the 1964 Civil Rights Act. That legislation, which permitted the federal government to withdraw federal funding from districts that still maintained de jure school segregation, took on new meaning with the 1965 passage of the Elementary and Secondary Education Act (ESEA). The ESEA provided the first major infusion of federal money into the public schools and required individual districts to submit desegregation plans before receiving those funds.[101]

In responding to federal pressure, Hickory first implemented a freedom-of-choice plan. Used by many southern districts, freedom-of-choice plans entailed no affirmative steps toward integration but simply opened up cross-racial transfers as an option that parents and students could choose; in effect, such approaches put the burden of desegregation entirely on black parents and students. Hickory's plan gave parents of students entering the seventh, tenth, or twelfth grades the option of choosing a school other than the one to which they had been assigned. In the spring of 1965, black students in those grades began applying to enter the white schools, but this limited approach to desegregation soon came under increased local and federal scrutiny. That summer, the interracial Community Relations Council went before the Hickory school board and questioned proposed additions to Ridgeview. The campus was already crowded, the group argued, and the elementary and high school grades should occupy separate campuses. Moreover, given that the white schools offered a broader curriculum, all students should "be allowed to attend another school where a more enriched program is offered." In September, several black parents whose children did not meet the freedom-of-choice criteria filed suit. The school board admitted these eight students to a white elementary school, but the suit continued because it broadly challenged discrimination within the system. In early 1966, the school board amended its compliance plan by immediately extending school choice to all students in grades eight and above and announcing that it would discontinue grades seven through twelve at Ridgeview at the end of the 1965–66 school year and transfer those students to white schools.[102]

In Hickory as in many other southern communities, desegregation largely traveled a one-way street, with black students transferring to white schools. Under the initial freedom-of-choice plan, for example, the local high schools integrated when nineteen black students chose to transfer to the white high school in the fall of 1965.[103] That plan had presented a particularly conflicted decision for rising seniors, who would only have one year to adjust to their new surroundings. Janice Lutz Johnson chose not to transfer to the white high school. She recalled that the black community was very supportive and proud of those few members of her class who did pave the way for full integration, explaining, "They were the trailblazers." At the same time, she never considered finishing anywhere but Ridgeview. Thanks to the dedication of Ridgeview parents and teachers, she recalled, "we thought we were rich. . . . We got the things we needed." Ridgeview, Johnson remembered, "was just a family affair." Classmates Judy Dula Mayhew and Mary Joice Jett shared Johnson's fondness for Ridgeview but nonetheless were among the six seniors who chose to transfer to Claremont Central. They approached the transfer as an opportunity to accept a challenge, "a chance to grow." They felt most at home, however, at Ridgeview, where they continued to attend sporting and social events. Mayhew recalled her decision to help integrate the schools as a way to demonstrate her "rebellious" streak and to open new doors, not as an effort to sever her ties to Ridgeview. In fact, having that home base meant that she had "the best of both worlds."[104]

In the spring of 1966, Ridgeview High graduated its last class. The school's alma mater, with its assertions of immortality, struck a particularly poignant note that year:

By the ridge of Blue Top Mountain,
Stands dear Ridgeview High
Whose fame and honor ever mounting,
Never ne'er will die.
Ridgeview, Ridgeview Alma Mater.
Your sons and daughters are true.
Long as the sun sinks o'er yon mountain,
We'll cheer the orange and blue.

In the years to come, after Ridgeview closed and the city had torn down its main classroom buildings, Janice Johnson took her daughter to the school's gymnasium to tell her about the pride students felt for their school. Reflected Johnson, "I know she'll never feel the joy, the pride that we had, but I was trying to give her a sense of it. And when you stand on those steps, . . . you can look over and see the mountains. . . . You just marveled at what you had. You knew you had a good education. . . . You had the teachers, you had the community behind you. . . . Everything was right there, encompassed in that little area."[105]

Subsequent generations of Hickory's black youth would not experience the unique Ridgeview environment, but there were many reasons for feeling confident in the spring of 1966 about the decision to forge ahead with integration. That April, federal judges declared North Carolina's Pearsall Plan unconstitutional. Though little actual use had been made of the plan's measures, it had served for a decade as an important symbol of state resistance to *Brown*.[106] Over the next year, two major federal research studies of U.S. education offered evidence that classroom diversity—both racial

Sign commemorating Ridgeview
School in Hickory, one of hundreds
of historically black schools in
North Carolina that closed during integration. (Photograph by
author)

and socioeconomic—mattered for improving the educational outcomes
of historically disadvantaged students.[107] While scholars most often measured desegregation's potential benefits in relation to black youth, some
integration proponents offered a more inclusive vision of *Brown*'s beneficiaries. Julius Chambers, who helped litigate Hickory's desegregation case
and ultimately contributed more than any other individual to the legal
battle for full school integration in North Carolina in the late 1960s and
1970s, explained his hopes to a white opponent of busing: "Perhaps your
children and mine . . . can begin to view each other as human beings with
faults, problems, hopes and aspirations no different from others."[108] That
vision seemed still remote in the mid-1960s. Yet in less than a generation,
the state would come closer than ever before to creating a school system
in which race and class posed no barrier to equal educational opportunity,
the possibilities for citizenship, and basic human understanding.

Most [black] parents felt that this is a good opportunity for my children
to get the best, . . . but they thought that they were really going to integrate the
whole thing. They had no idea that they were going to erase the buildings and
even the idea of Ridgeview ever being there.
—Educator Catherine Sudderth Tucker, on school desegregation in Hickory, 2010

We all learned and grew. We worked together to make
Broughton a more inclusive community and us more well-rounded individuals.
—Margaret Newbold, granddaughter of Nathan Newbold, on integration at
Raleigh's Broughton High, 2010

They are . . . tearing down what we have already built up.
—Hermena Hunter, mother of Raleigh integration pioneer Gloria Hunter, on the
opponents of Wake County's school diversity policy, September 2010

Epilogue

Despite *Brown*'s promise, many black students during the early days of
school desegregation felt less like first-class citizens than ever before. In
1969, when the Hickory Human Relations Council asked black pupils at
recently integrated Claremont Central High to offer anonymous feedback
on their experiences, one wrote that she had made a white friend but that
he was being teased as a "nigger lover." Another simply said, "My school
year at Hickory High has been one of Pure-D-Hell." In the spring of 1970,
although blacks comprised 15 percent of the student body, the student
council and varsity cheerleading team included no black members. In a
letter to the principal, the Black Student Union suggested several ways of
creating a more inclusive school: increasing black representation in student organizations, hiring a black high school coach and "human relations
counselor," and adding a course in black studies to the curriculum. Even
in terms of facilities, the move from Ridgeview had fallen short of black expectations. On one hand, the white school was better equipped and much
larger than Ridgeview. Mabel Sudderth, one of the first nineteen students
to integrate, recalled that each student in her Claremont Central science
classes enjoyed the use of a microscope, whereas everyone had crowded
around a single instrument at Ridgeview. On the other hand, the white
school's main building was four decades old, whereas Ridgeview built its
new high school addition in 1957. Ridgeview High students, then, left a
building that was less than a decade old to integrate a facility built in the
1920s. When Ridgeview teacher Janet Thompson began teaching at Clare-

mont Central, she "just couldn't believe that we would walk out of a new building and go into a building like that."[1]

Similar stories of disillusionment unfolded across North Carolina, where black high school students typically integrated historically white space. In cases where black high schools remained in use as educational facilities, they were often "demoted" from high schools to elementary schools or junior highs. Eighteen-year-old Ligon High, for example, became a middle school. In urging the Raleigh school board to retain Ligon as a high school, Charlotte attorney Julius Chambers argued, "The board's position is that it's all right to attend a previously black school, but not to graduate from there and bear the badge of having graduated from a previously black school." Since North Carolina had few black-majority school districts and black high schools therefore tended to be smaller than their white counterparts, size constraints certainly influenced building-use choices. Nonetheless, cultural ideas about race, identity, and public space also played a role. When the state's school superintendents were asked in 1954 whether whites would be willing to attend buildings once used for blacks, the unanimous answer was no. One wrote, "Phar[ao]h's Army could not make them enter a school building which has been used by the negroes." Another said, "The feeling of 95% of our parents would be, whether right or wrong, that it would be an unforgivable disgrace." Burke County's superintendent agreed: "No matter how adequate and if equal in all respects to the white ones, it would be next to impossible to get them to go."[2] These attitudes had a devastating effect on black high schools. In 1960, North Carolina had 248 black high schools; today, only 5 of the state's high schools are historically black institutions.[3] An irony of the school equalization movement was that many of the South's black schools that were closed during desegregation were relatively new—by one estimate, 57 percent were less than twenty years old. A 1971 report noted, "Physically adequate buildings have been made into warehouses and administration buildings, or sold to private interests. Black students from these schools have been transferred to overcrowded, tense, and—in many cases—inferior schools, which were previously all-white."[4] White disinclination to use relatively new "black" buildings for their original purpose reinforced the message that white rejection of black schools was not simply about the durability of bricks and mortar but also about power and the ownership of public space.

Even when students integrated seemingly neutral new buildings, the racial politics of Jim Crow continued to imprint school facilities. In 1966, Chapel Hill closed the city's white and black high schools and opened a fully integrated high school in a new building. The new school, however, retained the name of the white school, as well as its mascot and school colors. Its trophy case contained only mementos from the white school. The first yearbook was dedicated to two white staff members and bore the name of the white school's yearbook. Moreover, only a small number of black faces appeared among the school's faculty, and the longtime principal of the black high school was demoted to assistant principal. One of the three homecoming queens that year was black, but all of the cheerleaders were white. In both material and symbolic ways, black students had lost a sense of ownership over their school.[5]

Hickory also eventually built a new Hickory High School in 1972, but the contrasting fates of its two former segregated high schools speak to the role that white privilege played even in shaping public memories of the Jim Crow period. The city transformed the white high school into a widely used art and science museum adjacent to the city's main public library and razed Ridgeview's original and 1957 high school buildings. The only portions of the school that remain are the 1960 elementary classroom building and the gym and cafeteria complex, which today house child care, recreation, and senior citizen centers adjacent to the Ridgeview branch library. Some Ridgeview alumni tried to convince the city to salvage more of the Ridgeview campus. Longtime Hickory educator and Ridgeview graduate Catherine Sudderth Tucker advocated on behalf of school integration in the 1960s but later felt disillusioned by the ways that the desegregation process marginalized black students and eroded public memory of Ridgeview. Most black parents initially felt that desegregation was "a good opportunity for [their] children to get the best," she recalled, "but they thought that they were really going to integrate the whole thing. They had no idea that they were going to erase the buildings and even the idea of Ridgeview ever being there."[6]

For black communities, school integration entailed significant institutional losses and exacted a heavy human price. When the staffs of white and black schools were merged, the latter routinely lost out. In 1963, North Carolina had 620 black elementary school principals, a number that dropped to 170 in 1970. From 1963 to 1973, the number of black high school principals dropped from 209 to 3. And by 1972, 3,051 of the state's black teachers had lost their jobs as a result of integration. The state accomplished these dismissals in part by abolishing teacher tenure laws and requiring teachers to take the National Teachers Examination (NTE) for contract renewal. "School desegregation devastated black educational leadership," historian David Cecelski has concluded.[7]

In the context of these losses, some veteran integration activists began to reevaluate *Brown*'s benefits in light of its costs. Attorney and civil rights activist Floyd McKissick, who in the 1950s had integrated UNC's law school and whose daughter integrated Durham High School, later allied with the Black Power movement and embraced its concern for strengthening the black community. He continued to believe in the merits of integration, but not if it entailed closing black schools, firing black teachers, and subjecting black students to hostile environments. Legal scholar Charles Ogletree, who worked for the National Association for the Advancement of Colored People (NAACP) as a law student in Boston during the 1970s, wrestled with similar questions in hindsight. Why, he later wondered, had he and his peers labored exclusively for black children to attend school with whites without also "raising the question of more resources for black schools"?[8]

In terms of institutional survival, the state's historically black colleges and universities (HBCUs) fared better under desegregation than did black primary and secondary schools, but their long struggle for resources has persisted. Beginning in 1970, the University of North Carolina system was involved in a decadelong battle with the U.S. Department of Health, Education, and Welfare over whether the state had eliminated vestiges of segregation from higher education. Enrollment and staffing patterns as well as comparisons of resources and degree offerings pointed to a university system that was still in many ways separate and unequal. When department representatives toured the state's five HBCUs in 1979, they were appalled at conditions. At the school where James Shepard had dreamed more than a generation earlier of creating a university indistinguishable from white institutions, investigators were shocked to find leaky roofs and inadequate equipment. A tally of working autoclaves turned up none at North Carolina Central University (NCCU), two at A&T, and no fewer than forty at the historically white North Carolina State University. According to attorney Julius Chambers, who served as NCCU's chancellor from 1993 to 2001, the state simply never had committed itself "to bring[ing] the black institutions up to par."[9] Federal intervention did stimulate the state to expand programs and degree offerings at the HBCUs in the 1980s, but the schools continue to struggle with the legacy of historically weak public investment compounded by low endowments. On the eve of NCCU's centennial, NCCU chancellor Charlie Nelms called for a National HBCU Reinvestment Act, which in essence would confront anew the legacies of Jim Crow within higher education.[10]

At all levels of education, desegregation unfolded on white terms in part because black representation in policymaking bodies remained limited. Not until 1968, when Henry Frye won election to the state House of Representatives, did African Americans again sit in the General Assembly. Local school boards integrated more quickly, at least at the token level. As historian Helen Edmonds has pointed out, the appointment of "a token black" to local school boards became accepted practice in the South as early as the 1950s. Even so, in the mid-1970s, only about 2 percent of southern school board members were black. In the late 1970s, North Carolina had no black school superintendents, and nearly two-thirds of the state's school districts had no black administrators.[11]

In the context of black school closings, teacher dismissals and demotions, and student marginalization, it is no wonder that many veteran black educators experienced desegregation as a time of loss. As former Jeanes teacher Ruth Woodson put it, before integration "you didn't lose any children because the parents and the teachers worked so closely together. . . . So many children that are failures [now] would not have been failures then." Greensboro educator Nelle Artis Coley observed similar patterns during desegregation's first decade, but in the early 1980s, she cautiously hoped that a more cooperative era lay ahead. "I think it had to get worse before it can get better," she argued. "I don't know that it will be better than when it was all black. It will at least be equal to what it was; perhaps, it will get better. . . . Somewhere, short of eternity, we ought to learn to live with each other."[12]

Perhaps the central question facing policymakers and parents today is whether the situation did get better under integration, as Coley hoped. While there is no simple answer, a narrative of integration's losses and struggles certainly shortchanges many individual stories of black resilience as well as substantive evidence of integration's broader achievements. Even during integration's earliest days, there were stories that challenged the doomsayers. When Josephine Boyd became the first African American to graduate from an integrated high school in North Carolina in 1958, she did so with an academic average of 92.4, despite enduring a grueling year of harassment. At previously all-white Brunson School in Winston-Salem in 1963, twelve-year-old twins Harold Kennedy III and Harvey Kennedy were elected president and treasurer, respectively, of their classrooms. Two years later, when Harold was one of four black students at Wiley Junior High, he was elected secretary of the student body. Audrey Crawley Reeves, one of the first black students to integrate Claremont Central in Hickory in 1965, found that by the time she graduated in 1968, she had friends on both sides of the color line. In her view, integration enabled blacks and whites to "come together, sit down, and have a decent conversation." As black students integrated schools in larger numbers in the 1970s, they worked collectively for the democratic reclamation of school space. By the time Joanne Peerman graduated from Chapel Hill High School in 1973, youth-led protests had resulted in greater black representation in student organizations and a perceptible difference in black student attitudes. "We felt very powerful," Peerman recalled. "We felt like we had made change, we had made our stand. . . . We didn't feel intimidated or anything. We felt it was our school as much as theirs. We all came there together."[13]

In the fall of 1970, black students at Hickory High similarly organized after reaching a stalemate in negotiations with school officials over representation in student groups. When the principal appointed two black students to the varsity cheerleading squad, students rejected what they saw as tokenism and requested an election for at least four guaranteed slots. Denied this request, students turned to direct-action protest. Six black cheerleaders interrupted a football game by walking onto the field and leading several cheers. When the principal attempted to escort the cheerleaders off the field, a group of about one hundred black fans surrounded him. This confrontation ended peacefully, but fights broke out at halftime between black and white students. The local newspaper reported that after the game, black protesters poured onto the city streets, throwing rocks and bottles and damaging a number of local businesses and cars and injuring two white passengers. Soon thereafter, two whites were arrested for cross burnings in the Ridgeview neighborhood. When Hickory High principal Gene Miller suspended the six cheerleaders who interrupted the football game, nearly two hundred black students boycotted school. All of those students received a three-day suspension. Tensions eased when the mayor imposed a citywide curfew for several days, yet a state investigator judged that "the scar left on Hickory these past days has yet to heal." The work of interracial healing was indeed far from over, but student activism had raised awareness of black grievances and won some concessions from the administration. Miller agreed the following year to amend the student election process so that each class would be guaranteed at least one elected black student council representative and at least two elected black varsity cheerleaders. Moreover, the turmoil of early desegregation obscured the fact that the South's youth often were well ahead of their elders in the business of racial reconciliation. Despite—or perhaps because of—the tensions at Hickory High, investigators from the Southern Regional Council found in 1974 that "the majority felt race relations at the high school to be far superior to those in the community as a whole."[14]

Aside from these local battles, African Americans were also democratizing public education at the level of state policy. For example, under pressure from a wide range of national black protest organizations, the southern states by the 1970s increasingly adopted textbooks that gave greater attention to African American history.[15] African Americans also continued to fight for representation in school politics. North Carolina's two PTAS merged in 1969, and in 1970 the North Carolina Teachers Association (NCTA) merged with the North Carolina Education Association to form the North Carolina Association of Educators (NCAE). While the NCTA did not achieve all of its goals for the merger process, former NCTA executive secretary E. B. Palmer believes that overall, the NCAE's early power-sharing arrangements achieved more equitable leadership than did any other southern teachers' organization. African Americans have won seats on many local school boards since the 1970s, and in 2003, former state senator Howard Lee became the first black chair of the state board of education.[16] On many levels, then, African Americans resisted the inequities of the desegregation process and pushed for a system of shared school ownership.

Moreover, by both academic and economic measures, integration scored gains for black students. Studies have shown that when integration achieved its highest levels in the 1970s and 1980s, the racial achievement gap narrowed; when schools began to resegregate in the 1990s, the gap held fast or by some measures widened. Desegregation also appears to have had "an economically significant, positive effect" on narrowing the income gap between blacks and whites.[17] In assessing *Brown*'s accomplishments, some might ask whether black students would have scored similar gains if the Supreme Court in 1954 had demanded the strict enforcement of *Plessy* instead of overruling it. The answer is that entrenched white resistance to full educational equality surely would have stymied the ultimate realization of separate equality. But even if the region had removed all measurable racial differentials between black and white schools, the added resources likely would have had a positive effect on blacks' academic success and income potential—to a point. Decades of economic and sociological research indicate that school resources do improve poor and minority children's chances for success but that their chances are even greater in diverse schools.[18]

Moreover, the question of whether *Plessy*'s strict enforcement would have raised blacks' achievement and income levels misses two key points: desegregation benefited both black and white students, and not all the ways in which it did so are easily quantified. Research indicates that students of all races who attend diverse schools generally have higher graduation and college acceptance rates and are less likely to end up in the criminal justice system. More abstract but no less significant, students in integrated schools appear to gain an appreciation of diversity and a sensitivity to issues of exclusion. In other words, they learn to be citizens of a diverse world.[19] When a team of scholars interviewed more than five hundred members of the class of 1980 from six different integrated high schools, including West Charlotte High, they found that "despite pundits' claims that school desegregation is a failed social experiment, the millions of people who lived through this anomalous chapter of American history in the 1970s have a far more complicated tale to tell." That tale included stories of interracial friendships and increased cross-racial understanding as well as disappointment that school integration failed to translate into full integration within society at large.[20] In the words of Jennifer Hochschild and Nathan Scovronick, desegregation's "accomplishments were smaller than its advocates promised and less than they hoped for, but except when done irresponsibly or very unwisely, it improved the chances for black children to attain their dreams and did not diminish the chances for white children. Members of both races usually gained socially from the interaction." It was, "on balance, an educational success."[21]

After levels of school desegregation peaked in the 1970s and 1980s, the 1990s brought both gains and losses. On the one hand, that decade witnessed North Carolinians across racial lines cooperatively addressing unresolved educational inequities. In 1994, parents from five high-poverty rural counties (Hoke, Halifax, Robeson, Vance, and Cumberland) filed suit against the state, alleging that low local tax revenues resulted in inadequate schools and thereby violated state constitutional guarantees of an equal education. Plaintiffs from several wealthier urban districts eventually joined the suit, arguing that their high numbers of disadvantaged youth compromised their ability to offer equal opportunity. *Leandro v. State of North Carolina* brought new attention to the fact that North Carolina's educational inequalities never had fallen strictly along a black-white fault line. In addition to urban-rural educational differentials, *Leandro* addressed sharp disparities within urban districts, where it has become increasingly common to find schools with high concentrations of poor, minority, and limited-English-proficient students. In 1997, the state Supreme Court refused to require the state to equalize school funding, but it did affirm each child's constitutional right to an "equal opportunity to receive a sound basic education." The task of outlining the components of a "sound basic education" fell to Superior Court judge Howard Manning, who subsequently has led ongoing efforts to define and protect the "*Leandro* rights" of North Carolina's children.[22]

On the other hand, the 1990s also witnessed the first serious evidence of southern school resegregation. Disappointment with desegregation certainly could be found on both sides of the color line. Black disillusionment found expression in support for school choice programs such as charter schools and private school vouchers as well as in alumni efforts to commemorate the social and cultural strengths of historically black schools, which these graduates often perceived as missing from integrated schools.[23] Nonetheless, opinion polls reveal that a majority of African Americans—and a substantial percentage of whites—still believe that classroom diversity is important. In addition, more generalized support for an integrated society has remained strong across racial lines. At the same time, popular support—and, perhaps most significantly, judicial backing—for busing and other ways of maintaining integration has waned. In fact, scholar Gary Orfield has argued that school resegregation had less to do with "any negative turn in public opinion" and more with the courts "leading public opinion backward."[24]

The impact of recent court decisions was particularly evident in Charlotte, which in the 1970s received national acclaim as a model of southern school desegregation. A landmark Supreme Court decision, *Swann v. Charlotte-Mecklenburg Board of Education* (1971), had legitimated the use of busing in achieving school integration. One generation later, U.S. district judge Robert Potter seized what he saw as an opportunity to rescue the citizens of Charlotte, whose plight he compared to that of Sisyphus, the mythological King of Corinth who was condemned for eternity to push a heavy stone up a hill only to have it roll back down. Judging that the Charlotte system had removed "the vestiges of past discrimination," Potter ruled in 1999 that school officials should no longer be required to bus children to achieve racial balance. In other words, he argued that as long as all of the city's residents had access to quality schools, the government should not insist that those schools also be racially diverse. The Charlotte-Mecklenburg system appealed the decision, but the ruling had the backing of a predominantly white coalition of suburban parents who called for a return to "neighborhood schools." Teaming up against Potter's decision were Arthur Griffin, the black chair of the city's school board, and Eric Smith, the white superintendent of schools. Despite interracial efforts to maintain integration, when the Charlotte schools opened in the fall of 2002 with a new "neighborhood choice" school assignment plan, nearly a quarter of the district's schools had minority enrollments higher than 80 percent.[25] Today in Charlotte, as in many cities in the South and across the nation, the majority of public school students are both poor and either African American or Hispanic.[26]

Until recently, no city in North Carolina had bucked the resegregation trend more successfully than Raleigh. In an effort to create and maintain integrated schools, the city implemented a busing plan in 1971, merged with the Wake County Schools in 1976, and started a popular magnet program in the 1980s. In 2000, in response to the growing legal assault on desegregation, Wake officials became the first metropolitan system in the nation to use student family income rather than race as its chief criterion for assessing school diversity. The system received accolades as a model district, maintaining diverse schools while decreasing the racial achievement gap, winning high levels of parent satisfaction, and earning the support of the business community. The *Raleigh News and Observer* spoke for many when it argued that "a system that provides schools where students are in a diverse population better prepares those students for life and work in a very diverse country, and world."[27]

Nonetheless, in the fall of 2009, a small but highly organized group of citizens in four suburban voting districts elected to the school board opponents of the diversity plan, giving them a five to four majority.[28] Despite an outpouring of protest, the school board voted in the spring of 2010 to implement a choice-based assignment plan. The summer and fall brought more protests, arrests, candlelight vigils, and legal action by the NAACP. As the school system came under increasing scrutiny from the U.S. Department of Education and regional accrediting agencies—as well as lampooning by Comedy Central's Stephen Colbert and criticism from former president Bill Clinton—the opponents of Wake County's diversity plan lost their majority on the school board in the fall of 2011. The new board initially chose not to reinstate the socioeconomic integration plan, but within months preliminary enrollment patterns indicated increasing levels of racial and socioeconomic imbalance. In hopes of at least slowing that trend, the board voted in 2012 to end the choice plan, although it did not restore the county's original school diversity model.[29]

Opponents of integration plans in Raleigh and elsewhere have insisted that what really matters is school equality and effectiveness rather than diversity. Yet history suggests that these goals are inseparable. As Gary Orfield has recently written, "Our political leaders and our courts have failed to preserve the gains [of desegregation] and are spreading the false impression that *Plessy* can now work in a region where it failed comprehensively for more than sixty years."[30] In many ways, much of the current debate boils down to one question: Can a highly segregated public school system in the twenty-first century somehow free itself from the oppressive vestiges of the Jim Crow era? In 2001, Judge William B. Traxler Jr. wrote in upholding Potter's decision in Charlotte, "We are confident that *de jure* segregation is history." Venton Bell, the principal at West Charlotte High School at the time of the ruling and a student at that school during segregation, expressed qualified hopes about the fading influence of the past. "I think busing at the time was a good thing," he noted, "because there was no other way to change things. But the days of Jim Crow and apartheid are gone. I don't think this judge's decision is going to have a big effect—as long as we have equal facilities at all of our schools." By contrast, attorney Luke Largess, who represented black parents challenging Potter's ruling, warned, "The stubborn facts of history persist, and if they are left unattended, they fester." Wake County citizens also expressed divergent understandings of history. Ronald Margiotta, who chaired the Wake County School Board at the time of the policy shift, chafed at the suggestion that questions of segregation still merit a place on the educational agenda. "We're not talking about segregation," he asserted. "I don't see that here. It's never coming back. Race is not an issue as far as I'm concerned." State NAACP president William J. Barber II insisted, however, that the segregated past has not so much been buried as it has been repackaged and sanitized. "'Neighborhood schools,'" he recently cautioned, "is code for segregated schools."[31]

Wake County's integration pioneers have warned against a hasty dismissal or misappropriation of history. Joe Holt Jr. worries that his parents' initial arguments for sending him to white schools will be misremembered as a simple bid for "neighborhood schools." He predicts, "One day somebody's going to say, 'Wait a minute. Let's go back to this Holt case. . . . Wasn't what they were saying very much like what we are saying? Didn't they complain about the fact that their son had to go across town to school, okay, and isn't that all we are saying?'" Holt is quick to correct this misperception: "No, no, no. The objective here was to cast off the shackles of second-class citizenship." Gloria Hunter fears that her sacrifices as one of the Daniels Five may have been in vain. The recent bid to end the diversity policy "really hurts deeply to me," she said, "because I know what I have gone through to make [desegregation] happen." Her mother, Hermena Hunter, wonders whether many of the diversity plan's opponents are aware of what her daughter and other local integration pioneers endured. Noting that many of today's residents of Raleigh and its suburbs—including Margiotta, a New Jersey native—are relative new-comers to the South, Hermena Hunter fears that outsiders to the community "are coming down and tearing down what we have already built up."[32] The diversity plan's opponents included many regional natives, too, but the conspicuous role of northern transplants does point to an ironic twist in this story. Southern whites once warned that "outside agitators" would force integration on the region, but as it turns out, the South hardly held a monopoly on white ambivalence toward school integration.[33]

None of Raleigh's integration pioneers remembers desegregation as a panacea; rather, they see it as a process that brought significant gains along with sacrifices disproportionately shouldered by blacks. Larry Manuel, another of the Daniels Five, lost the close social network he had enjoyed in black schools but gained "tolerance, patience," and knowl-edge of "how to deal with diversity." Especially for desegregation's earli-est pioneers, one of the experience's chief shortcomings was its lack of reciprocity. Lillian Capehart feels that in integrating Broughton High, she "learned a lot about white people," but the white students learned far less "about African Americans and our history." By the time of full-scale integration in the 1970s and 1980s, the opportunities for mutual ex-change between black and white students increased. Lynn Parramore, a white student at Broughton High in the 1980s, recalls that her family re-gretted the long bus rides and assignment shifts that desegregation en-tailed, but they knew that they were a part of something "even more im-portant than the inconveniences." By that time, black and white students still often "existed in parallel universes. . . . But since we couldn't avoid each other altogether, something else happened. Slowly—sometimes painfully—we began to get used to each other. . . . Hardly a big post-racial bear hug. But better than the unbreachable divide that preceded busing. It was progress." About a decade earlier, another white student's reaction to integration at Broughton High offered a particularly poignant testament to the ways in which desegregation stimulated rapid generational shifts in racial attitudes. For Margaret Newbold, attending an integrated high school "was one of the best [experiences] of my life. . . . We all learned and grew. We worked together to make Broughton a more inclusive com-munity and us more well-rounded individuals." Only a generation earlier, Newbold's grandfather, Division of Negro Education director Nathan C. Newbold, had worked tirelessly to make the "separate but equal" system as equitable as possible, yet he found the collapse of the color line an unthinkable prospect. Today, Margaret Newbold finds it equally unimaginable that the Raleigh schools would choose to reverse the course of history. She hopes that the Wake County system will find a way to maintain school diversity "for the sake of humanity, for the sake of community and for basic fairness and the opportunity for each and every child to receive a high-quality education."[34]

At the very least, it seems that in charting future paths for public education, the present and the past should remain in close and meaningful dialogue, and the search for the vestiges of Jim Crow should include artifacts other than cast-off textbooks and worn-out buildings. Segregation's material markers vitally mattered and still do. But Jim Crow schooling was intimately bound up with a larger system of second-class citizenship that denied blacks full inclusion in American society. It was also bound up with a gulf of ignorance and misunderstanding between the races that permitted whites to hold unchallenged assumptions of superiority. Shortly after the *Brown* ruling, historian C. Vann Woodward warned against naturalizing the existence of segregation and denying that it had a relatively recent institutional history. Woodward later emphasized that in offering this admonition, he did not mean to suggest that segregation was "superficially rooted and could be readily eradicated by right-thinking reformers."[35] In reminding us of segregation's traceable yet deep roots, Woodward points the way for a new generation's struggle for schools—schools that represent both equality and a greater vision for democratic citizenship.

Notes

ABBREVIATIONS

ATA	Arch T. Allen
CAE	Clyde A. Erwin
CO	*Charlotte Observer*
DCT	*Durham Carolina Times*
DIS Papers	Department of Public Instruction, Division of Instructional Services Papers, State Archives, North Carolina Division of Archives and History, Raleigh
DMH	*Durham Morning Herald*
DNE Papers	Department of Public Instruction, Division of Negro Education Papers, State Archives, North Carolina Division of Archives and History, Raleigh
ECB	E. C. Brooks
GC DNE	General Correspondence of the Director Series, Department of Public Instruction, Division of Negro Education Papers, State Archives, North Carolina Division of Archives and History, Raleigh
GC SPI	General Correspondence Series, Department of Public Instruction, Superintendent of Public Instruction Papers, State Archives, North Carolina Division of Archives and History, Raleigh
GDN	*Greensboro Daily News*
GEB Papers	General Education Board Papers, Rockefeller Archive Center, Pocantico Hills, North Tarrytown, N.Y.
GHF	G. H. Ferguson
HDR	*Hickory Daily Record*
HLT	Herman L. Taylor
JES	James E. Shepard
LR	*Lumberton Robesonian*
MARS 104.3	Department of Public Instruction, State Superintendent's Office Papers, General Correspondence, Old Records Center, North Carolina Division of Archives and History, Raleigh
MARS 104.56	Department of Public Instruction, School Planning Section Papers, Application Folders for School Construction Funds, Old Records Center, North Carolina Division of Archives and History, Raleigh
NAACP Papers	National Association for the Advancement of Colored People Papers, Library of Congress, Washington, D.C.
NCC	North Carolina Collection, Louis R. Wilson Library, University of North Carolina, Chapel Hill

NCDAH   State Archives, North Carolina Division of Archives and History, Raleigh
NCN   Nathan C. Newbold
NCTR   *North Carolina Teachers Record*
Newbold A&S   Articles and Speeches of Nathan C. Newbold Series, Department of Public Instruction, Division of Negro Education Papers, State Archives, North Carolina Division of Archives and History, Raleigh
Newbold Papers   Nathan Carter Newbold Papers, Duke University, William R. Perkins Library, Special Collections, Durham, N.C.
NYT   *New York Times*
PC   *Pittsburgh Courier*
PTA Papers   North Carolina Congress of Colored Parents and Teachers Papers, North Carolina State Parent Teacher Association Headquarters, Raleigh
RC   *Raleigh Carolinian*
RN&O   *Raleigh News and Observer*
Shepard Papers   James E. Shepard Papers, North Carolina Central University, James E. Shepard Memorial Library, University Archives, Records and History Center, Durham, N.C.
SSF   Special Subject Files, Department of Public Instruction, Division of Negro Education Papers, State Archives, North Carolina Division of Archives and History, Raleigh
SSN   *Southern School News*
TM   Thurgood Marshall
WW   Walter White

Note: For some manuscript sources, I used both the archival and microfilm copies. Within the notes, the distinction is indicated by the fact that I have included reel numbers for the microfilm versions. For archival collections in which the folders are organized in an intuitive fashion—for example, the General Correspondence Series of the DNE Papers is generally organized by last name of correspondent—I have in most cases included only box numbers.

INTRODUCTION

1. Clotfelter, Ladd, and Vigdor, "Classroom-Level Segregation and Resegregation," 70–71; Traub, "Can Separate Be Equal?" 36; *Time*, 29 April 1996; Tim Simmons, "School Choice Is Resegregating Charlotte," *RN&O*, 3 November 2002, 1A, 12A.

2. In *Leandro v. State of North Carolina* (1997), the North Carolina Supreme Court affirmed the state's duty to provide each child with an "equal opportunity to receive a sound basic education."

3. Clotfelter, Ladd, and Vigdor, "Classroom-Level Segregation and Resegregation," 79–80; T. Keung Hui, "Is Diversity Worth the Effort?" a forum in the *RN&O*, 30 October 2005, 25A–26A.

4. Major works covering the early history of black education include James D. Anderson, *Education of Blacks*; Bullock, *History of Negro Education*; Harlan, *Separate and Unequal*; Heather Williams, *Self-Taught*; Span, *From Cotton Field to Schoolhouse*; Moss,

Schooling Citizens; Eric Anderson and Moss, *Dangerous Donations*. For black education in North Carolina during this period, see Leloudis, *Schooling the New South*, chapter 6; Westin, "State and Segregated Schools"; Boggs, "State Supported Higher Education." The literature on desegregation receives further attention in chapter 6.

5. Woodward, *Thinking Back*, 87; James D. Anderson, "Jubilee Anniversary," 155–56; Hall, "Long Civil Rights Movement." Studies that emphasize this middle period in educational history within the North Carolina context include Gavins, "Within the Shadow"; Walker, *Their Highest Potential*; Burns, "North Carolina and the Negro Dilemma." For recent case studies that have examined the long sweep of educational equalization efforts in other locations, see Scott Baker, *Paradoxes of Desegregation*; Bolton, *Hardest Deal of All*; Shabazz, *Advancing Democracy*; Sugrue, *Sweet Land of Liberty*, esp. chapter 6. For concurrent efforts to equalize segregated health facilities, see Thomas, *Deluxe Jim Crow*. Also important to my work is Adam Fairclough's long look at black educators, *Class of Their Own*.

6. The key study of the NAACP's equalization work is Tushnet, *NAACP's Legal Strategy*. See also Sullivan, "Prelude to *Brown*."

7. Cecelski, *Along Freedom Road*; Walker, *Their Highest Potential*.

8. Bell, *Silent Covenants*; Goluboff, *Lost Promise*. For counterpoints to Bell, see Ogletree, *All Deliberate Speed*; Cobb, *Brown Decision*, 51. Ogletree argues that the courts should have implemented *Brown* without delay.

9. Crow, Escott, and Hatley, *History of African Americans*, 77–79 (delegates quoted on 78); Heather Williams, *Self-Taught*, 72–74; Haley, *Charles N. Hunter*, 9–10.

10. My typology of citizenship rights draws on the classic work of T. H. Marshall (*Citizenship and Social Class*, esp. 10–11, 25), who identified three types of citizenship: civil, which encompassed legal rights such as freedom of speech and religion and property rights; political, marked by the right to vote and hold office; and social, which included access to education. He charted how civil rights evolved first, political rights followed, and social rights developed last. For the relationship between education and ideas of citizenship, see Moss, *Schooling Citizens*. For the South's delayed educational development, see Kaestle, *Pillars of the Republic*, 182–217; Leloudis, *Schooling the New South*, 3–17.

11. Crow, Escott, and Hatley, *History of African Americans*, 84–88.

12. *Laws and Resolutions*, 30; Noble, *History of the Public Schools*, 289–93, Hood quoted on 291; Crow, Escott, and Hatley, *History of African Americans*, 84–88, 154; McIver quoted in Haley, *Charles N. Hunter*, 31–32.

13. Douglas, *Reading, Writing, and Race*, 8–10; Leloudis, *Schooling the New South*, 121–23. The final blow to the Dortch Act ironically came when a coalition of whites opposed paying the higher tax rates that the measure imposed.

14. Crow, Escott, and Hatley, *History of African Americans*, 209–11.

15. Quotation from an 1888 issue of an early NCTA organ, *The Progressive Educator*, excerpted in "Looking Backward to Gain Perspective," *NCTR* 1 (January 1930): 11. On the NCTA's founding, see Percy Murray, *History*, 15–17; Haley, *Charles N. Hunter*, 59–61. Though the group at times called itself the North Carolina Negro Teachers Association, it was chartered simply as the "North Carolina Teachers' Association," and the apostrophe was generally dropped in later years. See Atkins, "President's Address."

16. Crow, Escott, and Hatley, *History of African Americans*, 112–18.

17. Kousser, *Shaping of Southern Politics*, 58; Gilmore, *Gender and Jim Crow*, chapters 4, 5, esp. 120–21. The amendment included a grandfather clause that allowed illiterates to

vote if they or their ancestors could vote on or before 1 January 1867. This clause expired in 1908, but it gave illiterate whites a window of opportunity to register.

18. Harlan, *Separate and Unequal*, 69, 131. On *Hooker*, see Douglas, *Reading, Writing, and Race*, 14–16.

19. Michael Katz has similarly revised T. H. Marshall's conception of citizenship, offering a modern example: "Immigrants admitted as resident aliens received social citizenship—access to the full benefits of the welfare state—before they qualified for political citizenship" (*Price of Citizenship*, 345).

CHAPTER ONE

1. Mary E. Sills to NCN, 26 July 1919, and enclosed broadside, box 4, GC DNE; "Report of NCN," August 1919, reel 93, series 1.1, GEB Papers.

2. Franklin and Moss, *From Slavery to Freedom*, 385. On efforts to enforce black loyalty, see Kornweibel, *"Investigate Everything."*

3. For analysis of how expressions of loyalty could serve as a strategy for liberation, I am indebted to my colleague David Sartorius and his work on nineteenth-century Cuba ("Limits of Loyalty").

4. "Raleigh Negroes Pledge Loyalty," *RN&O*, 7 April 1917, "Loyalty and the Negro," *RN&O*, 7 April 1917, both in Charles N. Hunter Scrapbooks, box 15, Charles N. Hunter Papers, Duke University, William R. Perkins Library, Special Collections, Durham, N.C.; Leuchtenburg, *Perils of Prosperity*, 11–29; Thomas Walter Bickett, "Loyalty of North Carolina," 7 April 1917, in Bickett, *Public Papers*, 270–71. For statistics on black service during the Civil War, see Crow, Escott, and Hatley, *History of African Americans*, 72.

5. Woodruff, "African American Struggles," 45–46.

6. Newbold, *Five North Carolina Negro Educators*, 49 (Dudley quote); C. W. McDevitt, "Kinston Negress Gives Seven Sons to America," *CO*, 3 October 1926, NCC Clipping File; Kate M. Herring, "Negro and War Savings"; Stephenson, "War Savings Campaign"; *Charlotte Observer* quoted in Lemmon, *North Carolina's Role*, 32.

7. Haley, *Charles N. Hunter*, 191–93 (Jordan quoted on 191); poster reprinted in Lemmon, *North Carolina's Role*, 37; Breen, "North Carolina Council of Defense," 25.

8. Haley, *Charles N. Hunter*, 187–88, 207; "The Negro and Politics," *CO*, reprinted in the *Raleigh Times*, 20 March 1916, Hunter Scrapbooks.

9. Franklin and Moss, *From Slavery to Freedom*, 352–54; Fairclough, *Better Day Coming*, 67–109 (Du Bois quoted on 98); Gavins, "NAACP in North Carolina," 107.

10. W. E. B. Du Bois, "Brothers, Come North," *The Crisis* 19 (January 1920): 105–6; Kornweibel, *"Investigate Everything,"* 2; Margo, *Race and Schooling*, 114–17; Crow, Escott, and Hatley, *History of African Americans*, 119–20, 130–33 (migrant quoted on 132). Black North Carolinians were slower to migrate than blacks from the Deep South. Five percent of the state's black population headed north in the 1910s; nearly 15 percent did so during the 1940s.

11. C. C. Spaulding to T. T. Thorne, 14 April 1921, enclosed in C. C. Spaulding to ECB, 13 April 1921, box 82, GC SPI. For northern school inequalities, see Grossman, *Land of Hope*, 246–58; Sugrue, *Sweet Land of Liberty*, esp. chapters 6, 13.

12. Bickett quoted in Haley, *Charles N. Hunter*, 215.

13. Franklin and Moss, *From Slavery to Freedom*, 385–88; "The Lynching Industry," *The Crisis* 19 (February 1920): 183–86; Bickett, "Loyal Order of Klansmen—A Very Foolish and

a Very Wicked Order," 30 June 1919, and "Negro Emigration," 4 August 1919, both in Bick-ett, *Public Papers*, 289–92; Moore quoted in *The Crisis* 18 (August 1919): 196.

14. [JES] to Westmoreland Davis, 4 August 1919, and accompanying proposals, box 69, GC SPI; JES to T. W. Bickett, 4 August 1919, folder Correspondence August 1919, box GB383, Governor Thomas Bickett Papers, NCDAH.

15. JES to NCN, 27 December 1923, box 7, GC DNE.

16. A. M. Moore to J. Y. Joyner, 19 December 1918, Joyner to Moore, 27 December 1918, Moore to ECB, 24 December 1918, ECB to Moore, 3 January 1919, all in box 71, GC SPI; ECB to JES, 15 September 1919, JES to ECB, 16 September 1919, ECB to "Sir," 20 Septem-ber 1919, all in box 69, GC SPI; Brooks quoted in "See Improvement in Negro Schools," *NYT*, 7 July 1919, 28.

17. Sosna, *In Search of the Silent South*, 20–41; Hall, *Revolt against Chivalry*, 62–65; Eleazer, *Adventure in Good Will*; H. H. Proctor, "The Atlanta Plan of Inter-Racial Co-operation," *Southern Workman* 49 (January 1920): 9–12; NCN, "Interracial Cooperation in the South," 3 December 1928, box 1, Newbold A&S.

18. "Suggestions for Conference, September 26," box 69, GC SPI; "A Declaration of Principles by Representative Negroes of North Carolina," NCC; NCN to William M. Cooper, 18 December 1942, box 2, Newbold A&S.

19. "A Declaration of Principles by Representative Negroes of North Carolina," NCC. See also Haley, *Charles N. Hunter*, 216–18; Gatewood, *Eugene Clyde Brooks*, 165; Boggs, "State Supported Higher Education," 198–99.

20. "A Declaration of Principles by Representative Negroes of North Carolina," NCC.

21. "Negroes Announce Definite Program of Race Activity," *RN&O*, 2 October 1919, 1, 12; "An Appeal to Common Sense," *RN&O*, 2 October 1919, 4; "Negroes of South More Prosperous Than Ever," *DMH*, 2 October 1919, 1, 8; "A Good Sign," *DMH*, 3 October 1919, 4; "Different Types of Leadership," *GDN*, 4 October 1919, 4; "For a Better Sentiment," *Salis-bury Evening Post*, 6 October 1919, 4; "The Race Problem," *CO*, 2 October 1919, 6; "Ex-ecutive Committee of the Teachers' Assembly Ask Teachers to Aid the Negroes," *North Carolina Education* 14 (February 1920): 3; J. E. Swearingen to ECB, 21 October 1919, box 72, GC SPI.

22. A. M. Moore to ECB, 26 September 1919, C. C. Spaulding to ECB, 13 October 1919, C. Dillard to ECB, 22 October 1919, E. E. Smith to ECB, 15 October 1919, C. M. Eppes to the Negro Citizens of North Carolina, 22 September 1919, all in box 69, GC SPI.

23. Charles Hunter to ECB and NCN, 22 October 1919, box 70, GC SPI; Haley, *Charles N. Hunter*, 219–20. On political activity among black men in early twentieth-century North Carolina, see Hornsby-Gutting, *Black Manhood and Community Building*; Zogry, "House That Dr. Pope Built."

24. Haley, *Charles N. Hunter*, 195; "Application for Charter," NAACP Raleigh Branch Files, 1916–39, NAACP Durham Branch Membership List, enclosed in J. M. Avery to John R. Shillady, 27 March 1919, scattered membership lists in NAACP Durham Branch Records, 1919–39, all in reel 18, series A, pt. 12, NAACP Papers; Johnson quoted in "Says North Carolina Race Relations Is Improving," *Norfolk Journal and Guide*, 10 May 1924, Hunter Scrapbooks. The five Raleigh men were T. L. McCoy, A. W. Pegues, James H. Young, Berry O'Kelley, and C. H. Boyer. Shepard appeared on the Durham NAACP's 1927 and 1931 membership lists.

25. Kenneth Warlick, entry on Dudley in Powell, *Dictionary of North Carolina Biog-raphy*, 2:113–14; Newbold, *Five North Carolina Negro Educators*, 33–59; Haley, *Charles N.*

Hunter, 117, 121, 175–76, 226–27, 253; Gilmore, *Gender and Jim Crow*, 212–13. For the *Crisis* controversy, see "Greensboro, N.C., and *The Crisis*," *The Crisis* 20 (May 1920): 46–47; Crow, Escott, and Hatley, *History of African Americans*, 126; ads for A&T in issues of the *Crisis*, June 1920–January 1921. Some southern cities, including Greenville, North Carolina, requested that the U.S. Post Office ban the delivery of select black periodicals (Jordan, *Black Newspapers*, 140).

26. Gilmore, *Gender and Jim Crow*, 149. The two women present at the 1919 meeting were Florence C. Williams, state director for Negroes of the State Bureau of Tuberculosis, and Jeanes supervisor Annie W. Holland.

27. Mrs. H. L. McCrorey to ECB, 22 September 1919, box 69, GC SPI; Gilmore, *Gender and Jim Crow*, 192–95, 203–11, 220; Margaret Supplee Smith and Wilson, *North Carolina Women*, 215–18; "Bickett Warns of Whisperers," *CO*, 13 October 1919, 7.

28. Margaret Supplee Smith and Wilson, *North Carolina Women*, 245–49; Gilmore, *Gender and Jim Crow*, 189–90, 213–14, 218–20; Wadelington and Knapp, *Charlotte Hawkins Brown*, 94–95; Charlotte Hawkins Brown to NCN, 25 October 1919, box 4, GC DNE.

29. Gilmore, *Gender and Jim Crow*, 207–24, quotation on 224.

30. Thomas Walter Bickett, "Legislation for Negroes," 23 August 1920, and "Tuskegee Institute," 25 January 1920, both in Bickett, *Public Papers*, 72–73, 297–98; "Ask Legislation for State Negroes," *RN&O*, 24 August 1920, 16. State representative William N. Everett from Richmond County chaired the panel. The other white members were state senator Lycurgus R. Varser of Lumberton and Judge George V. Cowper of Kinston. Simon G. Atkins, president of Slater Normal School in Winston-Salem, and Durham physician Aaron M. Moore comprised the commission's black minority. See T. W. Bickett to W. N. Everett, 22 November 1920, Commission on Negro Legislation to Bickett, 8 December 1920, both in box 9, GC DNE.

31. "A Division of Negro Education," n.d., folder 1920 Reports, box 76, GC SPI. This report is unsigned, but Newbold later mentioned authoring such a report (NCN to J. W. Seabrook, 27 April 1925, box 7, GC DNE).

32. For a general history of the state agents, see S. L. Smith, *Builders of Goodwill*; on Davis, see Fosdick, *Adventure in Giving*, 89–90. For Davis's influence on other agents, see Leo Favrot, "Reminiscences of Jackson Davis," 22 April 1947, folder 3038, box 291, series 1.2, GEB Papers; for the debate over black state agents, see Jackson Davis, "A Study of the West Virginia Schools," 27 October 1915, folder 3033, box 290, series 1.2, GEB Papers.

33. The best sketch of Newbold can be found in Leloudis, *Schooling the New South*, 183–85. See also entry by A. M. Burns in Powell, *Dictionary of North Carolina Biography*, 4:362–63; A. M. Proctor, "N. C. Newbold, '95, and Negro Education," *Trinity Alumni Register* 10 (January 1924): 158–60; "Dr. Newbold Dies in Raleigh," *RN&O*, 24 December 1957, NCC Clipping File.

34. Clippings from Newbold's years as a school superintendent, box 3, Newbold Papers; NCN to Eugenia Newbold, 14 June 1906, box 1, Newbold Papers.

35. NCN to Wickliffe Rose, 16 November 1923, box 7, GC DNE; NCN to CAE, 2 May 1950, box 188, GC SPI.

36. Correspondence about Newbold's job musings can be found in box 2, Newbold Papers; see esp. NCN to Wallace Buttrick, 7 June 1912. For recognition of Newbold's efforts to be of service to the Washington Colored Graded School, see "Many Attend Commencement Exercises," *Washington Daily News*, 13 May 1913, box 3, Newbold Papers;

Resolution from Teachers of the Washington Colored Graded School, 12 May 1913, box 2, Newbold Papers.

37. NCN to Wallace Buttrick, 27 February 1913, box 2, Newbold Papers; "Supt. Newbold Resigns His Position," *Washington Daily News*, 5 April 1913, box 3, Newbold Papers. Newbold recalls his job deliberations in "Outline—Talk, Superintendents' Conference," 27 July 1938, box 2, Newbold A&S.

38. NCN to Charles [?], 8, 11 March 1913, box 2, Newbold Papers.

39. Fosdick, *Adventure in Giving*, 96; C. H. Brown to NCN, 25 October 1919, A. M. Moore to NCN, 11 August 1920, both in box 4, GC DNE. For Newbold's early work as state agent, see Leloudis, *Schooling the New South*, 185–228.

40. Newbold signed a 1919 report as "state agent for rural schools" (NCN to ECB, 9 November 1919, GC DNE). Yet when "A Declaration of Principles" was published that fall, he was listed as "supervisor Negro rural schools."

41. *North Carolina Education* 15 (April 1921): 5–6, 13; Minutes of the State Board of Education, vol. 4, 2 June 1921, North Carolina State Board of Education Papers, NCDAH; NCN to F. Harrison Hough, 10 January 1924, box 7, GC DNE. For Newbold's outline of the division's staffing needs, see NCN to Abraham Flexner, 22 April 1921, reel 96, series 1.1, GEB Papers.

42. "Negro Teachers Hold Meeting in Greensboro," *RN&O*, 20 June 1921, 2. On black opportunities for state employment, see Burns, "North Carolina and the Negro Dilemma," 222–23; Crow, Escott, and Hatley, *History of African Americans*, 136. The DNE's initial salary schedule proposed for the agency's white employees annual salaries ranging from $3,500 to $3,000 and for its black employees salaries ranging from $2,250 to $1,800. See Minutes of the State Board of Education, vol. 4, 2 June 1921, North Carolina State Board of Education Papers, NCDAH. Newbold discusses the offices for black employees in NCN to ECB, 17 February 1922, box 5, GC DNE; see also NCN to Annie Holland, 13 February 1922 (enclosed in NCN to ECB, 17 February 1922), box 85, GC SPI; NCN to ATA, 6 January 1927, box 101, GC SPI.

43. "Negro Teachers Hold Meeting in Greensboro," *RN&O*, 20 June 1921, 2; JES to NCN, 8 March 1921, box 5, GC DNE; James Dudley to ECB, 17 June 1921, box 80, GC SPI; *Biennial Report*, 1920–21/1921–22, pt. 1, 34–35.

44. Newbold, for example, addressed blacks with courtesy titles, a small but rare gesture of respect among whites. See NCN, untitled address at Florida A&M College, 7–8 March 1948, box 4, SSF.

45. Clement, "History of Negro Education," 210.

46. Pearson, "Race Relations in North Carolina." For discussion of the 1921 meeting, see "Minutes of Committee Meeting on Negro Education in North Carolina, Shaw University Chapel, Raleigh, NC," 1 April 1927, box 8, SSF; Haley, *Charles N. Hunter*, 246; T. L. McCoy, "Inter-Racial Conference on Problems," *Norfolk Journal and Guide*, 24 September 1921, 1; NCN to W. R. Banks, 28 December 1929, box 10, GC DNE; NCN to Angus Wilton McLean, 30 October 1925, box 8, GC DNE. In 1921, the state allocated approximately $615,000 for permanent improvements at its three black normal schools and one black land-grant college; its total budget for higher education permanent improvements came to nearly $7 million. See "Permanent Improvements" Graph in "1947 Legislative Summary," *Popular Government* 13 (May 1947): 20; *Public Laws and Resolutions*, 1921, 440–41; Newbold, "Conference for Negro Education."

47. Lizzie Targinton to NCN, 15 March 1922, box 2, Newbold Papers.

48. North Carolina State Educational Commission, *Public Education in North Carolina*, 13-15, 41, 48, 77; U.S. Bureau of the Census, *Fourteenth Census of the United States*, 30. In 1920, 24.5 percent of blacks over age ten in North Carolina were illiterate; for native-born whites of native parentage, only 8.2 percent were illiterate.

49. *Biennial Report*, 1944-45/1945-46, pt. 1, 11, 1938-39/1939-40, pt. 1, 52-53; NCN to CAE, 25 July 1935, box 131, GC SPI.

50. Meier, *Negro Thought in America*, 42; Weare, "Charles Clinton Spaulding," 169; James D. Anderson, *Education of Blacks*, 185. Glenda Elizabeth Gilmore and James Leloudis have emphasized that Progressive-era self-help programs, despite their oppressive requirements, facilitated civic participation that paved the way for black reentry into politics. See Leloudis, *Schooling the New South*, 177-228; Gilmore, *Gender and Jim Crow*, 159-65.

51. Lance G. E. Jones, *Jeanes Teacher*; Arthur D. Wright, *Negro Rural School Fund*; James Dillard, "Circular Letter to Extension and Supervising Teachers and Organizers," 1911, box 5, State Supervisor of Elementary Instruction Series, DNE Papers; Jackson Davis, "The Jeanes Teachers," 27 May 1935 (published in pamphlet form by the Carnegie Corporation of New York, 1936), folder 2126, box 222, series 1.2, GEB Papers.

52. Annual Report of the Executive Director (J. Curtis Dixon) to the Southern Education Foundation, 14 October 1948, box 42, Southern Education Foundation Papers, Atlanta University Center, Robert W. Woodruff Library, Archives and Special Collections, Atlanta; NCN to James Dillard, 19 May 1919, box 4, GC DNE. For early Jeanes work in North Carolina, see Leloudis, *Schooling the New South*, 186-92, 201-4; Gilmore, *Gender and Jim Crow*, 161-65.

53. Pankey, "Life Histories," 71-72; NCN to P. H. Johnson, 16 May 1929, NCN to unknown, 19 April 1929, both in box 9, GC DNE; [Superintendent from Lincolnton, N.C.] to Annie Holland, 17 June 1926, box 2, SSF.

54. Leloudis, *Schooling the New South*, 187-88; NCN to J. C. Dixon, 24 June 1947, box 15, GC DNE.

55. On Holland, see Newbold, *Five North Carolina Negro Educators*, 63-85; Leloudis, *Schooling the New South*, 189-91; Debi Hamlin's entry in Gates and Higginbotham, *African American National Biography*, 4:271-73; Littlefield, " 'I Am Only One,' " chapter 1; Sarah Shaber's entry in Powell, *Dictionary of North Carolina Biography*, 3:174; DNE salaries for 1922-23 are listed in NCN to ATA, 27 June 1923, box 6, GC DNE. There is some discrepancy within the sources as to Holland's birth date and the spelling of her middle name (Welthy, alternately Wealthy). The most recent consensus favors Welthy and a birth date of approximately 1871.

56. Edith M. Thomas to NCN, 15 September 1924, box 7, GC DNE; NCN to Helen Hilts, 12 January 1934, box 11, GC DNE.

57. Sanders, *Negro Child Welfare*, 11-13, 309-10. For figures on PTA membership rates, see *Biennial Report*, 1928-29/1929-30, pt. 1, 50; "Report of Colored Parent Teacher Associations," 2 April 1927, PTA Papers.

58. Meier, *Negro Thought in America*, 100-118, quotation on 105. For comprehensive histories of the Rosenwald Fund, see Hoffschwelle, *Rosenwald Schools*; James D. Anderson, *Education of Blacks*, 148-85; Embree and Waxman, *Investment in People*. For a more focused look at Rosenwald work in North Carolina, see Hanchett, "Rosenwald Schools"; Leloudis, *Schooling the New South*, 211-28; Westin, "State and Segregated Schools," 350-70.

59. On Moore, see Leloudis, *Schooling the New South*, 215, 217, 218–19, 221–22; on the Chowan school, see Hanchett, "Rosenwald Schools," 407.

60. NCN to Abraham Flexner, 17 May 1919, NCN to Julius Rosenwald, 19 May 1919, box 4, both in GC DNE; Julius Rosenwald Fund, "Schoolhouse Construction Summary for 1923–1924," box 7, GC DNE.

61. NCN to Abraham Flexner, 18 June 1919, E. F. Upchurch to NCN, 12 May 1919, both in box 4, GC DNE; "Notes on the Rosenwald Work," n.d., folder Correspondence of NCN, Director of Division of Negro Education, 1923–25, box 7, GC DNE.

62. N. C. Newbold, *First Biennial Report of the State Agent of Negro Rural Schools*, 1915, reel 93, series 1.1, GEB Papers; NCN to Hurst, 30 April 1923, box 6, GC DNE; NCN to C. L. Cates, 13 March 1923, box 6, GC DNE; "Plan for Distribution of Aid for Building Rural Schoolhouses, Year Beginning July 1, 1927 and Ending June 30, 1928" (Rosenwald pamphlet), NCC.

63. *Report of Prof. Charles H. Moore, State Inspector of Negro Schools, Made Before the North Carolina State Teachers' Association, Assembled at Greensboro, June 23, 1916*, NCC; Hanchett, "Rosenwald Schools," 408–9; Leloudis, *Schooling the New South*, 221–23.

64. G. E. Davis, "Beginning of Activities of the Rosenwald Fund in North Carolina," *NCTR* 4 (January 1933): 3–5. For a sketch of Davis, see "Our Executive Secretary Emeritus," *NCTR* 16 (March 1945): frontispiece.

65. "Report of G. E. Davis," September 1924, box 8, SSF; Hart, "Negro Builds for Himself."

66. "Report of G. E. Davis," October 1922, box 8, SSF; G. E. Davis to GHF, 27 September 1923, box 1, Correspondence of the Supervisor of the Rosenwald Fund, DNE Papers; W. H. Credle to S. D. Stallings, 6 April 1927, Stallings to NCN, 3 May 1927, box 3, both in Correspondence of the Supervisor of the Rosenwald Fund, DNE Papers; James D. Anderson, *Education of Blacks*, 176; J. E. Debnam to NCN, 3 July 1919, box 4, GC DNE.

67. J. P. Law to NCN, 30 September 1920, box 5, GC DNE; Hanchett, "Rosenwald Schools," 401; "Report of W. F. Credle, July 1, 1921–July 1, 1922," box 8, SSF; "Old School Helped Generations; Former Students Want to Save Benefactor's Gift for a Community Center," *Winston-Salem Journal*, 8 March 1998, 1B.

68. *Biennial Report*, 1926–27/1927–28, pt. 1, 56.

69. G. E. Davis to W. F. Credle, 16, 25 January 1926, Credle to Davis, 18, 26 January 1926, all in box 2, Correspondence of the Supervisor of the Rosenwald Fund, DNE Papers.

70. G. E. Davis to NCN, 5, 11 October 1927, NCN to Davis, 12 October 1927, all in box 9, GC DNE.

71. "Report of G. E. Davis," March 1929, box 8, SSF.

72. "Newbold's Introductory Statement to the Conference on Negro Education in North Carolina, Shaw University, Nov. 3, 1923," NCC; Newbold, "Common Schools," 213.

73. Thomas J. Calloway to NCN, 12 May 1926, NCN to James H. Dillard, 11 August 1926, NCN to Josephus Daniels, 9 February 1927, all in box 8, GC DNE. For photos used in the exhibit, see box 8, SSF. For a history of the sesquicentennial, see Cleary, "Past Is Present," esp. chapter 5.

74. Charles Hunter, "Negro Teachers Open Sessions," *Goldsboro News*, 24 November 1927, Hunter Scrapbooks.

75. Julius Rosenwald to NCN, 12 April 1928, box 9, GC DNE; program from the Method dedication, box 8, SSF; NCN to Jackson Davis, 22 April 1930, box 10, GC DNE.

76. Leloudis, *Schooling the New South*, 225–26; fund official Thomas Jesse Jones

quoted in King, *Pan-Africanism and Education*, 55; NCN to Philipe Boden, 24 November 1925, box 8, GC DNE; NCN to Angus Wilton McLean, 3 February 1925, box 94, GC SPI; NCN to ATA, 2 November 1926, box 98, GC SPI; NCN, "North Carolina, A Way-Station for Caravans of Human Progress," 2 November 1928, box 1, Newbold A&S.

77. Angus Wilton McLean, "The Negro an Important Factor in the Industrial and Commercial Life in America," 22 October 1925, in McLean, *Public Papers*, 255–58; Oliver Max Gardner, "North Carolina's Attitude towards the Negro," 7 May 1929, in Gardner, *Public Papers*, 115–17.

78. "Report of W. F. Credle," June 1926, enclosed in NCN to ATA, 16 July 1926, ATA to NCN, 19 July 1926, both in box 98, GC SPI; NCN to ATA, 12, 17 January 1924, ATA to NCN, 14 January 1924, all in box 90, GC SPI.

79. Mabry, *Negro in North Carolina Politics*, 76–81.

80. [William A. Robinson] to W. E. B. Du Bois, 28 April 1926, box 8, GC DNE; W. E. B. Du Bois, "The Negro Common School in North Carolina," *The Crisis* 34 (June 1927): 135. After the bond passed, Raleigh blacks continued to press the school board to make necessary improvements to their schools (NCN to J. A. Ellis, 6 November 1926, box 8, GC DNE). A similar story came from Durham, where two thousand blacks donated one dollar each to defeat a discriminatory school bond (NCN to F. M. Martin, 22 April 1926, box 8, GC DNE).

81. NCN to ATA, 24 February 1925, box 7, GC DNE; "Report of Newbold," August 1925 (includes petitions from Johnston County citizens), box 94, GC SPI; NCN to ATA, 9 August 1926, box 98, GC SPI; NCN to B. C. Siske, 6 April 1927, box 8, GC DNE. Du Bois refers to what was most likely the Smithfield case in "The Negro Common School in North Carolina," *The Crisis* 34 (June 1927): 135.

82. C. C. Drew to State Board of Education, 2 October 1928 (enclosed in ATA to W. F. Credle, 4 October 1928), box 5, Correspondence of the Supervisor of the Rosenwald Fund, DNE Papers. On school terms and opportunities for black legal recourse, see Wager, *North Carolina*, 88; Douglas, *Reading, Writing, and Race*, 15–16.

83. "Summary of Jeanes Reports, December 1930," "Monthly Report of Jeanes Supervising Industrial Teacher," 5 December 1933, both in box 2, SSF; Ambrose Caliver, "Greetings from the United States Office of Education to the Jeanes Supervisors," *Tuskegee Messenger* 7 (November 1931): 10.

84. "Annual Report of the President to the Board of Trustees of the Negro Rural School Fund, Inc.," 28 April 1932, folder 2126, box 222, series 1.2, GEB Papers; Sanders, *Negro Child Welfare*, 313; "Summary of Annual Reports of Jeanes Teachers, 1932–33," box 2, SSF.

85. Caliver, *Rural Elementary Education*, 2–3; Lance G. E. Jones, *Jeanes Teacher*, 92, 113.

86. See series of letters from superintendents to Annie Holland, who requested their feedback in June 1926, box 2, SSF; Edwin R. Embree, "The School as a Social Force," *Tuskegee Messenger* 7 (November 1931): 4.

87. Embree and Waxman, *Investment in People*, 48, 57.

88. James Dillard to Wickliffe Rose, 25 October 1927, folder 2123, box 222, series 1.2, GEB Papers; see similar statement from GEB president Wallace Buttrick to Frank Chapman, 5 March 1920, folder 303, box 33, series 1.1, GEB Papers; "Report on the Conference of State Agents of Rural Schools for Negroes, 8–9 June 1928, Signal Mountain, Tennessee," folder 2000, box 208, series 1.2, GEB Papers. As Eric Anderson and Alfred Moss point out, the lack of black voting power in the South limited this private-to-public reform effort (*Dangerous Donations*, 101–2).

89. Fosdick, *Adventure in Giving*, 98; "Average Cost of Jeanes Teachers for 1926," folder 2122, box 221, series 1.2, GEB Papers; NCN to Leo Favrot, 7 March 1930, box 10, GC DNE. On the GEB's declining appropriations for Jeanes work, see "Annual Report to the Board of Trustees of the Negro Rural School Fund, Inc.," 28 April 1932, folder 2126, box 222, series 1.2, GEB Papers.

90. "Conference of State Superintendents and State Agents of Negro Schools," Edgewater Park, Mississippi, 15–17 December 1946, box 2, Newbold A&S; CAE to A. D. Wright, 27 May 1935, box 12, GC DNE.

91. James D. Anderson, *Education of Blacks*, 177; see several statements along these lines by Newbold: "North Carolina in Reverse Gear?" *NCTR* 1 (March 1930): 3; "Has North Carolina Made Any Real Progress in Negro Education?" *NCTR* 2 (January 1931): 3, 6; "Unfinished Tasks and New Opportunities in Education in North Carolina," *NCTR* 2 (October 1931): 66–67, 75–76.

92. Mrs. J. Buren Sidbury to Mrs. W. L. Wharton, 2 March 1938, PTA Papers.

93. NCN, "Notes for Lecture at Teachers College, New York," 11 February 1931, box 1, Newbold A&S. Newbold did not name the black educator in question, but most likely it was Brooks Dickens, who designated 1920–26 as a "Golden Period of Negro Education" in a study he wrote at Tennessee's historically black Lane College. See Cooke, *White Superintendent*, 19. For another invocation of this slogan, see Hugh Victor Brown, *E-Quality Education*, 111.

94. Gaines, *Uplifting the Race*, xii. For additional statistics on the Rosenwald Program, see "Report on Schoolhouse Construction Transportation and School Libraries to July 1, 1932," enclosed in S. L. Smith to NCN, 14 November 1932, box 11, GC DNE.

95. W. E. B. Du Bois, "The Negro Common School in North Carolina," *The Crisis* 34 (May 1927): 79–80, 96–97; 34 (June 1927): 117–18, 133–35.

CHAPTER TWO

1. Guion Johnson, Interview.

2. Lucy S. Herring, *Strangers No More*, 73; Harold Trigg to Charles Carroll, 18 February 1956, folder State Board of Education, box 40 (January–April 1956), MARS 104.3. On school terms, see NCN to ATA, 24 February 1925, box 7, GC DNE; NCN, "Two Urgent Educational Needs," 19 January 1933, box 1, Newbold A&S; "The Eight-Months School Term," *NCTR* 4 (January 1933); Newbold, "Some Achievements."

3. James D. Anderson, *Education of Blacks*, esp. chapters 2, 3; Kliebard, *Schooled to Work*, 13–16; North Carolina State Educational Commission, *Public Education in North Carolina*, 27–29, 37, 76.

4. Angus Wilton McLean, "The Negro an Important Factor in the Industrial and Commercial Life in America," 22 October 1925, in McLean, *Public Papers*, 255–58.

5. Eric Anderson and Alfred Moss argue that in the late nineteenth century, "the most consistent black demand was that their education should be similar to everyone else's" (*Dangerous Donations*, 13–14). On Washington, see Norrell, *Up from History*, 151–52. On the Wake County story, see "The Negro School an Asset to the State," *Hoke County News*, 19 April 1929, Charles N. Hunter Scrapbooks, box 15, Charles N. Hunter Papers, Duke University, William R. Perkins Library, Special Collections, Durham, N.C. For other examples of black educators using industrial work to win white support, see Principal and Teachers

of the Person County Training School to the White Families Employing Colored Servants, 12 November 1931, box 11, GC DNE; Mrs. M. C. Holliday, "Home-Makers' Classes in Iredell County," *NCTR* 4 (March 1933): 31.

6. *Second Biennial Report of the State Agent of Negro Schools* (Raleigh: Office of the Superintendent of Public Instruction, 1917), reel 93, series 1.1, GEB Papers; "Progress Letter," 6 March 1924, box 90, GC SPI; "Suggested Outline of Work for Jeanes Supervising Industrial Teachers," box 2, SSF.

7. "Memories They Cherish . . . A Symposium of Experiences as Jeanes Teachers," *Jeanes Supervisors Quarterly* 1 (September 1947): 21–22, copy in box 5, State Supervisor of Elementary Education Series, DNE Papers.

8. "General Education Board Sponsors Jeanes Conference," *Tuskegee Messenger* 7 (November 1931): 13; "Care of Schoolhouses and Grounds" (Rosenwald Fund pamphlet), 1923, box 2, SSF. Lu Ann Jones makes similar points about black home demonstration agents, many of whom doubled as Jeanes teachers ("Re-Visioning the Countryside," 244–45, 274–75, chapter 6).

9. "Progress Letter, 5 June 1924, Introductory Statement by N. C. Newbold," box 92, GC SPI; "A Suggestive Outline for Jeanes Supervising Teachers by Annie W. Holland," [4 February 1927], folder 2125, box 222, series 1.2, GEB Papers.

10. James Dillard, "Traditions of the Jeanes Fund," *Tuskegee Messenger* 7 (November 1931): 5; Jackson Davis, "The Jeanes Teachers," 27 May 1935 (published in pamphlet form by the Carnegie Corporation of New York, 1936), folder 2126, box 222, series 1.2, GEB Papers.

11. Lance G. E. Jones, *Jeanes Teacher*, 111–12.

12. Gilmore, *Gender and Jim Crow*, 160.

13. *Biennial Report*, 1922–23/1923–24, pt. 1, 10. See also N. W. Walker, "Public High School Development in North Carolina," *North Carolina High School Bulletin* 4 (January 1913): 10–24; Long, *Public Secondary Education*, 3–4. Public high schools proliferated much earlier in the North. The first opened in 1821; by the 1880s, they were commonplace (Reese, *Origins of the American High School*, xiii–xvii).

14. "Asheville's New High School," *High School Journal* 2 (November 1919): 216–17; "A Public High School for Person County," *Roxboro Courier*, 8 August 1906, box 3, Newbold Papers; James D. Anderson, *Education of Blacks*, 187.

15. "Annual Address of President O. R. Pope," *NCTR* 5 (May 1934): 49–50, 58–59; accredited high schools listed in *NCTR* 1 (October 1930): 22; *Biennial Report*, 1922–23/1923–24, pt. 3, Report of State Supervisor of Public High Schools, 7. For more on the organizations that founded private black high schools and colleges, see James D. Anderson, *Education of Blacks*, 238–45. Figures from 1916 found in James D. Anderson, *Education of Blacks*, 197.

16. W. A. Robinson, "Negro State Accredited Four-Year High Schools," box 8, GC DNE; *The Crisis* 34 (August 1927): 203–4; Long, *Public Secondary Education*, 31.

17. James D. Anderson, *Education of Blacks*, 110–47; Redcay, *County Training Schools*, 40; Sanders, *Negro Child Welfare*, 313; Walker, *Their Highest Potential*, 35; *Biennial Report*, 1934–35/1935–36, pt. 1, 84.

18. Eric Anderson and Moss, *Dangerous Donations*, 5; Hugh Victor Brown, *History*, 62; NCN to R. B. Eleazer, 7 April 1923, box 6, GC DNE.

19. T. S. Inborden to NCN, 20 May 1926, box 8, GC DNE; H. L. Trigg, "The Present Status of Tax-Supported High School Education for Negroes in North Carolina," *NCTR* 1 (Octo-

ber 1930): 4–6. On Brick School, see Hugh Victor Brown, *History*, 38, 60; Crow, Escott, and Hatley, *History of African Americans*, 157; "Changes at the Brick School," *NCTR* 4 (October 1933): 80.

20. Harold Trigg, "The Present Status of Tax-Supported High School Education for Negroes in North Carolina," *NCTR* 1 (October 1930): 4–6; NCN to Harry Howell, 25 March 1919, box 4, GC DNE; NCN to Harry Howell, 10 March 1921, box 5, GC DNE; W. A. Robinson, "Negro State Accredited Four-Year High Schools," box 8, GC DNE; see also *The Crisis* 34 (August 1927): 203–4. On Robinson, see Hugh Victor Brown, *History*, 142. On the role of black migration to cities, see Weinberg, *Chance to Learn*, 66; James D. Anderson, *Education of Blacks*, 202–4.

21. *Minutes of the Forty-Fourth Annual Session*; Perry, *History*, 172–75. For an earlier NCTA call on this issue, see James B. Dudley to ECB, 17 June 1921, box 80, GC SPI.

22. For the late 1920s survey, see Cooke, *White Superintendent*, 144; on the army tests, see Vander Zanden, *American Minority Relations*, 45–49.

23. Sanders, "Race Attitudes of County Officials." The State Board of Charities and Public Welfare, in conjunction with the Rosenwald Fund and UNC, planned for this work to be included in a larger study of black child welfare. Fifty-two fieldworkers—thirty-seven whites and fifteen blacks—visited local officials in more than fifty counties. Not revealing their official aim, they casually brought up topics of race. In the end, the researchers only compiled results from the white interviewers, as those comments were far more candid than those obtained by the black workers—so candid, in fact, that researchers omitted them from the published report. Sanders, *Negro Child Welfare*.

24. McKee, *Sociology and the Race Problem*, 55–102; Lee D. Baker, *From Savage to Negro*, 99–126; Boas, *Mind of Primitive Man*, 268–78; Singal, *War Within*, 302–38.

25. NCN to W. F. Credle, 4 May 1922, box 5, GC DNE; NCN, talk at Shaw University, 1922, box 1, Newbold A&S. The article that Newbold read was Cannon, "American Misgivings." The scholars he was reading included Charles A. Ellwood and Edward L. Thorndike, both of whom were moving toward a cultural conception of racial differences, albeit more cautiously than Boas. See Ellwood, *Introduction to Social Psychology*, 294–96; Thorndike, *Educational Psychology*, 243.

26. H. F. Srygley to NCN, 7 January 1924, NCN to Srygley, 9 January 1924, box 7, GC DNE; J. Douglas Smith, *Managing White Supremacy*, 136. For Newbold's full statement, see "Forward Stride in Education," *Norfolk Journal and Guide*, 22 November 1924, 12; "Asks for Equal Educational Opportunity," *Norfolk Journal and Guide*, 22 November 1924, 2. For another example of Newbold's promotion of curricular equality, see NCN to William Paul McDonough, 9 October 1926, box 10, GC DNE.

27. W. A. Robinson, "Four Year State Accredited High Schools for Negroes in 17 Southern States," [1926], reel 19, *Papers of W. E. B. Du Bois* (microfilm).

28. Charles S. Johnson, *Negro in American Civilization*, 253–54; Sanders, "Race Attitudes of County Officials"; Tarpley, Interview. For another story of white resignation to curricular equality, see Pope, *Chalk Dust*, 103–5.

29. "Annual Address of President O. R. Pope," *NCTR* 5 (May 1934): 49–50, 58–59; Report on the Conference of State Agents of Rural Schools for Negroes, 5–6 June 1930, Atlantic City, New Jersey, folder 2002, box 208, series 1.2, GEB Papers.

30. Biographical information on Pearson is found in Jean Bradley Anderson, *Durham County*, 258; Weare, *Black Business*, 14–15; Caldwell, *History of the American Negro*, 312–14; "Hillside History Book."

31. *DMH*, 1 June 1915, quoted in Westin, "History of the Durham School System," 82–83; see also 110–11.

32. On the school's curriculum, see "Hillside History Book"; W. G. Pearson, Report, 26 May 1925, box 1, High School Principals' Annual Reports, DNE Papers; W. G. Pearson, Report, 2 June 1932, box 4, High School Principals' Annual Reports, DNE Papers. Leslie Brown notes the rumors about blacks setting the fire that destroyed Whitted (*Upbuilding Black Durham*, 186). The three other state accredited black high schools were located at Reidsville, Wilmington, and Method. See report on high school development, n.d., folder Negro Education in N.C., 1925–49, box 4, SSF.

33. "Hillside History Book"; L. S. Cozart, Report, 11 June 1927, box 2, High School Principals' Annual Reports, DNE Papers.

34. Long, *Public Secondary Education*, 44, 49, 58 (includes 1928–29 figures); Caliver, *Secondary Education for Negroes*, 66–85; Pauli Murray, *Song*, 59.

35. "Hillside History Book"; *Minutes of the Forty-Fifth Annual Session*.

36. "Hillside History Book"; W. G. Pearson, Report, 26 May 1925, box 1, High School Principals' Annual Reports, DNE Papers; W. G. Pearson, Report, 2 June 1932, box 4, High School Principals' Annual Reports, DNE Papers; Brinton, "Negro in Durham," 392–93, 404–11.

37. Dorphenia Wingfield Hall, "Place of Extra-Curricular Activities in Secondary Schools," *NCTR* 4 (March 1933): 29–30; Pauli Murray, *Song*, 59–61.

38. William Kenneth Boyd, *Story of Durham*, 294; Westin, "History of the Durham School System," 111; Pauli Murray, *Song*, 67–70.

39. "Durham White Schools Get $155,000 from County but Negro Schools Get $21,000," *DCT*, 8 May 1937, 1, 8; "The Educational Rape of Negroes in North Carolina," *DCT*, 15 May 1937, 4, 8; "Representation Needed," *DCT*, 5 February 1938, 4; "The East Durham School," *DCT*, 18 September 1937, 1, 8; "Separate but Equal Educational Opportunities," *DCT*, 28 August 1937, 8.

40. *Biennial Report*, 1934–35/1935–36, pt. 1, 12; Louis Austin to WW, 4 March 1937, TM to Austin, 6 March 1937, Charles Houston to Austin, 4 May 1937, M. Hugh Thompson to Houston, 4 May 1937, Houston to Thompson, 5 May 1937, all in reel 5, series A, pt. 3, NAACP Papers; "Another Victory Won," *DCT*, 28 August 1937, 8.

41. See *Biennial Report*, 1928–29/1929–30, pt. 1, 31; Caliver, *Secondary Education for Negroes*, 14, 21, 23.

42. For a few examples of such alumni memories, see Clark, Interview; Mason, Interview; Meeks, Interview. The 1935 law can be found in Pauli Murray, *States' Laws*, 331. For state textbook practices, see "North Carolina Bids to Be Pioneer in Rental Textbooks, Erwin Thinks," *Gastonia Daily Gazette*, 17 May 1935, 11; *Handbook for Elementary and Secondary Schools*, 238–41. The study mentioned is Coleman et al., *Equality of Educational Opportunity*, 206, 211.

43. Long, *Public Secondary Education*, 36–42; W. A. Robinson, "The Present Status of High School Education among Negroes—A Factual and Critical Survey," *NCTR* 1 (October 1930): 8–11. Robinson routinely had found such conditions in North Carolina's black high schools. See reports in boxes 8 and 9, GC DNE.

44. Crow, Escott, and Hatley, *History of African Americans*, 159, 162, 173; "Hillside History Book," 18–20; Pauli Murray, *Song*, 64, 31.

45. On the NCTA's efforts, see Haley, *Charles N. Hunter*, 59–60. For Washington's views, see *My Larger Education*, chapter 11, "What I Learned About Education in Denmark."

For an overview of turn-of-the-century black nationalism, see Meier, *Negro Thought in America*, 50–58.

46. S. L. Smith, *Builders of Goodwill*, 164–67; Reuben, "Beyond Politics." For the state's early civics courses, see *Biennial Report*, 1896–97/1897–98, 217–23; *Study in Curriculum Problems*, 278–95.

47. On Woodson, see Goggin, *Carter G. Woodson*; Romero, "Carter G. Woodson." On the black history movement, see Brundage, *Southern Past*, chapter 4; Zimmerman, *Whose America?*, 42–54; Meier and Rudwick, *Black History*; Dagbovie, *Early Black History Movement*. On the ASNLH's founding, see Romero, "Carter G. Woodson," 88–91, Goggin, *Carter G. Woodson*, 32–35; Woodson quoted in Meier and Rudwick, *Black History*, 9.

48. Woodson, "Ten Years"; Carter G. Woodson, Interview by Leonard Outhwaite, 7 June 1926, folder 966, box 96, series III-8, Laura Spelman Rockefeller Memorial Papers, Rockefeller Archive Center, Pocantico Hills, North Tarrytown, N.Y.; "Proceedings of the Spring Conference of the Association for the Study of Negro Life and History Held at Durham, North Carolina, April 1 and 2, 1925," *Journal of Negro History* 10 (July 1925): 576–81; "Annual Report of the Director," *Journal of Negro History* 10 (October 1925): 590–97. In 1930, ASNLH salesman Lorenzo Greene found Newbold open to adopting the association's publications for use in black schools. By the mid-1930s, the state had adopted several of these texts as supplemental readings. See Lorenzo Greene, *Selling Black History*, 56–58. For the states that had adopted ASNLH publications, see "Notes on Books," *Negro History Bulletin* 1 (October 1937): 5, 7; "Books," *Negro History Bulletin* 2 (October 1938): 6.

49. *Minutes of the Forty-Sixth Annual Session*; H. L. Trigg, Report, 24 May 1926, box 1, High School Principals' Annual Reports, DNE Papers; Report of Dillard High Principal Hugh Brown, box 3, High School Principals' Annual Reports, DNE Papers; *Catalogue of the North Carolina College for Negroes*, 1927–28.

50. Brinton, "Negro in Durham," 393–95; Lorenzo Greene, *Selling Black History*, 54–58; "Enrollment by Subjects in North Carolina Accredited High Schools for Negroes, 1930–1931," box 1, Newbold A&S; Zimmerman, *Whose America?*, 46.

51. Caliver, *Secondary Education for Negroes*, 114, 118, 121; Woodson's speech in Theophilus McKinney, *Higher Education among Negroes*, 15–23; Woodson, *Mis-Education of the Negro*, 134–35.

52. NCN to Mrs. H. L. Hammond, 21 July, 4 August 1920, Hammond to NCN, 26 July 1920, all in box 4, GC DNE; "Race Literature in the Schools," *Norfolk Journal and Guide*, 12 March 1921, 2; "Notes on Books," *Negro History Bulletin* 1 (October 1937): 5, 7; *North Carolina State List*, 16. Approved texts included Giles B. Jackson and Davis, *Industrial History*; Edward A. Johnson, *School History*; Washington, *Up from Slavery*; Woodson, *Negro Makers of History*; Brawley, *Short History*.

53. "Negro History Week the Fourth Year," *Journal of Negro History* 14 (April 1929): 109–15; S. L. Smith, *Builders of Goodwill*, 167; "Report on Conference on Education and Race Relations," George Peabody College, 3–4 August 1933, box 1, Newbold A&S; Zimmerman, *Whose America?*, 45.

54. NCN to Hilda V. Grayson, 28 October 1938, box 13, GC DNE.

55. Zimmerman, *Whose America?*, 47–49; R. B. Eleazer, "School Books and Racial Antagonism," *High School Journal* 18 (October 1935): 197–99. For a similar survey by Newbold, see unsigned letter to Wade E. Miller, 26 October 1939, series 2 (Correspondence 1912–50), *Papers of Carter G. Woodson* (microfilm).

56. "Legislative Recommendations to the State Board of Education—Submitted,

April 11, 1952," *NCTR* 24 (January 1953): 7, 10; "Report of the Resolutions Committee," *NCTR* 28 (May 1957): 13.

57. On Woodson's motivations for founding the *Negro History Bulletin*, see Carter G. Woodson to Jackson Davis, 9 July 1937, folder 1959, box 205, series 1.2, GEB Papers; for illustrative articles, see "What Children Should Do in Observing Negro History Week," *Negro History Bulletin* 1 (February 1938): 12; C. L. Harper, "Making Negro History a More Important Part of the Curriculum," *Negro History Bulletin* 2 (May 1939): 71.

58. *Biennial Report*, 1940-41/1941-42, pt. 1, 58-60; *Biennial Report*, 1948-49/1949-50, pt. 1, 40; S. E. Duncan, "The Elective Offerings in 207 North Carolina High Schools," box 23, GC DNE; Zimmerman, *Whose America?*, 43, 110-12.

59. "Negro History Week: The Fifth Year," *Journal of Negro History* 16 (April 1931): 125-31; "Negro History Week," *Negro History Bulletin* 1 (January 1938): 3; Bulletin of No. 3 District of the North Carolina Congress of Colored Parents and Teachers, 1940-41, 1941-42, PTA Papers; "A Brief Summary of the Supervisory Activities Carried on in Granville County, 1949-1950," box 2, SSF; Woodson, Interview; Sutton and Attmore quoted in Chafe, Gavins, and Korstad, *Remembering Jim Crow*, 58, 154; N. C. Crosby, "Developing Leadership through History," *NCTR* 5 (January 1934): 7-8; Jones quoted in Elizabeth Wellington, "100 Years of Lifting Voices," *RN&O*, 6 February 2000, 1D, 6D.

60. Hilda Sharkey, "What a Ninth Grade Pupil of the Chapel Hill High School (white) Thinks of the Negro," *NCTR* 14 (March 1943): 10; R. Gregg Cherry, "Economic Opportunities of the Negro," 15 April 1945, in Cherry, *Public Addresses and Papers*, 126; "Negro History Week: The Fifth Year," *Journal of Negro History* 16 (April 1931): 125-31; Zimmerman, *Whose America?*, 49.

61. To take one example, even before the integration of Chapel Hill's historically black high school, black students there protested the school's "failure to observe National Negro History Week," an indication that within black communities, youth were vital in reviving the black history movement. See "Walkout Is Staged by Negro Students," *Chapel Hill Weekly*, 16 February 1964, 1, 2.

62. O. Max Gardner, "The Declaration of North Carolina Agricultural Independence," 23 June 1930, O. Max Gardner, "Educational and Economic Progress of the Negro Race," 3 June 1930, both in Gardner, *Public Papers*, 198-204, 186-95; "Live at Home," *Time*, 7 July 1930, 19-20; NCN to Roland McConnell, 5 April 1943, box 14, GC DNE; JES to Ralph Gardner, 9 February 1947, folder Hon. Ralph Gardner, box General Correspondence, A-P, Shepard Papers.

63. One notable exception is James D. Anderson, "Historical Development."

64. Kantor and Tyack, "Introduction," in Kantor and Tyack, *Work, Youth, and Schooling*, 1-13. Kantor and Tyack argue that "perhaps nowhere has there been a greater gap between rhetoric and reality than in the history of black vocational education" (10).

65. Kliebard, *Schooled to Work*, xiii; Fairclough, *Teaching Equality*, 60-61.

66. Kantor, "Vocationalism in American Education," 43; also see 14-44.

67. Ibid., 36; Kliebard, *Schooled to Work*, 132; *Biennial Report*, 1920-21/1921-22, pt. 1, 24-27; *Public Education in North Carolina*; *Biennial Report*, 1934-35/1935-36, pt. 1, 104.

68. *Study in Curriculum Problems*, 498-528; *Biennial Report*, 1934-35/1935-36, pt. 1, 9, 12, 101.

69. James D. Anderson, *Education of Blacks*, 199-237, esp. 226-27; W. A. Robinson to Alfred H. Stern, 17 January 1927, Stern to Robinson, 25 January 1927, both in box 3, Correspondence of the Supervisor of the Rosenwald Fund, DNE Papers.

70. Report beginning "The unprecedented development of high schools . . . ," n.d., folder Negro Education in North Carolina, 1925–49, box 4, SSF; NCN to Walter B. Hill, 14 June 1930, box 10, GC DNE; NCN, "Lecture Given at Peabody College," 15 July 1931, box 1, Newbold A&S.

71. "Summary of Jeanes Final Reports, 1930–1931," box 2, SSF; *Biennial Report*, 1934–35/1935–36, pt. 2, 55; NCN, "Founders' Day Address," 2 November 1936, box 2, Newbold A&S; *Report and Recommendations*, 23–24; NCN to John A. Lang, 12 October 1938, box 13, GC DNE.

72. Mid-1920s trends described in Long, *Public Secondary Education*, 40; *Report of the Governor's Commission*; Tarpley, "Some Aspects," 72; NCN to Walter B. Hill, 3 December 1935, box 12, GC DNE; Bond, *Education of the Negro*, 404–5. For another searing black critique of the state of black vocational training, see Horne, "'Dog House' Education."

73. James D. Anderson, "Historical Development," 203–6; "Editorial Comment," *Journal of Negro Education* 4 (January 1935), 2; H. L. Trigg, "Some Essentials of a Guidance Program for Negro Youth," *NCTR* 9 (October 1938): 3–4, 12, 15.

74. Martin, *Brown v. Board of Education*, 15–16; W. E. B. Du Bois, "The Right to Work," *The Crisis* 40 (April 1933): 93–94; W. E. B. Du Bois, "The Negro and Social Reorganization," *NCTR* 6 (May 1935): 43–44, 57–59.

75. "Editorial Comment," *Journal of Negro Education* 4 (January 1935), 4; Caliver, *Vocational Education and Guidance*, 119, 56–57; J. W. Groves Jr. to NCN, 3 October 1933, box 11, GC DNE; JES, "God Bless Old North Carolina," a 15 November 1934 talk, folder 374, Shepard Papers.

76. Long, *Public Secondary Education*, 41–42, 87–103, 110.

77. *Report and Recommendations*, 24–29.

78. Schulman, *From Cotton Belt to Sunbelt*, 13; Caliver, *Availability of Education*, 11; Gavin Wright, *Old South, New South*, 226–49; Larkins, *Negro Population*, 9.

79. Milton C. Calloway, "A Plea for Vocational Education for Negroes in Camden County and in North Carolina," *NCTR* 10 (March 1939): 3–4, 13–14; F. Davis Dennis to NCN, 26 February 1936, box 12, GC DNE; Monthly Report of GHF, November 1937, box 13, GC DNE; Minutes of the Membership Meeting of the Southern Education Foundation, 9 January 1941, box 44, Southern Education Foundation Papers, Atlanta University Center, Robert W. Woodruff Library, Archives and Special Collections, Atlanta.

80. A. D. Wright, "Annual Report of the President, SEF Inc.," 15 January 1943, box 42, Southern Education Foundation Papers; Marie McIver to NCN, 26 October 1937, box 13, GC DNE; V. V. Oak, review of *Tobe*, *NCTR* 10 (October 1939): 7; Sharpe, *Tobe*.

81. Myrdal, with Sterner and Rose, *American Dilemma*, 899, 906, 1417 (n. 22); *Biennial Report*, 1938–39/1939–40, pt. 3, 62; *Biennial Report*, 1944–45/1945–46, pt. 2, 42; Teachey, "Educational Opportunities," 98; "Annual Reports of Jeanes Teachers," 1948–49, box 2, SSF.

82. Statistics compiled from data in *Biennial Report*, 1944–45/1945–46, pt. 1, 39. On the growing numbers of women in clerical work, see Kessler-Harris, *Out to Work*, 303. On racial disparities in the clerical profession, see Conrad, "Changes in the Labor Market Status," 158–59.

83. *Biennial Report*, 1934–35/1935–36, pt. 1, 106. The idiosyncratic way that some high school principals submitted curricular reports makes exact comparisons of industrial arts offerings difficult. In 1943–44, a slightly higher percentage of black high schools reported offering "industrial arts" courses than did white high schools (13 compared to

9 percent), but 12 percent of white high schools, compared to 2 percent of black high schools, reported offering "other courses" such as fundamentals of machines and aeronautics that overlapped with the industrial arts curriculum. Statistics compiled from data in *Biennial Report*, 1942–43/1943–44, pt. 1, 60.

84. W. H. Green to NCN, 20 June 1944, box 15, GC DNE.

85. Watson, "Establishment of a Functional Guidance Program," 61–69.

86. Charles Wadelington, "North Carolina Agricultural and Technical State University," in Powell, *Encyclopedia of North Carolina*, 802–3; U.S. Bureau of Education, *Survey of Negro Colleges*; Holmes, *Evolution of the Negro College*, 150–56; James D. Anderson, "Historical Development," 190–95. A survey of A&T yearbooks reinforces this point. Of those seniors who indicated career plans, teaching and allied positions, such as home demonstration and extension agents, ranked as the most popular choices. See *Ayantee*, 1939, 1946, available at http://library.digitalnc.org/. Likewise, a roster of graduating seniors in 1946 indicated that the number of students getting degrees in education and the liberal arts was more than twice the number receiving degrees in agriculture, engineering, and the industrial arts combined (*Bulletin of the Agricultural and Technical College* 38 [May 1947]: 184–87).

87. "Minutes of Conference on Negro Education in North Carolina Hall of the House of Representatives," Raleigh, 23 October 1929, D. K. Cherry to NCN, 10 December 1931, both in box 8, SSF; JES to Clyde E. Hoey, 25 September 1936, box 12, GC DNE. Bluford used the so-called agricultural building, Shepard complained, for the liberal arts. Shepard's criticisms were no doubt fueled by his concerns that A&T would compete with his own liberal arts college.

88. "More Understanding Needed," *DCT*, 8 April 1939, 4; see also "The A. & T. College Muddle," *DCT*, 24 July 1937, 8; NCN to Walter John, 9 August 1937, box 13, GC DNE.

89. "Introductory Statement by N. C. Newbold," 23 October 1929, box 1, Newbold A&S; James D. Anderson, "Historical Development," 195–96.

90. James W. Turner to NCN, 24 February 1949, NCN to Turner, 1 March 1949, both in box 17, GC DNE.

91. Gibbs, *History of the North Carolina Agricultural and Technical College*, 68–69.

92. Larkins, *Negro Population*, 8, 35; U.S. Commission on Civil Rights, *Equal Protection of the Laws*, 68; *State School Facts*, May 1954, box 18, SSF; Margo, *Race and Schooling*, 107–8, 132–33.

93. Gene Roberts Jr., "Educated Negroes Forced to Seek Jobs Elsewhere," *RN&O*, 5 September 1961, 1–2. See also Gene Roberts Jr., "Lack of Economic Opportunity Chief Problem of N.C. Negro," *RN&O*, 4 September 1961, 1–2.

94. "Many Students Quit School Early," *SSN* 8 (January 1962): 7.

95. Gerrelyn Chunn Patterson, "*Brown* Can't Close Us Down," 98–101, 113–15.

96. Summons and Answer to Civil Action File No. 194, Durham Division, District Court of the United States, Middle District of North Carolina, 6 November 1952, in Person County Board of Education Minutes, County Records, Board of Education Records (Microfilm), NCDAH; Kansas witness quoted in Kluger, *Simple Justice*, 412; Kelly M. Alexander, speech at North Carolina State Conference of NAACP Branches, Winston-Salem, 20 October 1956, folder 3, box 1, Kelly Alexander Sr. Papers, Special Collections, J. Murrey Atkins Library, University of North Carolina, Charlotte.

97. "Over 700 Adkin High Students Parade in Protest on Facilities," *Kinston Daily Free Press*, 20 November 1951, 1, 10.

1. Carter, *Matter of Law*, 56; Tushnet, *NAACP's Legal Strategy*, 36; McNeil, *Groundwork*, 131–54.

2. Many of the school's early records were lost in a 1925 fire; its later records are located at North Carolina Central University's archives. General histories of the school include *Soaring on the Legacy*; Reid, *History of N.C. Central University*; Seay, "History of the North Carolina College for Negroes"; and Thorpe, *Concise History*.

3. Henry Drewry and Humphrey Doermann point out that in the early twentieth century it was, in fact, the black private colleges that were most likely to provide a true college curriculum, whereas the public colleges necessarily often adhered to white-approved programs for industrial education (*Stand and Prosper*, 50).

4. "The Luxury of Segregation," *DCT*, 19 September 1953, 2; "Equal Education Suits," *DCT*, 14 January 1950, 2, 6; Franklin, Interview. For other examples of black leaders blurring the line between accommodation and protest, see Meier, *Negro Thought in America*, 110–14. Meier notes that storied accommodationist Booker T. Washington "overtly . . . minimized the importance of the franchise and civil rights, [but] covertly he was deeply involved in political affairs and in efforts to prevent disfranchisement and other forms of discrimination" (110). Robert Norrell's more recent study of Washington questions the distinction between accommodation and protest: "The accommodationist-protest binary has obscured the fundamental similarity of the substance of Washington's action to the protest agenda put forward by the NAACP" (*Up from History*, 439). Adam Fairclough has made similar arguments about Robert Moton, Booker T. Washington's successor at Tuskegee (*Teaching Equality*, chapter 2). Finally, in discussing Virginia educator and journalist and Shepard contemporary Gordon B. Hancock, Raymond Gavins aptly argues, "The central problem confronting Hancock's generation was how to end segregation and achieve integration without sacrificing black identity or abandoning ideals of self-help and racial solidarity" (*Perils and Prospects*, xiii).

5. Crow, Escott, and Hatley, *History of African Americans*, 153; U.S. Bureau of Education, *Survey of Negro Colleges*, chapter 14; Savitt, "Education of Black Physicians." On the assimilationist worldview of black college students during Jim Crow, see Wolters, *New Negro on Campus*, 340–48.

6. For curricular battles in higher education, see James D. Anderson, *Education of Blacks*, chapter 7; Wolters, *New Negro on Campus*, introduction.

7. The first black state normal school opened in Fayetteville in 1877 and is now Fayetteville State University. Four normal schools founded in 1881 in New Bern, Plymouth, Franklinton, and Salisbury later closed. In 1891, the precursor to Elizabeth City State University was founded. Simon G. Atkins founded the school at Winston-Salem in 1892; it became a public institution in 1895 and was later renamed Winston-Salem State Teachers College. The state also founded a school for Native Americans in 1887, the Cherokee Indian Normal School of Robeson County, the precursor to the University of North Carolina at Pembroke. See Leloudis, *Schooling the New South*, 74, 192–93; Noble, *History of the Public Schools*, 422–27.

8. U.S. Bureau of Education, *Survey of Negro Colleges*, chapter 14; Holmes, *Evolution of the Negro College*, 150–56; Charles Wadelington, "North Carolina Agricultural and Technical State University," in Powell, *Encyclopedia of North Carolina*, 802–3. The First Morrill Act of 1862 provided the states with federal land-grant money to establish public agricul-

tural and technical colleges. In North Carolina, the legislature used this money in 1887 to establish what became North Carolina State University in Raleigh. With the Second Morrill Act of 1890 the federal government stipulated that states practicing segregation had to divide their federal funds evenly among the races.

9. James D. Anderson, *Education of Blacks*, 113. For Coon's comment, see W. A. Robinson, "A Campaign of Publicity for the State Negro Normal Schools of North Carolina," 1926, box 8, GC DNE. Newbold similarly noted in 1934 that "there was no higher education for Negroes provided by the State twenty-five years ago. . . . Careful investigation would reveal the fact that no[t] one of these state [normal] institutions at that date ranked even as a first-class high school" ("Higher Education for Negroes in North Carolina," WPTF, 4 December 1934, box 2, Newbold A&S). On A&T's curriculum, see Hugh Victor Brown, *History*, 95.

10. William A. Robinson, "A Campaign of Publicity," box 8, GC DNE.

11. "Report of the Superintendent of State Colored Normal Schools" in *Biennial Report*, 1918-19/1919-20; James B. Dudley to Charles N. Hunter, 2 March 1919, Charles N. Hunter Scrapbooks, box 6, Charles N. Hunter Papers, Duke University, William R. Perkins Library, Special Collections, Durham, N.C.

12. Much of Shepard's early correspondence was lost in the 1925 fire. The James E. Shepard Papers at North Carolina Central University cover primarily the last decade of his life. Biographical essays about Shepard include Beverly Jones, "James Edward Shepard"; George Reid's essay in Logan and Winston, *Dictionary of American Negro Biography*, 553-55; Charles Eagles's essay in Powell, *Dictionary of North Carolina Biography*, 5:328-29; Stan Brennan's essay in Covington and Ellis, *North Carolina Century*, 259-61; Caldwell, *History of the American Negro*, 423-26; Richardson, *National Cyclopedia*, 268-69; Sarah Thuesen's essay in Gates and Higginbotham, *African American Lives*, 764-66. See also Seay, "History of the North Carolina College for Negroes," chapter 1; "First Tree Felled for Famous N.C.C.N. Just 30 Years Ago," *Durham Herald-Sun*, 14 April 1940, NCC Clipping File; Weare, *Black Business*, 29-30, 46 (n. 53), 60, 227-31; Leslie Brown, *Upbuilding Black Durham*, 76-77. On Thomas Day, see Vicki Cheng, "Furniture Helps Tell Story of NCCU Founder's Kin," *RN&O*, 24 March 2003, 1B, 4B.

13. Crow, "'Fusion, Confusion, and Negroism'"; Eric Anderson, *Race and Politics*, 200, 228; Edmonds, *Negro and Fusion Politics*, 92; Floyd J. Calvin, "James E. Shepards' [*sic*] Friends Deplore Stand on Parker, but Refuse to Forsake Educator's Leadership," *PC*, 28 June 1930, 2.

14. Edmonds, *Negro and Fusion Politics*, 92; Shepard quoted in Greenwood, *Bittersweet Legacy*, 225-26.

15. Gaines, *Uplifting the Race*, xx, 16, 28 (Vardaman quoted on 28); Gilmore, *Gender and Jim Crow*, 139-40. Leslie Brown has pointed out that Shepard continued to vote after disfranchisement and was known to wield influence with whites in helping other blacks register to vote (*Upbuilding Black Durham*, 69, 281).

16. "Dr. James E. Shepard, Negro Educator, 72," *NYT*, 7 October 1947, 27; Tom MacCaughelty, "North Carolina College, One of Four Institutions of Kind in United States," *DMH*, 4 May 1947, NCC Clipping File.

17. Du Bois, "Upbuilding of Black Durham"; William Henry Lewis, "An Account of Washington's North Carolina Tour," *Boston Transcript*, 12 November 1910, in Washington, *Booker T. Washington Papers*, 10:455-69. For the national attention that Shepard was receiving, see "The Negro Has Accomplished Much since Emancipation," *NYT*, 22 Septem-

ber 1912, SM6. His school is cited along with Hampton and Tuskegee as "one of the three great centres of influence in the South in the work of uplifting the negro." See also "Judge J. C. Pritchard Comes to Aid Negro," *NYT*, 31 January 1911, 18. Shepard's early backers included industrialist and Confederate veteran Julian S. Carr and members of Durham's Duke family. See "For the Practical Uplift of the Negro," *Atlanta Georgian*, 12 August 1909, *Hampton University Newspaper Clipping File* (microform).

18. Studies of black life in Durham during this period include Leslie Brown, *Upbuilding Black Durham*; Weare, *Black Business*. For contemporary perspectives, see Frazier, "Durham," 333, 337, 338; "Whirl of Negro Business and Industry Centered in the City of Durham," *Norfolk Journal and Guide*, 7 July 1923, 1.

19. "National Religious Training School and Chautauqua," [1909], reel 92, series 1.1, GEB Papers; "For a Negro Chautauqua," *Washington Bee*, 9 January 1909, *Hampton University Newspaper Clipping File* (microform); JES to the President of the University of Chicago, 28 February 1914, reel 92, series 1.1, GEB Papers.

20. Endorsements in "An Appeal to the Public," issued by the Advisory Committee of the National Religious Training School, reel 92, series 1.1, GEB Papers. For the school's early years, see U.S. Bureau of Education, *Negro Education*, 2:401–3; Beverly Jones, "James Edward Shepard"; George Reid's essay in Logan and Winston, *Dictionary of American Negro Biography*, 553–55; Jean Bradley Anderson, *Durham County*, 258–60; "Alumni Trying to Save Home of NCCU Founder," *DMH*, 2 November 1975, NCC Clipping File; "A Brief History of the North Carolina College for Negroes," *NCTR* 5 (May 1934): 54; Westin, "State and Segregated Schools," 425–32; Boggs, "State Supported Higher Education," 214–23.

21. Du Bois, "Upbuilding of Black Durham"; Memorandum, 18 December 1916, reel 92, series 1.1, GEB Papers; Seay, "History of the North Carolina College for Negroes," chapter 2.

22. "National Religious Training School and Chautauqua, Durham, N.C.," Wallace Buttrick to JES, 28 October 1911, JES to E. C. Sage, 23 October 1916, Sage to JES, 29 January 1917, "National Religious Training School," 6 July 1921, all in reel 92, series 1.1, GEB Papers.

23. JES to ECB, 12 July 1920, box 4, GC DNE; JES to ECB, 4 December 1920, ECB to JES, 6 December 1920, both in box 76, GC SPI.

24. Ted Poston, "'He Never Lost Faith in 46 Years,' Says Wife of North Carolina's Famous Educator," *PC*, 20 April 1940, 8; Caldwell, *History of the American Negro*, 423–26; Asa T. Spaulding, "A Brief Sketch of the Early History of the National Training School—North Carolina Central University: My Connections and Impressions," 22 May 1976, in Records and History Center Vertical Files, North Carolina Central University, James E. Shepard Memorial Library, University Archives, Records and History Center, Durham, N.C.

25. Leloudis, *Schooling the New South*, 192; NCN to James Dillard, 19 May 1919, box 4, GC DNE; NCN, "Attempting to Solve Problems of Negro Education by Deliberative Processes in North Carolina: Explanation of Some Procedures That Have Been Used in This Interesting Enterprise," 13 August 1943, box 2, Newbold A&S.

26. Wolters, *New Negro on Campus*, 277; Holmes, *Evolution of the Negro College*, 203–4; Frank Foster to NCN, 28 March 1931, NCN to Foster, 15 April 1931, box 10, GC DNE.

27. For the issue of state involvement in private schools, see Newbold, talk at Shaw University, 1922, box 1, Newbold A&S; George E. Davis to NCN, 14 November 1922, NCN to Davis, 15 November 1922, box 6, GC DNE. For the question of Hampton's role, see NCN to Abraham Flexner, 7 May 1921, Flexner to NCN, 9 May 1921, Henry Doerman to NCN,

6 May 1921, enclosed in NCN to Flexner, 11 May 1921, Flexner to NCN, 13 May 1921, NCN to James E. Gregg, 28 June 1921, enclosed in NCN to Flexner, 28 June 1921, all in reel 96, series 1.1, GEB Papers.

28. NCN, "The Usefulness of Hampton-Trained Teachers to Negro Education in North Carolina," 26 April 192[8], box 1, Newbold A&S; "Report of the Superintendent of State Colored Normal Schools," in *Biennial Report*, 1918-19/1919-20, 6; *Biennial Report*, 1922-23/1923-24, 43; NCN to ATA, 6 January 1923, box 7, GC DNE; NCN to Mary Beattie Brady, 19 August 1929, box 9, GC DNE. For a sketch of Atkins and four other educators whom Newbold held up as model race leaders, see Newbold, *Five North Carolina Negro Educators*.

29. Fairclough, *Class of Their Own*, 182-84.

30. Minutes of the Board of Trustees Meeting of the Durham State Normal School, 28 August 1923, box 5, SSF; "National Religious Training School Is Now State Institution," *Durham Sun*, 31 August 1923, box 88, GC SPI. Shepard is listed as president of the National Religious Training School on the school letterhead used for miscellaneous correspondence from 1923 in box 7, GC DNE. For Shepard's involvement in the Masons, see undated/unsigned report, folder Correspondence of NCN, Director of Division of Negro Education, 1923-25, box 7, GC DNE. The curricular changes are discussed in Seay, "History of the North Carolina College for Negroes," 75-76.

31. Beverly Jones, "James Edward Shepard," 22; "N.C. College for Negroes Grows Greatly since Founding in 1910," *RN&O*, 22 November 1931, NCC Clipping File; "Large Numbers Witness N.T.S. Commencement," *Norfolk Journal and Guide*, 4 June 1921, 1, 4.

32. JES to ATA, 20 September 1923, box 90, GC SPI; NCN to JES, 5 December 1923, JES to NCN, 7, 8 December 1923, all in box 7, GC DNE; Hugh Victor Brown, *E-Qual-ity Education*, 119.

33. JES to NCN, 27 December 1923, NCN to JES, 1 January 1924, box 7, GC DNE. Following a January 1924 visit with Newbold, Jackson Davis of the GEB noted, "Dr. Shepard thinks the Durham School should become a college, but I think Mr. Newbold is inclined to Winston-Salem." See Report of Visit with Newbold, 16 January 1924, "National Training School, Now Durham State Normal School for Negroes," 2 July 1925, both in reel 92, series 1.1, GEB Papers.

34. For later discussion of Shepard's Mason work, see NCN, "A Statement," folder September 1927-28, box 9, GC DNE. For general context on the Masons, see Palmer, "Negro Secret Societies," 207-12; Muraskin, *Middle-Class Blacks*, 1-42, 219-50; Grimshaw, *Official History*, 258-62; Frazier, *Black Bourgeoisie*, 90-94; Kantrowitz, "'Intended for the Better Government of Man'"; Hornsby-Gutting, *Black Manhood and Community Building*, 104-29. For the links between NAACP chapters and Masonic lodges, see Juan Williams, *Thurgood Marshall*, 179-80; Activity Report of Charles McLean, 29 February 1956, folder 46, box 3, McLean to Gloster B. Current, 2 December 1957, folder 48, box 3, Charles A. McLean Papers, Special Collections, J. Murrey Atkins Library, University of North Carolina, Charlotte.

35. NCN to ATA, 31 July 1924, "Summary Situation at Negro and Indian State Normal Schools," 20 August 1924, NCN to ATA, 20 August 1924, all in box 7, GC DNE; *Minutes of the Forty-Fourth Annual Session*. On black empathy for Newbold, see "What Newbold Requires State Should Give," *Raleigh Times*, 11 November 1924, reel 96, series 1.1, GEB Papers. For Newbold's predictions, see his "Introductory Statement," 10 November 1924, box 92, GC SPI.

36. NCN to ATA, 29 January 1925, NCN to Frank Bachman, 11 March 1925, Frank Bachman, "Memorandum re. Durham (North Carolina) State College for Negroes," 10 July 1925, all in reel 92, series 1.1, GEB Papers; NCN to ATA, 24 February 1925, box 7, GC DNE.

37. "The Time and Place," *DMH*, 8 October 1924, 4; "The Negro College," *DMH*, 21 February 1925, 4.

38. "House Passes Measure for Negro College in Durham," *DMH*, 18 February 1925, 1; House Bill 498/Senate Bill 559, in reel 92, series 1.1, GEB Papers; U.S. Bureau of Education, *Survey of Negro Colleges*, chapter 14.

39. NCN to Frank Bachman, 11 March 1925, reel 92, series 1.1, GEB Papers; NCN, "Introductory Statement," 16 November 1925, box 1, Newbold A&S; "The Negro College," *DMH*, 21 February 1925, 4.

40. Conrad Pearson, Interview.

41. "Veritas," "A Legislative Joker Laden with Mischief," *GDN*, 3 March 1925; JES to NCN, 30 May 1925, NCN to JES, 1 June 1925, undated/unsigned report, folder Correspondence of NCN, Director of Division of Negro Education, 1923–25, all in box 7, GC DNE.

42. NCN, "A Statement," folder September 1927–28, box 9, GC DNE; NCN to Frank Bachman, 5 June 1925, Frank Bachman, "Memorandum re: Durham (North Carolina) State College for Negroes," 10 July 1925, reel 92, series 1.1, GEB Papers. For another exchange on this issue, see C. C. Spaulding to R. L. Flower[s], 29 May 1925, enclosed in Spaulding to ATA, 29 May 1925, box 95, GC SPI, and in NCN to C. C. Spaulding, 1 June 1925, box 7, GC DNE. Spaulding, president of North Carolina Mutual in Durham, insisted that Shepard's Masonic work was an "asset rather than a liability."

43. "The Auspicious Opening of the College for Negroes," *DMH*, 17 September 1925, clipping in reel 92, series 1.1, GEB Papers. In 1925, Johnson C. Smith University in Charlotte and Shaw University in Raleigh were the only black institutions to meet state requirements for an A-grade four-year college. See NCN, "Introductory Statement," 16 November 1925, box 1, Newbold A&S.

44. "North Carolina College for Negroes," [1926], reel 92, series 1.1, GEB Papers. See also GEB study on Negro Education in North Carolina, 1926–27, esp. 44–45, reel 83, series 1.1, GEB Papers; U.S. Bureau of Education, *Survey of Negro Colleges*.

45. *Appeal Supported by Facts and Reason*; "N.C. College for Negroes Grown Greatly since Founding in 1910," *RN&O*, 22 November 1931, NCC Clipping File; Jackson Davis, Memorandum on Conference in Governor's Office, Raleigh, North Carolina, 19 May 1927, reel 92, series 1.1, GEB Papers.

46. Copy of card from Dr. [James Hardy] Dillard about North Carolina College for Negroes at Durham, 14 February 1927, NCN to Wickliffe Rose, 16 May 1927, R. L. Flowers to Rose, 17 May 1927, Memorandum on Conference in Governor's Office, Raleigh, North Carolina, 19 May 1927, ATA to Frank P. Bachman, 4 October 1927, all in reel 92, series 1.1, GEB Papers; NCN to Flowers, 7 October 1927, NCN to ATA, 8 October 1927, NCN to Angus Wilton McLean, 8 October 1927, JES to ATA, 18 October 1927, JES to McLean, 15 October 1927 (encloses Luther M. Carlton to JES, 14 October 1927, Dennis Brummitt to JES, 28 January 1926), N. W. Walker to JES, 2 November 1927, enclosed in JES to ATA, 3 November 1927, all in box 103, GC SPI.

47. ATA to JES, 21 October 1927, box 9, GC DNE; "Survey of the North Carolina College for Negroes, Durham, North Carolina," 11 February 1928, box 5, SSF.

48. NCN to Frank Bachman, 23 July 1928, James H. Dillard to Bachman, 18 October 1928, Jackson Davis to Trevor Arnett, 16 November 1928, W. W. Brierly to ATA, 3 June 1929,

all in reel 92, series 1.1, GEB Papers. For mention of NCC's first graduating class, see *Biennial Report*, 1928-29/1929-30, pt. 1, 47.

49. Newbold, "North Carolina's Adventure," 122-23; "A Brief History of the North Carolina College for Negroes," *NCTR* 5 (May 1934): 54; "Special Committee of Governor Suggests That Negro School Be Left Here; Is Doing Good Work," *DMH*, 20 February 1929, clipping in reel 92, series 1.1, GEB Papers; "N.C. College for Negroes Grows Greatly since Founding in 1910," *RN&O*, 22 November 1931, NCC Clipping File; *DCT* quoted in Brinton, "Negro in Durham," 411.

50. NCN to C. T. Loram, 26 August 1929, box 9, GC DNE; List of Past Grand Masters, Official Website of the Most Worshipful Prince Hall Grand Lodge, http://www.mwphglnc.com/pastgrandmasters.html.

51. NCN, "Introductory Statement," 23 October 1929, box 1, Newbold A&S; JES to Jackson Davis, 5 November 1931, box 11, GC DNE.

52. Shepard draws these regional comparisons in "God Bless Old North Carolina," 15 November 1934, folder 374, Shepard Papers; J. H. Bias to J. C. B. Ehringhaus, 6 April 1932, folder 1, box 2, John Henry Bias Papers, University Archive, G. R. Little Library, Elizabeth City State University, Elizabeth City, N.C.

53. One exception was Meharry Medical College in Nashville, Tennessee. See Kluger, *Simple Justice*, 136-37.

54. The most extended treatment of the Hocutt case is Gershenhorn, *"Hocutt v. Wilson."* See also Ware, *"Hocutt"*; Janken, *White*, 184-85; Ware, *William Hastie*, 46-53; Boggs, "State Supported Higher Education," 248-53; Tushnet, *NAACP's Legal Strategy*, 52-53; Weare, *Black Business*, 232-35; Douglas, *Reading, Writing, and Race*, 18-19; Burns, "Graduate Education," 195-99; Kluger, *Simple Justice*, 155-58; Leslie Brown, *Upbuilding Black Durham*, 310-12. On Houston, see McNeil, *Groundwork*.

55. See scattered membership lists in NAACP Durham Branch Records, 1919-39, reel 18, series A, pt. 12, NAACP Papers. Mention of Shepard's friendship with Du Bois can be found in Gershenhorn, *"Hocutt v. Wilson,"* 282. For Du Bois's visits, see *Catalogue of the North Carolina College for Negroes*, 1930-31; JES to Du Bois, 7 January 1929, reel 28, *Papers of W. E. B. Du Bois* (microfilm); JES to Du Bois, 14 April 1942, reel 54, *Papers of W. E. B. Du Bois* (microfilm); Du Bois to JES, 2 February 1944, reel 56, *Papers of W. E. B. Du Bois* (microfilm). On the Parker affair, see Kluger, *Simple Justice*, 141-44, 157; Floyd J. Calvin, "James E. Shepards' [*sic*] Friends Deplore Stand on Parker, but Refuse to Forsake Educator's Leadership," *PC*, 28 June 1930, 2.

56. Gershenhorn, *"Hocutt v. Wilson,"* 291-96; Ware, *"Hocutt,"* 227-29; JES to ATA, 16 February 1933, box 123, GC SPI; JES to J. C. B. Ehringhaus, 16 February 1933, folder Governor John C. B. Ehringhaus (1933), box General Correspondence, A-P, Shepard Papers.

57. NCN to C. C. Spaulding, 14 March 1933, JES to NCN, 18 March 1933, NCN to JES, 22 March 1933, all in box 11, GC DNE.

58. Bystanders and Hastie quoted in Ware, *William Hastie*, 49; Brummitt quoted in Gershenhorn, *"Hocutt v. Wilson,"* 299-300.

59. Gershenhorn, *"Hocutt v. Wilson,"* 300, 303-4; White, *Man Called White*, 158; Cecil McCoy to WW, 10 June 1933, reel 15, series A, pt. 3, NAACP Papers. Hocutt tried once again in 1946, while still working as a waiter in Durham, to secure NAACP legal assistance in a fight to get into the UNC pharmacy school, but the case never materialized. He later moved to New York, where he worked for the city transit until his death in 1974. Gilbert

Ware described Hocutt as a "modest man" who rarely spoke of his moment in the spot-light. See Gershenhorn, *"Hocutt v. Wilson,"* 306 (n. 139); Ware, *"Hocutt,"* 233.

60. White, *Man Called White*, 159; Thompson, "Court Action," 426.

61. JES to Frank Porter Graham, 26 January 1934, folder 252, series 1.1, Frank Porter Graham Papers, Southern Historical Collection, Louis R. Wilson Library, University of North Carolina, Chapel Hill; Charlotte Hawkins Brown to NCN, 5 December 1936, Brown to Graham, 5 December 1936, folder 471, series 1.1, both in Graham Papers. Brown also proposed the establishment of a "State College for Negro Women" comparable to the one for white women at Greensboro.

62. Burns, "Graduate Education," 200–201; *Report and Recommendations*, 49.

63. Jules B. Warren to Jackson Davis, 24 January 1936, reel 92, series 1.1, GEB Papers; NCN to JES, 7 December 1936, box 12, GC DNE; "Training, Number, and Salaries of In-structional Staffs in Four-Year Negro Colleges Approved by the Southern Association," enclosed in Fred McCuistion to NCN, 23 May 1938, box 13, GC DNE.

64. Taylor, *History of the North Carolina Communist Party*, 129; "Trustees in Meet Re-ceive Report on Needs of the College," *Register*, December 1936, 1; John W. Mitchell to NCN, 2 June 1938, box 13, GC DNE.

65. Boggs, "State Supported Higher Education," 242; NCN to F. L. Atkins, 18 February 1937, box 12, GC DNE; *Catalogue of the North Carolina College for Negroes*, 1940–41, 17; *Public Laws and Resolutions*, 1938, 5–6; *Soaring on the Legacy*, 46–47.

66. Fred McCuistion to JES, 12 April 1938, box 13, GC DNE; "Negro College Wins Top Rank," *RN&O*, 2 April 1938, NCC Clipping File; Membership History for North Carolina Central University, Southern Association of Colleges and Schools, http://sacscoc.org /details.asp?instid=52960.

67. Murray, Interview; Pauli Murray, *Song*, 65–70, 92–110; W. W. Pierson to Pauli Murray, 14 December 1938, reel 18, series A, pt. 3, NAACP Papers. For extended treatment of Murray, including her efforts to enter UNC, see Gilmore, *Defying Dixie*, esp. chapter 6.

68. Tushnet, *NAACP's Legal Strategy*, 70–77.

69. Pauli Murray to Frank P. Graham, 17 December 1938, W. W. Pierson to Murray, 20 December 1938; Murray to Pierson, 31 December 1938, Murray to Franklin D. Roosevelt, 31 December 1939, all in reel 18, series A, pt. 3, NAACP Papers; Pauli Murray, *Song*, 111–13.

70. Pauli Murray, *Song*, 114–19; Clyde Hoey, "Biennial Message," 5 January 1939, in Hoey, *Public Addresses, Letters, and Papers*, 38; Pauli Murray to Frank P. Graham, 17 January 1939, Graham to Murray, 5 February 1939, both in reel 18, series A, pt. 3, NAACP Papers; on Odum's stand, see Gilmore, *Defying Dixie*, 281–82.

71. Pauli Murray, *Song*, 119–20; Pauli Murray to JES, 6, 31 December 1938, Murray to Carl DeVane, 22 February 1939, all in reel 18, series A, pt. 3, NAACP Papers.

72. Hugh Victor Brown, *History*, 97; "Negro Law Department to Open September 25," *RN&O*, 5 September 1939, NCC Clipping File; Boggs, "State Supported Higher Education," 268; W. T. Bost, "Among Us Tar Heels," *GDN*, 26 January 1941, NCC Clipping File. An early proposal for out-of-state tuition aid came from Durham businessman C. C. Spaulding. See Spaulding to Howard Odum, 23 January 1935, folder O–R, box 1, Division of Coopera-tion in Education and Race Relations Series, DNE Papers. For more on the out-of-state grants, see CAE to R. Gregg Cherry, 9 September 1948, folder Public Schools, box 73, Sub-ject Files, Governor R. Gregg Cherry Papers, NCDAH; Nelson Harris, "The Present Status of Higher Education among Negroes in North Carolina," 38. The grants covered trans-

portation and "the difference between the tuition at the University of North Carolina and the out of the state university at which the Negro may matriculate." The papers of the state superintendent of public instruction include hundreds of applications for this program, which continued to operate into the 1960s.

73. Roy Wilkins to WW, 21 January 1939, WW to Wilkins, 23 January 1939, both in reel 18, series A, pt. 3, NAACP Papers; Gilmore, *Defying Dixie*, 286–89.

74. Pauli Murray, *Song*, 125–29.

75. Pauli Murray to TM, 13 April 1940, reel 18, series A, pt. 3, NAACP Papers; JES to CAE, 22 April 1942, folder Clyde A. Erwin, box General Correspondence, A–P, Shepard Papers; see also JES to Forrest Pollard, 28 January 1941, folder Forrest Pollard, box General Correspondence, P–Z, Shepard Papers; JES to Audrey Krueger, 6 June 1944, folder Prof. S. E. Warren, box General Correspondence, P–Z, Shepard Papers. On Shepard's plans for graduate education, see JES to A. R. Mann, 22 September 1939, reel 92, series 1.1, GEB Papers. On the medical school question, see JES to Fred McCuistion, 14 October 1941, reel 92, series 1.1, GEB Papers; JES to NCN, 15 February 1945, box 15, GC DNE. For Shepard's dream of parallelism, see "First Tree Felled for Famous NCC Just 30 Years Ago," *Durham Herald-Sun*, 14 April 1940, NCC Clipping File.

76. "Graduate Courses for Negroes," *DCT*, 14 January 1939, 4. For the Texas poll, see Shabazz, *Advancing Democracy*, 55.

77. "National Training School, Now Durham State Normal School for Negroes," 2 July 1925, reel 92, series 1.1, GEB Papers; Green, Interview; Beverly Jones, "James Edward Shepard," 18, 27–28; George Reid's essay in Powell, *Dictionary of American Negro Biography*, 553–55; Boggs, "State Supported Higher Education," 230–31, 269–70. For a broader discussion of discipline practices at black schools, see Wolters, *New Negro on Campus*, 12–13. For the student tribute, see "Tribute to a Builder of Dreams," *Campus Echo*, October 1947, 2. On Hurston, see Eubanks, "Women Writers of Hayti"; Valerie Boyd, *Wrapped in Rainbows*, 327, 337–41.

78. JES to NCN, 27 December 1923, box 7, GC DNE; Faggett, "Shepard Tradition."

79. JES, "Let's Win the War," 21 October 1942, folder 380, Shepard Papers.

80. Rampersad, *Life of Langston Hughes*, 2:83–84; Faggett, "Shepard Tradition," 484–88; *People's Voice*, 26 February 1944, clipping in folder 631, Shepard Papers.

81. JES to WW, 26 June 1943, as well as similar letters in folder WW, box General Correspondence, P–Z, Shepard Papers; Christina Greene, *Our Separate Ways*, 24–25.

82. JES to NCN, 21 August 1947, box 17, GC DNE; also see Gordon Gray to R. Gregg Cherry, 18 July 1947, NCN to Gray, 20 August 1947, NCN to Frank P. Graham, 22 August 1947, NCN to Gray, 22 August, 22 September 1947, all in box 16, GC DNE; NCN to JES, 19, 22 August 1947, both in box 17, GC DNE.

83. JES to R. Gregg Cherry, 8 October 1946, box 36, Cherry Papers. Mention of the gifts is found in scattered thank you notes from Cherry to Shepard during 1945–47. For the name change, see JES to Members of the Board of Trustees, 10 September 1946, box 173, GC SPI; Shepard's comments to the school board in "An Editorial," [*DCT*, 1947], NCC Clipping File.

84. Charles Ray, "Last Rites Held for Noted Educator Here Thursday; Many Notables Pay Tribute," *DCT*, 11 October 1947, NCC Clipping File; "Final Rites Held for Dr. Shepard," 10 October 1947, *RN&O*, NCC Clipping File; "Last Rites Held for Dr. Shepard," *PC*, 18 October 1947, 1; program for Shepard's memorial service, 9 October 1947, box 17, GC DNE.

85. Editorial, *GDN*, 9 October 1947, 6.

86. "James E. Shepard Memorial Foundation, Inc." (pamphlet), box 18, GC DNE.

87. W. T. Bost, "Among Us Tar Heels," *GDN*, 31 December 1948, 6.

88. Benjamin E. Mays, "Jim Shepard," *PC*, 1 November 1947, 6; Conrad Pearson, Interview; Weare, *Black Business*, 228 (n. 41).

89. Green, Interview.

90. Tushnet, *NAACP's Legal Strategy*, 120–32; Sullivan, *Lift Every Voice*, 337–39; Fisher, *Matter of Black and White*, 145–47.

91. "Regional Colleges Charted for South," *NYT*, 9 February 1948, 15; Thompson, "Why Negroes Are Opposed"; "Race Leaders Asleep, N.C. Okays Regional Schools," *PC*, 26 March 1949, 2; Thomas, "Dr. Jim Crow"; "Report of the Resolutions Committee," *NCTR* 19 (May 1948): 17; "Resource Use Education and Regional Disgrace," *NCTR* 21 (January 1950): 9; "Segregation Is Doomed," *DCT*, 3 September 1949, 2.

92. "Southern Professors Vote to End Segregation in Professional Schools," *Southern Patriot* 6 (November 1948): 1. The other state universities where faculty favored integration included Arkansas, Florida, Oklahoma, Tennessee, Texas, and Virginia. At three southern universities—Georgia, Mississippi, and South Carolina—a majority of the faculty favored the establishment of segregated regional black graduate and professional schools.

93. "Appropriations," *Popular Government* 13:1-A (May 1947): 14–15; *Soaring on the Legacy*, 47–48; Boykin, *Separate . . . but Equal*; *Asheville Citizen* reprinted in "Other Papers Say: Not Much Discrimination," *LR*, 20 September 1950, 4.

94. James T. Patterson, *Brown v. Board of Education*, 16–17; NCN to Frank P. Graham, 10 January 1950, NCN, "North Carolina Moves Positively toward Equality in Public Education as between White and Colored People," 4 January 1950, both in box 18, GC DNE.

95. Burns, "Graduate Education," 209–11; McKissick, Interview by Kalk; "N.C. Whites Fighting to Keep Jim-Crow Law School," *PC*, 3 September 1949, 2; "More Plaintiffs Are Permitted in U.N.C. Case," *DMH*, 9 February 1950, "Negro Denied Study at UNC," *RN&O*, 13 June 1951, both in NCC Clipping File; David E. Brown, "Grudging Acceptance"; Wallenstein, "Higher Education," 284–85; Snider, *Light on the Hill*, 246–49. There are some discrepancies within both primary and secondary sources as to whether all five of the abovementioned law students began in June 1951, but UNC General Alumni Association records indicate that all five entered at that time. I am grateful to Reginia Oliver and Joan Pendergraph of the University of North Carolina General Alumni Association for their assistance on this question.

96. "A Statement of the Need to the Advisory Budget Commission from the North Carolina College at Durham," September 1950, box 19, SSF; "Information about Out-of-State Aid for Students Who Go Out of the State," 18 January 1956, box 18, SSF; Harris, "Publicly-Supported Negro Higher Institutions," 291.

97. Gershenhorn, "Stalling Integration"; Crow, Escott, and Hatley, *History of African Americans*, 173–74.

98. One of the more famous, if short-lived, expressions of that impulse was Malcolm X Liberation University, a school formed in 1969 in Durham (later relocated to Greensboro) by a group of black activists and Duke University students. See Christina Greene, *Our Separate Ways*, 186–89.

99. Ferguson, Interview; Lisa Watters, "Peaceful Warriors," *Mountain Xpress*, 26 Octo-

ber 2005, http://www.mountainx.com/news/2007/1026ascore.php. Lightner made his comments at a 1984 symposium held at North Carolina Central University. See Reid, *History of N.C. Central University*, 143–47.

100. Leoneda Inge, "NCCU Turns 100," WUNC, 9 July 2010, http://wunc.org/programs/news/archive/Nli0709_NCCU_Birthday_website.mp3/view.

CHAPTER FOUR

1. Langston Hughes, "Cowards from Colleges," *The Crisis* 41 (August 1934), reprinted in Aptheker, *Documentary History*, 101–9. For the larger context of Hughes's southern tour, see Rampersad, *Life of Langston Hughes*, 1:214–15, 224–26; Gilmore, *Defying Dixie*, 207–9.

2. "Report of Committee on Teachers' Salaries," *NCTR* 1 (March 1930): 8; *Biennial Report*, 1942–43/1943–44, pt. 1, 98. As Robert Margo has shown, other southern states underwent a similar widening of the racial gap in teacher salaries. The most egregious case was in Alabama, where in 1890 black teachers received 119 percent of the average white salary; in 1910 that figure was 39 percent (*Race and Schooling*, 54).

3. Discussions of North Carolina's salary campaign can be found in Leslie Brown, *Upbuilding Black Durham*, 312–21; Percy Murray, *History*, 44–50; Gershenhorn, "Courageous Voice," 72–74. For more general discussions of teacher salary equalization suits, see Fairclough, *Class of Their Own*, 309–11, 344–53; Tushnet, *NAACP's Legal Strategy*, 58–65, 78–80, 89–92, 95–99, 102–3. For case studies of salary suits outside of North Carolina, see Lewis, *In Their Own Interests*, 155–66; Scott Baker, *Paradoxes of Desegregation*, 44–62; Charron, *Freedom's Teacher*, 149–78; Kirk, "NAACP Campaign."

4. There may have been an isolated but successful teacher salary lawsuit prior to the NAACP's 1933 campaign. In August 1933, Newbold noted that in the preceding twenty years, there had been "only two definite law suits, one about a high school, the other a teacher suing for an equal salary. These were won by the Negroes concerned" (NCN to [Members of the State School Commission], 30 August 1933, box 122, GC SPI).

5. Fairclough, *Class of Their Own*, 309.

6. In addition to the role that gender played in shaping the fault lines of the salary fight, Leslie Brown found that the struggle in Durham represented "a generational power struggle and an insider/outsider contest for authority" (*Upbuilding Black Durham*, 320).

7. The 1930–44 cohort of NCTA presidents included state Rosenwald supervisor George E. Davis (b. 1862), Rocky Mount principal Oliver R. Pope (b. 1876), Elizabeth City State Teachers College president John H. Bias (b. 1879), Palmer Memorial Institute president Charlotte Hawkins Brown (b. 1883), North Carolina College for Negroes president James E. Shepard (b. 1875), Jeanes supervisor Rose Aggrey (b. 1882), Fayetteville State Teachers College president James W. Seabrook (b. 1886), and Greensboro principal John A. Tarpley (b. 1900). See Percy Murray, *History*, 51–55.

8. Frazier, *Black Bourgeoisie*, 235. For one source that points out the caution of North Carolina's black educational leadership, see Tushnet, *NAACP's Legal Strategy*, 58. Davison Douglas found teachers impeding and instigating litigation at different moments (*Reading, Writing, and Race*, 21, 111–12). Adam Fairclough acknowledges that many teachers resisted confrontational legal battles but argues that they were still key players in facilitating the civil rights movement (*Class of Their Own*). For a more general look at black female professionals, see Shaw, *What a Woman Ought to Be*. Shaw argues that black

women embraced, in lieu of bourgeois individualism, "socially responsible individualism."

9. *Minutes of the Forty-Fourth Annual Session; Minutes of the Forty-Fifth Annual Session; Minutes of the Forty-Sixth Annual Session;* Delany, Interview.

10. Supervisor of High Schools [William A. Robinson] to W. E. B. Du Bois, 28 April 1926, box 8, GC DNE. At the time, Robinson was furnishing Du Bois with information about the North Carolina schools for use in *The Crisis.* See scattered correspondence in reels 16 and 19, *Papers of W. E. B. Du Bois* (microfilm).

11. Atkins, "President's Address," includes an abstract of Newbold's address, "Definite Gains That Have Been Made and a Look Ahead," NCC.

12. Clement, "History of Negro Education," 239–40; "A Report of Progress," *NCTR* 1 (January 1930): 10–11; Benjamin Brawley, "Response to Address of Welcome at Rocky Mount," *NCTR* 1 (May 1930): 3; "Surety, Economy, and Co-operation," *NCTR* 2 (October 1931): 68–69.

13. The timing of this meeting is unclear. In one recollection, Newbold placed it in 1925. Yet in a 1930 letter, Newbold referred to the meeting as having taken place a year and a half earlier. See document beginning, "So far as my work in North Carolina is concerned . . . ," folder S (July 1948–June 1949), box 17, GC DNE; NCN to ATA, 24 September 1930, box 10, GC DNE. The 1948–49 document is unsigned, but the content points to Newbold since he describes a similar story in the 1930 letter.

14. NCN to ATA, 24 September 1930, ATA to NCN, 25 September 1930, both in box 10, GC DNE. On the Parker affair, see Kluger, *Simple Justice,* 141–44, 157; Boggs, "State Supported Higher Education," 246–47.

15. NCN to ATA, 12 September 1931, box 11, GC DNE. On the matter of school tax law, see Leloudis, *Schooling the New South,* 121–22; NCN to Tyre Taylor, 31 May 1930, box 10, GC DNE; NCN, "Report on the Negro," 15 April 1930, box 1, Newbold A&S.

16. Form letter from ATA and NCN, 12 November 1931, box 8, SSF; NCN, "Introductory Address," 27 November 1931, box 1, Newbold A&S; Typescript of the Meeting's Minutes and a Statement Adopted by the Participants, 27 November 1931, box 8, SSF; "Do Negroes Study Details, Work Out Definite Requests and Proposals on Local Situations and Then Present These Formally to Local, County, and State Authorities?," box 8, SSF.

17. NCN to ATA, 21 June 1932, box 11, GC DNE; *Biennial Report,* 1934–35/1935–36, pt. 1, 89–90; Newbold, "Public Education of Negroes."

18. J. T. Taylor, "Inequalities in Educational Opportunity," *NCTR* 4 (October 1933): 62, 68; "Report of Committee on Teachers' Salaries," *NCTR* 1 (March 1930): 8. Regional figures were even more stark. In 1932, the average rural black teacher in the South had 70 percent as much training as her white counterpart but only received 40 percent of the average white salary (Miller and Gregg, "Teaching Staff").

19. Prior to the twentieth century, the southern black teaching force actually had a greater proportion of males than the region's white teaching force, a trend partly explained by the paucity of professional options for black men. It was not until the salaries began to fall in the twentieth century that the profession matched—and eventually eclipsed—white patterns of feminization. See Fultz, "African-American Teachers in the South, 1890–1940: Growth Feminization, and Salary Discrimination," 548–53.

20. *DCT,* 15 February 1930, quoted in Brinton, "Negro in Durham," 381; Raper and Reid, *Sharecroppers All,* 104.

21. Weare, *Black Business*, 236–39.

22. Korstad, *Civil Rights Unionism*, 127–30; see also Sullivan, *Days of Hope*, chapter 2.

23. Fairclough, *Class of Their Own*, 341–44; Hall et al., *Like a Family*, chapter 6, worker quoted on 349.

24. "Evolution of the Governor's Commission on the Study of Problems in Negro Education," *NCTR* 6 (March 1935): 32–34.

25. "Asks Equality in Negro Education," *RN&O*, 23 May 1933, clipping in NAACP Raleigh Branch Files, 1916–39, reel 18, series A, pt. 12, NAACP Papers; WW to J. N. Mills, 29 May 1933, WW to Richard L. McDougald, 8 June 1933, McDougald to WW, 21 July 1933, all in NAACP Durham Branch Files, 1919–39, reel 18, series A, pt. 12, NAACP Papers.

26. Ware, *William Hastie*, 56.

27. Ibid., 55–60; George Streator to WW, 1 September 1933, Streator to WW, [September 1933], both in reel 17, series A, pt. 12, NAACP Papers; JES to NCN, 6 September, 19 October 1933, both in box 11, GC DNE.

28. Weare, *Black Business*, 238–39; "Negro Teachers' Salary," reel 17, series A, pt. 12, NAACP Papers; C. C. Spaulding to WW, 24 October 1933, reel 18, series A, pt. 12, NAACP Papers.

29. "A Glance at the Status of the Negro Teacher in North Carolina," *NCTR* 4 (October 1933): 72–74. See also J. T. Taylor, "Inequalities in Educational Opportunity," *NCTR* 4 (October 1933): 62, 68.

30. NAACP Press Release, 31 October 1933, WW to George E. Nightengale, 30 October 1933, both in reel 17, series A, pt. 12, NAACP Papers; "Negro Group to Back Pay Issue," *RN&O*, 29 October 1933, 1, 2; "Militant Speech Made to Negroes," *RN&O*, 30 October 1933, 1, 2; "A Clever Propagandist," *RN&O*, 31 October 1933, 4; "Commission Will Discuss Salaries," *RN&O*, 1 November 1933, 2; George Streator, "The Colored South Speaks for Itself," *The Crisis* 40 (December 1933), reprinted in Aptheker, *Documentary History*, 40–45. On the number of teachers at the rally, see Gershenhorn, "Courageous Voice," 72 (n. 50).

31. "Older Negroes Not Supporting Present School Salary Issue" (typescript), WW to George Nightengale, 13 November 1933, both in reel 17, series A, pt. 12, NAACP Papers; G. A. Edwards to NCN, 2 November 1933, box 11, GC DNE. On Eppes, see "Negro Educator Dies in Raleigh," *RN&O*, 1 August 1942, NCC Clipping File. On Nightengale's origins, see 1930 U.S. Federal Census, High Point, Guilford County, N.C., Roll 1695, p. 14A, Enumeration District 55, http://search.ancestry.com/cgibin/sse.dll?h=76750696&db=1930usfedcen&indiv=try.

32. WW to George Nightengale, 22 November 1933, "'Boogey Man' Cry by North Carolina Amuses N.A.A.C.P.," 10 November [1933], both in reel 17, series A, pt. 12, NAACP Papers; George Streator, "The Colored South Speaks for Itself," *The Crisis* 40 (December 1933), reprinted in Aptheker, *Documentary History*, 40–45.

33. JES to J. C. B. Ehringhaus, 31 October 1933, folder Governor J. C. B. Ehringhaus, box General Correspondence, A–P, Shepard Papers; JES to NCN, 1 November 1933, JES to NCN, 13 November 1933 (encloses WW to JES, 11 November 1933), both in box 11, GC DNE.

34. W. J. Trent Jr. to WW, 17 November 1933, reel 17, series A, pt. 12, NAACP Papers. On the younger Trent, see "William Trent, 83, Director of Negro College Fund," *NYT*, 29 November 1993, D8. On both Trents, see essays by Andre Vann in Jones-Wilson et al., *Encyclopedia of African-American Education*, 476–78.

35. A copy of this statement was enclosed in JES to NCN, 17 November 1933, box 11,

GC DNE. A published copy can be found in "Negro Citizens' Appeal to North Carolinians," *GDN*, 17 December 1933, NCC Clipping File. On the excision of the statement about court action, see George Nightengale to WW, 17 November 1933, reel 17, series A, pt. 12, NAACP Papers.

36. George Nightengale to WW, 17 November 1933, "North Carolina Factions Uniting behind Program," 24 November [1933], both in reel 17, series A, pt. 12, NAACP Papers; "N.C. Factions Unite behind NAACP Program," *Norfolk Journal and Guide*, 2 December 1933, A19. For a list of state NAACP officers, see reel 18, series A, pt. 12, NAACP Papers.

37. Daisy E. Lampkin to WW, 27 November 1933, reel 17, series A, pt. 12, NAACP Papers.

38. Gavins, "Within the Shadow," 80; O. R. Pope to "Fellow Teachers," December 1933, folder 1, Oliver R. Pope Papers, Southern Historical Collection, Louis R. Wilson Library, University of North Carolina, Chapel Hill; Pope, *Chalk Dust*, 152–53.

39. "Evolution of the Governor's Commission on the Study of Problems in Negro Education," *NCTR* 6 (March 1935): 32–34; *Report of the Governor's Commission*.

40. "Some Plain Facts about Negro Education in North Carolina," *NCTR* 5 (March 1934): 32; "Annual Address of Pres. O. R. Pope," *NCTR* 5 (May 1934): 49–50, 58–59.

41. Leslie Brown, *Upbuilding Black Durham*, 69, 281; Weare, *Black Business*, 240–50; Mabry, *Negro in North Carolina Politics*, 76–81; Sanders, "Race Attitudes of County Officials."

42. For statements by Shepard on voting, see "Racial Discriminations," 28 April 1936, folder 376, Shepard Papers; "Our Mutual Tasks," 16 February 1946, folder 387, Shepard Papers.

43. Burns, "North Carolina and the Negro Dilemma," 205–6; "Iredell Case May Figure in Nat. Election," *Statesville Record*, 7 February 1936, 1, 8; T. E. Allison Jr., "News of Statesville Colored People," *Statesville Record*, 17 April 1936, 2.

44. Lawson, *Black Ballots*, table 2, 284.

45. Newbold, "More Money," 506; "Dean" [William Pickens] to WW and Roy Wilkins, 8 December 1936, reel 18, series A, pt. 12, NAACP Papers; *DCT* editorial quoted in Tindall, *Emergence of the New South*, 568.

46. Gilmore, *Gender and Jim Crow*, 218–23.

47. "North Carolina Negro Teachers Association Closes Its Fifty-Fourth Annual Session," *NCTR* 6 (May 1935): 52; "Message from the President of the N.C. Teachers Association," *NCTR* 10 (October 1939): 3. On Brown's efforts to court public funding, see Wadelington and Knapp, *Charlotte Hawkins Brown*, 82, 161–63, 170–71.

48. Newbold, "Equalization of Teachers' Salaries," 164–65; Clara D. Mann, "The Salary Scale and Salary Differential," *NCTR* 8 (January 1937): 5–6.

49. Its five members were two state senators (J. W. Noell of Roxboro and J. H. McDaniel of Cabarrus County) and three state representatives (Hugh G. Horton of Williamston, F. H. Brooks of Smithfield, and George R. Uzzell of Salisbury). Newbold served as secretary. See NCN, "Yesterday, Today, and Tomorrow," 15 April 1938, box 2, Newbold A&S.

50. "The Commission on Negro Education," *DCT*, 29 May 1937, 2; JES to NCN, 2 December 1938, box 13, GC DNE. For the publication of that committee, see *Report and Recommendations*.

51. *Salary Schedule and Classification of Schools*; ECB to County Superintendents, 13 May 1920, box 74, GC SPI.

52. M. Hugh Thompson to TM, 11 November 1937, reel 5, series A, pt. 3, NAACP Papers;

NCN to B. T. Harvey, 9 August 1937, JES to NCN, 7 April 1938, both in box 13, GC DNE; Bond, *Education of the Negro*, 255–56. By the late 1930s, the State School Commission's salary scales did employ the racially neutral "maximum" and "minimum" recommendations. However, the intended meaning behind those designations was thinly disguised. For example, in 1939, the estimated costs for teachers paid at the "maximum" level were labeled "white"; the totals for those paid at the "minimum" level were labeled "colored." See Minutes of the State School Commission, 10 August 1939, vol. 8, North Carolina State Board of Education Papers, NCDAH.

53. For discussion of the Maryland and Virginia cases, see Tushnet, *NAACP's Legal Strategy*, 58–65, 77–81, 102–3; Lewis, *In Their Own Interests*, 155–66; Winston Douglas, "Annual Address of the Virginia State Teachers Association," *Virginia Teachers Bulletin* 15 (January 1938): 7.

54. WW to P. B. Young, 24 April 1939, reel 5, series A, pt. 3, NAACP Papers; "Welcome Teachers, the Hour Has Come!," *DCT*, 16 April 1938, 4; "Conservative Leadership and the General Assembly," *DCT*, 4 March 1939, 4; "The Teachers Salary Question," *DCT*, 25 March 1939, 4.

55. Minutes of the State School Commission, 9 February 1939, North Carolina State Board of Education Papers, NCDAH; JES, untitled address, November 1939, folder 392, Shepard Papers.

56. Newbold, "Equalization of Teachers' Salaries," 164–65.

57. NCN to Joseph Melville Broughton, 3 June 1944, box 15, GC DNE; A. H. Anderson to TM, 4 November 1941, TM to Anderson, 1 December 1941, reel 9, series B, pt. 3, NAACP Papers.

58. "North Carolina State School Commission Raises Teachers Salaries," *NCTR* 12 (October 1941): 10.

59. "Our Duty in the Present Crisis," *NCTR* 13 (January 1942): 8; for the Durham manifesto, see *Basis for Inter-Racial Cooperation*; Sosna, *In Search of the Silent South*, 116–18; Egerton, *Speak Now against the Day*, 305–7; Gavins, *Perils and Prospects*, 128–32; Hall, *Revolt against Chivalry*, 258–59; Crow, Escott, and Hatley, *History of African Americans*, 150–51.

60. For a sketch of Seabrook, see Percy Murray, *History*, 54–55; J. W. Seabrook to Nathan Yelton, 5 June 1942, box 14, GC DNE.

61. "Presentation of the Plea of the Negro Teachers Association to the Joint Appropriations Committee," *NCTR* 14 (March 1943): 8–10; "Equalized Salaries," *CO*, 11 February 1943, 10, reprinted in *NCTR* 14 (March 1943): 9.

62. Report of NAACP Charlotte Branch, 1943, reel 20, series A, pt. 25, NAACP Papers; A. H. Anderson to TM, 20 April 1942, 16 April 1943, Hosea V. Price to TM, 9 April 1943, Price to E. F. Tullock, 14 April 1943, all in reel 9, series B, pt. 3, NAACP Papers.

63. Korstad, *Civil Rights Unionism*; Korstad and Lichtenstein, "Opportunities Found and Lost," 788–93; Franklin and Moss, *From Slavery to Freedom*, 496; Joseph Melville Broughton, "John Merrick: Pioneer and Builder," 11 July 1943, in Broughton, *Public Addresses, Letters, and Papers*, 250.

64. Newbold, "Equalization of Teachers' Salaries," 164–65; "Equal Pay for N.C. Teachers," *Norfolk Journal and Guide*, 17 June 1944, B1–B2; Tarpley, Interview; Streator to WW, [September 1933], reel 17, series A, pt. 12, NAACP Papers; "Report of the Legislative Committee of the North Carolina College Conference," *NCTR* 15 (May 1944): 12, 14.

65. Tushnet, *NAACP's Legal Strategy*, 58–65, 77–81, 102–3; Lewis, *In Their Own Inter-*

ests, 154–65; Shircliffe, "Rethinking *Turner v. Keefe*"; Charron, *Freedom's Teacher*, 149–78, esp. 175; Scott Baker, *Paradoxes of Desegregation*, 44–62.

66. Weare, *Black Business*, 239.

67. CAE to B. M. Grier, 12 January 1946, box 171, GC SPI; HLT to State Board of Education, 26 October 1948, CAE to HLT, 27 November 1948, both in box 181, GC SPI; "Problems That Still Remain in the Education of Negroes in North Carolina," [1948], box 18, SSF. NAACP state president Kelly Alexander noted that the town of Monroe distributed discriminatory local supplements in 1949 (Kelly Alexander, "The Task of the NAACP in North Carolina," 23 June 1949, folder 2, box E87, Group II, NAACP Papers). In the mid-1950s, about one-third of all state school personnel received local supplements. See *North Carolina Public School Survey*, Fall 1956, box 18, SSF.

68. NCN to O. Arthur Kirkman, 15 March 1949, enclosed in NCN to CAE, 15 March 1949, box 184, GC SPI.

69. CAE to John Stennis, 15 September 1948, box 18, SSF; "School Ratings Low for Negroes," *RN&O*, 16 October 1946, 1. North Carolina's use of the National Teachers Examination is discussed in the epilogue.

70. Adam Fairclough has pointed out that some black teachers mistrusted the quality of their training, as some had raised their certification levels by attending weakly funded summer schools (*Class of Their Own*, 368).

CHAPTER FIVE

1. Dabney quoted in NCN, "How Can Race Relations Be Improved?," 5 November 1943, box 2, Newbold A&S; "Negro Rights," *Life*, 24 April 1944, 32; Margo, *Race and Schooling*, 21–22.

2. Cultural affairs officer Clifford Manshardt quoted in Dudziak, *Cold War Civil Rights*, 59.

3. Meier and Rudwick, *Along the Color Line*, 359. On pre-*Brown* school protests in the North, see Sugrue, *Sweet Land of Liberty*, 163–81.

4. Case studies of pre-*Brown* equalization efforts include Bolton, *Hardest Deal of All*, esp. chapter 2; Scott Baker, *Paradoxes of Desegregation*, esp. chapters 2, 5; Walker, *Their Highest Potential*, esp. chapter 2. For an overview of pre-*Brown* activism in North Carolina, see Gavins, "Within the Shadow"; Burns, "North Carolina and the Negro Dilemma," chapter 2.

5. Lau, *Democracy Rising*, 212. The key study of the national NAACP's equalization work is Tushnet, *NAACP's Legal Strategy*. See also Kluger, *Simple Justice*, esp. pt. 1. Tushnet has argued that the national NAACP was sensitive to the goals of local communities and that the group's successful litigation necessarily reflected grassroots imperatives (146–58). More recent studies have emphasized tensions between the national NAACP agenda and local concerns. See Shabazz, *Advancing Democracy*, esp. chapter 2; Goluboff, *Lost Promise*, chapter 9; Fairclough, *Class of Their Own*, 375–76; Turner, "'It Is Not at Present a Very Successful School,'" chapter 5; Korstad and Lichtenstein, "Opportunities Found and Lost," esp. 808–9. For NAACP executive secretary Walter White's discomfort with grassroots mobilization, see Janken, *White*, 265, 370–71.

6. *Biennial Report*, 1918–19/1919–20, pt. 3, 9–15; Newbold, "Some Achievements," 457; *Report and Recommendations*, 11; P. J. Long to NCN, 31 August 1938, box 13, GC DNE; *Biennial Report*, 1944–45/1945–46, pt. 2, 105.

7. NCN to Clyde R. Hoey, 23 February 1939, box 13, GC DNE; *Biennial Report*, 1944–45/1945–46, pt. 2, 67, 91; Marie McIver, "Special Needs of Negro Children," 6 February 1941, box 14, GC DNE.

8. Newbold, "Some Achievements," 463; "Report of the Committee on Negro Education of the State Board of Education," folder Committee on Negro Education (Reports 1944–45), box 1, SSF; E. L. Cundiff to NCN, 15 June 1938, Annie B. Wade to NCN, 14 October 1938, box 13, GC DNE; *Biennial Report*, 1944–45/1945–46, pt. 2, 98.

9. In 1944–45, there were 2,690,066 library books for whites and 507,867 for blacks (*Biennial Report*, 1944–45/1945–46, pt. 2, 106).

10. Oscar Chapman to NCN, 7 January 1946, DNE Memorandum, 7 March 1946, Grade Mothers of Franklin County Training School to NCN, [1946 or 1947], all in box 15, GC DNE; W. H. Green to NCN, 11 December 1941, box 14, GC DNE.

11. JES, "Racial Discriminations," 28 April 1936, folder 376, Shepard Papers; Foreman, *Environmental Factors*, esp. 52. On Foreman, see Sullivan, *Days of Hope*, 24–40. On diverging achievement levels, see "Report on the North Carolina Annual Statewide Testing Program for 1946–1947," folder Analysis of Data, 1946–47, box 1, Elementary and Secondary Education Section, Analysis of Data, DIS Papers; Joseph H. Douglass, "Certain Implications of the North Carolina Educational Commission Study to the Education of Negroes within the State," *NCTR* 20 (January 1949): 13–16.

12. *Bulletin*, No. 3 District, 1941–42, PTA Papers; "Excerpts from Annual Reports of Jeanes Supervisors in North Carolina [1942–43], box 15, GC DNE.

13. Myrdal, with Sterner and Rose, *American Dilemma*, esp. chapter 41; Logan, *What the Negro Wants*. For the history of Logan's book, see Janken, *Rayford W. Logan*, chapter 6; for the history of *An American Dilemma*, see Walter A. Jackson, *Gunnar Myrdal and America's Conscience*.

14. NCN to W. T. Couch, 16, 18, 20 October 1943, all in reel 93, series 1.1, GEB Papers. See also Couch to NCN, 8 November 1943, NCN to Couch, 22 January 1944, both in box 15, GC DNE.

15. NCN, "How Can Race Relations Be Improved?," 5 November 1943, box 2, Newbold A&S; NCN to C. C. Spaulding, 17 January 1944, box 15, GC DNE.

16. NCN to James Dillard, 25 June 1929, box 9, GC DNE; NCN to CAE, 25 July 1935, box 131, GC SPI. For a similar pattern in Mississippi, see Bolton, *Hardest Deal of All*, 40–41.

17. "Representation Needed," *DCT*, 22 May 1937, 2. For discussion of school financing and governing practices, see Newbold, "Some Achievements," 457–58; Wager, *North Carolina*, 32, 88–93; NCN to W. A. Schiffley, 19 April 1938, box 13, GC DNE. In 1929–30, state funds accounted for about 23 percent of school budgets; by 1934–35, that figure had jumped to 89 percent. The state's share of school financing would gradually decrease; by 1966, the breakdown was state, 69 percent; local, 16 percent; federal, 15 percent. See *Biennial Report*, 1940–41/1941–42, pt. 1, 62; *Biennial Report*, 1966–67/1967–68, pt. 1, 16.

18. "Negro Children Protest Conditions at Two Lumberton School Units," *LR*, 1 October 1946, 1, 4; "Strike Planned," *LR*, 2 October 1946, 1; McQueen, Interview; Gus Bullock to R. Gregg Cherry, 2 October 1946, box 11, Governor R. Gregg Cherry Papers, NCDAH. The first newspaper article misidentifies Gus Bullock as "Gus Bullard." The Lumberton strike is briefly discussed in Burns, "North Carolina and the Negro Dilemma," 89–92; Fairclough, *Better Day Coming*, 203; Tushnet, *Making Civil Rights Law*, 152–53; Scott Baker, *Paradoxes of Desegregation*, 87; Gavins, "NAACP in North Carolina," 117; Meier and Rudwick, *Along the Color Line*, 359–61.

19. R. Gregg Cherry to Gus Bullock, 4 October 1946, box 11, Cherry Papers; "Negro Students Strike in Protest of Building Status," *LR*, 7 October 1946, 1, 2; "400 Negro Youths Strike at Schools in Lumberton," *RN&O*, 8 October 1946, 1, 2; "School Strike Continued by Negroes in Lumberton," *RN&O*, 9 October 1946, 1, 2; "Thompson Institute to Resume Classes Tomorrow as School Strike Ends," *LR*, 16 October 1946, 1. For national mention of the strike, see "Strike for Negro School Repair," *NYT*, 10 October 1946, 19; "Pupils' Protest Parade Hits School Conditions," *PC*, 12 October 1946, 14.

20. Lowery, *Lumbee Indians*, 21, 36–37; Morgan, "Racial Comparison," 19, 28, 30. For discussion of hostility between blacks and Indians, see Lily E. Mitchell to NCN, 12 February 1929, NCN to Mitchell, 14 February 1929, box 9, GC DNE.

21. Lowery, *Lumbee Indians*, 31–33; Morgan, "Racial Comparison," 169–70; W. F. Credle to NCN, 10 October 1946, box 16, GC DNE; "Lumberton Is Proud of Splendid New High School Building," *LR*, 11 September 1924, 1. Lumberton student population statistics found in *Biennial Report*, 1950–51/1951–52, pt. 3, 10. Drawing comparisons between the black and Indian schools is complicated by changes in how the state classified Indians. In the state superintendent's *Biennial Report* for 1928–29/1929–30, statistics on Indian schools were included with those for blacks; in the following *Biennial Report*, Indian statistics were included with white figures.

22. HLT to Robert L. Carter, 8 May 1947, folder 2, box B146, group II, NAACP Papers.

23. Kemp, Interview; McQueen, Interview. On black school conditions, see complaint filed by Lawrence S. Stephens, Sam Bullock, and Bessie Thompson, reel 3, series B, pt. 3, NAACP Papers; see also "Resolutions by Lumberton Parents," n.d., box 16, GC DNE; HLT to Robert L. Carter, 8 May 1947, reel 4, series B, pt. 3, NAACP Papers.

24. U.S. Bureau of Education, *Negro Education*, 2:433; Caldwell, *History of the American Negro*, 142–44; Whitted, *History of Negro Baptists*, 178–79, Documenting the American South, http://docsouth.unc.edu/church/whitted/whitted.html; "Dr. William H. Knuckles Was Pioneer in Negro Education," *LR*, 30 May 1971, 8A; Alice Briley, "Former Slave A. H. Thompson was Leader, Builder," *LR*, 5 February 2012, http://www.robesonian .com/pages/full_story/push?article-Former+slave+A-H-+Thompson+was+leader -+builder%20&id=17390996.

25. U.S. Bureau of Education, *Negro Education*, 2:455–56; Caldwell, *History of the American Negro*, 606–7; "Will Replace Buildings," *LR*, 13 December 1915, 1; "A Worthy Cause," *LR*, 25 November 1915, 2; "Fine Record of Service," *LR*, 15 June 1933, 4; "Thompson-Hayswood," *LR*, 14 September 1933, 7; "Resolution by City Council Praises Hayswood's Service," *LR*, 2 February 1953, 1, 4; "Rev. Dr. John H. Hayswood Reaches End of Useful Life," *LR*, 1 April 1958, 1; "Dr. Hayswood, Teacher Extraordinary, Was a Vanguard of Local Community," *LR*, 16 May 1971, 9D; S. J. Fisher, "Tried by Fire," *Home Mission Monthly* 30 (April 1916): 145; Kemp, Interview.

26. For early black efforts to petition authorities, see Minutes of the Robeson County Board of Education, 1 March, 12 April, 2 July 1937, 13 April 1944, 29 April 1946, County Records, Board of Education Records (Microfilm), NCDAH; "Petition to the Lumberton School Board and the Board of County Commissioners," folder Robeson County, 1945–1949, box 20, County Files, Department of Public Instruction, Superintendent of Public Instruction Papers, NCDAH; HLT to Robert L. Carter, 8 May 1947, reel 4, series B, pt. 3, NAACP Papers. For Credle's 1940 visit, see "Negro Schools 'Disgrace' State Health Head Says," *RN&O*, 11 October 1946, 1, 3; for Newbold's visit, see NCN to Judge L. R. Varser, 25 March 1941, box 14, GC DNE.

27. V. J. Thompson to NAACP, 7 February 1944, Vernie C. Grady to NAACP, 17 March 1944, both in folder Robeson County, N.C., 1944, box C138, group II, NAACP Papers; Thompson and Thompson, Interview.

28. Gavins, "NAACP in North Carolina," 108–10, 120; Christina Greene, *Our Separate Ways*, 42.

29. Robeson Youth Council Membership Lists, 1946, folder 4, box E106, group II, NAACP Papers; "Suggested Goals—1946 Membership Campaign," n.d., folder 4, box E31, group II, NAACP Papers; "NAACP Youth to Make Vote Study," *LR*, 24 February 1947, 2; "NAACP Youth Have Education Program," *LR*, 11 March 1947, 6. For the significance of the Youth Councils and of youth protest generally, see Lovell, "Youth Programs," 383–84; de Schweinitz, *If We Could Change the World*, 171–78; Bynum, "'We Must March Forward!'" The founding date of Lumberton's youth council was determined from Bullock's invitation to Governor Cherry to speak at the youth chapter's fourth anniversary in the fall of 1947. The governor declined. See Gus Bullock to R. Gregg Cherry, 3 September 1947, Cherry to Bullock, 9 September 1947, box 11, Cherry Papers.

30. McQueen, Interview.

31. Ibid.; "Thompson Institute to Resume Classes Tomorrow as School Strike Ends," *LR*, 16 October 1946, 1; "Redstone P.T.A. Does Not Endorse School Strike," *LR*, 16 October 1946, 6; "School Strike Continued by Negroes in Lumberton," *RN&O*, 9 October 1946, 1, 2; "Prove or Retract," *LR*, 4 October 1946, 1; "Thompson School Committee Asks Proof of Charge," *LR*, 7 October 1946, 2; J. H. Hayswood to the editor, *LR*, 8 October 1946, 4.

32. Kemp, Interview.

33. Lillian McQueen to Ruby Hurley, 11 October 1946, Hurley to McQueen, 17 October 1946, both in folder 2, box B146, group II, NAACP Papers.

34. "400 Students Strike," *PC*, 19 October 1946, 1, 4; on Rivera, see Rivera, Interview.

35. McQueen, Interview; "Time to Call Halt," *LR*, 9 October 1946, 4; "Liberal for Schools," *LR*, 17 October 1946, 4.

36. "Must Be Remedied," *RN&O*, 9 October 1946, 4; "Students Remain out of Schools," *RN&O*, 10 October 1946, 1, 2; "Disgrace to the State," *RN&O*, 10 October 1946, 4; "Worse and Worse," *RN&O*, 11 October 1946, 4.

37. Gus Bullock to R. Gregg Cherry, 12 October 1946, Cherry to Bullock, 16 October 1946, box 11, Cherry Papers; "400 Negro Youths Strike at Schools in Lumberton," *RN&O*, 8 October 1946, 1, 2; "Students Remain out of Schools," *RN&O*, 10 October 1946, 1, 2.

38. "School Ratings Low for Negroes," *RN&O*, 16 October 1946, 1, 2; *Educational Directory*, 1945–46, 88.

39. NCN, "Report: Lumberton Negro School Strike," 21 October 1946, enclosed in NCN to CAE, 24 October 1946, box 172, GC SPI; "Negro Schools 'Disgrace' State Health Head Says," *RN&O*, 11 October 1946, 1, 3.

40. "Lumberton Strike Ended, Classes Will Be Resumed," *RN&O*, 17 October 1946, 3; "No More School Strikes," *RN&O*, 18 October 1946, 4; "Lumberton and North Carolina," *RC*, 26 October 1946, 4; TM to Gloster B. Current, 20 January 1947, folder 2, box B146, group II, NAACP Papers.

41. Ruby Hurley to Lillian McQueen, 17 October 1946, HLT to TM, 28 October 1946, TM to HLT, 4 November 1946, HLT to Curtiss Todd, 11 November 1946, all in reel 4, series B, pt. 3, NAACP Papers.

42. HLT to TM, 8 May 1943, HLT to Board of Directors, NAACP, 3 August 1945, both in folder 9, box B173, group II, NAACP Papers. For Taylor's career, see North Carolina Asso-

ciation of Black Lawyers, *Chronicle*, 1:23; *No Crystal Stair* (video); Kearns and Dayton, *Capital Lawyers*, 71, 75–76.

43. Taylor quotations from *No Crystal Stair* (video); HLT to Robert L. Carter, 19 May 1947, folder 2, box B146, group II, NAACP Papers.

44. HLT to Robert L. Carter, 8, 19 May 1947, both in folder 2, box B146, group II, NAACP Papers; HLT to Marian Wynn Perry, 21 June 1947, folder 3, box B146, group II, NAACP Papers.

45. "Negro Parents File Civil Suit against School Authorities Here Charging Unequal Facilities," *LR*, 8 July 1947, 1; HLT to Robert L. Carter, 17 July 1947, folder 2, box B146, group II, NAACP Papers; Case Complaints and Court Dockets, folder 3, box B146, group II, NAACP Papers.

46. "Parents Sue School Board, Charge Inferior Facilities," *PC*, 12 July 1947, 1, 4.

47. Sugrue, *Sweet Land of Liberty*, 169–70; "Poor Schools Becoming No. 1 Dixie Headache," *PC*, 26 July 1947, 5; Obituary for Lawrence Stephens, *LR*, 28 April 1974, 2A; Obituary for Samuel Bullock Jr., *LR*, 21 September 1956, 5; Obituary for Bessie Thompson, *LR*, 21 January 1963, 9; Obituary for Sherman Thompson, *LR*, 15 December 1961, 17.

48. David Mitchell to T. V. Mangum, 26 December 1946, Gloster B. Current to Mangum, 8 January 1947, both in folder 11, Southern Robeson County, box C139, group II, NAACP Papers; Ruby Hurley to TM, 5 February 1947, TM to Hurley, 6 February 1947, both in folder 2, box B146, group II, NAACP Papers. Tensions between the parent and youth branches persisted, as the latter felt that the former was too controlling. In 1949, the national office intervened again, telling the new president of the Robeson County branch, "There is no reason for the Branch to interfere with the youth council. . . . If the young people are ever to develop leadership ability they must be given proper opportunity to express themselves" (Lucille Black to S. T. Brooks, 12 May 1949, folder N.C. State Conference, box E87, group II, NAACP Papers).

49. Marian Wynn Perry to TM, 29 January 1948, folder 2, box B146, group II, NAACP Papers; Ruby Hurley to Kelly Alexander, 7 January 1949, folder 2, box E87, group II, NAACP Papers.

50. "Demurrers in School Action Argued," *LR*, 13 January 1948, 6; "Judge Grady's School Ruling Favors Negroes," *LR*, 16 January 1948, 1; "Suit in N.C. Hits School Facilities," *PC*, 24 January 1948, 20; HLT to Marian Wynn Perry, 24 January 1948, enclosing copy of the complaint, folder 2, box B146, group II, NAACP Papers; "Negroes Seek to Add State School Officials as Defendants in Suits for Equal Facilities," *LR*, 10 May 1948, 2; "Court Allows New Complaint in School Suit," *LR*, 18 May 1948, 1.

51. "Negro School Suit Demurrer Is Sustained," *LR*, 13 July 1948, 1; "Negro School Suit Brought in Fayetteville Federal Court," *LR*, 4 August 1948, 1; "Grand Jury and School Suit to Occupy Court," *LR*, 13 August 1948, 1; "Fund Available to Erect Local Negro School," *LR*, 19 October 1948, 1; "Handsome J. H. Hayswood School Opens on Site Just East of City Limits," *LR*, 3 January 1949, 2; Robert L. Carter to TM, 28 April 1948, folder 11, box B145, group II, NAACP Papers; HLT to Carter, 26 April 1949, folder 2, box B146, group II, NAACP Papers; "Equal School Facilities Suit Dismissed in District Court," *LR*, 27 September 1950, 1. The plaintiffs in the federal case were Waldean Stephens and Verdall Stephens (children of Lawrence S. Stephens); James S. Bullock and Margaret Anna Bullock (children of Sam Bullock); Addie Mae Thompson, Lue Frances Thompson, Annie Lee Thompson, Carean Thompson, Mildred Elizabeth Thompson, Sherman Thompson Jr., David Thompson, and Mary Jane Thompson (children of Bessie Thompson). See *Stephens et al.*

v. Board of Graded School Trustees of Lumberton, Civil Action File No. 237 (E.D.N.C., Fayetteville Division, 22 September 1950), copy of judgment in Record Group 21, National Archives, Atlanta.

52. Kemp, Interview; "School Officials Blamed for Lack of Improvements," *LR*, 14 March 1951, 1; B. E. Lohr, "Schools in the Days Ahead," *LR*, 14 November 1952, 11; "Overcrowded Schools," *LR*, 1 March 1953, 4.

53. "Contracts Awarded for Negro School Building in Lumberton," *LR*, 17 January 1949, 1; "Negroes First in Improvement for Lumberton," *LR*, 24 September 1951, 6; "Asks Race Cooperation at Rites Dedicating New Negro School," *LR*, 8 May 1950, 1.

54. B. E. Lohr to Charles Carroll, 30 November 1953, folder Li, box 10, MARS 104.3; B. E. Lohr, "Schools in the Days Ahead," *LR*, 14 November 1952, 11.

55. "Overcrowded Schools," *LR*, 1 March 1953, 4; W. H. Spearman to editor, *LR*, 3 March 1953, 4. On Spearman, who in 1961 was elected to the Lumberton City Council, see "Ex-Councilman Spearman Dies," *LR*, 23 January 1967, 1.

56. "City Negro Schools to Open Sept. 9, Facilities Ready," *LR*, 17 August 1954, 6; "Lumberton in Dire Need of New High School Plant," *LR*, 6 April 1955, 8; *State School Facts* 28 (September 1956); "One Problem among Many," *LR*, 8 September 1955, 14.

57. "Conference Report at NAACP Council Meet," *LR*, 28 April 1948, 7; Dorothy Leggett, "Lumberton Girl Attends NAACP Youth Council," *Norfolk Journal and Guide*, 1 May 1948, A19.

58. NCN, "Today, Yesterday, and Tomorrow," 7 August 1947, box 2, Newbold A&S; W. F. Credle to CAE, 31 May 1949, box 182, GC SPI.

59. T. T. Murphy to NCN, 23 October 1947, box 16, GC DNE; "Poor Schools Becoming No. 1 Dixie Headache," *PC*, 26 July 1947, 5; NCN to R. Gregg Cherry, 8 July 1948, folder Public Schools, box 73, General Correspondence Series, Cherry Papers.

60. C. C. Spaulding to NCN, 15 July 1947, box 17, GC DNE.

61. Kelly Alexander to TM, 24 August, 3 October 1948, TM to Alexander, 6 October 1948, "A Survey of the Public Schools of Charlotte, North Carolina," May 1948, all in reel 3, series B, pt. 3, NAACP Papers. For newspaper coverage of this case, see "Charlotte Survey Cites Educational Inequality," *PC*, 17 July 1948, 24; "Inferior Educational Facilities Charged," *Charlotte News*, 12 July 1948; "Myers Park High School Plans to Get Further Study by Board," *Charlotte News*, 28 September 1948, reel 20, series A, pt. 25, NAACP Papers. For a precursor to this action, see "Memo from the Committee on Education of the Inter-Group Council to Supt. H. P. Harding and E. H. Garinger of the Charlotte School Board," 24 March 1947, box 16, GC DNE.

62. "Report of Conference with the Honorable Governor W. Kerr Scott" and "A Brief Report of Activities of the North Carolina State Conference of NAACP Branches, 1949," both in folder 2, box E87, group II, NAACP Papers; "Protest March Is Planned by N.C. NAACP Chapters," *Wilmington Journal*, 30 October 1948, clipping in folder 3, box C141, group II, NAACP Papers; "N. Carolina's New Governor Blasts Racial Inequalities," *PC*, 22 January 1949, 2; "Negroes Present Legislative Plan," *RN&O*, 27 January 1949, 1, 2; W. Kerr Scott to Mrs. R. L. Welsh, 31 January 1949, box 26, General Correspondence Series, Governor W. Kerr Scott Papers, NCDAH.

63. "Education Well Served," *GDN*, 26 April 1949, "This Appointment Will Be Commended," *Asheville Citizen-Times*, 24 April 1949, "The Ways of Snakes and Mad Dogs," *DCT*, 25 June 1949, all in NCC Clipping File. For an additional critical assessment of Trigg, see "What's Wrong with Saint Augustine?," *Afro-American*, 1 July 1950, 13, Mollie Huston

Lee Collection, Richard B. Harrison Library, Raleigh, N.C. For personal endorsements of Trigg's appointment, see folder "Dr. Trigg," box 10, Subject Files, Scott Papers. For Trigg's career, see Lawrence London's essay in Powell, *Dictionary of North Carolina Biography*, 6:52.

64. "Tar Heels Converge on Raleigh Hearing," 3 March 1949, *LR*, 1; "Governor Scott Campaigns for Better Rural Roads and Schools," 23 May 1949, *LR*, 1; "Road-School Bonds Issues at Stake in Election Today," 4 June 1949, *RN&O*, 1, 2; "Governor Speaks on Negro Schools," *RN&O*, 11 October 1949, NCC Clipping File.

65. "The Ballot Box Is the Solution," *DCT*, 11 March 1950, 2.

66. "N. Carolina Teachers Buy $55,000 Building," *PC*, 30 November 1946, 14; "Story of a Building Project," *NCTR* 18 (March 1947): 1-2.

67. "The President's Annual Address," *NCTR* 21 (1950): 2-3, 7; "Resolutions of N.C. Congress Colored Parents and Teachers, November 1946," *NCTR* 18 (March 1947): 6; "Educational Organizations and Educational Policy Making," *NCTR* 16 (January 1945): 8-9; "The Report of the Resolutions Committee," *NCTR* 18 (May 1947): 17.

68. Crow, Escott, and Hatley, *History of African Americans*, 149; Korstad, *Civil Rights Unionism*, 306-10; NCN to P. D. Snipes, 16 February 1949, box 17, GC DNE; *NCTR* 20 (March 1949): cover; Larkins, *Negro Population*, 43; "Naming of Negro Lawyer to School Board Well Received in Tar Heel Capital City," *Raleigh Times*, 26 May 1949, clipping in Lee Collection.

69. NCN to J. W. Wilson, 3 February 1949, box 17, GC DNE.

70. Hugh Thompson to TM, 25 May 1949, J. H. Wheeler and Thompson to CAE, 18 October 1949, enclosed in Wheeler to Kelly Alexander, 19 October 1949, all in folder 1, box B146, group II, NAACP Papers; "Durham Leaders File Suit," *PC*, 25 May 1949, 11; "Education Board in Plea for Dismissal in School Bias Suit," *DCT*, 6 August 1949, 1; "Seek to Hold School Funds in Bias Case," *DCT*, 22 October 1949, 1, 8; "State Education Officials Denied Dismissal from School Suit by Ruling," *DCT*, 5 November 1949, 1; "Negroes Press School Charge," *Statesville Daily Record*, 28 June 1950, 3. Lead plaintiffs in the case were Carolyn J. Blue, Donald W. Blue, and Portia C. Blue, the children of Margaret Blue. See state's 1949 Motion to Dismiss enclosed in Harry McMullan to Members of the State Board of Education, 7 June 1949, folder State Board of Education, box 185, GC SPI.

71. "Judge Rules Discrimination in Durham School Suit," *RN&O*, 27 January 1951, "Warning from a Friend," *RN&O*, 27 January 1951, both in NCC Clipping File.

72. "Say Negroes Get Equal Fund Share," *DCT*, 19 November 1949, 1; "Misinforming the Governor," *DCT*, 26 November 1949, 2, 6.

73. "Durham Leaders File Suit," *PC*, 25 May 1949, 11; Kelly Alexander, "The Task of the NAACP in North Carolina," 23 June 1949, folder 2, box E87, group II, NAACP Papers.

74. My attention to this region of the state follows the lead of David Cecelski, who has argued that historians should not neglect the state's eastern Black Belt in searching for the roots of black protest (*Along Freedom Road*, 13).

75. "State to Face 2 School Suits," *DCT*, 7 January 1950, 1, 8; *Winborne et al. v. Taylor et al.*, 195 F.2d 649, 651 (4th Cir. 1952). In 1952, Washington County applied for $234,485.18 in state bond money to build a new black high school, Washington County Union School. See State Board of Education Minutes, 20 June 1952, North Carolina State Board of Education Papers, NCDAH.

76. Charles McKinney has noted that a 1947 suit organized by working-class citizens of Wilson County in 1947 was dropped when officials promised to build two new schools

("'Our People Began to Press,'" 105–9, 118 [n. 66]). For discussion of the 1950 suit, see W. F. Credle to CAE, 29 September 1949, enclosing 28 September 1949 statement by Credle, box 182, GC SPI; B. O. Barnes to NCN, 22 December 1949, enclosing circular letters from the Citizens' Committee, 9 November, 20 December 1949, NCN to Barnes, 11 January, 7 February, 22 May, 28 June 1950, Barnes to NCN, 24 January, 20 May 1950, NCN to A. J. Hutchins, 16 February, Barnes to NCN, 10 May 1950, enclosing "Open Letter to the Citizens of Wilson" and local newspaper editorials, all in box 18, GC DNE.

77. "The President's Annual Address," *NCTR* 21 (May 1950): 2–3, 7; "Resolutions of the North Carolina Teachers Association for the Year 1950–1951," *NCTR* 21 (May 1950): 15; "N.C. Teachers Association Repudiates Trigg; Gives $500 for Aid to Suit," *DCT*, 8 April 1950, 1, 8; "The President's Annual Address," *NCTR* 22 (May 1951): 2–3, 14–16; "Proceedings of the Seventieth Annual Convention of the North Carolina Teachers Association," *NCTR* 22 (March 1951): 11–13; "Can We Achieve First-Class Citizenship through Education?" *NCTR* 22 (March 1951): 8. For further evidence of NCTA support for the NAACP, see W. L. Greene to Kelly Alexander, 12 October 1951, folder 4, box 19, Kelly Alexander Sr. Papers, Special Collections, J. Murrey Atkins Library, University of North Carolina, Charlotte; Alexander to Greene, 5, 16 October 1951, both in folder 7, box 19, Alexander Papers.

78. Obituaries and funeral programs for Oliver R. Pope (1876–1973) can be found in the vertical files at Braswell Memorial Library, Rocky Mount, North Carolina. For Anderson (1906–62), see Certificate of Death, http://search.ancestry.com/cqi-bin/sse.dll?h+1887957&db=NCdeathCerts&indiv=try; Obituary in *Winston-Salem Journal*, 14 February 1962, 2.

79. NCN, "How Christian Can I Afford to Be?," 21 August 1950, "Banquet Honors Dr. Newbold" (clipping), n.d., "Remarkable Progress in a Hard Task," *Winston-Salem Journal*, 15 July 1950, "He Served the State," *RN&O*, 10 July 1950, all in box 3, Newbold Papers; J. C. Dixon to All State Agents, 7 July 1950, reel 93, series 1.1, GEB Papers; NCN to Fred McCuistion, 29 June 1950, box 19, GC DNE. On Newbold's death, see "Doctor Newbold Dies in Raleigh," *RN&O*, 24 December 1957, NCC Clipping File.

80. Woodson, Interview; Annie Wade Biggers and S. E. Biggers to NCN, 30 August 1950, box 2, Newbold Papers; Mrs. L. B. Yancey and W. L. Greene, "Thirty-Seven Years of Progress: A Tribute to Dr. N. C. Newbold," *NCTR* 22 (January 1951): 2, 16; Lucy Herring to GHF, [1955], box 23, GC DNE.

81. "Newbold Steps Down," *RC*, [July 1950], 4, clipping in box 3, Newbold Papers; "Negro Education Foisted: Successor to N. C. Newbold Is Appointed," *DCT*, 5 August 1950, 1; "N. C. Newbold Quits; Is Trigg Next?," *DCT*, 8 July 1950, 1; "Trigg May Succeed Newbold Says Capitol City Rumor," *DCT*, 17 December 1949, 1, 8. On Ferguson, see folder GHF, box 19, GC DNE. On discussion of the DNE, see D. L. Allen to NCN, 27 January 1936, box 134, GC SPI; CAE to Fred McCuistion, 17 May 1951, box 19, GC DNE; Woodson, Interview; "Resolutions Adopted by the 71st Annual Convention of the North Carolina Teachers Association," *NCTR* 23 (May 1952): 7. For a look at administrative practices in other southern and border states, see S. E. Duncan, "A Brief Report on Activities and Observations with Travel Fellowship Sponsored by the Southern Education Foundation," 12 April–14 May 1953, box 21, GC DNE.

82. For cases from Chapel Hill and Davidson, New Hanover, Perquimans, Martin, Cumberland, and Person Counties, see "Chapel Hill Plans to Sue," *DCT*, 26 August 1950, 1; "No Radical Solutions," unidentified newspaper, 12 June 1951, NCC Clipping File; Eaton, *"Every Man Should Try,"* 41–52; Annual Report of the Perquimans Branch of the NAACP,

1950, reel 20, series A, pt. 25, NAACP Papers; "Negro Leaders Denounce NAACP Petition Submitted to Martin School Board," *RN&O*, 13 August 1951, "Negroes File Cumberland Petition," *RN&O*, 11 June 1951, both in NCC Clipping File; "Person Negroes File Suit to Enter White Schools," *DMH*, 6 November 1952, 1, 3.

83. Cecelski, *Along Freedom Road*, 28. The first case came from Clarendon County, South Carolina, and became one of the component cases of *Brown v. Board of Education*.

84. Daisy Walker, Report from Pamlico County, 8 December 1950, box 8, State Supervisor of Elementary Education Files, DNE Papers; Pamlico County Board of Education Minutes, 7 April 1952, County Records, Board of Education Records (Microfilm), NCDAH; Fulcher, Interview; Himbry, Interview. For state official discussion of the lawsuit, see correspondence between attorney Hugh Thompson and state superintendent Clyde Erwin, box 193, GC SPI. For newspaper coverage, see "Pamlico Negroes Endorse Segregation," *RN&O*, 12 August 1951, "Court Suit Asks Action at Oriental," *RN&O*, 14 September 1951, "School Suit Complaint Cited," *RN&O*, 14 October 1951, "Responsibility Begins at Home," *Asheville Citizen*, 11 December 1951, "Oriental School Suit and Others Still Idle Pending in U.S. Courts," *RN&O*, 8 November 1953, all in NCC Clipping File; "Pamlico County Citizens OK School Segregation Despite Inequalities," *RC*, 18 August 1951, 1; "Negroes File School Suit," *Statesville Daily Record*, 20 October 1951, 2; "Suit Brought Results in Pamlico," *RN&O*, 23 September 1956, I-9; Cecelski, *Along Freedom Road*, 180 (n. 30).

85. Perquimans Chapter of the NAACP, Annual Report, 1950, reel 20, series A, pt. 25, NAACP Papers; Eaton, *"Every Man Should Try,"* 41–52; Segregation Questionnaires, 1954, box 2, North Carolina State Attorney General Papers, NCDAH.

86. "Segregation in Schools," *Kinston Daily Free Press*, 16 March 1951, NCC Clipping File; "Over 700 Adkin High Students Parade in Protest on Facilities" and "An Ill Advised and Dangerous Movement on Part of Negro Students," *Kinston Daily Free Press*, 20 November 1951, 1, 10; "Adkin's Students Return Here Monday A.M.," *Kinston Daily Free Press*, 26 November 1951, 1; "Carolina Students Strike for New School," *Jet*, 6 December 1951, 17; CAE to J. P. Booth, 7 December 1951, along with Booth's Talk on Radio Station WFTC, 21, 25 November 1951, box 190, GC SPI. For discussion of the 1952 lawsuit, see "School Suit at Kinston," *DCT*, 8 March 1952, 1, 8; J. P. Booth to CAE, 7 March 1952, CAE to Booth, 12 March 1952, box 194, GC SPI. On the new school additions, see "Last Students Leave Old Adkin School," *Kinston Daily Free Press*, 10 June 1979, 1C. In 1963, Kinston replaced Adkin with a completely new building. See Hugh Victor Brown, *E-Quality Education*, 161–63. Student recollections included in Joyner, "Adkin High School," 80–81. Adkin alumni recently commemorated the strike with a reenactment. See "Adkin High School Reunites to Remember Class of 1952," *Kinston Free Press*, 1 September 2010, www.kinston .com/articles/school-67926-adkin-high.html.

87. Kluger, *Simple Justice*, chapters 19, 20, esp. 474–79.

88. Kelly Alexander to Gloster B. Current, 12 September 1950, Alexander to TM, 18 September 1950, both in folder 5, box C141, group II, NAACP Papers; Alexander to Ruby Hurley, 11 June 1949, folder N.C. State Conference, box E87, group II, NAACP Papers. For additional wrangling between NAACP officials and Taylor and Mitchell, see TM to HLT, 10 January 1957, enclosed in TM to Alexander and C. O. Pearson, 10 January 1957, folder 8, box 2, Alexander Papers; HLT to Alexander, 12 August 1955, folder 8, box 19, Alexander Papers.

89. "Negro Leaders Denounce NAACP Petition Submitted to Martin School Board," *RN&O*, 19 August 1951, NCC Clipping File; "Equality or Integration Sought in Martin

County" and "School Jimcrow Again under Fire by NAACP Head," *RC*, 8 September 1951, 1, 8.

90. See Summons and Answer to Civil Action File No. 194, Durham Division, District Court of the United States, Middle District of North Carolina, 6 November 1952, copy in Person County Board of Education Minutes, County Records, Board of Education Records (Microfilm), NCDAH.

91. Douglas, *Reading, Writing, and Race*, 260 (n. 113); "It Could Happen Here," *RN&O*, 8 July 1951, NCC Clipping File; Benjamin Fine, "Negro Education in South on Rise," *NYT*, 16 March 1952, 82; Hill quoted in Kluger, *Simple Justice*, 291; W. E. Abernethy to CAE, 19 December 1950, box 186, GC SPI; "State School Program Narrowing Gap between White and Negro Facilities," *DMH*, 17 April 1951, NCC Clipping File.

92. *Biennial Report*, 1952–53/1953–54, pt. 1, 39; M. Ruth Lawrence, "Monthly Report," April 1950, box 18, GC DNE. See also scattered reports by Daisy Walker, 1951–55, box 8, State Supervisor of Elementary Education Files, DNE Papers.

93. CAE to Robert M. Thompson, 26 June 1952, box 197, GC SPI; "Tar Heels Take Look at System," *High Point Enterprise*, 30 May 1951, 1; "Estimates Equal School Costs at $80 Millions," *High Point Enterprise*, 7 July 1951, 1, 8; D. Hiden Ramsey to CAE and Santford Martin, 17 December 1951, "Our School Building Problem," *Winston-Salem Journal and Sentinel*, 13 April 1952, included with CAE to Santford Martin, 22 April 1952, all in folder State Board of Education, box 197, GC SPI.

94. For white views, see Robert Proctor to Brandon Hodges, 31 August 1953, folder Catawba, box 85, Public Schools and Mental Care Series, Governor William B. Umstead Papers, NCDAH; William W. Taylor Jr. to William B. Umstead, 21 July 1953, folder T, box 86, Public Schools and Mental Care Series, Umstead Papers; "Vote in the Dark," *LR*, 18 August 1953, "School Bond Issue," *LR*, 14 September 1953, both in folder Newspaper Clippings, box 87, Public Schools and Mental Care Series, Umstead Papers. For black views, see "Bond Issue Support Begins to Take Shape," *DCT*, 15 August 1953, 1, 8.

95. "State to Vote on Big Bond Issue," 22 July 1953, *Statesville Daily Record*, 1; "Bond Vote Set October 3," *RN&O*, 22 July 1953, 1; "Bond Election Set Tomorrow," *Gastonia Gazette*, 2 October 1953, 1; "Tar Heels Decide Saturday on $72 Million Bond Issues," *RN&O*, 2 October 1953, 1, 6; "School and Hospital Bonds Approved by Wide Margin," *RN&O*, 4 October 1953, 1, 4. For state promotional materials, see boxes 85–87, Public Schools and Mental Care Series, Umstead Papers; John Kerr Jr. to Luther Hodges, 22 April 1954, folder K, box 14, MARS 104.3. For black support, see "Negroes Should Support the $72 Million Bond Issue," *DCT*, 12 September 1953, 2; "Durham Group Votes Support of Bond Issue," *DCT*, 26 September 1953, 1; Helen G. Edmonds to Brandon Hodges, 20 September 1953, folder Durham, box 85, Public Schools and Mental Care Series, Umstead Papers. "Spending the Bond Money," *DCT*, 10 October 1953, 2.

CHAPTER SIX

1. "North Carolina NAACP Meet to Be Held in Lumberton," *LR*, 5 October 1954, 1; "'Meaning of Segregation' Is Theme of NAACP Meet," *LR*, 16 October 1954, 1; "Eastern Carolinas Hurricane Damage Expected to Run into Many Millions," *LR*, 16 October 1954, 1, 10; "11th Annual Convention of North Carolina NAACP Ends 3-Day Session," *LR*, 18 October 1954, 10. The most extensive history of *Brown* remains Kluger's *Simple Justice*.

For a more recent overview, see James T. Patterson, *Brown v. Board of Education*. For the text of the decision, see Martin, *Brown v. Board of Education*, 168–74.

2. Chafe, *Civilities and Civil Rights*, 7–8, chapters 1–2. Chafe's study of Greensboro is a critical starting point for understanding school desegregation in North Carolina. See also Davison Douglas's study of Charlotte, *Reading, Writing, and Race*, which argues that the concerns of Charlotte's business leaders for maintaining a progressive image were instrumental in facilitating desegregation. On the question of white attitudes, Matthew Lassiter and Andrew Lewis point out that even in Virginia, the heart of Massive Resistance, whites collectively held a broad spectrum of opinion on *Brown*. Most were neither staunch segregationists nor committed integrationists. See "Massive Resistance Revisited."

3. The schools at Fort Bragg integrated in 1951, and the first black teacher in North Carolina to work in a white school taught in a federally controlled school at Camp Lejeune. See Lutz, *Homefront*, 116; "'Merely a Change of Jobs,' Says First Negro Teacher in White Elementary School in North Carolina," *DCT*, 26 June 1954, 1; "North Carolina's First Negro Teacher in a White School," *DCT*, 3 July 1954, 2. For desegregation statistics, see U.S. Commission on Civil Rights, *Public Education: 1964 Staff Report*, 156.

4. Historians have disagreed over the extent to which *Brown* offered inspiration to black communities and accelerated the civil rights movement. A key critic of this idea is Michael Klarman, "How *Brown* Changed Race Relations." While I think it important not to exaggerate *Brown*'s influence, *Brown* was critical in both legitimizing and galvanizing black concerns regarding civic inclusion.

5. For two critical case studies from North Carolina that demonstrate African Americans' enduring interest in their school communities, see Cecelski, *Along Freedom Road*; Walker, *Their Highest Potential*. For studies outside of North Carolina that show the overlap between activism for equalization and integration, see Scott Baker, *Paradoxes of Desegregation*; Bolton, *Hardest Deal of All*; Turner, "'It Is Not at Present a Very Successful School'"; Walker, *Hello Professor*; Ramsey, *Reading, Writing, and Segregation*. Risa Goluboff has argued more generally that *Brown* compromised efforts to frame the civil rights struggle around questions of material equality and economic justice. As she puts it, "When the NAACP pressed, and the *Brown* Court accepted, stigmatic harm as the essence of Jim Crow, the image of civil rights the Court projected eclipsed the deep and abiding material inequalities that characterized the nation's caste system for most African Americans" (*Lost Promise*, 245).

6. Legal scholar and former NAACP Legal Defense Fund attorney Derrick A. Bell argued that *Brown*'s lack of attention to these political questions constituted one of its key shortcomings. He contended that the ruling should have required school boards to be representative of the student populations they governed. See Balkin, *What Brown v. Board of Education Should Have Said*, 197.

7. For a discussion of the "damage imagery" in *Brown*, see Scott, *Contempt and Pity*, 119–36. As Michael Fultz has pointed out, this idea of segregation's damaging effects predated *Brown* and extended to black teachers as well as students. Both white and black intellectuals had long characterized black teachers as tragic (and somewhat ineffective) figures. See Fultz, "African American Teachers in the South, 1890–1940: Powerlessness and the Ironies of Expectations and Protest."

8. In assessing *Brown*'s merits and limitations, I drew inspiration from the compilation of critiques in Balkin, *What Brown v. Board of Education Should Have Said*. I find

most compelling Jack Balkin's suggestion that *Brown* should have affirmed the goals of equalization and integration and required both equal educational opportunity and the elimination of "racially identifiable schools" (68, 88–90). Of the volume's nine contributors, Derrick Bell was unique in arguing that instead of overruling *Plessy*, the court should have required its strict enforcement. For Bell's full critique, see *Silent Covenants*. For a critique of Bell, see Cobb, *Brown Decision*, 50–51.

9. *DCT*, 22 May 1954, 1; Pauli Murray, "Open Letter to Citizens of Durham," *DCT*, 12 June 1954, 2, 7; Breathett, "Black Educators"; "Campus Hails Anti-Bias Ruling" and "Supreme Court Decision Opens Way for 'Liberty, Equality, Fraternity,'" both in *Campus Echo*, 25 May 1954, 1, 2; "A New Kind of Leadership for a New Day," *DCT*, 3 July 1954, 2.

10. Mosnier, "Crafting Law," 68–85 (Chambers quoted on 85); Hargraves, Interview; *Echo* (Lincoln High), vol. 23, October 1954, 2.

11. Du Bois, "Does the Negro Need Separate Schools?," 335.

12. "No Immediate School Change Seen in Gaston," *Gastonia Gazette*, 18 May 1954, 1, 5; "Segregation in the Schools" (video). I thank the staff at UNC's North Carolina Collection for converting their film reel copy of this segment to VHS for my use.

13. "Arndt Weighs NAACP Plea on Segregation," *HDR*, 11 October 1954; "School Advisory Unit Named, Protest Filed," *HDR*, 19 August 1955; "Leave Schools Alone, Maiden Negroes Urge," *HDR*, 7 December 1954; "Maiden Negroes Make Courageous and Sensible Step in School Matters," *Observer and Catawba News-Enterprise*, 8 December 1954, all in vertical files, Patrick Beaver Memorial Library, Hickory, N.C.; "Maiden N.C., Negroes Ask for Jim Crow Schools," *Jet*, 30 December 1954, 24; *SSN* 1 (6 January 1955): 12. In 1954, state inspectors prioritized the Maiden school as one of five that most needed upgrades. See "Negro Schools Get Priority in County," *HDR*, 17 May 1954, 1, 13. Catawba Negro School received more than one hundred thousand dollars for a new lunchroom and home economics facility in 1952. See State Board of Education Minutes, 1 May 1952, North Carolina State Board of Education Papers, NCDAH.

14. "The Lethargy of Negro Voters," *DCT*, 5 June 1954, 2; Kelly Alexander to State Officers and Branch Officials of the N.C. State Conference of the NAACP, 13 July 1954, reel 2, series C, pt. 3, NAACP Papers.

15. *SSN* 1 (4 November 1954): 13; petition from Harnett County NAACP, filed with GHF to G. T. Proffit, 5 October 1954, box 22, GC DNE.

16. Editorial, *DMH*, 14 August 1954, reel 2, series C, pt. 3, NAACP Papers; "Umstead Names Group to Study Segregation," *Statesville Record and Landmark*, 5 August 1954, 1; Chafe, *Civilities and Civil Rights*, 50; Edwin A. Penick, Memorandum, [September 1954], folder 12, box 1, Thomas J. Pearsall Papers, Southern Historical Collection, Louis R. Wilson Library, University of North Carolina, Chapel Hill.

17. Lamanna, "Negro Public School Teacher," 59; "Resolutions of the Twenty-Seventh Annual Convention," North Carolina Congress of Colored Parents and Teachers, 19–20 November 1954, PTA Papers; "Our Executive Committee Accepts the Supreme Court's Challenge," *NCTR* 25 (October 1954): 8.

18. Edward Jackson to Thomas Pearsall, 7 August 1954, folder 5, box 1, Pearsall Papers; Segregation Questionnaires, 1954, box 2, North Carolina State Attorney General Papers, NCDAH; Dallas Herring to Charles F. Carroll, 3 December 1954, enclosing confidential statement and letter to the Pearsall Committee, 29 November 1954, folder Segregation, box 23, MARS 104.3. Herring was appointed to the state board of education in 1955 and served as its chair from 1957 to 1977. For more on Herring, see Batchelor, "Save Our

Schools." Batchelor argues that while Herring opposed integration, he was adamant that the state not go the way of Massive Resistance. Herring later argued that he did not oppose integration but rather "was trying to find a way through the maze that we were confronted with" (Interview).

19. "Pearsall Group's Segregation Report Endorsed by Governor," *Rocky Mount Evening Telegram*, 6 January 1955, 1, 9; Hugh Victor Brown, *E-Quality Education*, 142; U.S. Commission on Civil Rights, *Civil Rights U.S.A.*, 65; "To Uphold or to Upset," *NCTR* 26 (January 1955): 8; "A Report to the Joint Committee on Education of the North Carolina Legislature by a Group of Representative Negro Citizens Drawn from Various Parts of North Carolina," [1955], reel 3, series C, pt. 3, NAACP Papers; Chafe, *Civilities and Civil Rights*, 50.

20. James T. Patterson, *Brown v. Board of Education*, 82–85 (Marshall quoted on 85); "What the NAACP Means to You," *Wilmington Journal*, 10 June 1955, reel 2, series C, pt. 3, NAACP Papers.

21. Korstad and Leloudis, *To Right These Wrongs*, 34; "Report on North Carolina," n.d., reel 2, series C, pt. 3, NAACP Papers; "The Segregation Problem in the Public Schools of North Carolina" (pamphlet), box 26, GC DNE; Chafe, *Civilities and Civil Rights*, 50–51; "Voluntary Segregation Course Urged by Hodges as Best Plan," *LR*, 9 August 1955, 1, 7; "Negro Teachers Turn Thumbs Down on Hodges' Voluntary Segregation," *LR*, 29 August 1955, 5; "Setting the Record Straight," *NCTR* 26 (October 1955): 8.

22. GHF to J. C. Dixon, 8 January 1960, box 26, GC DNE. On teacher contracts, see "Carroll Suggests Teacher Election Held in Abeyance," *LR*, 4 April 1955, 9; "School Teacher Contracts Will Be Terminated," *Statesville Record and Landmark*, 20 April 1955, 1; Fultz, "Displacement of Black Educators," 19; "Negro Teachers for the North?," *U.S. News and World Report*, 27 August 1954, 35–37; GHF to Charles Carroll, 27 May 1957, folder F, box 56, MARS 104.3. For more on black supervisor reductions, see Smathers, "History of the Supervision of Instruction," 135–36; GHF to J. C. Dixon, 23 June 1955, box 22, GC DNE; GHF to Charles Carroll, 21 March 1958, box 24, GC DNE; GHF to Carroll, 13 February 1959, GHF to Dixon, 16 February 1959, GHF to T. T. Murphy, 17 June 1959, all in box 25, GC DNE; Nile F. Hunt to Jeanes Supervisors, 18 April 1961, box 26, GC DNE.

23. Loftus Carson, Field Notes, [1955], reel 2, series C, pt. 3, NAACP Papers; "Negro Teachers Face Cut in Jobs," *NYT*, 23 October 1955, 80.

24. Adam Fairclough has similarly argued that black teachers' ambivalence regarding *Brown* reflected divisions within the larger black community (*Teaching Equality*, 65).

25. "A Discussion of the NAACP Program to Desegregate Public Schools in North Carolina," 16 July 1955, folder 5, box C142, group II, NAACP Papers; Christina Greene, *Our Separate Ways*, 42–44.

26. Martin, *Brown v. Board of Education*, 220–23; Franklin and Moss, *From Slavery to Freedom*, 513; Douglas, *Reading, Writing, and Race*, 32–34; Chafe, *Civilities and Civil Rights*, 54–60.

27. "The Principle of Integration Must Be Established," *NCTR* 27 (May 1956): 8; "Report of the Legislative Committee," *NCTR* 27 (May 1956): 16; "Recommendations on School Reorganization," *NCTR* 27 (October 1956): 15–16; "Assembly Told Bills Wouldn't Be Held Valid," *Statesville Record and Landmark*, 24 July 1956, 1, 2; "Move Launched to Sidetrack Pearsall Bills," *Statesville Record and Landmark*, 25 July 1956, 1, 7; Douglas, *Reading, Writing, and Race*, 32–34; Chafe, *Civilities and Civil Rights*, 54–60.

28. Myrtle Brittain to S. E. Duncan, 27 August 1948, NCN to Brittain, 9 November 1948,

Brittain to NCN, 14 November 1948, all in box 17, GC DNE; George W. Sandlin to W. Kerr Scott, CAE, J. B. Johnson, H. F. Beam, N. F. Stepp[e], 22 August 1950, CAE to J. L. [G. W.] Sandlin, 24 August 1950, Sandlin to CAE, 31 August 1950, S. E. Duncan, "A Report to State Superintendent Clyde A. Erwin and G. H. Ferguson on the School Controversy Involving Old Fort, Marion, and McDowell County," 21–22 September 1950, all in box 188, GC SPI.

29. D. Hiden Ramsey to Charles Carroll, 25 November 1952, enclosing Ramsey to N. F. Steppe, 25 November 1952, folder State Board of Education, box 197, GC SPI; "Discrimination Suit Is Filed," *Statesville Daily Record*, 12 August 1953, 12; "McDowell Man Says Race Schools Inferior," *DCT*, 22 August 1953, 1, 8; "Judge Rules against New School Plan," *Rocky Mount Evening Telegram*, 6 July 1955, 1, 5; "Negroes Petition for Integration," *LR*, 14 July 1955, 14; News Brief Datelined Marion, N.C., *LR*, 21 July 1955, 1; *Carson v. Board of Education of McDowell County*, 227 F.2d 789 (4th Cir. 1955).

30. "5 Negro Children Denied Admission to White School," *LR*, 24 August 1955, 1, 3; "Old Fort Police Chief Denies Race Tension in Assault Case" and "Hodges Attends Battleboro Event; Deplores Violence in Old Fort Case," both in *Rocky Mount Evening Telegram*, 3 September 1955, 1; "White Man, Negro Charged in Affray in Old Fort Case," *LR*, 5 September 1955, 5; "N.C. School Bars 5 Negroes as 500 Whites Look On," *Jet*, 8 September 1955, 19; "Violence Flares in N.C.," *Jet*, 22 September 1955, 22; "White Man Fined $15 for Hitting Negro in N.C.," *Jet*, 6 October 1955, 55.

31. U.S. Commission on Civil Rights, *Civil Rights U.S.A.*, 65–67; *Carson v. Board of Education of McDowell County*, 227 F.2d 789 (4th Cir. 1955); "N.C. Pupils Must 'Exhaust Remedies,'" *SSN* 3 (December 1956): 6; George B. Patton to Members, North Carolina Advisory Committee on Education, 7 February 1957, folder Segregation—Advisory Committee, box 229, Governor Luther H. Hodges Papers, NCDAH.

32. "Old Fort Negro Suit Dismissed," *LR*, 6 March 1956, 5; "Ask Quick SEG Ruling in McDowell," *LR*, 21 March 1956, 11; *Carson v. Warlick*, 238 F.2d 724 (4th Cir. 1956); "Negroes Rejected by School Boards," *Gastonia Gazette*, 15 October 1957, 5; *Statistical Summary*, 1964–65, 39. For the legal implications of this case, see Peltason, *Fifty-Eight Lonely Men*, 81–82; Tushnet, *Making Civil Rights Law*, 242–44.

33. Luther Hodges to Thomas Pearsall, 25 October 1956, folder Public Instruction, General, A–Z, box 75, Hodges Papers.

34. On the mountain situation, see P. Brown [pseud.] to Claude Ramsey, 27 September 1956, enclosed in Robert Bunnelle to Ed Rankin, 28 September 1956, Rankin to Bunnelle, 3 October 1956, Russell Lowell to Luther Hodges, 22 October 1956, Hodges to Lowell, 25 October 1956, Hodges to Charles Carroll, 25 October 1956, Hodges to Loster Love, 25 October 1956, Love to Hodges, 30 October 1956, Carroll to Hodges, 31 October 1956, all in folder Public Instruction, General, A–Z, box 75, Hodges Papers; George Johnson to S. E. Duncan, 8 November 1956, enclosed in GHF to J. Everett Miller, 24 January 1957, S. E. Duncan to GHF, 27 November 1956, all in box 24, GC DNE.

35. Executive Committee of the Southport Citizens League to J. T. Denning, 22 October 1949, box 18, GC DNE; Southport Colored Citizens League to Luther Hodges, 10 October 1956, Charles Carroll to Hodges, 18 October, 26 November 1956, Hodges to Robert McKenzie, 23 October 1956, McKenzie to Hodges, 12 November 1956, all in folder Public Instruction, General A–Z, box 75, Hodges Papers. For photos of Brunswick County Training School, see Southport Colored Citizens League to Hodges, 10 October 1956, folder Ho, box 48, MARS 104.3.

36. Raleigh had established its first public white high school in 1905, almost two decades before building Washington High School. Soon thereafter, the city constructed two new white high schools, Morson in 1925 and Broughton in 1929. See Barbee, *Historical Sketches*, 41–42, 52, 59, 66.

37. On Ligon's opening, see "Schools Ready for Record Opening," *RN&O*, 30 August 1953, 1–2; "Ligon Jr.-Sr. High to Be Dedicated," *RC*, 7 November 1953, 1; "Ligon School Dedicated," *RN&O*, 9 November 1953, 24. For alumni recollections, see Mackie et al., "Capturing the Past." I am grateful to Candy Beal and Marsha Alibrandi for sharing these materials with me.

38. Between 1951 and 1956, Raleigh built nine new schools: two black schools (Ligon Junior-Senior High and Mary Phillips Elementary) and seven white schools (Daniels Junior High and Joyner, Lacy, Sherwood-Bates, Conn, Longview Garden, and Poe Elementary Schools). See *Raleigh–Wake County Public Schools*, 204–5.

39. "Full Equality throughout for New Race School at Raleigh," *RC*, 13 June 1953, 1. Broughton—and to a lesser extent Morson (which closed in 1955) and Enloe (which opened in 1962)—offered a broader range of electives, including more professionally oriented vocational courses. In 1969, a survey of the Raleigh schools judged that Ligon's facilities were "good" but that its original site was too small (*Raleigh–Wake County Public Schools*, 209). For curricular comparisons, see High School Principals Annual Reports, 1954–55, box 22, DIS Papers; 1961–62, box 75, DIS Papers; 1965–66, box 166, DIS Papers.

40. Raleigh City School Board Minutes, 2 August 1955, Wake County Public Schools Administrative Building, Raleigh, N.C.; "Citizens Will File School Petitions Here," *RC*, 23 July 1955, 1, 11; "Raleigh Board Gets Petitions," *RC*, 30 July 1955, 1, 11; "Negroes Turned Down Here on Petition Integration," *RN&O*, 3 August 1955, 22.

41. Benjamin, "Suburbanizing Jim Crow." For reflections on the Oberlin community by a former resident, see Peebles-Wilkins, *Look to the Rainbow*, 17–19. On Chavis Heights, see "Good Homes for Raleigh," Annual Report of the Housing Authority of the City of Raleigh, North Carolina, [1944–45], NCC. On the schools' namesakes, see Richard L. Watson, "Josephus Daniels," in Powell, *Dictionary of North Carolina Biography*, 2:13–14; Maye E. Ligon, interview by Tim Tyson, 12 July 1988, in Simmons-Henry and Edmisten, *Culture Town*, 85–87; and Zogry, "House That Dr. Pope Built," 220–21.

42. Raleigh City School Board Minutes, 13 December 1955, 3 April, 7 August 1956; Holt, Interview; Joseph H. Holt Jr., "The First Brave Step," 2000, copy in author's possession; "Negro Teacher Discloses Job Threat in Wake," *Burlington Daily Times-News*, 5 November 1956, 5; *SSN* 3 (December 1956): 6–7. For the Holt case, see *Exhausted Remedies* (video), http://www.joeholtstory.org/. See also McEntarfer, "Catching Hell"; Peebles, "School Desegregation," 95–103; McElreath, "Cost of Opportunity," 158–59, 165, 187.

43. Holt, Interview; Holt, correspondence with author, 9 June 2011; "Negro Dad May Sue on School Application," *Raleigh Times*, 3 November 1956, 1.

44. Holt, Interview; Raleigh City School Board Minutes, 6 November 1956.

45. "Negro Dad May Sue on School Application," *Raleigh Times*, 3 November 1956, 1; "Free School Bus Transportation Is Contrary to Public Interest" and "End Secrecy on the School Board," *Raleigh Times*, 1 November 1956, 4; Holt, Interview.

46. "Negro Asks to Enter Broughton," *RN&O*, 11 June 1957, 20; "Anonymous Call Threatens Bombing Negro Home Here," *Raleigh Times*, 24 July 1957, 1; "Bomb Threat Made in City," *RC*, 27 July 1957, 1, 2; "City School Board Turns Down Negro's Bid to Enter

Broughton," *RN&O*, 2 August 1957, 1, 2; Raleigh City School Board Minutes, 6 August 1957; "Joseph Holt Jr. Seeks 'Permanent Injunction' for City School Board," *Raleigh Times*, 29 August 1957, 1; Taylor quoted in *Exhausted Remedies* (video).

47. Holt, Interview. While most of Holt's supporters were black, his cause also won a small number of white allies, including the family of novelist Anne Tyler. See "School Integration Enters Its 50th Year," *RN&O*, 15 January 2011, http://www.newsobserver.com /2010/09/06/667066/school-integration-enters-its.html.

48. Holt, Interview.

49. Ibid.; "School Segregation Trial Opened by Judge Stanley," *RN&O*, 15 July 1958, NCC Clipping File; "Judge Rules against Holt in Integration Case Here," *RN&O*, 2 September 1958, 1, 2; "Negro Pupil Is Refused," *CO*, 2 September 1958, 3A; *Holt v. Raleigh City Board of Education*, 265 F.2d 95 (4th Cir. 1959); "Supreme Court Refuses to Review Holt Case," *RN&O*, 13 October 1959, 1; "'End of the Road,' Holt Lawyer Says," *RN&O*, 13 October 1959, 1, 2; Marshall quoted in Greenberg, *Crusaders in the Courts*, 260. James T. Patterson points out that after *Brown II*, the Supreme Court began "to turn controversies involving school segregation over to the lower courts. . . . [T]he last thing the justices were prepared to do was to act as a gigantic school board" (*Brown v. Board of Education*, 117). The NAACP condemned the Supreme Court's decision not to review the Holt case (Statement, 15 October 1959, reel 8, series D, pt. 3, NAACP Papers).

50. "Negroes Enrolled in Charlotte Schools," *Burlington Daily Times-News*, 4 September 1957, 1A, 10B; "Integration at a Glance" and "Winston-Salem School Integration Is Peaceful," *Burlington Daily Times-News*, 5 September 1957, 1; "First School Year Now Completed," *Sunday Telegram*, 1 June 1958, 1–2A; "Troubles Beset School Opening," *Life*, 16 September 1957, 24–31; "National Affairs: Advance in North Carolina," *Time*, 16 September 1957, 27. For the Charlotte pioneers, see Polly Paddock, "On Sept. 4, 1957, Four Young Charlotte Students Braved Fear and Uncertainty to Take Their Place in History as School Desegregation Pioneers: Somebody Had to Be First," *CO*, 12 April 1992, http:// www.cmstory.org/aaa2/heritage/4_desegregation/update.htm. For Josephine Boyd's experience, see Kevin Sack, "For Civil Rights Pioneer, a Life of Quiet Struggle," *Los Angeles Times*, 9 May 2004, http://articles.latimes.com/2004/may/09/nation/na-josephine9.

51. Gaillard, *Dream Long Deferred*, 3–11; Counts-Scoggins, Interview.

52. Counts-Scoggins, Interview; "25,726 Stuffed into Schools," *Charlotte News*, 8 September 1954, 1B; photo in *Charlotte News*, 10 September 1954, 1B. West Charlotte received accolades for its architectural design. See "School Building in North Carolina," *Southern Architect* 1 (October 1954): 15; "Charlotte School Provides Maximum Flexibility," *Southern Architect* 1 (March 1955): 9–12; *North Carolina Architect* 12 (January 1965): 8–9. There were curricular differences between the two schools in 1957–58, although mainly at the level of electives. Harding offered electives not found at West Charlotte (mechanical drawing, Latin II, orchestra), yet West Charlotte offered some not found at Harding (dramatics, speech, Spanish). See High School Annual Reports, 1957–58, box 43, High School Principals Annual Reports Series, DIS Papers.

53. A discussion of Dorothy Pitman's 1959 dissertation on Alamance County can be found in Lamanna, "Negro Public School Teacher," 57–58. For NAACP branch reports, see Wilson Branch of the NAACP, 1961 Annual Report, Wilmington Branch of the NAACP, 1961 Annual Report, Wendell–Wake County Branch of the NAACP, 1962 Annual Report, all in reel 15, series B, pt. 25, NAACP Papers; "NAACP Announces Plans to Push Pace of School Desegregation," *SSN* 11 (August 1964): 12.

54. Many of Raleigh's middle-class blacks, unlike their Durham counterparts, were state employees and thus directly beholden to the white power structure. See McElreath, "Cost of Opportunity," 175–76; Loftus Carson, Field Report, n.d., reel 2, series C, pt. 3, NAACP Papers.

55. Petition from Representatives of the Durham NAACP, Durham Committee on Negro Affairs, Ministerial Alliance, Durham Business and Professional Chain, PTA Council, East End Betterment League, Executive Committee of the Negro Labor Unions, AFL to the Board of Education of the Public School District of Durham, 11 July 1955, folder Correspondence 1956, box 2, Rencher Harris Papers, Special Collections, William R. Perkins Library, Duke University, Durham, N.C.; McElreath, "Cost of Opportunity," 169–70; *McKissick v. Durham City Bd. of Education*, 176 F. Supp. 3, 7–8 (M.D.N.C. 1959); Christina Greene, "'New Negro Ain't Scared No More!,'" 249; U.S. Commission on Civil Rights, *Equal Protection of the Laws*, 122.

56. Lamanna, "Negro Public School Teacher," 54–55.

57. U.S. Commission on Civil Rights, *Equal Protection of the Laws*, 122; Douglas, *Reading, Writing, and Race*, 46.

58. Raleigh City School Board Minutes, 6 September 1960; "Negro Student Gets Assignment to White Elementary School Here," *RN&O*, 7 September 1960, 1, 2; "Negro Pupil Is Enrolled at Murphey School Here," *RN&O*, 10 September 1960, 18; Holt, Interview; "Signal for Reappraisal," *RN&O*, 2 September 1958, 4.

59. Raleigh City School Board Minutes, 1 June 1961; Gloster B. Current to Robert L. Carter, 16 April 1962, reel 8, series D, pt. 3, NAACP Papers; *Hunter v. Raleigh City Bd. of Education*, Civil Case 1308, U.S. District Court for the Eastern District of North Carolina, Raleigh Division, Records of the District Courts of the United States, Record Group 21, National Archives at Atlanta; U.S. Commission on Civil Rights, *Civil Rights U.S.A.*, 93–95; "Student Assignment Act Challenged Here," *RN&O*, 1 June 1961, 1, 2; "Much to Consider," *RN&O*, 2 June 1961, 4.

60. Covington and Ellis, *Terry Sanford*, 250–51; "Sanford's Children Enter School," *High Point Enterprise*, 9 January 1961, 1; Chafe, *Civilities and Civil Rights*, 102–7. For Sanford's evolution on race, see Korstad and Leloudis, *To Right These Wrongs*, 46–55.

61. Raleigh City School Board Minutes, 1 August 1961; "8 Negroes Assigned to White Schools Here," *RN&O*, 2 August 1961, 1, 2; "Negro Lawyers Study Raleigh Move," *RN&O*, 3 August 1961, 3; "2 Schools to Receive Students," *RC*, 5 August 1961, 1, 2; Capehart, Interview; Sommer Brokaw, "Teens First to Integrate Broughton," *Triangle Tribune*, 22 March 2009, http://www.triangletribune.com/clientuploads/TTPDFs/tt032209A; Sommer Brokaw, "Recalling a Time of Firsts for Blacks," *Triangle Tribune*, 29 March 2009, http://www.triangletribune.com/clientuploads/TTPDFs/tt032909A; L. W. Purdy to Editor, *RN&O*, 22 August 1961, 4.

62. Campbell, Interview; Capehart, Interview; Hermena Hunter, Interview; Gloria Hunter, Interview; Willis, Interview; Manuel, Interview.

63. U.S. Commission on Civil Rights, *Equal Protection of the Laws*, 122; Raleigh City School Board Minutes, 3 July 1962; "Negro Pupils Turned Down," *RN&O*, 8 August 1962, 24.

64. "Report of Resolutions Committee," *NCTR* 29 (May 1958): 17, 20; NCTA Resolutions from the 1961 Annual Meeting, *NCTR* 32 (May 1961): 11–13; NCTA Resolutions from the 1963 Annual Meeting, *NCTR* 33 (May 1963): 25. For the survey of black teachers, see Lamanna, "Negro Public School Teacher," 103, 116–17, 218–19.

65. Phairlever Pearson, Interview; Tarpley, Interview; Mask, Interview; Bartley, *Rise of Massive Resistance*, 212–13 (n. 7).

66. "Report of the Resolutions Committee," *NCTR* 26 (May 1955): 11–13; S. E. Duncan to GHF, 10 February 1957, box 23, GC DNE; GHF to Charles Carroll, 21 January 1958, box 24, GC DNE; James T. Taylor to Carroll, 6 March 1959, box 25, GC DNE; Woodson, Interview.

67. Ida H. Duncan, "The Work of the Teacher in Educating for Full Participation in American Life," *NCTR* 26 (May 1955): 2–4; James T. Taylor, "Your Call to Citizenship Action," *NCTR* 26 (March 1955): 5; "We Face Old Problems in New Form," *NCTR* 30 (January 1959): 8; "Report of Intergroup Relations Committee," *Bulletin* 20 (March–April 1957): 8; Report of North Carolina Congress of Colored Parents and Teachers, 1958–59, PTA Papers.

68. Hugh Victor Brown, *E-Quality Education*, 144–45; Mask, Interview.

69. Scott Baker, *Paradoxes of Desegregation*, 94–107; Dobrasko, "South Carolina's Equalization Schools"; *Statistical Summary*, 1963–64, 38; Bolton, *Hardest Deal of All*, 33–60, 76–88, 134–40; *Southern Schools*, 150.

70. Simmons Fentress, "Greatest Overcrowding Yet Forecast for N.C. Schools," *RN&O*, 27 August 1953, transcript in folder Public Schools and Mental Care, box 11, MARS 104.3.

71. "Integration of Teachers Important," *NCTR* 36 (May 1966): 18–19. Prior to 1954, the state compiled racial breakdowns of how the bond money was allocated, and by 1954, blacks had received 43 percent, slightly more than their 30 percent of the school population. See *Biennial Report*, 1952–53/1953–54, 39–42. For the remainder of the decade, I calculated racial breakdowns using the State Board of Education Minutes, which recorded individual applications for state bond funds. By my best estimation, black schools received around 43 percent of the total bond funds spent between 1949 and 1961.

72. North Carolina's two U.S. senators did support the bill, but to no avail. See "School Aid Gets Little N.C. Support," *CO*, 17 January 1960, N.C. Schools, 1959–60, NCC Clipping File. On southern attitudes toward federal aid, see Orfield, *Reconstruction of Southern Education*, 1–46.

73. Turner, "'It Is Not at Present a Very Successful School,'" chapter 5; Scott Baker, *Paradoxes of Desegregation*, chapter 5; Jones-Wilson and Davis, *Paul Laurence Dunbar High School*, 140–44; Jacoway, *Turn away Thy Son*, 164. Elizabeth Jacoway points out that Little Rock officials bragged about the new Horace Mann High School as a "million dollar school" even though its actual cost was $773,799.32 (403 [n. 3]).

74. Edmonds quoted in Chafe, *Civilities and Civil Rights*, 62–63; Ramsey, *Reading, Writing, and Segregation*, 81, 137–38. Charles Bolton has made similar points about Mississippi (*Hardest Deal of All*, 55–60).

75. Walker, *Their Highest Potential*, 8, 41–63, 171–219; "Caswell County Spends $1,649,917 on School Building Construction during Period, 1949–1957," *Caswell Messenger*, 22 August 1957, 1; "Local School Officials Ponder Moves in County School Segregation Suit," *Caswell Messenger*, 20 December 1956, 1; "Caswell Suit Answer Filed," *Statesville Record and Landmark*, 15 January 1957, 4; "One Negro Pupil Applies for Admittance to Bartlett Yancey High School," *Caswell Messenger*, 1 August 1957, 1; "Board Interviews Negro Parents of Pupils Applying for Transfers," *Caswell Messenger*, 28 August 1957, 1, 4; "Negro Parents Tell Board They Bitterly Oppose Segregation," *Caswell Messenger*, 5 September 1957, 1, 4; "County Schools Get Under Way with All Pupils Enrolled as Assigned," *Caswell Messenger*, 12 September 1957, 1; *Jeffers v. Whitley*, 309 F.2d 621, 625, 628 (4th Cir. 1962); U.S. Commission on Civil Rights and Richard Day, *Civil Rights U.S.A.*, 18–39, 51–53.

76. U.S. Commission on Civil Rights, *Civil Rights U.S.A.*, 97–100; Gerald Cowan to Charles Carroll, 9 July 1953, folder State Board of Education, box 8, MARS 104.3.

77. "N.C. Pupils Who Refuse to Go 80 Miles to School," *Jet*, 8 October 1959, 22–25; Robert E. Giles to Luther H. Hodges, 6 October 1959, D. Hiden Ramsey to Dallas Herring, 23 September [1959], both in folder Education, Board of, box 375, Hodges Papers; "Carolina Pupils Demand Integration," *Southern Patriot* 17 (November 1959): 1; "Carolina Mother Opposes Segregation," *Southern Patriot* 18 (February 1960): 3; NAACP advertisement, *NYT*, 1 December 1959, 26; "Pupil Assignment Law Upset," *The Crisis* 67 (November 1960): 596–97; U.S. Commission on Civil Rights, *Public Education: 1964 Staff Report*, 159. During their long struggle, Yancey County's black citizens received aid from the NAACP, local white allies, and the American Friends Service Committee, which raised money for tutoring programs. See Letters from the Burnsville Educational Project, reel 13, series D, pt. 3, NAACP Papers; Bill Bagwell to Jean Fairfax, 27 February 1962, reel 8, series D, pt. 3, NAACP Papers.

78. "Wilmington Pupil's Transfer Brings First Desegregation," *SSN* 9 (September 1962): 17. The pace of integration in eastern North Carolina was somewhat slower than in the rest of the state. That section, with its smaller black middle class, possessed fewer resources for litigation. Also, rural white elites in this section did not have the same need to create the progressive image and friendly business climate that Davison Douglas has shown was so critical in Charlotte ("Quest for Freedom").

79. *SSN* 6 (June 1960): 13; Greene County Branch of the NAACP, Annual Reports, 1956, 1959, reel 15, series B, pt. 25, NAACP Papers; Gloster B. Current to Roy Wilkins, 2 March 1959, reel 8, series D, pt. 3, NAACP Papers; Charles A. McLean to Current, 8 July 1959, folder 49, box 3, Charles A. McLean Papers, Special Collections, J. Murrey Atkins Library, University of North Carolina, Charlotte; Greene County School Board Minutes, 10–12 February 1959, County Records, Board of Education Records (Microfilm), NCDAH; "Greene County Negro Schools Shut Down as Students Strike," *RN&O*, 11 February 1959, 1, 12; "Board's Offer Fails to End Pupil Strike," *RN&O*, 12 February 1959, 1, 6; "The Grapevine in Greene," *RN&O*, 12 February 1959, 4; "Strikers' Parents Turn Conciliatory," *LR*, 13 February 1959, 1.

80. Greene County School Board Minutes, 3, 14 August, 23 September 1959, 22, 23 April 1964; C. O. Pearson to John Morsell, 19 October 1959, Charles A. McLean to Roy Wilkins, 23 October 1959, both in reel 8, series D, pt. 3, NAACP Papers; *Becton v. Greene County Board of Education* (Civil Case No. 458, U.S. District Court, Eastern District, Washington Division, May 1960), copy in folder Education: Public Instruction, General, A–Z, box 473, Hodges Papers; *Becton v. Greene County Board of Education*, 32 F. R. D. 220 (E.D.N.C. 1963); Dora M. Farmer to Charles A. McLean, 4 January 1965, folder 2, box 2, McLean Papers.

81. Cecelski, *Along Freedom Road*, 28; "Negro Boycott of Schools Denounced," *SSN* 10 (October 1963): 5; "Martin County Threatens to Shut Down Schools in Face of Boycott," *Burlington Daily Times-News*, 10 September 1963, 8B; "School Boycotts Are Called Off," *LR*, 11 September 1963, 1.

82. "Negro Students Boycott School," *RN&O*, 2 September 1961, 1–2; "Two School Boycotts in Warren End," *RN&O*, 12 September 1961, 1; "Protest and Signal," *RN&O*, 4 September 1961, 4; "Sanford Assures Integration Leader," *High Point Enterprise*, 30 March 1964, 6A; "Boycott Set for Schools of Warren," *Rocky Mount Evening Telegram*, 31 March 1964, 1; "Warren Boycott to Continue," *Burlington Daily Times-News*, 1 April 1964, 1; *SSN*

10 (April 1964): 17–18; "East N.C. Schools Are Desegregated," *High Point Enterprise*, 24 July 1964, 6A. For the Warren County litigation, begun in 1963, see *Turner v. Warren County Board of Education*, 313 F. Supp. 380 (E.D.N.C. 1970); Charles A. McLean to Ruby Hurley, Gloster B. Current, and Kelly Alexander, 24 August 1964, folder 50, box 3, McLean Papers.

83. Rencher Harris to Lew Hanne, 15 February 1960, folder Board of Education (1959), box 5, Harris Papers; Jean Bradley Anderson, *Durham County*, 434. Anderson notes that the bond passed, and Durham used some of the funds to build a school named for Harris.

84. This effort to block the building of new segregated schools may in part have failed because at least one prominent NAACP leader backed the bond. A new black school (South Lumberton Junior-Senior High) and new white school (Lumberton High) were constructed in 1965–66, but by then the desegregation process had begun. See "Board Orders Bond Vote; County Residents Object," *LR*, 26 February 1963, 1; "Negro Leader Urges School Bond Passage," *LR*, 10 April 1963, 1; "Landslide Vote Okays School Bond Issues," *LR*, 17 April 1963, 1; "Nice, Cool Schools Planned but Funds Could Force Cuts," *LR*, 31 July 1963, 1; "New High School Opening Monday," *LR*, 6 October 1965, 1; "Delay Again Faces New High School," *LR*, 4 February 1966, 1; "Faculty Integration Start OK'd by City School Board," *LR*, 13 May 1966, 1.

85. Asheville did not build the proposed addition to Stephens-Lee but instead closed the school and opened a new black school, South French Broad High, in 1965. When the high schools integrated several years later, South French Broad became a junior high. See Ferguson, Interview; *Southern News*, 23 October 1965, clipping in Heritage of Black Highlanders Collection, Special Collections, D. H. Ramsey Library, University of North Carolina, Asheville; Johnnie Grant, "South French Broad Class of 1969—The End of a Valuable Heritage," *Urban News*, 9 July 2009, http://www.theurbannews.com/content /view/819/61/.

86. Moody, *Coming of Age in Mississippi*, 229; Eaton, *"Every Man Should Try,"* 81–120; "Williston School Dedicated Today," *Wilmington Sunday Star-News*, 16 May 1954, 14A; Godwin, *Black Wilmington*, 237–38.

87. "Negro Parents Request Segregated High School," *Concord Tribune*, 8 July 1963, 1; "'Separate' High School Is Requested," *Concord Tribune*, 9 July 1963, 1; "Negro Parents, NAACP Refute School Survey," *Concord Tribune*, 12 July 1963, 1; "NAACP Holds Meeting," *Concord Tribune*, 17 July 1963, 7; "Segregation Suit Is Formally Filed," *Concord Tribune*, 24 October 1963, 1; Cabarrus County School Board Minutes, 8 July, 4 November 1963, County Records, Board of Education Records (Microfilm), NCDAH; *SSN* 10 (August 1963): 19; "Lawsuit against Cabarrus County Asks 1964 School Desegregation," *SSN* 10 (November 1963): 4; U.S. Commission on Civil Rights, *Public Education: 1964 Staff Report*, 159.

88. *Biennial Report*, 1962–63/1963–64, pt. 1, 37; U.S. Commission on Civil Rights, *Equal Protection of the Laws*, 102–3.

89. *Biennial Report*, 1962–63/1963–64, pt. 1, 44. Fifty-one percent of Ligon's faculty had graduate degrees; the next-highest school was Broughton High with 36 percent (*Raleigh–Wake County Public Schools*, 163).

90. U.S. Bureau of the Census, *Census of Population: 1950*, 44 (table 20), and *Census of Population: 1970*, 564–65 (table 148).

91. "N.C. Has Low Ratio of Whites in Accredited High Schools," *SSN* 7 (February 1961): 15. In twenty-five of North Carolina's counties, the percentage of blacks in accredited high schools was greater than the percentage of whites, and in forty-three counties, no

students of either race attended accredited high schools. See Report by the North Carolina Advisory Committee on Public High School Enrollment in Accredited Schools, 22 May 1961, reel 13, series D, pt. 3, NAACP Papers. At this time, the Southern Association of Colleges and Secondary Schools did not offer formal membership to black schools. Until the early 1960s, black schools that met its standards were designated "approved" rather than "accredited." From 1934 to 1964, a black accrediting agency, the Association of Colleges and Secondary Schools, used the same standards as the white agency but offered black schools full membership. See Walker, *Hello Professor*, 81, 112.

92. *Biennial Report*, 1962-63/1963-64, pt. 1, 37. The school year 1963-64 was the last one for which the state published racial breakdowns of this data and the last year that its *Educational Directory* categorized schools as "white schools" and "Negro schools." For the 1960s southern trend of not reporting statistics by race, see "Records by Race: To Keep or Not," *Southern Education Report* 2 (September 1966): 29-32; "Faster Pace, Scarcer Records," *Southern Education Report* 1 (January–February 1966): 28-32. For statewide data on curricula, see *Biennial Report*, 1962-63/1963-64, pt. 1, 57-58.

93. No statewide testing program existed until the 1970s, so comprehensive data are limited for the period under study. For one example of test results from the 1950s, see *Goldsboro Township Schools*, 102-3, 106-7, 114-15, 117-25. For a broader discussion of achievement test results in the mid-1960s, see Jim Leeson, "Some Basic Beliefs Challenged," *Southern Education Report* 2 (May 1967): 4. The differences between the achievement levels of blacks in segregated schools and black students in integrated schools helped inspire Judge James B. McMillan to support the implementation of busing in Charlotte (Watters, "Charlotte, North Carolina," 29).

94. *Biennial Report*, 1962-63/1963-64, pt. 1, 42.

95. Freeze, *Catawbans*, 199, 339-40; "Modern Vocational Education Building among Most Urgent Needs at Ridgeview School," *HDR*, 20 September 1949, in Vertical Files, Beaver Memorial Library; U.S. Bureau of the Census, *Census of Population: 1950*, 33; Tucker et al., Interview; Drucella Sudderth Hartsoe, "The Hill: Memories of the Ridgeview Community," 2001, Ridgeview Branch, Hickory Public Library, Hickory, N.C.

96. "Negro Schools Get Priority in County," *HDR*, 17 May 1954, 1, 13; "Funds Allotted Ridgeview Will Have Big Job to Do," *HDR*, 12 December 1954; "School Addition Dedicated Here," *HDR*, 13 November 1957, 1, 22; "School Board Lets Contract for Addition," *HDR*, 6 April 1960, 1, 26, all in Vertical Files, Beaver Memorial Library. See also Hickory City School Board Minutes, 1 June 1954, Hickory City Schools Administrative Offices, Hickory, N.C.; Catawba County File, MARS 104.56.

97. Tucker et al., Interview.

98. Tucker et al., Interview; Janice Lutz Johnson, Interview; "Index of Instructional Personnel in N.C.," *Newsletter of the Institute for Research in Social Science, University of North Carolina*, 25 February 1953, box 18, SSF; "Hickory Teacher Presented Award," *HDR*, 11 June 1980, Vertical Files, Beaver Memorial Library; Thompson quoted in *Unintended Consequences?* (video); *Proceedings of the Sixty-Seventh Annual Meeting*, 99.

99. "Ridgeview Overcame Obstacles," *HDR*, 27 June 1993, Vertical Files, Beaver Memorial Library; Grundy, *Learning to Win*, 161-63, 179.

100. Catawba County File, MARS 104.56; W. S. Hamilton to Charles Carroll, 7 November 1952, Carroll to Hamilton, 20 November 1952, both in box 196, GC SPI; *Hickory, North Carolina Public Schools*, 64, 134-35, 141-42. As a consequence of its small size, Ridgeview

had a higher book-to-pupil ratio (8.7:1) than Claremont Central (6.75:1), but the latter had nearly 9,000 books, while Ridgeview had only 2,268 for its twelve grades. See High School Preliminary Reports, 1965–66, box 149, DIS Papers.

101. Historians have generally argued that the federal legislation of the 1960s helped stimulate desegregation, but many districts found ways of delaying full-scale integration. Flagrant abuses of federal funds were common. Warren County used ESEA funds to purchase trailers to relieve overcrowding at a black school even though an underpopulated white school was right down the road. See Jeffrey, *Education for Children of the Poor*, 107–10; James T. Patterson, *Brown v. Board of Education*, 136–41; Schulman, *From Cotton Belt to Sunbelt*, 195–96.

102. Hickory City School Board Minutes, 6 May, 10 August, 13, 21 September, 5 October, 2 November 1965, 11 January, 21 February, 5 April 1966; "Hickory School Board Alters Compliance Plan," *HDR*, 7 May 1965, 1, 18; "Administrative School Personnel Get Pay Hike," *HDR*, 11 August 1965, 25; *Wilson v. Hickory City Board of Education*, Complaint filed in U.S. District Court for the Western District of North Carolina (Statesville Division), 10 September 1965, Civil Action No. 529, U.S. District Court Records, Record Group 21, National Archives, Atlanta. The eight students represented in this suit were L'Tanya Fish, Barbara Phillips, Lorene Phillips, Marie Phillips, Charles Wilson, Diane Wilson, Elfreda Wilson, and Thomas Wilson. The suit led to a 1966 court order for full desegregation. See Paul Johnson, "School Turmoil Recalled," *HDR*, 20 October 1986, 1A, 7A.

103. For a list of the nineteen black students who integrated Claremont Central, see Suzanne Jackson, "To Those Who Helped Pave the Way, You Won't Be Forgotten," *HDR*, 1 March 2005, A4. I am grateful to Hickory High School principal Ann Stalnaker and Hickory integration pioneer Audrey Crawley Reeves for their help in verifying this information.

104. Janice Lutz Johnson, Interview; Mayhew, Interview; Jett, Interview.

105. Janice Lutz Johnson, Interview; *Ridgeview Alma Mater* (yearbook, commemorative edition), Ridgeview Branch, Hickory Public Library.

106. "No Surprise Involved in End to Plan," *RN&O*, 5 April 1966, NCC Clipping File.

107. The first study was sociologist James Coleman et al., *Equality of Educational Opportunity*, also known as the Coleman Report. Harvard psychologist Thomas Pettigrew served as a chief consultant on the second study, *Racial Isolation in the Public Schools*. For a discussion of both, see Jeffrey, *Education for Children of the Poor*, 144–78. As Jeffrey points out, the Coleman Report has received numerous critiques, but its basic arguments still hold sway. See also Hochschild and Scovronick, *American Dream*, 26.

108. For more on Chambers, particularly his litigation against employment discrimination, see Mosnier, "Crafting Law" (Chambers quoted on 292). Attorneys Jack Greenberg and Derrick Bell of New York and Conrad Pearson of Durham joined Chambers in representing the Hickory plaintiffs. Chambers is best known for the landmark *Swann v. Charlotte-Mecklenburg Board of Education* case (1971), which legitimated the use of busing in achieving school integration.

EPILOGUE

1. Anonymous Letters collected at Hickory High, folder High School Student Response Letters, 1969, box 4, Educational Institutions File, Department of Administration, Human Relations Council Papers, NCDAH; Albert Nelson, Report on "Crisis Situation," 1–11 Sep-

tember 1970, folder Catawba County, box 1, Educational Institutions File, Human Relations Council Papers; "Negroes Ask Shifts," *HDR*, 12 February 1969, 1, 36; Sudderth quoted in Suzanne Jackson, "Breaking Racial Barriers," *HDR*, 23 February 2005, A1, A8; Thompson quoted in *Unintended Consequences?* (video). Student Larry Pope similarly remembered the white high school as being "not as nice as the school we had left" ("Board of the Past," *Hickory News Extra*, 20–27 May 2004, 7).

2. "Use Busing, City Schools Told," *RN&O*, 14 July 1971, NCC Clipping File; superintendents representing Montgomery County, Fairmont City, and Burke County quoted in Segregation Questionnaires, 1954, box 2, North Carolina State Attorney General Papers, NCDAH.

3. *Biennial Report*, 1958–59/1959–60, pt. 1, 29; Cindy George, "Alumni Cherish School's Heritage," *RN&O*, 3 May 2003, 1B, 7B. The five are Hillside High School in Durham, E. E. Smith High School in Fayetteville, Dudley High School in Greensboro, Carver High School in Winston-Salem, and West Charlotte High.

4. Mike Honey, "Report on Schools," *Southern Patriot* 28 (January 1971): 4. The Coleman Report similarly found that in the rural South, 79 percent of black schools and just 52 percent of white schools were less than twenty years old. See Jim Leeson, "Some Basic Beliefs Challenged," *Southern Education Report* 2 (May 1967): 4. The two schools that boycotters in Hyde County in 1968–69 wished to preserve had received upgrades between 1953 and 1964 (Cecelski, *Along Freedom Road*, esp. 29–30).

5. I am drawing on the Southern Oral History Program's series on desegregation in Chapel Hill, which I surveyed in 2004 under George Noblit and James Leloudis's direction. See also Noblit and Leloudis, "What Was Lost"; *Hillife* (Chapel Hill High yearbook), 1967, NCC.

6. "Ridgeview Bids Opened," *HDR*, 3 February 1977, Vertical Files, Patrick Beaver Memorial Library, Hickory, N.C.; Tucker et al., Interview.

7. Cecelski, *Along Freedom Road*, 8; "Negro Teachers' Status Becomes Statewide Issue," *SSN* 11 (June 1965): 16. North Carolina began using the NTE on a statewide basis in the early 1960s for teacher certification purposes. Widely criticized by black teachers, the exam came under court challenge in the 1970s. See Fultz, "Displacement of Black Educators," 27; Fairclough, *Class of Their Own*, 407–8; Robert W. Hooker, "Displacement of Black Teachers in the Eleven Southern States," 1970, folder "Teachers: Displacement of Black Teachers, 1970," box 5, Educational Institutions File, Human Relations Council Papers; "National Teachers Examination," *NCTR* 37 (March 1967): 43; Herring, Interview; "Certifying Teachers," *High Point Enterprise*, 15 December 1972, 4A; "Study Okays Teacher Test," *Gastonia Gazette*, 9 October 1976, 1.

8. Jeffrey, *Education for Children of the Poor*, 187; McKissick, Interview by Bass and De Vries; Ogletree, *All Deliberate Speed*, 77.

9. Link, *William Friday*, chapter 11, esp. 320–21, 446 (n. 40); Snider, *Light on the Hill*, 307–9; Chambers, Interview.

10. Neil Offen, "NCCU Making Financial Gains," *Durham Herald-Sun*, 21 November 2009, http://www.heraldsun.com/view/full_story/4664103/article-NCCU-making-financial-gains; Charlie Nelms, "Measuring Up!: Assessing Institutional Effectiveness," 11 August 2009, http://www.nccu.edu/formsdocs/proxy.cfm?file_id=1278; Marybeth Gasman, "A Call to Action," *Chronicle of Higher Education*, 12 September 2011, http://chronicle.com/blogs/innovations/a-call-to-action/30291. In 2006, historically white state universities in North Carolina held a median endowment per full-time student of

$17,579; at the state's HBCUs, that figure was $2,183. See Charlie Nelms, "HBCU Reconstruction," *NCCU NOW*, Summer 2010, 36.

11. Luebke, *Tar Heel Politics*, 144–47; Edmonds, *Black Faces in High Places*, 220–21; Cecelski, *Along Freedom Road*, 8–9, 176 (n. 12).

12. Woodson, Interview; Coley quoted in Wilson, *Hope and Dignity*, 108. Several veteran black educators in this oral history collection expressed similar sentiments.

13. Press Release on Boyd, 12 June 1958, reel 8, series D, pt. 3, NAACP Papers; *SSN* 10 (October 1963): 5–6; *SSN* 11 (June 1965): 16–17; Reeves quoted in Paul Johnson, "School Turmoil Recalled," *HDR*, 20 October 1986, 1A, 7A; Peerman, Interview. The Kennedy twins were the sons of Winston-Salem attorneys Annie Brown Kennedy and Harold L. Kennedy Jr.

14. Albert Nelson, "Crisis Situation," 1–11 September 1970, folder Catawba County, box 1, Educational Institutions File, Human Relations Council Papers; "North Carolina Students Rebel against Exclusion from School Activity," *Southern Patriot* 28 (October 1970): 7; "Blacks Break Windows Here," *HDR*, 7 September 1970, 1, 25; "Fiery Crosses Show Tension Remains High," *HDR*, 7 September 1970, 1, 18; "Hickory School Board Weighs Disciplinary Issue," *HDR*, 8 September 1970, 1; "Group Balks at Returning to HHS Today," *HDR*, 8 September 1970, 1; "3-Day Suspensions Handed Blacks Who Left School," *HDR*, 9 September 1970, 1; "High School Representation Assured Blacks, Board Told," *HDR*, 3 March 1971, Vertical Files, Beaver Memorial Library; Southern Regional Council, "Tension and Conciliation," 38.

15. Jonathan Zimmerman points out that the "integration of textbooks" also had the unintended result of sanitizing or blunting analysis of racial oppression, as black activists "sometimes pressed their own distortions upon the nation's textbooks" and whites resisted "any negative material about their own past" (*"Brown*-ing the American Textbook," 50).

16. "This Too, Is Our Heritage" (pamphlet), PTA Papers; Percy Murray, *History*, 111–37; Palmer, Interview; Todd Silberman, "Lee Named to State Board," *RN&O*, 30 April 2003, B1.

17. Hochschild and Scovronick, *American Dream*, 39; Orfield, "Lessons Forgotten," 4; David L. Kirp, "Making Schools Work," *NYT*, 20 May 2012, 1, 7 (Sunday Review section); Ashenfelter, Collins, and Yoon, "Evaluating the Role of *Brown*," 243.

18. In 1966, James Coleman et al. made the case that peer interactions and family background have an even greater influence on student achievement than does school quality, although they did not dismiss the importance of school resources (*Equality of Educational Opportunity*, esp. 302). Economists have shown that the postwar improvement of segregated schools had at least a small positive effect on student earnings. See Card and Krueger, "School Resources and Student Outcomes"; Card and Krueger, "School Quality and Black-White Relative Earnings." Robert Margo has argued that equalized segregated schools alone would not have "fully equalize[d] educational outcomes" (*Race and Schooling*, 86).

19. Robbie Brown, "School District in North Carolina Considers Ending Busing for Economic Diversity," *NYT*, 28 February 2010, A14, A20; Mickelson, "Subverting *Swann*"; Killen, Crystal, and Ruck, "Social Developmental Benefits."

20. Wells et al., *Both Sides Now*, 5–8, 19.

21. Hochschild and Scovronick, *American Dream*, 29.

22. Superfine, *Courts and Standards-Based Education Reform*, 133–39; "What the Courts Decided in the Leandro Case: A Brief History," *Educate!*, 8 April 2005, http://www

.swannfellowship.org/Educate/PDF2005/Educate!%20050408.pdf; Martha Waggoner, "Judge: 'Academic Genocide' in Halifax Schools," *RN&O*, 19 March 2009, http://www.newsobserver.com/2009/03/19/38345/judge-academic-genocide-in-halifax.html.

23. Tim Simmons, "Black Parents Seek a Better Choice," *RN&O*, 23 November 1999, 1A, 10A–11A; Shokaraii, "Free at Last"; MacLean, "Conservative Quest"; Vanessa Siddle Walker, Interview, in Bates, "Remembering the Good"; Dougherty, "From Anecdote to Analysis"; Reed, "Romancing Jim Crow"; Shircliffe, "'We Got the Best of That World.'"

24. Hochschild and Scovronick, *American Dream*, 48; Orfield, "Southern Dilemma," 9, 14; Jonathan Kozol, "Overcoming Apartheid," *The Nation*, 19 December 2005, http://www.thenation.com/doc/20051219/kozol.

25. Chris Burritt, "Charlotte Faces New Challenge as Bus Order Lifted," *Atlanta Journal-Constitution*, 12 September 1999, 5B; *Capacchione v. Charlotte-Mecklenburg Schools*, 57 F. Supp. 2d 228 (W.D.N.C. 1999); Tim Simmons, "Ruling Ends Busing Order," *RN&O*, 22 September 2001, 3A; "Judge to Schools: No Racial Assignment," *CO*, 11 September 1999, 1; "Historic Era Dawns in CMS Classrooms," *CO*, 18 August 2002, 1A, 11A; Tim Simmons, "School Choice Is Resegregating Charlotte," *RN&O*, 3 November 2002, 1A, 12A.

26. "CMS' Shifting Enrollment," *CO*, 7 October 2011, 1B, 4B; Fannie Flono, "The South's Changing Public Schools," *CO*, 8 January 2010, 17A. Other North Carolina districts have experienced rapid school resegregation. Within one summer, a school choice plan transformed Winston-Salem's Atkins Middle School from an enrollment that was two-thirds white to one that was 96 percent black ("Separate and Unequal, Again," *RN&O*, 18 February 2001, 1A). This story was part of a four-part series in the *Raleigh News and Observer* on the "new segregation."

27. "Standing Strong," *RN&O*, 11 April 2009, 10A. Gerald Grant offers a thoughtful assessment of Raleigh's income-based plan in *Hope and Despair*. See also Alan Finder, "Integrating Schools by Income Is Cited as Success in Raleigh," *NYT*, 25 September 2005, 1, 13; Tim Simmons, "Wake Clings Tenaciously to Diversity," *RN&O*, 20 February 2001, 1A, 6A; Emily Bazelon, "The Next Kind of Integration," *NYT Magazine*, 29 July 2008, 38–43; "Wake Schools Get Diversity Kudos," *RN&O*, 9 April 2009, 3B; "School Diversity: Why Does Wake Keep Trying?," *RN&O*, 11 January 2009, 13A.

28. "Truitt: 'Forced Busing Is Dead,'" *RN&O*, 8 October 2009, 1A, 5A; "School District in North Carolina Considers Ending Busing for Economic Diversity," *NYT*, 28 February 2010, A14, A20. In early 2010, Wake superintendent and diversity plan supporter Del Burns resigned when it became clear that the new board did not share his priorities ("Citing Conscience, Wake Schools Chief Resigns," *RN&O*, 17 February 2010, 1A, 8A).

29. "Diversity Policy Voted down in Raucous, Tense, Meeting," *RN&O*, 3 March 2010, 1A, 8A; "Tumultuous Session Ends Diversity Policy," *RN&O*, 24 March 2010, 1A, 8A; "Diversity Policy Tossed; Tough Decisions Loom," *RN&O*, 19 May 2010, 1A, 6A; "Schools Fight Stays Hot," *RN&O*, 21 June 2010, 1A, 6A; "Fear of 'Resegregation' Fuels Unrest in Raleigh," *CO*, 19 July 2010, 8B; "A Day of Protest, Arrests, and a Promise," *RN&O*, 21 July 2010, 1A, 6A; "Rights Leaders, Clergy Rally for Diversity," *RN&O*, 21 July 2010, 6A; "NAACP Takes Wake to Feds," *RN&O*, 26 September 2010, 1A, 10A; "Goldman: Dump the Assignment Plan, Start Over," *RN&O*, 5 October 2010; "Wake Schools Catch Bill Clinton's Eye," *RN&O*, 24 February 2011, 1A, 8A; Michael Winerip, "Seeking Integration, Whatever the Path," *NYT*, 28 February 2011, A11, A13; "Parental Choice Poised to Win the Nod in Wake," *RN&O*, 22 June 2011, 1A, 8A; "Democrats Again Control Wake School Board," *RN&O*, 9 November 2011, 1A, 8A; "Schools Plan to Go Forward," *RN&O*, 11 January 2012, 1A, 7A; "Wake Offers

Incentives on Schools," *RN&O*, 12 April 2012, 1A, 7A; "Shift Seen in Kindergarten," *RN&O*, 28 June 2012, 1A, 6A; "Wake School Board Approves 2013–14 Assignment Plan," *RN&O*, 12 December 2012, http://www.newsobserver.com/2012/12/11/2539222/wake-school-board-approves-2013.html. For new evidence that Wake's former diversity plan may have raised overall student achievement levels, see "Report Links Diversity, Higher Grades," *RN&O*, 19 April 2012, 1A, 9A.

30. Orfield, "Southern Dilemma," 24. Richard Kahlenberg of the Century Foundation has made similar points, saying of the Raleigh case, "It's not as if this is a new idea, 'Let's experiment and see what happens when poor kids are put together in one school.' We know. The results are almost always disastrous" (Stephanie McCrummen, "Republican School Board in N.C. Backed by Tea Party Abolishes Integration Policy," *Washington Post*, 12 January 2011, http://www.washingtonpost.com/wp-dyn/content/article/2011/01/11/AR2011011107063.html).

31. "Ruling Ends Busing Order," *RN&O*, 22 September 2001, 3A; "Charlotte Contemplates Life after School Busing," *NYT*, 13 September 1999, http://www.nytimes.com/library/national/091399busing-edu.html; Araminta Johnston, "Any Vestiges of Old Segregation?," *Educate!*, 4 March 2001, http://www.swannfellowship.org/Educate/PDF2001/Educate!%20010304.pdf; Anne Blythe, "Two Men Shape Fight over Diversity," *RN&O*, 7 September 2010, 1A, 8A.

32. Holt, Interview; Gloria Hunter, Interview; Hermena Hunter, Interview.

33. Historians recently have stressed the ways in which resistance to desegregation transcended region. Matthew Lassiter, for example, has argued that integration opponents were united less by a regional identity and more by a suburban one (*Silent Majority*).

34. Manuel, Interview; Capehart, Interview; Lynn Parramore, "Tea Party Plans Scrap Integration Policy at N.C. Schools," *Huffington Post*, 12 January 2011, http://www.huffingtonpost.com/lynn-parramore/tea-party-north-carolina-integration_b_808201.html; Margaret Newbold, "We Can't Let Integration Slide," *RN&O*, 30 April 2010, 11A.

35. Woodward, *Strange Career*; Woodward, *Thinking Back*, 94.

Bibliography

MANUSCRIPT COLLECTIONS

Asheville, North Carolina
    University of North Carolina at Asheville, D. H. Ramsey Library, Special Collections
        Heritage of Black Highlanders Collection
Atlanta, Georgia
    Atlanta University Center, Robert W. Woodruff Library, Archives and Special
        Collections
        Southern Education Foundation Papers
    National Archives at Atlanta
        Records of the District Courts of the United States, Record Group 21
Chapel Hill, North Carolina
    University of North Carolina, Louis R. Wilson Library, North Carolina Collection
        North Carolina Collection Clipping File
    University of North Carolina, Louis R. Wilson Library, Southern Historical Collection
        Frank Porter Graham Papers
        Thomas J. Pearsall Papers
        Oliver R. Pope Papers
        Southern Oral History Program Collection
Charlotte, North Carolina
    University of North Carolina at Charlotte, J. Murrey Atkins Library, Special
        Collections
        Kelly Alexander Sr. Papers
        Charles A. McLean Papers
Durham, North Carolina
    North Carolina Central University, James E. Shepard Memorial Library, University
        Archives, Records and History Center
        Records and History Center Vertical Files
        James E. Shepard Papers
    Duke University, William R. Perkins Library, Special Collections
        William H. Chafe Oral History Collection
        Rencher Harris Papers
        Charles N. Hunter Papers
        Nathan Carter Newbold Papers
Elizabeth City, North Carolina
    Elizabeth City State University, G. R. Little Library, University Archive
        John Henry Bias Papers

Hickory, North Carolina
    Hickory City Schools Administrative Offices
        Minutes of the Hickory City School Board
    Patrick Beaver Memorial Library
        Local History Clipping File
    Ridgeview Branch Library
        Ridgeview High School Yearbook
Pocantico Hills, North Tarrytown, New York
    Rockefeller Archive Center
        General Education Board Papers
        Laura Spelman Rockefeller Memorial Papers
Raleigh, North Carolina
    North Carolina Division of Archives and History, Old Records Center
        Department of Public Instruction, School Planning Section Papers
            Application Folders for School Construction Funds (MARS 104.56)
        Department of Public Instruction, State Superintendent's Office Papers
            General Correspondence (MARS 104.3)
    North Carolina Division of Archives and History, State Archives
        County Records, Board of Education Records (Microfilm)
            Cabarrus County, North Carolina, Board of Education Minutes
            Greene County, North Carolina, Board of Education Minutes
            Pamlico County, North Carolina, Board of Education Minutes
            Person County, North Carolina, Board of Education Minutes
            Robeson County, North Carolina, Board of Education Minutes
        Department of Administration, Human Relations Council Papers
        Department of Public Instruction, Division of Instructional Services Papers
        Department of Public Instruction, Division of Negro Education Papers
        Department of Public Instruction, Superintendent of Public Instruction Papers
        Governor Thomas Bickett Papers
        Governor R. Gregg Cherry Papers
        Governor Luther H. Hodges Papers
        Governor W. Kerr Scott Papers
        Governor William B. Umstead Papers
        North Carolina State Attorney General Papers
        North Carolina State Board of Education Papers
    North Carolina State Parent Teacher Association Headquarters
        North Carolina Congress of Colored Parents and Teachers Papers
    Richard B. Harrison Library
        Mollie Huston Lee Collection
    Wake County Public Schools Administrative Building
        Raleigh City School Board Minutes
Rocky Mount, North Carolina
    Braswell Memorial Library
        Local History Vertical Files
Washington, D.C.
    Library of Congress
        National Association for the Advancement of Colored People Papers

MICROFORM COLLECTIONS

General Education Board Archives. New York: Rockefeller University; Wilmington, Del.:
   Scholarly Resources, 1993.
Hampton University Newspaper Clipping File. Alexandria, Va.: Chadwyck-Healey, 1987.
National Association for the Advancement of Colored People Papers. Frederick, Md.:
   University Publications of America, 1991.
*Papers of Carter G. Woodson and the Association for the Study of Negro Life and History,
   1915–1950*. Bethesda, Md.: University Publications of America, 1998.
Papers of W. E. B. Du Bois at University of Massachusetts, Amherst. Sanford, N.C.:
   Microfilming Corporation of America, 1980–81.

INTERVIEWS

Campbell, William. Interview by David Crabtree, WRAL (Raleigh), 3 September 2010,
   http://www.wral.com/news/local/video/8242327/#/vid8242327.
Capehart, Myrtle Lillian. Interview by author, Raleigh, N.C., 25 August 2010.
Chambers, Julius. Interview by William Link, 18 June 1990, Southern Oral History
   Program Collection, Southern Historical Collection, Louis R. Wilson Library,
   University of North Carolina, Chapel Hill.
Clark, Rebecca. Interview by Bob Gilgor, 21 June 2000, Southern Oral History Program
   Collection, Southern Historical Collection, Louis R. Wilson Library, University of
   North Carolina, Chapel Hill.
Counts-Scoggins, Dorothy. Telephone interview by author, 23 June 2011.
Delany, Lemuel. Interview by Kimberly Hill, 15 July 2005, Southern Oral History
   Program Collection, Southern Historical Collection, Louis R. Wilson Library,
   University of North Carolina, Chapel Hill.
Ferguson, James. Interview by Rudolph Acree Jr., 3, 17 March 1992, Southern Oral
   History Program Collection, Southern Historical Collection, Louis R. Wilson Library,
   University of North Carolina, Chapel Hill.
Franklin, John Hope. Interview by John Egerton, 27 July 1990, Southern Oral History
   Program Collection, Southern Historical Collection, Louis R. Wilson Library,
   University of North Carolina, Chapel Hill.
Fulcher, James. Interview by Sandra B. Hawkins, 1 June 2007, Southern Oral History
   Program Collection, Southern Historical Collection, Louis R. Wilson Library,
   University of North Carolina, Chapel Hill.
Green, Carolyn Smith. Interview by author, Durham, N.C., 6 May 2011.
Hargraves, Frances. Interview by Bob Gilgor, 22 January 2001, Southern Oral History
   Program Collection, Southern Historical Collection, Louis R. Wilson Library,
   University of North Carolina, Chapel Hill.
Herring, Dallas. Interview by Jay Jenkins, 16 May 1987, Southern Oral History Program
   Collection, Southern Historical Collection, Louis R. Wilson Library, University of
   North Carolina, Chapel Hill.
Himbry, Joseph, Jr. Interview by Linda Henry, 28 June 2007, Southern Oral History
   Program Collection, Southern Historical Collection, Louis R. Wilson Library,
   University of North Carolina, Chapel Hill.
Holt, Joseph H., Jr. Interview by author, Raleigh, N.C., 17 August 2010.

Hunter, Gloria, and Hermena Hunter. Interview by author, Raleigh, N.C., 22 September 2010.

Jett, Mary Joice. Telephone interview by author, 27 August 2010.

Johnson, Guion. Interview by Mary Frederickson, 28 May 1974, Southern Oral History Program Collection, Southern Historical Collection, Louis R. Wilson Library, University of North Carolina, Chapel Hill.

Johnson, Janice Lutz. Interview by author, Hickory, N.C., 26 July 2010.

Kemp, Elizabeth. Interview by author, Lumberton, N.C., 13 August 2008.

Manuel, Larry. Telephone interview by author, 23 September 2010.

Mask, J. W. Interview by Goldie Wells, 15 February 1991, Southern Oral History Program Collection, Southern Historical Collection, Louis R. Wilson Library, University of North Carolina, Chapel Hill.

Mason, John. Interview by Kate Goldstein, 1 March 2001, Southern Oral History Program Collection, Southern Historical Collection, Louis R. Wilson Library, University of North Carolina, Chapel Hill.

Mayhew, Judy Dula. Interview by author, Newton, N.C., 27 August 2010.

McKissick, Floyd B., Sr. Interview by Bruce Kalk, 31 May 1989, Southern Oral History Program Collection, Southern Historical Collection, Louis R. Wilson Library, University of North Carolina, Chapel Hill.

McKissick, Floyd B., Sr. Interview by Jack Bass and Walter De Vries, 6 December 1973, Southern Oral History Program Collection, Southern Historical Collection, Louis R. Wilson Library, University of North Carolina, Chapel Hill.

McQueen, Lillian Bullock. Interview by author, Lumberton, N.C., 8 December 2008.

Meeks, Rosalie. Interview by Matt West, 27 February 2001, Southern Oral History Program Collection, Southern Historical Collection, Louis R. Wilson Library, University of North Carolina, Chapel Hill.

Murray, Pauli. Interview by Genna Rae McNeil, 13 February 1976, Southern Oral History Program Collection, Southern Historical Collection, Louis R. Wilson Library, University of North Carolina, Chapel Hill.

Palmer, Elliott Brown. Interview by author, Raleigh, N.C., 8 April 2011; telephone interview by author, 23 June 2011.

Pearson, Conrad. Interview by Walter Weare, 18 April 1979, Southern Oral History Program Collection, Southern Historical Collection, Louis R. Wilson Library, University of North Carolina, Chapel Hill.

Pearson, Phairlever. Interview by Cecile Bost, reprinted in *Past Times*, the quarterly newsletter of the Catawba County Historical Association, July–December 2005, 14–22.

Peerman, Joanne. Interview by Bob Gilgor, 24 February 2001, Southern Oral History Program Collection, Southern Historical Collection, Louis R. Wilson Library, University of North Carolina, Chapel Hill.

Rivera, Alex M., Jr. Interview by Kieran Taylor, 30 November 2001, Southern Oral History Program Collection, Southern Historical Collection, Louis R. Wilson Library, University of North Carolina, Chapel Hill.

Tarpley, John A. Interview by William Chafe, ca. 1975, William Chafe Oral History Collection, Duke University; digitized transcript, Civil Rights Greensboro, http://library.uncg.edu/dp/crg/oralhistitem.aspx?i=683.

Thompson, Angus, Sr., and Lillian Thompson. Interview by Malinda Maynor, 21 October 2003, Southern Oral History Program Collection, Southern Historical Collection, Louis R. Wilson Library, University of North Carolina, Chapel Hill.

Tucker, Catherine Sudderth, Larry Johnson, Flossie Waller Saddler, and Billy Sudderth. Interview by author, Newton, N.C., 17 June 2010.

Willis, Rebecca Bryant. Interview by author, Raleigh, N.C., 11 October 2010.

Woodson, Ruth Lawrence. Interview by author, Raleigh, N.C., 14 June 2002.

GOVERNMENT AND SCHOOL DOCUMENTS

Biennial Report of the State Superintendent of Public Instruction of North Carolina. Various Publishers, 1896–1964.

Bulletin of the Agricultural and Technical College of North Carolina 38 (May 1947).

Caliver, Ambrose. *Availability of Education to Negroes in Rural Communities.* U.S. Bureau of Education Bulletin, 1935, No. 12. Washington, D.C.: U.S. Government Printing Office, 1936.

———. *Rural Elementary Education among Negroes under Jeanes Supervising Teachers.* U.S. Bureau of Education Bulletin, 1933, No. 5. Washington, D.C.: U.S. Government Printing Office, 1933.

———. *Secondary Education for Negroes.* U.S. Bureau of Education Bulletin, 1932, No. 17, Monograph No. 7. Washington, D.C.: U.S. Government Printing Office, 1933.

———. *Vocational Education and Guidance of Negroes: Report of a Survey Conducted by the Office of Education.* U.S. Bureau of Education Bulletin, 1937, No. 38. Washington, D.C.: U.S. Government Printing Office, 1938.

Catalogue of the North Carolina College for Negroes. Durham, various years.

Educational Directory of North Carolina. Raleigh: State Superintendent of Public Instruction, various years.

The Goldsboro Township Schools: Report of a Cooperative Survey, 1954–1956. Chapel Hill: Bureau of Educational Research and Service, School of Education, University of North Carolina, 1956.

Handbook for Elementary and Secondary Schools. Publication 235. Raleigh: North Carolina State Superintendent of Public Instruction, 1953.

Hickory, North Carolina Public Schools: A Survey Report. Nashville, Tenn.: George Peabody College for Teachers, Division of Surveys and Field Services, 1964.

Larkins, John R. *The Negro Population of North Carolina, 1945–1955.* Raleigh: North Carolina State Board of Public Welfare, 1957.

Laws and Resolutions of the State of North Carolina, Passed by the General Assembly at Its Session, 1876–77. Raleigh: News Publishing, 1877.

North Carolina State Educational Commission. *Public Education in North Carolina.* New York: General Education Board, 1921.

The North Carolina State List of Approved High School Text-Books for County Adoptions, 1929–1934. Educational Publication 129. Raleigh: North Carolina State Superintendent of Public Instruction, n.d.

Public Laws and Resolutions of the State of North Carolina Passed by Its General Assembly at Its Session of 1921. Raleigh: Mitchell, 1921.

Public Laws and Resolutions of the State of North Carolina Passed by the General

Assembly at Its Extra Session of 1938 . . . And at Its Regular Session of 1939. Chapel Hill: Orange, 1939.

Raleigh–Wake County Public Schools: A Survey Report. Nashville, Tenn.: George Peabody College for Teachers, Division of Surveys and Field Services, 1969.

Report and Recommendations of the Commission to Study Public Schools and Colleges for Colored People in North Carolina. Raleigh: n.p., n.d.

Report of the Governor's Commission for the Study of Problems in the Education of Negroes in North Carolina. Raleigh: North Carolina State Superintendent of Public Instruction, 1935.

The Salary Schedule and Classification of Schools. Educational Publication 51. Raleigh: North Carolina State Superintendent of Public Instruction, [1922].

Southern Schools: Progress and Problems. Nashville, Tenn.: Southern Education Reporting Service, 1959.

A Study in Curriculum Problems of the North Carolina Public Schools: Suggestions and Practices, 1935. Raleigh: North Carolina State Superintendent of Public Instruction, n.d.

United States Bureau of Education. *Negro Education: A Study of the Private and Higher Schools for Colored People in the United States*. 2 vols. Washington, D.C.: Government Printing Office, 1917.

————. *Survey of Negro Colleges and Universities: Section of Bulletin, 1928, No. 7, Chapter XIV, North Carolina*. Washington, D.C.: Government Printing Office, 1928.

United States Bureau of the Census. *Fourteenth Census of the United States: State Compendium, North Carolina*. Washington, D.C.: Government Printing Office, 1925.

————. *Census of Population: 1950*. Vol. 2, *General and Detailed Characteristics of the Population*. Part 33, *North Carolina*. Washington, D.C.: Government Printing Office, 1952.

————. *Census of Population: 1970*. Vol. 1, *Characteristics of the Population*. Part 35, *North Carolina*. Washington, D.C.: Government Printing Office, 1973.

United States Commission on Civil Rights. *Civil Rights U.S.A.: Public Schools, Southern States, 1962*. Washington, D.C.: Government Printing Office, 1962.

————. *Equal Protection of the Laws in North Carolina: Report of the North Carolina Advisory Committee to the United States Commission on Civil Rights, 1959–1962*. Washington, D.C.: Government Printing Office, 1962.

————. *Public Education: 1964 Staff Report*. Washington, D.C.: Government Printing Office, 1964.

————. *Racial Isolation in the Public Schools: A Report*. Washington, D.C.: Government Printing Office, 1967.

United States Commission on Civil Rights and Richard E. Day. *Civil Rights U.S.A., Public Schools, Southern States, 1963: North Carolina*. [Washington, D.C., 1963].

DIRECTORIES, BIOGRAPHICAL DICTIONARIES, AND GENERAL REFERENCE WORKS

Caldwell, A. B., ed. *History of the American Negro: North Carolina Edition*. Vol. 4. Atlanta: Caldwell, 1921.

Covington, Howard E., Jr., and Marion A. Ellis, eds. *The North Carolina Century: Tar Heels Who Made a Difference*. Charlotte: Levine Museum of the New South, 2002.

Gates, Henry Louis, Jr., and Evelyn Brooks Higginbotham, eds. *African American Lives*. New York: Oxford University Press, 2004.

———. *African American National Biography*. 8 vols. New York: Oxford University Press, 2008.

Jones-Wilson, Faustine C., Charles A. Asbury, Margo Okazawa-Rey, D. Kamili Anderson, Sylvia M. Jacobs, and Michael Fultz. *Encyclopedia of African-American Education*. Westport, Conn.: Greenwood, 1996.

Logan, Rayford W., and Michael R. Winston, eds. *Dictionary of American Negro Biography*. New York: Norton, 1982.

North Carolina Association of Black Lawyers. *Chronicle of Black Lawyers in North Carolina*. Vol. 1, *The Pioneers: 1865–1950*. Durham: North Carolina Association of Black Lawyers, 1981.

Powell, William S., ed. *Dictionary of North Carolina Biography*. 7 vols. Chapel Hill: University of North Carolina Press, 1979–96.

———. *Encyclopedia of North Carolina*. Chapel Hill: University of North Carolina Press, 2006.

Richardson, Clement, ed. *The National Cyclopedia of the Colored Race*. Montgomery, Ala.: National, 1919.

Smith, Margaret Supplee, and Emily Herring Wilson. *North Carolina Women Making History*. Chapel Hill: University of North Carolina Press, 1999.

NEWSPAPERS AND PERIODICALS

Asheville Citizen

Asheville Citizen-Times

Asheville Mountain Xpress

Asheville Southern News

Asheville Urban News

Atlanta Georgian

Atlanta Journal-Constitution

Baltimore Afro-American

Bulletin (North Carolina Congress of Colored Parents and Teachers)

Burlington Daily Times-News

Campus Echo (North Carolina College)

Carolina Alumni Review (University of North Carolina at Chapel Hill)

Charlotte News

Charlotte Observer

Chicago Defender

Chronicle of Higher Education

Concord Tribune

The Crisis (National Association for the Advancement of Colored People)

Durham Carolina Times

Durham Herald-Sun

Durham Morning Herald

Durham Sun

Durham Triangle Tribune

Echo (Lincoln High School, Chapel Hill)

Educate! (Swann Fellowship, Charlotte)

Gastonia Gazette

Goldsboro News

Greensboro Daily News

Greensboro News and Record

Hickory Daily Record

Hickory News Extra

High Point Enterprise

High School Journal (University of North Carolina School of Education)

Hoke County News

Home Mission Monthly (Presbyterian Church in the U.S.A.)

Huffington Post (http://www .huffingtonpost.com/)

Jeanes Supervisors Quarterly

Jet

Kinston Daily Free Press

Kinston Free Press

Life

Los Angeles Times

Lumberton Robesonian

The Nation

NCCU NOW (North Carolina Central University)

Negro History Bulletin

Newton Observer and Catawba News Enterprise

New York Times

Norfolk (Va.) Journal and Guide

North Carolina Architect

North Carolina Education (North Carolina Education Association)

North Carolina High School Bulletin

North Carolina Teachers Record (North Carolina Teachers Association)

Pittsburgh Courier

Popular Government (University of North Carolina, Institute of Government)

Raleigh Carolinian

Raleigh News and Observer

Raleigh Times

Register (North Carolina A&T)

Rocky Mount Evening Telegram

Rocky Mount Sunday Telegram

Roxboro Courier

Salisbury Evening Post

Southern Architect

Southern Education Report (Southern Education Reporting Service)

Southern Patriot (Southern Conference Educational Fund)

Southern School News (Southern Education Reporting Service)

Southern Workman (Hampton Institute)

State School Facts (North Carolina State Superintendent of Public Instruction)

Statesville Daily Record

Statesville Record

Statesville Record and Landmark

Statistical Summary (Southern Education Reporting Service)

Time

Tuskegee Messenger

U.S. News and World Report

Virginia Teachers Bulletin (Virginia Teachers Association)

Washington Bee

Washington (N.C.) Daily News

Washington Post

Wilmington Journal

Wilmington Sunday Star-News

Winston-Salem Journal

Winston-Salem Journal and Sentinel

Yanceyville Caswell Messenger

PAMPHLETS, ADDRESSES, AND CONFERENCE PROCEEDINGS

An Appeal Supported by Facts and Reason. Durham: Durham Negro Business League, n.d.

Atkins, S. G. "President's Address." Speech to the North Carolina Negro Teachers' Association, Goldsboro, November 23, 1927. N.p., [1927].

A Basis for Inter-Racial Cooperation and Development in the South: A Statement by Southern Negroes. Norfolk, Va.: Journal and Guide, [1942].

Bickett, Thomas Walter. Public Papers of Thomas Walter Bickett, Governor of 1917– 1921. Compiled by Santford Martin. Edited by R. B. House. Raleigh: Edwards and Broughton, 1923.

Boykin, James H. Separate . . . but Equal: A Comparative Study of Appropriations for Negro and White Institutions of Higher Learning in North Carolina. Raleigh: Carolinian, 1951.

Broughton, Joseph Melville. Public Addresses, Letters, and Papers of Joseph Melville Broughton, Governor of North Carolina, 1941–1945. Edited by David Leroy Corbitt. Raleigh: Council of State, 1950.

Cherry, Robert Gregg. Public Addresses and Papers of Robert Gregg Cherry, Governor of

North Carolina, 1945–1949. Edited by David Leroy Corbitt. Raleigh: Council of State, 1951.

A Declaration of Principles by Representative Negroes of North Carolina, Raleigh, September 26, 1919. Raleigh: North Carolina Superintendent of Public Instruction, [ca. 1919].

Eleazer, Robert B. *An Adventure in Good Will*. Atlanta: Commission on Interracial Cooperation, n.d.

Gardner, Oliver Max. *Public Papers and Letters of Oliver Max Gardner: Governor of North Carolina, 1929–1933*. Edited by David Leroy Corbitt. Raleigh: Council of State, State of North Carolina, 1937.

Hoey, Clyde Roark. *Public Addresses, Letters, and Papers of Clyde Roark Hoey, Governor of North Carolina, 1937–1941*. Edited by David Leroy Corbitt. Raleigh: Council of State, State of North Carolina, 1944.

McKinney, Theophilus, ed. *Higher Education among Negroes: Addresses Delivered in Celebration of the Twenty-Fifth Anniversary of the Presidency of Dr. Henry Lawrence McCrorey of Johnson C. Smith University*. Charlotte: Johnson C. Smith University, 1932.

McLean, Angus Wilton. *Public Papers and Letters of Angus Wilton McLean, Governor of North Carolina, 1925–29*. Edited by David Leroy Corbitt. Raleigh: Council of State, State of North Carolina, 1931.

Minutes of the Forty-Fourth Annual Session of the North Carolina Negro Teachers' Association. Wilmington, North Carolina, 26, 27, 28 November 1924. North Carolina Collection, Louis R. Wilson Library, University of North Carolina, Chapel Hill.

Minutes of the Forty-Fifth Annual Session of the North Carolina Negro Teachers' Association. Greensboro, North Carolina, 25, 26, 27 November 1925. North Carolina Collection, Louis R. Wilson Library, University of North Carolina, Chapel Hill.

Minutes of the Forty-Sixth Annual Session of the North Carolina Negro Teachers' Association. Salisbury, North Carolina, 24, 25, 26 November 1926. North Carolina Collection, Louis R. Wilson Library, University of North Carolina, Chapel Hill.

Proceedings of the Sixty-Seventh Annual Meeting of the Southern Association of Colleges and Schools. N.p.: Southern Association of Colleges and Schools, 1962.

Public Education in North Carolina. Bulletin prepared for the Sesquicentennial Exposition, Philadelphia, 15 July 1926. Raleigh: State Superintendent of North Carolina, [ca. 1926].

Reid, George W., ed. *A History of N.C. Central University: A Town and Gown Analysis*. Proceedings of a symposium held at North Carolina Central University, 1984. Durham: North Carolina Central University, 1985.

BOOKS AND ARTICLES

Anderson, Eric. *Race and Politics in North Carolina, 1872–1901: The Black Second*. Baton Rouge: Louisiana State University Press, 1981.

Anderson, Eric, and Alfred A. Moss. *Dangerous Donations: Northern Philanthropy and Southern Black Education, 1902–1930*. Columbia: University of Missouri Press, 1999.

Anderson, James D. *The Education of Blacks in the South, 1860–1935*. Chapel Hill: University of North Carolina Press, 1988.

————. "The Historical Development of Black Vocational Education." In *Work, Youth, and Schooling: Historical Perspectives on Vocationalism in American Education*, edited by Harvey Kantor and David Tyack, 180–222. Stanford: Stanford University Press, 1982.

————. "The Jubilee Anniversary of *Brown v. Board of Education*: An Essay Review." *History of Education Quarterly* 44 (2004): 149–57.

Anderson, Jean Bradley. *Durham County: A History of Durham County, North Carolina*. Durham: Duke University Press, 1990.

Aptheker, Herbert, ed. *A Documentary History of the Negro People in the United States, 1933–1945*. Secaucus, N.J.: Citadel, 1974.

Ashenfelter, Orley, William J. Collins, and Albert Yoon. "Evaluating the Role of *Brown v. Board of Education* in School Equalization, Desegregation, and the Income of African Americans." *American Law and Economics Review* 8 (2006): 183–212.

Baker, Lee D. *From Savage to Negro: Anthropology and the Construction of Race, 1896–1954*. Berkeley: University of California Press, 1998.

Baker, Scott. *Paradoxes of Desegregation: African American Struggles for Educational Equity in Charleston, South Carolina, 1926–1972*. Columbia: University of South Carolina Press, 2006.

Balkin, Jack M., ed. *What Brown v. Board of Education Should Have Said: The Nation's Top Legal Experts Rewrite America's Landmark Civil Rights Decision*. New York: New York University Press, 2001.

Barbee, Jennie M. *Historical Sketches of the Raleigh Public Schools, 1876–1941–1942*. Raleigh: Barbee Pupils Association, 1943.

Bartley, Numan V. *The Rise of Massive Resistance: Race and Politics in the South during the 1950s*. Baton Rouge: Louisiana State University Press, 1969.

Bates, Eric. "Remembering the Good." *Southern Exposure*, Summer 1994, 24–29.

Bell, Derrick. *Silent Covenants: Brown v. Board of Education and the Unfulfilled Hopes for Racial Reform*. New York: Oxford University Press, 2004.

Benjamin, Karen. "Suburbanizing Jim Crow: The Impact of School Policy on Residential Segregation in Raleigh." *Journal of Urban History* 38 (2012): 225–46.

Boas, Franz. *The Mind of Primitive Man*. New York: Macmillan, 1911.

Bolton, Charles C. *The Hardest Deal of All: The Battle over School Integration in Mississippi, 1870–1980*. Jackson: University Press of Mississippi, 2005.

Bond, Horace Mann. *The Education of the Negro in the American Social Order*. New York: Prentice-Hall, 1934.

Boyd, Valerie. *Wrapped in Rainbows: The Life of Zora Neale Hurston*. New York: Scribner, 2003.

Boyd, William Kenneth. *The Story of Durham: City of the New South*. Durham: Duke University Press, 1925.

Brawley, Benjamin. *A Short History of the American Negro*. New York: Macmillan, 1917.

Breathett, George. "Black Educators and the United States Supreme Court Decision of May 17, 1954." *Journal of Negro History* 68 (1983): 201–8.

Breen, William J. "The North Carolina Council of Defense during World War I, 1917–1918." *North Carolina Historical Review* 50 (1973): 1–31.

Brown, David E. "A Grudging Acceptance." *Carolina Alumni Review* 91 (May–June 2002): 20–29.

Brown, Hugh Victor. *E-Quality Education in North Carolina among Negroes*. Raleigh: Irving-Swain, 1964.

———. *A History of the Education of Negroes in North Carolina*. Raleigh: Irving-Swain, 1961.

Brown, Leslie. *Upbuilding Black Durham: Gender, Class, and Black Community Development in the Jim Crow South*. Chapel Hill: University of North Carolina Press, 2008.

Brundage, W. Fitzhugh. *The Southern Past: A Clash of Race and Memory*. Cambridge: Belknap Press of Harvard University Press, 2005.

Bullock, Henry Allen. *A History of Negro Education in the South: From 1619 to the Present*. Cambridge: Harvard University Press, 1967.

Burns, Augustus M., III. "Graduate Education for Blacks in North Carolina, 1930–1951." *Journal of Southern History* 46 (1980): 195–218.

Bynum, Thomas L. "'We Must March Forward!': Juanita Jackson and the Origins of the NAACP Youth Movement." *Journal of African American History* 94 (2009): 487–508.

Cannon, Cornelia James. "American Misgivings." *Atlantic Monthly* 129 (February 1922): 145–57.

Card, David, and Alan B. Krueger. "School Quality and Black-White Relative Earnings: A Direct Assessment." *Quarterly Journal of Economics* 107 (1992): 151–200.

———. "School Resources and Student Outcomes: An Overview of the Literature and New Evidence from North and South Carolina." *Journal of Economic Perspectives* 10 (1996): 31–50.

Carter, Robert. *A Matter of Law: A Memoir of Struggle in the Case of Equal Rights*. New York: New Press, 2005.

Cecelski, David. *Along Freedom Road: Hyde County, North Carolina, and the Fate of Black Schools in the South*. Chapel Hill: University of North Carolina Press, 1994.

Chafe, William. *Civilities and Civil Rights: Greensboro, North Carolina, and the Black Struggle for Freedom*. New York: Oxford University Press, 1981.

Chafe, William, Raymond Gavins, and Robert Korstad, eds. *Remembering Jim Crow: African Americans Tell about Life in the Segregated South*. New York: New Press, 2001.

Charron, Katherine Mellen. *Freedom's Teacher: The Life of Septima Clark*. Chapel Hill: University of North Carolina Press, 2009.

Clotfelter, Charles, Helen F. Ladd, and Jacob L. Vigdor. "Classroom-Level Segregation and Resegregation in North Carolina." In *School Resegregation: Must the South Turn Back?*, edited by John Charles Boger and Gary Orfield, 70–86. Chapel Hill: University of North Carolina Press, 2005.

Cobb, James C. *The Brown Decision, Jim Crow, and Southern Identity*. Athens: University of Georgia Press, 2005.

Coleman, James S., Ernest Q. Campbell, Carol J. Hobson, James McPartland, Alexander M. Mood, Frederic D. Weinfeld, and Robert L. York. *Equality of Educational Opportunity*. Washington, D.C.: Government Printing Office, 1966.

Conrad, Cecelia A. "Changes in the Labor Market Status of Black Women, 1960–2000." In *African Americans in the U. S. Economy*, edited by Cecelia A. Conrad, John Whitehead, Patrick Mason, and James Stewart, 157–62. Oxford: Rowman and Littlefield, 2005.

Cooke, Dennis Hargrove. *The White Superintendent and the Negro Schools in North Carolina*. Nashville, Tenn.: George Peabody College for Teachers, 1930.

Covington, Howard E., Jr., and Marion A. Ellis. *Terry Sanford: Politics, Progress, and Outrageous Ambitions*. Durham: Duke University Press, 1999.

Crow, Jeffrey J. "'Fusion, Confusion, and Negroism': Schisms among Negro Republicans in the North Carolina Election of 1896." *North Carolina Historical Review* 53 (1976): 364–84.

Crow, Jeffrey J., Paul D. Escott, and Flora J. Hatley. *A History of African Americans in North Carolina*. Raleigh: North Carolina Division of Archives and History, 1992.

Dagbovie, Pero Gaglo. *The Early Black History Movement, Carter G. Woodson, and Lorenzo Johnston Greene*. Urbana: University of Illinois Press, 2007.

De Schweinitz, Rebecca. *If We Could Change the World: Young People and America's Long Struggle for Racial Equality*. Chapel Hill: University of North Carolina Press, 2009.

Dougherty, Jack. "From Anecdote to Analysis: Oral Interviews and New Scholarship in Educational History." *Journal of American History* 86 (1999): 712–23.

Douglas, Davison M. "The Quest for Freedom in the Post-*Brown* South: Desegregation and White Self-Interest." *Chicago-Kent Law Review* 70 (1994): 689–755.

———. *Reading, Writing, and Race: The Desegregation of the Charlotte Schools*. Chapel Hill: University of North Carolina Press, 1995.

Drewry, Henry N., and Humphrey Doermann, in collaboration with Susan H. Anderson. *Stand and Prosper: Private Black Colleges and Their Students*. Princeton: Princeton University Press, 2001.

Du Bois, W. E. B. "Does the Negro Need Separate Schools?" *Journal of Negro Education* 4 (1935): 328–35.

———. "The Upbuilding of Black Durham." *World's Work* 23 (1912): 334–38.

Dudziak, Mary L. *Cold War Civil Rights: Race and the Image of American Democracy*. Princeton: Princeton University Press, 2000.

Eaton, Hubert A. *"Every Man Should Try."* Wilmington, N.C.: Bonaparte, 1984.

Edmonds, Helen G. *Black Faces in High Places: Negroes in Government*. New York: Harcourt Brace Jovanovich, 1971.

———. *The Negro and Fusion Politics in North Carolina, 1894–1901*. Chapel Hill: University of North Carolina Press, 1951.

Egerton, John. *Speak Now against the Day: The Generation before the Civil Rights Movement in the South*. New York: Knopf, 1994.

Eleazer, R. B. "School Books and Racial Antagonism." *High School Journal* 18 (1935): 197–99.

Ellwood, Charles A. *An Introduction to Social Psychology*. New York: Appleton, 1917.

Embree, Edwin R., and Julia Waxman. *Investment in People: The Story of the Julius Rosenwald Fund*. New York: Harper, 1949.

Eubanks, Georgann. "Women Writers of Hayti." *Our State* 78 (2010): 72–74, 76, 78–79.

Faggett, Harry L. "The Shepard Tradition." *Journal of Negro Education* 18 (1949): 484–88.

Fairclough, Adam. *Better Day Coming: Blacks and Equality, 1890–2000*. New York: Viking, 2001.

———. *A Class of Their Own: Black Teachers in the Segregated South*. Cambridge: Harvard University Press, 2007.

———. *Teaching Equality: Black Schools in the Age of Jim Crow*. Mercer University Lamar Memorial Lectures 43. Athens: University of Georgia Press, 2001.

Fisher, Ada Lois Sipuel. *A Matter of Black and White: The Autobiography of Ada Lois Sipuel Fisher*. Norman: University of Oklahoma Press, 1996.

Foreman, Clark. *Environmental Factors in Negro Elementary Education*. New York: Norton, 1932.

Fosdick, Raymond B. *Adventure in Giving: The Story of the General Education Board*. New York: Harper and Row, 1962.

Franklin, John Hope, and Alfred A. Moss. *From Slavery to Freedom: A History of African Americans*. 8th ed. New York: Knopf, 2001.

Frazier, E. Franklin. *Black Bourgeoisie*. 1957; New York: Free Press, 1997.

———. "Durham: Capital of the Black Middle Class." In *The New Negro: An Interpretation*, edited by Alain Locke, 333–40. 1925; New York: Johnson, 1968.

Freeze, Gary. *The Catawbans*. Vol. 2, *Pioneers in Progress*. Newton, N.C.: Catawba County Historical Association, 2002.

Fultz, Michael. "African-American Teachers in the South, 1890–1940: Growth, Feminization, and Salary Discrimination." *Teachers College Record* 96 (1995): 544–68.

———. "African American Teachers in the South, 1890–1940: Powerlessness and the Ironies of Expectations and Protest." *History of Education Quarterly* 35 (1995): 401–22.

———. "The Displacement of Black Educators Post-*Brown*: An Overview and Analysis." *History of Education Quarterly* 44 (2004): 11–45.

Gaillard, Frye. *The Dream Long Deferred*. Chapel Hill: University of North Carolina Press, 1988.

Gaines, Kevin K. *Uplifting the Race: Black Leadership, Politics, and Culture in the Twentieth Century*. Chapel Hill: University of North Carolina Press, 1996.

Gatewood, Willard B., Jr. *Eugene Clyde Brooks: Educator and Public Servant*. Durham: Duke University Press, 1960.

Gavins, Raymond. "The NAACP in North Carolina during the Age of Segregation." In *New Directions in Civil Rights Studies*, edited by Armstead L. Robinson and Patricia Sullivan, 105–25. Charlottesville: University Press of Virginia, 1991.

———. *The Perils and Prospects of Southern Black Leadership: Gordon Blaine Hancock, 1884–1970*. Durham: Duke University Press, 1977.

———. "Within the Shadow of Jim Crow: Black Struggles for Education and Liberation in North Carolina." In *From the Grassroots to the Supreme Court: Brown v. Board of Education and American Democracy*, edited by Peter Lau, 68–87. Durham: Duke University Press, 2004.

Gershenhorn, Jerry. "A Courageous Voice for Black Freedom: Louis Austin and the *Carolina Times* in Depression-Era North Carolina." *North Carolina Historical Review* 87 (2010): 57–92.

———. "*Hocutt v. Wilson* and Race Relations in Durham, North Carolina, during the 1930s." *North Carolina Historical Review* 78 (2001): 275–308.

———. "Stalling Integration: The Ruse, Rise, and Demise of North Carolina College's Doctoral Program in Education, 1951–1962." *North Carolina Historical Review* 82 (2005): 156–92.

Gibbs, Warmoth T. *History of the North Carolina Agricultural and Technical College: Greensboro, North Carolina*. Dubuque, Iowa: W. C. Brown, 1966.

Gilmore, Glenda Elizabeth. *Defying Dixie: The Radical Roots of Civil Rights, 1919–1950*. New York: Norton, 2008.

———. *Gender and Jim Crow: Women and the Politics of White Supremacy in North Carolina, 1896–1920*. Chapel Hill: University of North Carolina Press, 1996.

Godwin, John L. *Black Wilmington and the North Carolina Way: Portrait of a Community in the Era of Civil Rights Protest*. Lanham, Md.: University Press of America, 2000.

Goggin, Jacqueline. *Carter G. Woodson: A Life in Black History*. Baton Rouge: Louisiana State University Press, 1993.

Goluboff, Risa. *The Lost Promise of Civil Rights*. Cambridge: Harvard University Press, 2007.

Grant, Gerald. *Hope and Despair in the American City: Why There Are No Bad Schools in Raleigh*. Cambridge: Harvard University Press, 2009.

Greenberg, Jack. *Crusaders in the Courts: How a Dedicated Band of Lawyers Fought for the Civil Rights Revolution*. New York: Basic Books, 1994.

Greene, Christina. "'The New Negro Ain't Scared No More!': Black Women's Activism in North Carolina and the Meaning of *Brown*." In *From the Grassroots to the Supreme Court: Brown v. Board of Education and American Democracy*, edited by Peter Lau, 245–69. Durham: Duke University Press, 2004.

———. *Our Separate Ways: Women and the Black Freedom Movement in Durham, North Carolina*. Chapel Hill: University of North Carolina Press, 2005.

Greene, Lorenzo. *Selling Black History for Carter G. Woodson: A Diary, 1930–1933*. Edited by Arvarh Strickland. Columbia: University of Missouri Press, 1996.

Greenwood, Janette Thomas. *Bittersweet Legacy: The Black and White Better Classes in Charlotte, 1850–1910*. Chapel Hill: University of North Carolina Press, 1994.

Grimshaw, William H. *Official History of Freemasonry among the Colored People in North America*. 1903; New York: Negro Universities Press, 1969.

Grossman, James. *Land of Hope: Chicago, Black Southerners, and the Great Migration*. Chicago: University of Chicago Press, 1989.

Grundy, Pamela. *Learning to Win: Sports, Education, and Social Change in Twentieth-Century North Carolina*. Chapel Hill: University of North Carolina Press, 2001.

Haley, John. *Charles N. Hunter and Race Relations in North Carolina*. Chapel Hill: University of North Carolina Press, 1987.

Hall, Jacquelyn Dowd. "The Long Civil Rights Movement and the Political Uses of the Past." *Journal of American History* 91 (2005): 1233–63.

———. *Revolt against Chivalry: Jessie Daniel Ames and the Campaign against Lynching*. Rev. ed. New York: Columbia University Press, 1993.

Hall, Jacquelyn Dowd, James Leloudis, Robert Korstad, Mary Murphy, Lu Ann Jones, and Christopher B. Daly. *Like a Family: The Making of a Southern Cotton Mill World*. Chapel Hill: University of North Carolina Press, 1987.

Hanchett, Thomas W. "The Rosenwald Schools and Black Education in North Carolina." *North Carolina Historical Review* 65 (1988): 388–427.

Harlan, Louis R. *Separate and Unequal: Public School Campaigns and Racism in the Southern Seaboard States, 1901–1915*. Chapel Hill: University of North Carolina Press, 1958.

Harris, Nelson H. "The Present Status of Higher Education among Negroes in North

Carolina." In *Proceedings of the Fourth Meeting of the Association of Business Officers in Schools for Negroes*, 28–45. 1942.

———. "Publicly-Supported Negro Higher Institutions of Learning in North Carolina." *Journal of Negro Education* 31 (1962): 284–92.

Hart, Joseph K. "The Negro Builds for Himself." *Survey*, September 1924, 563–67, 596.

Herring, Kate M. "The Negro and War Savings in North Carolina." *South Atlantic Quarterly* 18 (1919): 36–40.

Herring, Lucy S. *Strangers No More: Memoirs by Lucy S. Herring*. New York: Carlton, 1983.

"Hillside History Book." *Hillside Chronicle* 49, no. 7 (June 1979) (special issue). North Carolina Collection, Louis R. Wilson Library, University of North Carolina, Chapel Hill.

Hochschild, Jennifer L., and Nathan Scovronick. *The American Dream and the Public Schools*. Oxford: Oxford University Press, 2003.

Hoffschwelle, Mary S. *The Rosenwald Schools of the American South*. Gainesville: University Press of Florida, 2006.

Holmes, Dwight Oliver Wendell. *The Evolution of the Negro College*. New York: Teachers College, Columbia University, 1934.

Horne, Frank S. "'Dog House' Education." *Journal of Negro Education* 5 (1936): 359–68.

Hornsby-Gutting, Angela. *Black Manhood and Community Building in North Carolina, 1900–1930*. Gainesville: University Press of Florida, 2009.

Jackson, Giles B., and D. Webster Davis. *The Industrial History of the Negro Race of the United States*. Richmond: Virginia Press, 1908.

Jackson, Walter A. *Gunnar Myrdal and America's Conscience: Social Engineering and Racial Liberalism, 1938–1987*. Chapel Hill: University of North Carolina Press, 1990.

Jacoway, Elizabeth. *Turn away Thy Son: Little Rock, the Crisis That Shocked the Nation*. New York: Free Press, 2007.

Janken, Kenneth R. *Rayford W. Logan and the Dilemma of the African American Intellectual*. Amherst: University of Massachusetts Press, 1993.

———. *White: The Biography of Walter White, Mr. NAACP*. New York: New Press, 2003.

Jeffrey, Julie Roy. *Education for Children of the Poor: A Study of the Origins and Implementation of the Elementary and Secondary Education Act of 1965*. Columbus: Ohio State University Press, 1978.

Johnson, Charles S. *The Negro in American Civilization: A Study of Negro Life and Race Relations in the Light of Social Research*. New York: Holt, 1930.

Johnson, Edward A. *A School History of the Negro Race in America from 1619 to 1890, with a Short Introduction as to the Origin of the Race, Also a Short Sketch of Liberia*. Rev. ed. Raleigh: Edwards and Broughton, 1891.

Jones, Beverly. "James Edward Shepard, the Founder." In *A History of N.C. Central University: A Town and Gown Analysis*, ed. George W. Reid, 11–46. 1984; Durham: North Carolina Central University, 1985.

Jones, Lance G. E. *The Jeanes Teacher in the United States, 1908–1933: An Account of Twenty-Five Years' Experience in the Supervision of Negro Rural Schools*. Chapel Hill: University of North Carolina Press, 1937.

Jones-Wilson, Faustine C., and Erma Glasco Davis. *Paul Laurence Dunbar High School of Little Rock, Arkansas*. Virginia Beach, Va.: Donning, 2003.

Jordan, William G. *Black Newspapers and America's War for Democracy, 1914–1920.* Chapel Hill: University of North Carolina Press, 2001.

Kaestle, Carl. *Pillars of the Republic: Common Schools and American Society, 1780–1860.* New York: Hill and Wang, 1983.

Kantor, Harvey. "Vocationalism in American Education: The Economic and Political Context, 1880–1930." In *Work, Youth, and Schooling: Historical Perspectives on Vocationalism in American Education,* edited by Harvey Kantor and David B. Tyack, 14–44. Stanford: Stanford University Press, 1982.

Kantor, Harvey, and David B. Tyack. "Introduction: Historical Perspectives on Vocationalism in American Education." In *Work, Youth, and Schooling: Historical Perspectives on Vocationalism in American Education,* edited by Harvey Kantor and David B. Tyack, 1–13. Stanford: Stanford University Press, 1982.

Kantrowitz, Stephen. "'Intended for the Better Government of Man': The Political History of African American Freemasonry in the Era of Emancipation." *Journal of American History* 96 (2010): 1001–26.

Katz, Michael. *The Price of Citizenship: Redefining the American Welfare State.* New York: Holt, 2001.

Kearns, Kathleen, and Michael J. Dayton. *Capital Lawyers: A Legacy of Leadership.* Birmingham, Ala.: Association, 2004.

Kessler-Harris, Alice. *Out to Work: A History of Wage-Earning Women in the United States.* 20th anniv. ed. New York: Oxford University Press, 2003.

Killen, Melanie, David S. Crystal, and Martin Ruck. "The Social Developmental Benefits of Intergroup Contact among Children and Adolescents." In *Lessons in Integration: Realizing the Promise of Racial Diversity in American Schools,* edited by Erica Frankenberg and Gary Orfield, 57–73. Charlottesville: University of Virginia Press, 2007.

King, Kenneth. *Pan-Africanism and Education: A Study of Race Philanthropy and Education in the Southern United States of America and East Africa.* Oxford: Oxford University Press, 1971.

Kirk, John A. "The NAACP Campaign for Teachers' Salary Equalization: African American Women Educators and the Early Civil Rights Struggle." *Journal of African American History* 94 (2009): 529–52.

Klarman, Michael. "How *Brown* Changed Race Relations: The Backlash Thesis." *Journal of American History* 81 (1994): 81–118.

Kliebard, Herbert M. *Schooled to Work: Vocationalism and the American Curriculum, 1876–1946.* New York: Teachers College Press, 1999.

Kluger, Richard. *Simple Justice: The History of Brown v. Board of Education and Black America's Struggle for Equality.* New York: Vintage, 1975.

Kornweibel, Theodore, Jr. *"Investigate Everything": Federal Efforts to Compel Black Loyalty during World War I.* Bloomington: Indiana University Press, 2002.

Korstad, Robert. *Civil Rights Unionism: Tobacco Workers and the Struggle for Democracy in the Mid-Twentieth Century South.* Chapel Hill: University of North Carolina Press, 2003.

Korstad, Robert, and James Leloudis. *To Right These Wrongs: The North Carolina Fund and the Battle to End Poverty and Inequality in 1960s America.* Chapel Hill: University of North Carolina Press, 2010.

Korstad, Robert, and Nelson Lichtenstein. "Opportunities Found and Lost: Labor,

Radicals, and the Early Civil Rights Movement." *Journal of American History* 75 (1988): 786–811.

Kousser, J. Morgan. *The Shaping of Southern Politics: Suffrage Restriction and the Establishment of the One-Party South, 1880–1910.* New Haven: Yale University Press, 1974.

Lassiter, Matthew D. *The Silent Majority: Suburban Politics in the Sunbelt South.* Princeton: Princeton University Press, 2006.

Lassiter, Matthew D., and Andrew B. Lewis. "Massive Resistance Revisited: Virginia's White Moderates and the Byrd Organization." In *The Moderates' Dilemma: Massive Resistance to School Desegregation in Virginia,* edited by Matthew D. Lassiter and Andrew B. Lewis, 1–21. Charlottesville: University Press of Virginia, 1998.

Lau, Peter F. *Democracy Rising: South Carolina and the Fight for Black Equality since 1865.* Lexington: University Press of Kentucky, 2006.

Lawson, Steven F. *Black Ballots: Voting Rights in the South, 1944–1969.* Lanham, Md.: Lexington Books, 1999.

Leloudis, James L. *Schooling the New South: Pedagogy, Self, and Society in North Carolina, 1880–1920.* Chapel Hill: University of North Carolina Press, 1996.

Lemmon, Sarah McCulloh. *North Carolina's Role in the First World War.* Raleigh: North Carolina Department of Cultural Resources, Division of Archives and History, 1975.

Leuchtenburg, William E. *The Perils of Prosperity, 1914–1932.* 2nd ed. Chicago: University of Chicago Press, 1993.

Lewis, Earl. *In Their Own Interests: Race, Class, and Power in Twentieth-Century Norfolk, Virginia.* Berkeley: University of California Press, 1991.

Link, William A. *William Friday: Power, Purpose, and American Higher Education.* Chapel Hill: University of North Carolina Press, 1995.

Locke, Alain, ed. *The New Negro: An Interpretation.* 1925; New York: Johnson Reprint, 1968.

Logan, Rayford, ed. *What the Negro Wants.* Chapel Hill: University of North Carolina Press, 1944.

Long, Hollis Moody. *Public Secondary Education for Negroes in North Carolina.* New York: Teachers College, Columbia University, 1932.

Lovell, John, Jr. "Youth Programs of Negro Improvement Group." *Journal of Negro Education* 9 (1940): 379–87.

Lowery, Malinda Maynor. *Lumbee Indians in the Jim Crow South: Race, Identity, and the Making of a Nation.* Chapel Hill: University of North Carolina Press, 2010.

Luebke, Paul. *Tar Heel Politics 2000.* Chapel Hill: University of North Carolina Press, 1998.

Lutz, Catherine. *Homefront: A Military City and the American Twentieth Century.* Boston: Beacon, 2001.

Mabry, William Alexander. *The Negro in North Carolina Politics since Reconstruction.* New York: AMS, 1940.

Margo, Robert A. *Race and Schooling in the South, 1880–1950: An Economic History.* Chicago: University of Chicago Press, 1990.

Marshall, T. H. *Citizenship and Social Class and Other Essays.* Cambridge: Cambridge University Press, 1950.

Martin, Waldo E., Jr., ed. *Brown v. Board of Education: A Brief History with Documents.* Boston: Bedford/St. Martin's, 1998.

McEntarfer, Heather Killelea. "Catching Hell: The Joe Holt Integration Story." *Terrain.
org.* 2008. http://www.terrain.org/essays/22/mcentarfer.htm.

McKee, James B. *Sociology and the Race Problem: The Failure of a Perspective.* Urbana:
University of Illinois Press, 1993.

McNeil, Genna Rae. *Groundwork: Charles Hamilton Houston and the Struggle for Civil
Rights.* Philadelphia: University of Pennsylvania Press, 1983.

Meier, August. *Negro Thought in America, 1880–1915: Racial Ideologies in the Age of
Booker T. Washington.* Ann Arbor: University of Michigan Press, 1963.

Meier, August, and Elliott Rudwick. *Along the Color Line: Explorations in the Black
Experience.* Urbana: University of Illinois Press, 1976.

———. *Black History and the Historical Profession, 1915–1980.* Urbana: University of
Illinois Press, 1986.

Mickelson, Roslyn Arlin. "Subverting *Swann*: First- and Second-Generation
Segregation in the Charlotte-Mecklenburg Schools." *American Educational Research
Journal* 38 (2001): 215–52.

Miller, Carroll L., and Howard D. Gregg. "The Teaching Staff of the Negro Elementary
School." *Journal of Negro Education* 1 (1932): 220–23.

Moody, Anne. *Coming of Age in Mississippi.* New York: Dial, 1968.

Moss, Hilary J. *Schooling Citizens: The Struggle for African American Education in
Antebellum America.* Chicago: University of Chicago Press, 2009.

Muraskin, William A. *Middle-Class Blacks in a White Society: Prince Hall Freemasonry in
America.* Berkeley: University of California Press, 1975.

Murray, Pauli. *Song in a Weary Throat: An American Pilgrimage.* New York: Harper and
Row, 1987.

———, ed. *States' Laws on Race and Color.* 1951; Athens: University of Georgia Press,
1997.

Murray, Percy. *History of the North Carolina Teachers Association.* Washington, D.C.:
National Education Association, 1984.

Myrdal, Gunnar, with Richard Sterner and Arnold Rose. *An American Dilemma: The
Negro Problem and Modern Democracy.* New York: Harper, 1944.

Newbold, Nathan Carter. "Common Schools for Negroes in the South." *Annals of the
American Academy of Political and Social Science* 140 (1928): 209–23.

———. "Conference for Negro Education in Raleigh." *Journal of Social Forces* 1 (1923):
145–47.

———. "Equalization of Teachers' Salaries in North Carolina." *Opportunity* 22 (1944):
164–65.

———. "Financial History of State Institutions of Higher Education for Negroes in
North Carolina." In *Proceedings of the Fourth Annual Meeting of the Association of
Business Officers in Schools for Negroes*, 17–27. 1942.

———. "More Money for and More Emphasis upon Negro Education—Not
Reorganization and Redirection." *Journal of Negro Education* 5 (1936): 502–7.

———. "North Carolina's Adventure in Good-Will." *High School Journal* 13 (1930):
119–23.

———. "The Public Education of Negroes and the Current Depression." *Journal of
Negro Education* 2 (1933): 5–15.

———. "Some Achievements in the Equalization of Educational Opportunities in
North Carolina." *Educational Forum* 9 (1945): 451–66.

————, ed. *Five North Carolina Negro Educators*. Chapel Hill: University of North Carolina Press, 1939.

Noble, M. C. S. *A History of the Public Schools of North Carolina*. Chapel Hill: University of North Carolina Press, 1930.

Norrell, Robert. *Up from History: The Life of Booker T. Washington*. Cambridge: Harvard University Press, 2009.

Ogletree, Charles. *All Deliberate Speed: Reflections on the First Half-Century of Brown v. Board of Education*. New York: Norton, 2004.

Orfield, Gary. "Lessons Forgotten." In *Lessons in Integration: Realizing the Promise of Racial Diversity in American Schools*, edited by Erica Frankenberg and Gary Orfield, 1–6. Charlottesville: University of Virginia Press, 2007.

————. *The Reconstruction of Southern Education: The Schools and the 1964 Civil Rights Act*. New York: Wiley-Interscience, 1969.

————. "The Southern Dilemma: Losing *Brown*, Fearing *Plessy*." In *School Resegregation: Must the South Turn Back?*, edited by John Charles Boger and Gary Orfield, 1–25. Chapel Hill: University of North Carolina Press, 2005.

Palmer, Edward N. "Negro Secret Societies." *Social Forces* 23 (1944): 207–12.

Patterson, James T. *Brown v. Board of Education: A Civil Rights Milestone and Its Troubled Legacy*. Oxford: Oxford University Press, 2001.

Pearson, C. Chilton. "Race Relations in North Carolina: A Field Study of Moderate Opinion." *South Atlantic Quarterly* 23 (1924): 1–9.

Peebles-Wilkins, Wilma. *Look to the Rainbow: Early African American Recollections*. Bloomington, Ind.: Xlibris, 2010.

Peltason, Jack Walter. *Fifty-Eight Lonely Men: Southern Federal Judges and School Desegregation*. Urbana: University of Illinois Press, 1971.

Perry, Thelma D. *History of the American Teachers Association*. Washington, D.C.: National Education Association, 1975.

Pope, Oliver R. *Chalk Dust*. New York: Pageant, 1967.

Proctor, A. M. "N. C. Newbold, '95, and Negro Education." *Trinity Alumni Register* 10 (1924): 158–60.

Rampersad, Arnold. *The Life of Langston Hughes*. Vol. 1, *1902–1941: I, Too, Sing America*. New York: Oxford University Press, 1986.

————. *The Life of Langston Hughes*. Vol. 2, *1941–1967: I Dream a World*. New York: Oxford University Press, 1988.

Ramsey, Sonya. *Reading, Writing, and Segregation: A Century of Black Women Teachers in Nashville*. Urbana: University of Illinois Press, 2008.

Raper, Arthur F., and Ira DeA. Reid. *Sharecroppers All*. Chapel Hill: University of North Carolina Press, 1941.

Redcay, Edward E. *County Training Schools and Public Secondary Education for Negroes in the South*. Washington, D.C.: Slater Fund, 1935.

Reed, Adolph, Jr. "Romancing Jim Crow." *Village Voice*, 16 April 1996, 24–29.

Reese, William. *The Origins of the American High School*. New Haven: Yale University Press, 1995.

Reuben, Julie A. "Beyond Politics: Community Civics and the Redefinition of Citizenship in the Progressive Era." *History of Education Quarterly* 37 (1997): 399–420.

Sanders, Wiley B. *Negro Child Welfare in North Carolina: A Rosenwald Study*. Chapel Hill: University of North Carolina Press, 1933.

Savitt, Todd L. "The Education of Black Physicians at Shaw University, 1882–1918." In *Black Americans in North Carolina and the South*, edited by Jeffrey J. Crow and Flora J. Hatley, 160–88. Chapel Hill: University of North Carolina Press, 1984.

Schulman, Bruce J. *From Cotton Belt to Sunbelt: Federal Policy, Economic Development, and the Transformation of the South, 1938–1980*. Durham: Duke University Press, 1994.

Scott, Daryl Michael. *Contempt and Pity: Social Policy and the Image of the Damaged Black Psyche, 1880–1996*. Chapel Hill: University of North Carolina Press, 1997.

Shabazz, Amilcar. *Advancing Democracy: African Americans and the Struggle for Access and Equity in Higher Education in Texas*. Chapel Hill: University of North Carolina Press, 2004.

Sharpe, Stella Gentry. *Tobe*. Chapel Hill: University of North Carolina Press, 1939.

Shaw, Stephanie. *What a Woman Ought to Be and to Do: Black Professional Women Workers and the Jim Crow Era*. Chicago: University of Chicago Press, 1996.

Shircliffe, Barbara. "Rethinking *Turner v. Keefe*: The Parallel Mobilization of African-American and White Teachers in Tampa, Florida, 1936–1946." *History of Education Quarterly* 52 (2012): 99–136.

———. "'We Got the Best of That World': A Case for the Study of Nostalgia in the Oral History of School Segregation." *Oral History Review* 28 (2001): 59–84.

Shokaraii, Nina. "Free at Last: Black America Signs Up for School Choice." *Policy Review* 80 (1996): 20–26.

Simmons-Henry, Linda, and Linda Harris Edmisten. *Culture Town: Life in Raleigh's African American Communities*. Raleigh: Raleigh Historic Districts Commission, 1993.

Singal, Daniel. *The War Within: From Victorianism to Modernism in the South, 1919–1945*. Chapel Hill: University of North Carolina Press, 1982.

Smith, J. Douglas. *Managing White Supremacy: Race, Politics, and Citizenship in Jim Crow Virginia*. Chapel Hill: University of North Carolina Press, 2002.

Smith, Rogers M. *Civic Ideals: Conflicting Visions of Citizenship in U. S. History*. New Haven: Yale University Press, 1997.

Smith, S. L. *Builders of Goodwill: The Story of the State Agents of Negro Education in the South, 1910 to 1950*. Nashville: Tennessee Book, 1950.

Snider, William D. *Light on the Hill: A History of the University of North Carolina at Chapel Hill*. Chapel Hill: University of North Carolina Press, 1992.

Soaring on the Legacy: A Concise History of North Carolina Central University, 1910–2010. Durham: North Carolina Central University, 2010.

Sosna, Morton. *In Search of the Silent South: Southern Liberals and the Race Issue*. New York: Columbia University Press, 1977.

Span, Christopher M. *From Cotton Field to Schoolhouse: African American Education in Mississippi, 1862–1875*. Chapel Hill: University of North Carolina Press, 2009.

Stephenson, Gilbert. "The War Savings Campaign in 1918." *North Carolina Historical Review* 1 (1924): 26–34.

Sugrue, Thomas. *Sweet Land of Liberty: The Forgotten Struggle for Civil Rights in the North*. New York: Random House, 2008.

Sullivan, Patricia. *Days of Hope: Race and Democracy in the New Deal Era*. Chapel Hill: University of North Carolina Press, 1996.

———. *Lift Every Voice: The NAACP and the Making of the Civil Rights Movement*. New York: New Press, 2009.

————. "Prelude to *Brown*: Education and the Struggle for Racial Justice during the NAACP's Formative Decades, 1909-1934." In *From the Grassroots to the Supreme Court: Brown v. Board of Education and American Democracy*, edited by Peter Lau, 154-72. Durham: Duke University Press, 2004.

Superfine, Benjamin Michael. *The Courts and Standards-Based Education Reform*. New York: Oxford University Press, 2008.

Tarpley, John A. "Some Aspects of Education among Negroes in North Carolina." *Quarterly Review of Higher Education among Negroes* 6 (1938): 68-72.

Taylor, Gregory S. *The History of the North Carolina Communist Party*. Columbia: University of South Carolina Press, 2009.

Thomas, Karen Kruse. *Deluxe Jim Crow: Civil Rights and American Health Policy, 1935-1954*. Athens: University of Georgia Press, 2011.

————. "Dr. Jim Crow: The University of North Carolina, the Regional Medical School for Negroes, and the Desegregation of Southern Medical Education, 1945-1960." *Journal of African American History* 88 (2003): 223-44.

Thompson, Charles H. "Court Action the Only Reasonable Alternative to Remedy Immediate Abuses of the Negro Separate School." *Journal of Negro Education* 4 (1935): 419-34.

————. "Why Negroes Are Opposed to Segregated Regional Schools." *Journal of Negro Education* 18 (1949): 1-8.

Thorndike, Edward L. *Educational Psychology*. Vol. 1, *The Original Nature of Man*. New York: Teachers College, Columbia University, 1921.

Thorpe, Earl E. *A Concise History of North Carolina Central University*. Durham: Harrington, 1984.

Tindall, George Brown. *The Emergence of the New South, 1913-1945*. Baton Rouge: Louisiana State University Press, 1967.

Traub, James. "Can Separate Be Equal?: New Answers to an Old Question about Race and Schools." *Harper's Magazine*, June 1994, 36-47.

Tushnet, Mark V. *Making Civil Rights Law: Thurgood Marshall and the Supreme Court, 1936-1961*. New York: Oxford University Press, 1994.

————. *The NAACP's Legal Strategy against Segregated Education, 1925-1950*. Chapel Hill: University of North Carolina Press, 1987.

Vander Zanden, James W. *American Minority Relations: The Sociology of Race and Ethnic Groups*. New York: Ronald, 1966.

Wadelington, Charles W., and Richard F. Knapp. *Charlotte Hawkins Brown and Palmer Memorial Institute*. Chapel Hill: University of North Carolina Press, 1999.

Wager, Paul W. *North Carolina: The State and Its Government*. New York: Oxford, 1947.

Walker, Vanessa Siddle. *Hello Professor: A Black Principal and Professional Leadership in the Segregated South*. Chapel Hill: University of North Carolina Press, 2009.

————. *Their Highest Potential: An African American School Community in the Segregated South*. Chapel Hill: University of North Carolina Press, 1996.

Wallenstein, Peter. "Higher Education and the Civil Rights Movement: Desegregating the University of North Carolina." In *Warm Ashes: Issues in Southern History at the Dawn of the Twenty-First Century*, edited by Winfred B. Moore Jr., Kyle S. Sinisi, and David H. White Jr., 280-300. Columbia: University of South Carolina Press, 2003.

Ware, Gilbert. "*Hocutt*: Genesis of *Brown*." *Journal of Negro Education* 52 (1983): 227-33.

————. *William Hastie: Grace under Pressure*. New York: Oxford University Press, 1984.

Washington, Booker T. *Booker T. Washington Papers*. Edited by Louis R. Harlan. 14 vols. Urbana: University of Illinois Press, 1972–89.

———. *My Larger Education: Being Chapters from My Experience*. New York: Doubleday, Page, 1911.

———. *Up from Slavery: An Autobiography*. Garden City, N.Y.: Doubleday, 1901.

Watters, Pat. "Charlotte, North Carolina: 'A Little Child Shall Lead Them.'" In *The South and Her Children: School Desegregation, 1970–1971*. Atlanta: Southern Regional Council, 1971.

Weare, Walter B. *Black Business in the New South: A Social History of the North Carolina Mutual Life Insurance Company*. 1973; Durham: Duke University Press, 1993.

———. "Charles Clinton Spaulding: Middle-Class Leadership in the Age of Segregation." In *Black Leaders of the Twentieth Century*, edited by John Hope Franklin and August Meier, 166–90. Urbana: University of Illinois Press, 1982.

Weinberg, Meyer. *A Chance to Learn: The History of Race and Education in the United States*. Cambridge: Cambridge University Press, 1977.

Wells, Amy Stuart, Jennifer Jellison Holme, Anita Tijerina Revilla, and Awo Korantemaa Atanda. *Both Sides Now: The Story of School Desegregation's Graduates*. Berkeley: University of California Press, 2009.

White, Walter. *A Man Called White: The Autobiography of Walter White*. New York: Viking, 1948.

Whitted, J. A. *A History of the Negro Baptists in North Carolina*. Raleigh: Edwards and Broughton, 1908.

Williams, Heather. *Self-Taught: African American Education in Slavery and Freedom*. Chapel Hill: University of North Carolina Press, 2005.

Williams, Juan. *Thurgood Marshall: American Revolutionary*. New York: Three Rivers, 1998.

Wilson, Emily Herring. *Hope and Dignity: Older Black Women of the South*. Philadelphia: Temple University Press, 1983.

Wolters, Raymond. *The New Negro on Campus: Black College Rebellions of the 1920s*. Princeton: Princeton University Press, 1975.

Woodruff, Nan Elizabeth. "African American Struggles for Citizenship in the Arkansas and Mississippi Deltas in the Age of Jim Crow." *Radical History Review* 55 (1993): 33–51.

Woodson, Carter G. *The Mis-Education of the Negro*. 1933; New York: AMS, 1977.

———. *Negro Makers of History*. Washington, D.C.: Associated, 1928.

———. "Ten Years of Collecting and Publishing the Records of the Negro." *Journal of Negro History* 10 (1925): 598–605.

Woodward, C. Vann. *The Strange Career of Jim Crow*. New York: Oxford University Press, 1957.

———. *Thinking Back: The Perils of Writing History*. Baton Rouge: Louisiana State University Press, 1986.

Wright, Arthur D. *The Negro Rural School Fund*. Washington, D.C.: Negro Rural School Fund, 1933.

Wright, Gavin. *Old South, New South: Revolutions in the Southern Economy since the Civil War*. Baton Rouge: Louisiana State University Press, 1986.

Zimmerman, Jonathan. "*Brown*-ing the American Textbook: History, Psychology, and the Origins of Modern Multiculturalism." *History of Education Quarterly* 44 (2004): 46–69.

———. *Whose America?: Culture Wars in the Public Schools*. Cambridge: Harvard University Press, 2002.

DISSERTATIONS, THESES, AND PAPERS

Batchelor, John. "Save Our Schools: Dallas Herring and the Governor's Special Advisory Committee on Education." Master's thesis, University of North Carolina at Greensboro, 1983.

Boggs, Wade Hamilton, III. "State Supported Higher Education for Blacks in North Carolina, 1877–1945." Ph.D. diss., Duke University, 1972.

Brinton, Hugh Penn. "The Negro in Durham: A Study of Adjustment to Town Life." Ph.D. diss., University of North Carolina at Chapel Hill, 1930.

Burns, Augustus M., III. "North Carolina and the Negro Dilemma, 1930–1950." Ph.D. diss., University of North Carolina at Chapel Hill, 1969.

Cleary, Calista K. "The Past Is Present: Historical Representation at the Sesquicentennial International Exposition." Ph.D. diss., University of Pennsylvania, 1999.

Clement, Rufus Early. "A History of Negro Education in North Carolina, 1865–1928." Ph.D. diss., Northwestern University, 1930.

Jones, Lu Ann. "Re-Visioning the Countryside: Southern Women, Rural Reform, and the Farm Economy in the Twentieth Century." Ph.D. diss., University of North Carolina at Chapel Hill, 1996.

Joyner, Rita. "Adkin High School and the Relationships of Segregated Education." Ph.D. diss., University of North Carolina at Chapel Hill, 2009.

Lamanna, Richard A. "The Negro Public School Teacher and Desegregation: A Survey of Negro Teachers in North Carolina." Ph.D. diss., University of North Carolina at Chapel Hill, 1965.

Leloudis, James, and George Noblit. "What Was Lost: African American Accounts of School Desegregation." Paper presented at the Organization of American Historians Annual Meeting, Boston, March 2004.

Littlefield, Valinda. "'I Am Only One, but I Am One': Southern African-American Women Schoolteachers, 1884–1954." Ph.D. diss., University of Illinois at Urbana-Champaign, 2003.

Mackie, Betty, Greta Deerson, Eric Dill, and Shannon Fyfe, eds. "Capturing the Past to Guide the Future: A Continuing Legacy of Ligon High School." Oral history of Ligon School. Copy in possession of Candy Beal and Marsha Alibrandi. 1999.

MacLean, Nancy. "The Conservative Quest to 'Make Democracy Safe for the World': Privatization as the Sequel to Massive Resistance." Paper presented at the Long Civil Rights Movement Conference, University of North Carolina at Chapel Hill, 3 April 2009.

McElreath, J. Michael. "The Cost of Opportunity: School Desegregation and Changing Race Relations in the Triangle since World War II." Ph.D. diss., University of Pennsylvania, 2002.

McKinney, Charles. "'Our People Began to Press for Greater Freedom': The Black

Freedom Struggle in Wilson, North Carolina, 1945–1970." Ph.D. diss., Duke University, 2003.

Morgan, Ernest West. "A Racial Comparison of Education in Robeson County (North Carolina)." Master's thesis, University of North Carolina at Chapel Hill, 1940.

Mosnier, L. Joseph. "Crafting Law in the Second Reconstruction: Julius Chambers, the NAACP Legal Defense Fund, and Title VII." Ph.D. diss., University of North Carolina at Chapel Hill, 2004.

Pankey, George E. "Life Histories of Rural Negro Teachers in the South." Master's thesis, University of North Carolina at Chapel Hill, 1927.

Patterson, Gerrelyn Chunn. "*Brown* Can't Close Us Down: The Invincible Pride of Hillside High School." Ph.D. diss., University of North Carolina at Chapel Hill, 2005.

Peebles, Wilma C. "School Desegregation in Raleigh, North Carolina, 1954–1964." Ph.D. diss., University of North Carolina at Chapel Hill, 1984.

Romero, Patricia Watkins. "Carter G. Woodson: A Biography." Ph.D. diss., Ohio State University, 1971.

Sanders, Wiley B., ed. "Race Attitudes of County Officials." 1933. Typescript copy in North Carolina Collection, Louis R. Wilson Library, University of North Carolina, Chapel Hill.

Sartorius, David. "Limits of Loyalty: Race and the Public Sphere in Cienfuegos, Cuba, 1845–1898." Ph.D. diss., University of North Carolina at Chapel Hill, 2003.

Seay, Elizabeth Irene. "A History of the North Carolina College for Negroes." Master's thesis, Duke University, 1941.

Smathers, Keener McNeal. "A History of the Supervision of Instruction in Schools for Negroes in North Carolina." Ed.D. diss., Duke University, 1969.

Southern Regional Council. "Tension and Conciliation: A Report by the Southern Regional Council on Contributing Factors Causing Racial Disagreements and Conflicts within the Hickory, North Carolina City Schools." 11 August 1974. Copy in North Carolina Collection, Louis R. Wilson Library, University of North Carolina, Chapel Hill.

Teachey, Guy B. "Educational Opportunities for Negroes in the Public High Schools of Sampson County, North Carolina." Master's thesis, University of North Carolina at Chapel Hill, 1945.

Thuesen, Sarah C. "Classes of Citizenship: The Culture and Politics of Black Public Education in North Carolina, 1919–1960." Ph.D. diss., University of North Carolina at Chapel Hill, 2003.

Turner, Kara Miles. "'It Is Not at Present a Very Successful School': Prince Edward County and the Black Educational Struggle, 1865–1995." Ph.D. diss., Duke University, 2001.

Watson, William H. "The Establishment of a Functional Guidance Program in the Rural Negro High Schools of Eastern North Carolina." Ph.D. diss., New York University, 1948.

Westin, Richard Barry. "A History of the Durham School System, 1882–1933." Master's thesis, Duke University, 1960.

———. "The State and Segregated Schools: Negro Public Education in North Carolina, 1863–1923." Ph.D. diss., Duke University, 1966.

Zogry, Kenneth. "The House That Dr. Pope Built: Race, Politics, Memory, and the Early

Struggle for Civil Rights in North Carolina." Ph.D. diss., University of North Carolina at Chapel Hill, 2008.

FILMS AND VIDEOS

Exhausted Remedies: Joe Holt's Story. Produced by Deborah L. Holt, 1995.

No Crystal Stair: Stories from North Carolina's Minority Lawyers. Produced by the Minority History Committee of the North Carolina Bar Association, Young Lawyer's Division, 2001.

"Segregation in the Schools" (episode of *See It Now*). Produced by Edward R. Murrow and Fred W. Friendly of the Columbia Broadcasting System, broadcast 25 May 1954.

Unintended Consequences?: Black Educators Recount Their Experiences. Produced by the Wildacres Leadership Initiative, 2002.

WEBSITES

Charlotte-Mecklenburg Public Library. "The Charlotte-Mecklenburg Story." http://www.cmstory.org/.

Dobrasko, Rebekah. "South Carolina's Equalization Schools, 1951–1960." http://scequalizationschools.org/default.aspx.

Free and Accepted Masons of North Carolina and Jurisdictions. "The Official Website of the Most Worshipful Prince Hall Grand Lodge." http://www.mwphglnc.com/.

Holt, Joe, Jr. "Exhausted Remedies: The Joe Holt Story." http://www.joeholtstory.org/.

North Carolina Collection, University of North Carolina at Chapel Hill Libraries. "Digital NC." http://library.digitalnc.org/.

University Library, University of North Carolina at Chapel Hill. "Documenting the American South." http://docsouth.unc.edu/.

University of North Carolina at Greensboro Libraries. "Civil Rights Greensboro." http://library.uncg.edu/dp/crg/.

Index

Bias, John Henry, 108, 288 (n. 7)
Bickett, Thomas, 15, 17, 21, 23, 24
Biddle Institute, 91
Birmingham Post, 120
Birth of a Nation (film), 66
Black, Aline, 155
Black Belt, 190–91, 215, 235, 237, 299 (n. 74)
Black deference: and black loyalty, 15, 18; and citizenship, 61; and Shepard, 98, 101, 102, 104, 120, 180; and Atkins, 100; and local/national black leadership, 132; and NCTA, 134; and teacher salary equalization, 138, 144; and NAACP Youth Council, 173; and school facility equalization, 175
Black educators: and black history movement, 9, 65–69; and teacher salary equalization, 10, 63, 64, 145, 149–50, 240; and interracial dialogues, 19–21; and NAACP, 22, 130–31, 132, 133, 181, 230; and Newbold, 27, 193; and Division of Negro Education, 27–28, 140; Jeanes teachers, 31–32; and Rosenwald Fund, 35; achievements in black public education, 46; and school equalization campaigns, 47, 234; and academics, 54; and public funding of education, 56; and black public high school development, 56–57, 59; educational background of, 61; adaptation of white-authored courses of study, 65, 68; on curriculum committees, 68; and vocational education, 73, 76–80; and Masonic activities, 102–3; white fears of northern-trained teachers, 106; college faculty teaching load, 112; Langston Hughes's observations on, 129–30; black and white teachers' salaries, 130, 288 (n. 2); and litigation, 131–32, 288–89 (n. 8); and civil rights movement, 132, 230, 288–89 (n. 8); certification requirements, 137, 150, 249, 293 (n. 70), 315 (n. 7); feminization of, 137–38, 289 (n. 19); and black voting rights, 147; and school facility equalization, 171, 197–98; and school integration, 197, 209–10, 229, 230–31, 249, 250, 251; and

Brown decision, 204, 205, 207, 209–11, 305 (n. 24); annual teaching contracts for, 209–10; and desegregation of educational leadership, 230, 249; qualifications of, 240, 242, 293 (n. 70); and effects of school segregation, 303 (n. 7). *See also* North Carolina Teachers Association
Black entrepreneurship, 84, 93–94, 96–97
Black history movement: and curricular equalization, 9, 50, 65–71; and black public high schools, 67, 69, 276 (n. 61); and Newbold, 67, 275 (n. 48)
Black home demonstration agents, 272 (n. 8)
Black identity, 16, 66–67, 69–70, 248, 279 (n. 4)
Black juvenile delinquents, 23
Black loyalty: fears of black insurgency, 14, 17; and Shepard, 14–15, 17, 18, 105, 119, 120; and World War I, 14–24; and political citizenship, 16, 17, 21–24; and interracial dialogues, 17–22; and women's activism, 23; and Division of Negro Education, 28; and Bolshevism, 40; and higher education equalization, 103, 104; and teacher salary equalization, 134, 146, 148; and World War II, 152; and school facility equalization, 178; and "voluntary segregation," 209
Black men: and labor market, 78–79; as teachers, 137, 289 (n. 19). *See also* Black women
Black middle class, 94, 96, 132, 147, 309 (n. 54), 311 (n. 78)
Black normal schools, 18, 40–41, 55, 56, 92, 98, 99–106, 267 (n. 46)
Black parents: and Newbold, 27; and Rosenwald Fund, 36, 37; and litigation for school equalization, 43–44, 63, 157, 181; and school equalization campaigns, 47, 172, 234; and vocational education, 76; and Lumberton black student strike, 174–75; and school integration, 224, 225, 229, 231, 235, 237, 238, 244, 311 (n. 77); school involvement of, 251

and black public high school development, 57; and Shepard, 105, 109; and
Langston Hughes, 129; and NCTA, 132;
and Robinson, 133, 289 (n. 10); and
teacher salary equalization, 143
Curricular equalization: black advocacy
of, 2, 54, 271 (n. 5); and black public
high schools, 9, 49, 50, 54–55, 59–61,
64–65, 187, 216; white concessions
to, 9, 49, 90; and black history movement, 9, 50, 65–71; and white assumptions of black intellectual inferiority,
49, 50, 53–54, 55, 57–58, 59, 62–63; and
industrial curricula, 49, 51–54, 57, 59,
60, 61; and academics, 49, 53–54, 55,
56, 60–61, 76, 77, 83, 97–98, 99, 101,
102, 103, 104–5; implementation of,
49–50; and distribution of curricular
resources, 50, 54, 64–65; and North
Carolina Teachers Association, 57,
65–66; Newbold on, 58–60; and vocational education, 71–88; and school
integration, 87–88, 224, 228, 243, 244,
308 (n. 52); and black normal schools,
102; and electives, 240, 313 (n. 92)

Dabney, Virginius, 159
Daly, Samuel F., 217
Daniels, Josephus, 217
Davis, George E., 27, 36, 38–40, 288 (n. 7)
Davis, Harold, 222
Davis, Jackson, 25, 32, 107, 282 (n. 33)
Davis, Sam, 243
Day, Thomas, 94
"A Declaration of Principles by Repre-
sentative Negroes of North Carolina,"
19–21, 22
De jure segregation, 3, 243, 257
Delany, Julia, 145
Democratic Party, 6, 7, 8, 17, 94–95, 170,
217
Denmark, 65–66, 77–78
Dickens, Brooks, 271 (n. 93)
Diggs, Edward O., 124
Dillard, Clarence, 21
Dillard, James Hardy, 32, 45, 53, 107
Dillard High School, Goldsboro, 67

Direct-action protest: and closing of black
schools, 3; and Lumberton black student strike, 10, 160, 168–79, 183; white
fears of, 14, 15–16; and NAACP, 16, 22,
161, 176, 187, 279 (n. 4); and Adkin High
School black student boycott, 88, 196,
301 (n. 86); threats of, 114; and North
Carolina College of Negroes, 123–24;
and unions, 154; and school equalization, 157, 160, 161, 195; and Lumberton
litigation for school facility equalization, 179–86; and Lumberton legacy,
186–99; and school integration, 213,
229, 235, 237, 238–39; and sit-in movement, 226; and integrated black students, 252; national black protest
organizations, 253; and black history
movement, 276 (n. 61)
Division of Instructional Service, 178
Division of Negro Education (DNE): and
white management of black schools,
9, 26–27, 40, 194; and fears of black insurgency, 14; and Newbold, 24, 26–28,
186, 192–94, 266 (n. 31), 267 (n. 42);
purposes of, 24–25; black educators
employed by, 27–28, 140; salary schedule of, 28, 33, 267 (n. 42); offices for
black employees, 28, 230, 267 (n. 42);
and Langston Hughes, 129; and school
facility equalization, 164–65
Dockery, Robert, 147
Doermann, Humphrey, 279 (n. 3)
Domestic service, 75, 78
Dortch Act (1883), 6, 263 (n. 13)
Douglas, Davison, 225, 288 (n. 8), 303
(n. 2), 311 (n. 78)
Douglas, Winston, 150
Drew, C. C., 44
Drewry, Henry, 279 (n. 3)
Du Bois, W. E. B.: and race pride, 16; and
Mary McCrorey, 23; and progressivism
in North Carolina, 47; and racial dif-
ference, 58; and economic separatism,
77–78; and Shepard, 96, 97, 109; and
Robinson, 133, 289 (n. 10); on school
integration, 205; on Smithfield case,
270 (n. 81)

Shepard, 9–10, 88, 90–91, 95–98, 100–101, 104–8, 111, 112, 114–17, 119, 125, 250; and appropriations for permanent improvements, 29, 40, 267 (n. 46); and boosterism, 40–41; and economic citizenship, 83–84; and parallelism, 92; and black normal schools, 99–106; and state funding, 99–109, 111–12, 122; and Great Depression, 108–9; graduate and professional education, 109–14, 122, 125, 140, 146, 161, 187, 287 (n. 92); and grants for out-of-state tuition, 115, 125, 285–86 (n. 72); white commitment to true parity, 117; and integration, 121–27; primary and secondary school equalization compared to, 161

High Point, 145, 229

Highsmith, J. Henry, 178

Hill, Herbert, 197

Hill, John Sprunt, 60

Hill, Oliver, 189

Hillside High School, Durham, 60–64, 65, 86, 96, 112–13, 315 (n. 3)

Himbry, Joseph, 195

Historically black colleges and universities (HBCUs), 90, 91–99, 250, 279 (n. 3), 315–16 (n. 10)

Historically black schools: preservation of, 3–4; effect of *Brown* ruling on, 11, 203, 239–43, 248; integration of, 121, 250; and civil rights movement, 124–25, 126; black parents' continued support for, 231, 237; social and cultural strengths of, 255

Hochschild, Jennifer, 254

Hocutt, Thomas Raymond, 65, 109–11, 113, 118, 120, 136, 284–85 (n. 59)

Hocutt case, 109–11, 118, 136, 138

Hodges, Luther, 199, 209, 211, 213–15

Hoey, Clyde R., 114, 148–49, 185

Holland, Annie Welthy, 27, 32–34, 53, 266 (n. 26), 268 (n. 55)

Holley, Ophelia, 72

Holliday, Mary, 52

Holt, Elwyna H., 217–19, 221–22, 257

Holt, Joseph H., Jr., 217–22, 225–26, 227, 228, 257, 308 (n. 47)

Holt, Joseph H., Sr., 218–22, 224, 257

Home-Makers' Clubs, 52

Hood, James Walker, 5, 6, 102–3

Hooker v. Town of Greenville (1902), 7

Hoover, Herbert, 109, 135

Horton, Hugh G., 291 (n. 49)

Houston, Charles Hamilton, 109

Howard, Dorothy, 227

Howard University, 30

Hughes, Charles Evan, 113

Hughes, Langston, 118, 129–30

Hunter, Charles, 21, 23

Hunter, Gilbert, Jr., 228

Hunter, Gilbert, Sr., 228

Hunter, Gloria, 227, 228, 257–58

Hunter, Hermena, 228, 257–58

Hunter College, New York, 113

Hunter v. Raleigh City Board of Education (1961), 226

Huntley, Delois, 222

Hurley, Ruby, 176, 179, 182

Hurricane Hazel, 201

Hurston, Zora Neale, 118

Hyde County, 315 (n. 4)

Ickes, Harold, 112

Inborden, T. S., 56

Industrial curricula: and self-determination strategies, 42, 51; and curricular equalization, 49, 51–54, 57, 59, 60, 61; and Hampton Institute, 51, 55, 73, 75, 92, 99, 100; vocational education distinguished from, 73

Industrialization, 73–74

International Labor Defense, 140

International Sunday School Association, 96

Interracial dialogues, 17–21, 23, 28, 29, 152, 156, 266 (n. 26), 267 (n. 44)

James A. Whitted School, Durham, 60, 274 (n. 32)

Jarnagin, Ada, 166

Jeanes, Anna T., 31–32

Jeanes Fund, 32–34, 41, 43, 44–46, 51, 53–54, 80

Jeanes teachers: and self-help institutions, 31, 32–34, 44–45, 46; and black rural schools, 31–33; Holland's leadership of, 32–34, 53; and curricular equalization, 50, 53–54; and industrial curricula, 51, 52–53; and black history movement, 69; and vocational education, 79–80, 81; and budget cuts, 136; Aggrey as supervisor, 148; and teacher salary equalization, 148; and school bus availability, 163–64; and Redstone Academy, 172; firing of black supervisors, 209

Jeffrey, Julie Roy, 314 (n. 107)

Jett, Mary Joice, 245

J. H. Hayswood School, Lumberton, 183, 184, 185

Jim Crow social and political order: NAACP's attack on, 3, 196; in North Carolina, 4; legitimizing of, 7; and citizenship, 8; and curricular equalization, 9; and black loyalty, 16; and Great Migration, 17; and Commission on Interracial Cooperation, 19; blacks denouncing, 21; politics of, 27, 102, 232–33, 241, 248–49; and Newbold, 28; inequalities of, 45, 63, 91, 160, 166; and assumptions of black intellectual inferiority, 49, 50, 53–54, 55, 57–58, 59, 62–63, 208; and industrial curricula, 51; and vocational education, 71; and employment discrimination, 85; and politics of black school ownership, 90; and Shepard, 95, 105; and higher education equalization, 109, 250; and Langston Hughes, 129; and regional progressivism, 159; and school equalization, 160; and school facility equalization, 185; and *Brown* decision, 201, 204, 303 (n. 5); challenges to, 215, 224, 225; and federal education funding, 232–33, 243–44, 310 (n. 72); public memories of, 249; vestiges of, 259

John Chavis School, Cherryville, 83

Johnson, Charles S., 59

Johnson, Dwayne, 127

Johnson, Guion Griffis, 49

Johnson, Guy Benton, 113

Johnson, James Weldon, 22, 70

Johnson, Janice Lutz, 242, 244–45

Johnson, J. H., 29

Johnson, Larry, 242

Johnson C. Smith University, 91, 224, 283 (n. 43)

Johnston County Training School, 43

John W. Ligon Junior-Senior High School, Raleigh, 215–21, 222, 227–28, 240, 248, 307 (nn. 38, 39)

Joint Appropriations Committee of the General Assembly, 153

Jones, Arnell, 227

Jones, Louise, 69–70

Jones, Lu Ann, 272 (n. 8)

Jordan, D. J., 15

Joseph Keasly Brick Agricultural, Industrial, and Normal School, 56

Josephus Daniels Junior High School, Raleigh, 217–18, 219, 227, 228–29, 257, 258

Journal of Negro Education, 77, 111

Journal of Negro History, 66

Joyner, Albert, 213

Justice, Hubert, 235

Kahlenberg, Richard, 318 (n. 30)

Kantor, Harvey, 73, 276 (n. 64)

Katz, Michael, 264 (n. 19)

Kemp, Elizabeth, 171, 172, 175

Kennedy, Harold, III, 251

Kennedy, Harvey, 251

King, Martin Luther, Jr., 121

Kinston, 196

Klarman, Michael, 303 (n. 4)

Knuckles, William H., 171

Korstad, Robert, 138

Ku Klux Klan, 17, 122, 228

Labor market segregation: and vocational education, 9, 50, 71–73, 77, 78, 81, 83; and North, 14, 17; and curricular equalization, 51; and urban areas, 79; and lack of black employment diversification, 85–86; and black women, 137–38. *See also* Employment discrimination

Lake, I. Beverly, 209

McKissick, Evelyn, 225
McKissick, Floyd, 123, 124, 225, 250
McKissick, Joycelyn, 224–25
McLaurin, George, 122
McLean, Angus W., 42, 51, 106
McQueen, Lillian Bullock, 169, 171, 174, 176, 182
Mechanics and Farmers Bank, 96
Meier, August, 31, 34, 160, 279 (n. 4)
Michael, Leila B., 145
Miller, Gene, 252
Mississippi, 231, 239
Mitchell, David, 182
Mitchell, John W., 112
Mitchell, Samuel, 196, 220, 222, 226
Moody, Anne, 239
Moore, Aaron M., 18, 21, 22, 27, 266 (n. 30)
Moore, Charles H., 17, 35, 36
Morgan, Anna, 227
Morrison, Cameron, 23
Morson High School, Raleigh, 307 (n. 39)
Moss, Alfred A., Jr., 14, 270 (n. 88), 271 (n. 5)
Moton, Robert, 279 (n. 4)
Murphey Elementary School, Raleigh, 225–26, 228
Murphy, T. T., 186
Murphy Bill, 115
Murray, Donald, 111
Murray, Pauli, 61, 62–63, 65, 86, 113–17, 118, 148, 204
Murrow, Edward R., 205
Myrdal, Gunnar, 81, 166

Nashville, Tennessee, 233
National Association for the Advancement of Colored People (NAACP): and teacher salary equalization, 3, 4, 10, 130–32, 136, 138, 139–45, 150–52, 153, 154–55, 288 (n. 4); school equalization strategy, 3, 10, 160; and higher education equalization, 3, 89–90, 109–11, 113, 115, 117, 284 (n. 59); Legal Defense and Education Fund (LDF), 3–4, 10, 202; Youth Councils, 10, 119, 168–69, 173–76, 179, 182, 185, 238, 296 (n. 29), 297 (n. 48); chapters in South, 16, 21–22, 24, 265 (n. 24); and North Carolina chap-

ters, 16, 21–22, 130, 142, 143, 173, 182, 196, 216–17; and textbooks, 68; and Negro National Anthem, 70; and legal equality, 77; and school integration, 88, 109–11, 182, 183, 187, 190, 196–97, 205, 206–7, 210–11, 224, 225–26, 228, 235, 237, 238; and Masonic activities, 103; regional campaign for graduate and professional education integration, 109, 140; and litigation, 130, 134–35, 138, 141, 142, 143, 144, 145, 146, 150–51, 153, 154–55, 160, 161, 179, 181, 220, 233, 235, 293 (n. 5); State Conference of Branches, 142, 148, 173; and women's suffrage, 148; and school facility equalization, 179, 181, 183, 186–87; and tensions in parent and youth branches, 182, 297 (n. 48); North Carolina Conference, 201; and civil rights movement, 230; and protest agenda, 279 (n. 4); and U.S. Supreme Court, 308 (n. 49). See also *The Crisis*
National Association of Teachers in Colored Schools, 57
National Education Association, 188
National HBCU Reinvestment Act, 250
National Labor Relations Board, 154
National Recovery Administration (NRA), 138, 148
National Religious Training School and Chautauqua for the Colored Race, 90, 96–101, 102, 281 (n. 17), 282 (n. 30)
National Teachers Examination (NTE), 155, 156, 249, 315 (n. 7)
Native Americans, 169–70, 172, 238, 279 (n. 7), 295 (n. 21)
Negro Citizens' Committee (Wilson), 190–91
Negro History Bulletin, 68–69
Negro History Week, 66, 69, 276 (n. 61)
Negro Rural School Fund, 32
Negro State Fair (1925), 42
Neighborhood schools, 255–56, 257
Nelms, Charlie, 250
Newbold, Margaret, 258–59
Newbold, Nathan Carter: and interracial dialogues, 19, 28, 29, 267 (n. 44);

lic school funding, 8, 42, 55–56; decline in funding from, 45–46, 167; and black private higher education, 91, 99, 109. *See also specific philanthropies*

Phillips, Barbara, 314 (n. 102)

Phillips, Lorene, 314 (n. 102)

Phillips, Marie, 314 (n. 102)

Pickens, William, 147

Piedmont Junior High School, Charlotte, 222

Pierson, W. W., 113–14

Pittsburgh Courier, 176, 181

Plessy v. Ferguson (1896), 4, 7, 167, 253–54, 257, 304 (n. 8). *See also* Separate but equal doctrine

Political citizenship: rights of, 5, 8, 263 (n. 10), 264 (n. 19); and black voting rights, 5, 96, 147, 280 (n. 15); voter literacy restrictions, 7, 24, 54, 147, 264 (n. 17); and disfranchisement, 7–8, 22, 29, 92, 103, 112, 130, 131, 142, 144, 170, 186, 264 (n. 17), 280 (n. 15); and black loyalty, 16, 17, 21–24; voter registration movements, 23; and radicalism, 24, 25, 140, 142, 175, 179; self-help institutions as substitute for, 31, 268 (n. 50); and black history movement, 66–67; and Masonic activities, 102–3, 108; and NCTA, 134; white assumptions concerning, 134; and teacher salary equalization, 146–47; limitations of, 147, 270 (n. 88); and NAACP, 160; and state and local political representation, 188; and school facility equalization, 188, 191, 195, 215; and school integration, 197; and black representation on school boards, 206; and voter registration, 230

Poll taxes, 7

Pope, Larry, 301 (n. 86)

Pope, Oliver R., 54, 59, 145–47, 192, 288 (n. 7)

Populist Party, 7, 94

Potter, Robert, 255–56, 257

Powell, Adam Clayton, Jr., 118

Press. *See* Black press; White press; *and specific newspapers*

Price, Hosea V., 154

Prince Hall Free and Accepted Masons of North Carolina, 98, 101, 102–3, 120

Progressivism: and NAACP, 16; and black respectability, 95; and self-help institutions, 268 (n. 50)

Protest. *See* Direct-action protest

Public education: in South, 4, 5, 8; as right of citizenship, 5, 6–8, 14, 24–30, 43, 47; and school segregation, 5–6; NCTA's promotion of, 6; and black and white fusionists, 7; and paternalism, 24, 29–30, 42, 46, 188; blacks' enthusiasm for, 37–38. *See also* Black public high schools; White public high schools

Public Works Administration, 167

Pupil Assignment Act, 208, 213, 220, 221–22, 226

Pupil-teacher ratio: racial gap in, 112, 130, 131, 240, 313–14 (n. 100)

Race relations: racial management, 8, 25, 28, 42, 57, 104, 146, 148; in post–World War I era, 14, 17–18; white supremacy, 16, 23, 30, 95, 217; interracial dialogues, 17–21, 23, 28, 29, 152, 156, 266 (n. 26), 267 (n. 44); and Shepard, 18, 120; educational progress as evidence of, 42; and assumptions of black cultural dependence, 70; and Live-at-Home campaign, 71–72; Myrdal on, 81; and higher education equalization, 100, 104; personal nature of, 107; study of, 113; and pragmatism, 152; and unions, 154; and World War II, 166; and Lumberton black student strike, 176; and teacher salary equalization, 181; and *Brown* decision, 212; and separate but equal doctrine, 238; and school desegregation, 239, 248, 252–53, 254, 255; and public space, 248. *See also* Paternalism

Racial collectivism, 77–78

Racial difference: alternative theories of, 58, 273 (n. 25); Newbold on, 58–59, 273 (n. 25); and higher education equalization, 92; and high school graduation rates, 161, 164; and achievement, 161,

165–66, 240, 253–54, 256, 313 (n. 93), 316 (n. 18); in educational attainment, 240–41, 312–13 (n. 91)

Racial integration: of educational leadership, 27–28, 119–20, 146, 148, 152, 168, 187–88, 190–91, 194, 206–7, 230, 241, 251, 253. *See also* School integration

Racial order: and "A Declaration of Principles by Representative Negroes of North Carolina," 20–21; and Newbold, 28, 129–30; and male leadership, 103; and Brummitt, 110; and higher education equalization, 114; black impatience with, 166. *See also* Black deference; Black loyalty

Racial segregation: generational differences in, 1–2; and black history movement, 71; Shepard's attitude toward, 91; and assimilation within white society, 92, 234, 239; and pragmatism, 152; professional segregation, 194, 230; and public accommodation, 238; material markers of, 259. *See also* Labor market segregation; School segregation

Racial uplift, 94, 96, 97, 118, 120, 281 (n. 17)

Racial violence: and Wilmington riot, 7, 142, 195; and Red Summer of 1919, 17; of disfranchisement era, 131, 142; and school integration, 252

Raleigh Citizens Association, 216–17, 220, 226

Raleigh Institute, 91

Raleigh Ministerial Alliance, 216–17, 220

Raleigh News and Observer: and Declaration of Principles, 20; and NAACP, 142; and teacher salary equalization, 156; and Lumberton black student strike, 176–79; and school facility equalization, 189, 197; and Newbold, 193; and Daniels, 217; and school integration, 226, 238, 256

Raleigh School Board, 220, 226–27, 229

Raleigh schools: and curricular equalization, 61; and school integration, 215–22, 226–29, 240, 248, 257–59, 307 (nn. 36, 38, 39), 318 (n. 30)

Raleigh Times, 220

Ramsey, D. Hiden, 198, 235

Ramsey, Sonya, 233

Randolph, Virginia Estelle, 32

Raper, Arthur F., 137–38

Rayford, Alice, 44

Reconstruction, 51

Red Shirts, 17

Redstone Academy, Lumberton, 168–72, 174–75, 177, 178, 179, 183, 184

Red Summer of 1919, 17–18

Reeves, Audrey Crawley, 251–52, 314 (n. 103)

Reid, Ira DeA., 137–38

Reid, Paul, 177

Republican Party, 7, 8, 21, 94

Reuben, Julie, 66

Reynolds, Carl, 178

Reynolds High School, Winston-Salem, 75, 222

Richardson, Elaine, 225

Richardson, Rachel, 225

Richmond Times-Dispatch, 159

Ridgeview School, Hickory, 241–46, 247–48, 249, 313–14 (n. 100)

Rivera, Alex, Jr., 176

R. J. Reynolds Tobacco Company, 154

Roberts, Girvaud, 222

Roberts, Gustavus, 222

Robeson County, 169–70, 173, 176, 179–86

Robesonian, 172, 174, 183, 184–85

Robinson, William A., 27, 56–57, 64–65, 75, 133, 274 (n. 43), 289 (n. 10)

Rocky Mount Evening Telegram, 142–43

Roosevelt, Eleanor, 112, 114

Roosevelt, Franklin, 112, 114, 138, 165, 167

Roosevelt, Theodore, 97

Rosenwald, Julius, 34–35, 37, 41

Rosenwald Fund: and school facility equalization, 34–40, 41, 43, 45, 46, 170, 186, 238; and industrial curriculum, 51; and vocational education, 75–76; and study of black child welfare, 273 (n. 23)

Rosenwald High School, Camden County, 79

Rowland-Norment School, Lumberton, 184

Rudwick, Elliott, 160

authored plans, 11, 207–9, 211–12, 229, 231; and black history movement, 71; and curricular equalization, 87–88, 224, 228, 243, 244, 308 (n. 52); and litigation, 88, 190, 194, 197, 202, 213, 216–18, 225–28, 233–35, 237–39, 244, 246, 311 (n. 78), 314 (nn. 102, 108); and NAACP, 160, 182, 183, 187, 190, 196–97, 205, 206–7, 210–11, 224, 225–26, 228, 235, 237, 238; black attitudes toward, 197, 233–34, 239–40, 247; shift from school equalization, 199, 203, 231–39; federal enforcement of, 202, 209, 243–44, 314 (n. 101); merits of, 205–6; black input on, 206–7; white resistance to, 207–8, 239, 253, 258, 318 (n. 33); and white assumptions of black intellectual inferiority, 208; grassroots movements for, 212; and citizenship, 219, 225, 257; token integration, 222, 226; Counts's experience of, 222–24; and harassment and social isolation of black students, 228–29, 234, 247, 251; and race relations, 239, 248, 252–53, 254, 255; freedom-of-choice plans, 244; and black representation on school boards, 251, 253; accomplishments of, 251–54, 256, 258

School policy: black representation in policymaking, 27–28, 119–20, 146, 148, 152, 168, 187–88, 190–91, 194, 206–7, 230, 241, 251, 253

School segregation: and taxation, 6, 263 (n. 13); and "shoe-stringed" town limits, 38; and higher education equalization, 89, 109; costs of upholding, 161; and school equalization, 167, 193; and school facility equalization, 185, 191, 198; "voluntary segregation," 209, 215; residential segregation, 217; and Second Morrill Act, 280 (n. 8)

Scott, W. Kerr, 187–88, 189, 198

Scovronick, Nathan, 254

Seabrook, James W., 153, 207, 208, 288 (n. 7)

Second Morrill Act of 1890, 92, 280 (n. 8)

Self-determination strategies, 9, 14, 42, 51, 97, 132

Self-help institutions: and black public school funding, 8, 9, 30, 31, 44, 46–47; and Jeanes teachers, 31, 32–34, 44–45, 46; as substitute for political citizenship, 31, 268 (n. 50); and Holland, 34; and Rosenwald Fund, 34–39, 46; whites' recognition of, 42; and school facility equalization, 171–72; and integration, 279 (n. 4)

Separate but equal doctrine: and U.S. Supreme Court, 1, 7, 113, 121–22; rehabilitation of, 2; and educational policy studies, 4; and black citizenship rights, 7, 8; and higher education equalization, 90, 109, 113, 122; and school equalization, 167; and school facility equalization, 181, 190, 195, 198, 232, 258–59; and race relations, 238

Sharpe, C. R., 147

Sharpe, Stella Gentry, 80

Shaw, Stephanie, 288–89 (n. 8)

Shaw University, 44, 91, 92, 93, 99, 109, 283 (n. 43)

Shepard, Annie Day, 95

Shepard, Annie Day Robinson, 94, 98

Shepard, Augustus, 93

Shepard, Hattie Whitted, 93

Shepard, James E.: and higher education equalization, 9–10, 88, 90–91, 95–98, 100–101, 104–8, 111, 112, 114–17, 119, 125, 250; and black loyalty, 14–15, 17, 18, 105, 119, 120; on interracial dialogue, 17–18; and NAACP, 22, 109–11, 119, 143–44, 265 (n. 24); and Newbold, 28, 90–91, 100, 101–7, 108, 110, 119, 120, 141; and black history movement, 67; and liberal arts, 84, 97–98, 278 (n. 87); and institutional autonomy, 91, 96, 104, 105; conservatism of, 91, 121, 122; and interracial diplomacy, 93, 94, 95–96, 97, 101–6, 120–21, 143–44, 151, 180; investments of, 93–94; political appointments of, 94–95; church work of, 96; and black voting rights, 96, 147, 280 (n. 15); Masonic involvement of, 98, 101, 102–3, 105, 106–7, 108, 120, 283 (n. 42); resistance of, 101–2, 120; oratorical talents

Tunstall, Melvin, 238

Turner, James W., 85

Tushnet, Mark V., 293 (n. 5)

Tuskegee Institute, 32, 42, 51, 55, 73, 75, 92, 100

Tyack, David, 276 (n. 64)

Tyler, Anne, 308 (n. 47)

Umstead, William B., 199, 206, 207, 209

Unions, 73, 139–40, 154

University of Maryland, 111

University of Missouri, 113

University of North Carolina at Chapel Hill: NAACP's integration efforts at, 10, 109–11, 284 (n. 59); integration efforts at, 65, 90, 112–15, 117, 118, 121, 124, 125, 136, 250; and higher education equalization, 88, 89, 99, 108, 109–10, 113–16, 180; graduate and professional education, 109–11, 113–16, 125, 189; integration of Law School, 121, 124, 250, 287 (n. 95); state funding of, 123; degree programs of, 125; study of black child welfare, 273 (n. 23)

University of North Carolina Press, 166

University of Oklahoma, 122

University of Texas, 117, 123

Urban areas: and black public high school development, 56–57; rural migration to, 71, 79–80; and teacher salary equalization, 155–56; and scholastic achievement test results, 165; and NAACP members, 173; and equal opportunity, 254

U.S. Army intelligence tests, 57, 58

U.S. Bureau of Education, 41, 67, 78, 106

U.S. Congress, 4, 14–15

U.S. Department of Education, 44, 256

U.S. Department of Health, Education, and Welfare, 250

U.S. Department of Justice, 40

U.S. sesquicentennial celebration (1926), 40–41

U.S. Supreme Court: and separate but equal doctrine, 1, 7, 113, 121–22; and school integration in higher education, 121–22, 123, 124; and school facility equalization, 199; and school assignment matters, 222, 308 (n. 49)

Uzzell, George R., 291 (n. 49)

Vardaman, James, 95

Varser, Lycurgus R., 266 (n. 30)

Virginia, 150–51, 155, 303 (n. 2)

Virginia Teachers Association, 150

Vocational education: and labor market segregation, 9, 50, 71–73, 77, 78, 81, 83; and economic citizenship, 9, 50, 71–88; and curricular equalization, 71–88; rhetoric and reality of, 73, 276 (n. 64); industrial arts curriculum, 74, 75, 82, 87, 277–78 (n. 83); home economics curriculum, 74, 75–76, 78, 86–87; agricultural curriculum, 74, 78, 79–83, 88; and black public high schools, 75, 76–83, 86–87, 88, 277–78 (n. 83); and NCTA, 146; and Lumberton black student strike, 171

Voter literacy restrictions, 7, 24, 54, 147, 264 (n. 17)

Voter registration movements, 23

Voting rights, 5, 96, 147, 280 (n. 15)

Wake County, 256, 259

Wake County Training School, 51–52

Wake County Twentieth Century Voter's Club, 16

Walker, James, 124

Walker, Vanessa Siddle, 3, 234

Walstonburg High School, Greene County, 237

Ware, Gilbert, 284–85 (n. 59)

Warlick, Wilson, 213

Washam, Troy, 243

Washington, Booker T., 32, 34, 51, 65–66, 71, 76, 96, 167, 279 (n. 4)

Washington, John C., 228

Washington County Union School, 299 (n. 75)

Washington High School, Raleigh, 61, 215, 307 (n. 36)

Watts, Grace, 217–18